Laughter is the Best Medicine

Confessions of a Young Surgeon

By

Peter Sykes

Published by New Generation Publishing in 2021

Copyright © Peter Sykes 2021

First Edition

The author asserts the moral right under the Copyright, Designs and Patents Act 1988 to be identified as the author of this work.

All Rights reserved. No part of this publication may be reproduced, stored in a retrieval system or transmitted, in any form or by any means without the prior consent of the author, nor be otherwise circulated in any form of binding or cover other than that in which it is published and without a similar condition being imposed on the subsequent purchaser.

ISBN: 978-1-80031-285-2

www.newgeneration-publishing.com

New Generation Publishing

Acknowledgements

I wish to thank my wife Jane for her patience and for the numerous cups of tea (and the occasional glass of wine) that have sustained me whilst writing this novel.

I also offer my thanks to the many patients it has been my privilege to serve for giving me the inspiration to write this book.

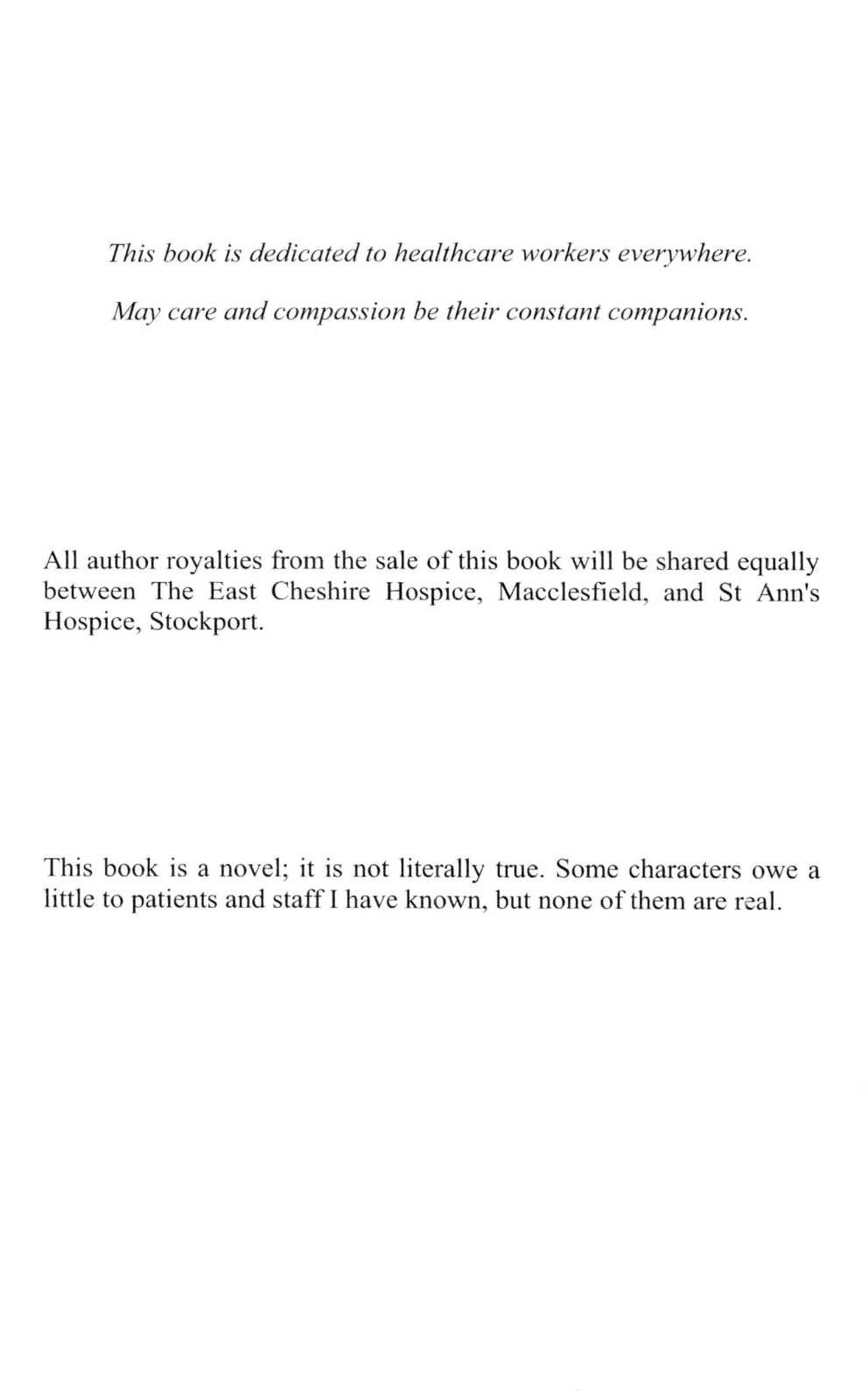

This book is dedicated to healthcare workers everywhere.

May care and compassion be their constant companions.

All author royalties from the sale of this book will be shared equally between The East Cheshire Hospice, Macclesfield, and St Ann's Hospice, Stockport.

This book is a novel; it is not literally true. Some characters owe a little to patients and staff I have known, but none of them are real.

By the same author

The 'Doctor Paul – Nurse Kate' Series of Novels

Peter's first novel **'The First Cut'** was published in 2011. It described Paul Lambert's medical misadventures as he was thrown, bewildered and unprepared, onto a busy surgical ward as a newly qualified doctor.

This was followed in 2013 by **'Behind the Screens'** which tells real-life tales at a time when care and compassion ruled supreme in British hospitals. Some of the stories are humorous, some sad, others poignant, but all are very 'human'. The novel also follows Paul's chequered love life, and unveils some of the 'high jinks' that doctors get up to when off-duty.

'First Do No Harm' published in 2015, is set against the political disputes that beset the National Health Service between 1974 and 1976. Again, the narrative is interspersed with numerous fascinating tales of the patients treated by Paul and his medical and nursing colleagues.

'Invisible Scars' was published in 2017. Paul, now training to become a surgeon, and his wife Nurse Kate, work alongside each other on a surgical unit. Strains in their relationship emerge. And when Kate's baby dies and Paul's inexperience costs lives, doubt and despair hang in the air, and their marriage appears to be doomed. However, in a dramatic turn of events, Paul saves the life of a critically ill patient, and Kate is finally able to bid an emotional farewell to the child she has lost.

Also written by Peter Sykes

'All in a Doctor's Day' is a 'coffee table' collection of 45 individual light-hearted stories all with a medical theme. They feature a variety of healthcare workers and settings. Humour is prominent throughout.

Preface

Peter Sykes has been steeped in medicine from the day he was born. His father was a doctor who consulted from the family home and his mother was a nurse, so it was perhaps no surprise when he too studied to be a doctor. Jane, his wife, is also medically qualified, and their marriage has been blessed with three sons, all of whom currently work for the NHS: as a physiotherapist, a general practitioner and as a clinical academic. Now retired, Peter has a wide breadth of experience having served as a hospital consultant, as medical director to an NHS Trust that provided hospital, community and mental health services and as a consultant to the Healthcare Commission.

This book is a collection of the best of the patient stories featured in the Paul and Kate series of novels that Peter has published during the last ten years. They embrace a wide variety of healthcare personnel and clinical situations. A few of the tales are tragic; many are humorous and some have an unexpected twist in the tail. All are accompanied by a quotation which draws a moral from the story.

Peter continues to publish new stories on his blog at www.medicaltales.org where you can Sign On/Subscribe and receive all future tales, free of charge, direct to your email in-box.

List of Chapters

Part 1 1966 1

    Chapter 1   An Eventful First Day 2

    Chapter 2   An Embarrassing Mistake 15

    Chapter 3   The Patient who was B. I. D. 17

    Chapter 4   Mr Quigley's Nasogastric Tube 21

    Chapter 5   Fun with Magic Markers 26

    Chapter 6   Suppositories 32

    Chapter 7   Mrs Ann Brown 43

    Chapter 8   The Medical Detective 57

    Chapter 9   Sue Weston 62

    Chapter 10   A Humble Hero 75

    Chapter 11   Cash or Conscience 91

    Chapter 12   The Biter gets Bit 96

    Chapter 13   A Life Changing Decision 100

    Chapter 14   Paul gains Sister's respect 110

    Chapter 15   Rosie 116

Part 2 1970 129

    Chapter 16   Mr Mills' Stomach Ulcer 130

    Chapter 17   Dr Elizabeth Webb 140

    Chapter 18   The International Soccer Star 159

    Chapter 19   Harry Grimshaw M.P. 171

    Chapter 20   Queenie 189

    Chapter 21   Mrs Twigg 211

    Chapter 22   Mr Walton's Party Trick 229

    Chapter 23   Mr Cullen's Vasectomy Operation 234

    Chapter 24   Lodgers 244

    Chapter 25   Dr Janet Smith 256

Chapter 26	Cedric Brown: (A Drama in Three Acts)	262
Chapter 27	Cedric King Act Two: Trial by Jury	274
Chapter 28	Cedric King Act Three: Litigation	289
Chapter 29	Malcolm's Toolbox	297
Chapter 30	A Game of Cricket brings a Moral Dilemma	312
Chapter 31	The Lady with the Lump	327

Part 1

The City General Hospital   1966

Chapter 1   An Eventful First Day

1st August 1966

Paul, quietly apprehensive of the task that lay ahead, was on his way to report for duty on his first morning as a doctor; he was to be the new house officer on the Surgical Five Unit at The City General Hospital. As he left the residency, he walked along the short-covered passage that led to the main hospital corridor. There he joined the morning rush heading for the wards; porters in brown overalls pushing large, heated, metal trolleys containing the patients' breakfasts, cleaners sporting pink aprons, carrying their buckets and mops, and nurses wearing their smart blue uniforms and starched caps preparing to relieve the night staff. At the crossroads where the casualty staff went straight on and the managers turned left into the administrative block, Paul turned right into the surgical corridor. Then, eschewing the lift, since it was always quicker to take the stairs, he reached the corridor leading to the Surgical Five wards. Nervously, he approached Sister's office.

'Dr Paul Lambert, House Surgeon to Mr Potts'. Paul found it hard to believe, yet the name badge on the lapel of his freshly-laundered white coat, confirmed that it was true. One pocket held a copy of the British National Formulary which listed all the drugs licensed for use in the UK, a second pocket held his stethoscope and tendon hammer, symbolic instruments of his trade, and a third pocket held pens and pencils and the hospital bleep, which he had been so proud to receive from the hospital switchboard. How naïve he had been not to recognise that this was, in reality, not a modern aid to good communication, but an instrument of torture, a demanding taskmaster, a destroyer of sleep; something which, in less than a month, he would gladly have thrown from the highest cliff into the deepest sea!

Arriving on the ward on that first morning, Paul felt a sense of pride in his new found status; he had graduated from medical student to medical practitioner. But he was also acutely aware of the many challenges that lay ahead, and conscious that this pride might be shattered in an instant by being faced with a situation, perhaps an emergency, with which he couldn't cope.

Paul was joined by Mr Khan, the registrar on the surgical unit.

'Welcome Paul,' he said, 'I'm pleased to see you, and I hope you'll enjoy your time with us. Will you be working for Sir William or Mr Potts?'

Sir William Warrender and Mr Leslie Potts were the two consultants in charge of the unit.

'For Mr Potts, Sir,' Paul replied.

The registrar laughed. 'Oh please don't call me 'Sir'. Everyone calls me 'Mo', its short for Mohammed of course, but I'm very happy to be known as 'Mo'.

'Right,' Mr Khan continued, 'let's take a quick look at Mr Potts' patients before he arrives,' and with that, he led Paul out of the office and onto the ward.

The ward was of a 'Nightingale' design; a large, open-plan rectangular room, with a line of a dozen beds down each side. With its large windows and high ceiling, it was light and airy, with just a slight scent of antiseptic in the air. For convenience, each consultant was allocated beds on one side of the ward: Mr Potts' patients on the left side, and Sir William's patients on the right.

'Since this is your first morning on the ward,' Mr Khan continued, 'I'll present the patients to Mr Potts today, but of course, in future that will be your responsibility.'

Starting with the first bed on the left, Mr Khan picked up the observation chart from the rail on the foot of the bed, glanced at it briefly, and then addressed the patient.

'Good morning, Mr Needham, and how are you feeling this morning?'

'Fine, Doctor, thank you.'

'Your rupture operation appears to have gone very well, and as you know, we're planning to let you go home today. Do you have your post-operative instruction sheet?'

'Yes, I do, thanks.'

'And you understand that the district nurse will call next week to take out your stitches?'

The patient nodded.

'Are there any questions you want to ask before you leave?'

'None at all, thank you. And Doctor, thank you for all your help these last few days.'

'You're welcome.'

They moved on to the next bed. Again, Mr Khan addressed the patient by name, asked how he was feeling and whether he had enjoyed a comfortable night.

'I feel well enough, thank you, but in the night the nurses seemed a bit anxious about this wound in my groin.'

'Paul, perhaps you could screen the patient, so that we can have a look?'

The screens had four cotton panels printed with a floral design, each panel held within folding, rectangular, metal frames mounted on casters. Three such screens were required to provide adequate privacy for the patient. A great deal of time was spent both by nurses and junior doctors moving these screens during the course of every working day. When Paul had arranged the screens around the bed, Mr Khan looked at the dressing covering the varicose vein wound in the groin. Although the nurses had put an extra pad over the wound, the amount of blood visible on the dressing was minimal. Mr Khan reassured the patient.

'There's no cause for any concern, Mr Taylor,' he said, 'it's quite common for there to be a bit of oozing after a varicose vein operation. The nurses will put a fresh dressing on the wound for you, and you'll be able to go home tomorrow as planned.'

The patient clearly looked relieved.

'Do you have any questions?' asked Mr Khan.

'No thanks, Doc,' came the reply, and again they moved on.

Mr Khan's conduct on the ward round was exemplary. He was open and personable with the patients, and spoke to them in language that they understood. Having been a surgical registrar for many years, he was completely comfortable with these clinical situations which were, for him, quite routine.

It was obvious that Mr Quigley in the third bed was far from well. He had been admitted having vomited fresh blood, and he looked pale and anxious. His charts revealed a low blood pressure despite the blood that was being administered through a drip in his arm. Mr Khan took a careful history of the patient's longstanding dyspepsia. Mr Quigley had experienced indigestion for many years, which had been particularly severe in the last few weeks. He blamed his problems on stress at work, but admitted to smoking thirty cigarettes a day. Mr Khan inquired about any drugs that he might have taken, knowing that a number of tablets, even common ones such as aspirin, may cause ulcers on the lining of the stomach.

After completing his history and examination, Mr Khan spoke to the patient.

'As you know, there's some bleeding going on, probably from the stomach or the duodenum. We're going to replace the blood that you've lost with these blood transfusions,' he indicated the drip in the patient's right arm, 'but should the bleeding continue, then I'm afraid it may mean an operation.'

'Does that mean that it's serious?' Mr Quigley asked.

'Clearly, any bleeding has to be taken seriously,' came the reply. 'If you were bleeding from the surface of the skin, we could easily stop it, simply by stitching it up, or by applying some pressure, but because your bleeding is internal, we would need to give you an anaesthetic and perform an operation to reach the bleeding point. Mr Potts, your consultant, will be here to see you in about an hour, and we will be asking him for advice.'

He turned to Paul. 'Please find out how many pints of blood we still have available, and whatever the number, make it up to four. In addition, make sure they've got plenty of serum in the lab, so that if we need to cross-match any more blood, there won't be a delay whilst we take a further blood sample. Also, if the blood pressure drops below 90, or the pulse goes above 110, you must call me at once.'

They had spent quite some time with Mr Quigley, but fortunately the remaining male patients were straightforward. Mr Khan's review of the patients on the female ward was equally efficient, and in less than an hour they had returned to the clinical office on the male ward to await Mr Potts' arrival.

While they were waiting, Mo Khan took the opportunity to give Paul some general advice about his role as house officer, and the responsibilities that he would have for the next six months. Essentially, it was Paul's job to know everything that was clinically relevant about every one of Mr Potts' patients at all times. That included the patient's history, details of abnormal physical findings, and, particularly, their investigations.

'Also,' Mo Khan added, 'there will be times when you'll need to be the spokesman for the patient. Sometimes patients are a little timid, particularly when faced with some of our more formidable colleagues. If a patient fails to tell a consultant something that you know to be important, you will have to speak up for them.

There is one point however that I particularly need to emphasise. Should you feel uncertain about anything, at any time, if for example you feel that you are out of your depth, then you must call someone more senior for support. It's better to call unnecessarily than not to seek advice when it is truly needed.'

As Paul and Mo were talking, Mr Potts arrived. Although slightly less than average height and stockily built, with his immaculate suit, erect posture and broad shoulders, he was an impressive figure despite his lack of inches. Paul judged him to be forty or forty-five years of age. His dark hair was well oiled and swept back, but showed a hint of grey around the edges. His face, though lined, was tanned, or possibly weather-beaten, from a weekend spent sailing in Scotland.

Awaiting his arrival, the junior doctors had been reclining in their chairs, but now they jumped promptly and smartly to their feet.

'Good morning, Sir,' said Mr Khan. 'I trust that you've had a good weekend?'

'Yes, thanks,' boomed Mr Potts, in a deep voice that seemed unnecessarily loud in the confines of the office. 'Good weather, calm seas and a fresh breeze, perhaps blowing four or five from the west. We tried out the new spinnaker on the run from East Loch Tarbert to the Isle of Arran, and it worked a treat; a great improvement on the old jenny. So, yes, I've had an excellent weekend, thank you.'

He paused and looked around. 'Now I see that we have a new face with us this morning. Who have we here?'

'Yes,' responded Mr Khan, 'Our new house officer has arrived. Can I introduce you to Dr Paul Lambert?'

There is a convention that surgeons are referred to as *'Mister'*, whereas physicians and all other doctors are called *'Doctor'*. This distinction is historical; it goes back to the days of untrained barber surgeons who were much despised by the medical establishment of the time. They cut hair, but did 'extras' on the side, such as stitching wounds, pulling teeth and splinting broken bones. Referring to them as *'Mister'* was a deliberate slight, and implied that they were not proper doctors. Over the years, the status of surgery has changed, such that when a doctor passes the examination to become a Fellow of the Royal College of Surgeons, as Mo Khan had done several years previously, he is entitled, indeed pleased and proud, to be called *'Mister'*. Paul would therefore be called *'Doctor'*, but the more senior members of the team would be called *'Mister'*.

'I'm pleased to meet you,' said Mr Potts. 'Now, we are running behind schedule. So, let's get on with the ward round.'

Led by Mr Potts, Mr Khan and Paul, together with the ward Sister, Jean Ashbrook, her staff nurse and one of the student nurses, took the trolley containing the medical notes, and went, in procession on to the ward. It was immediately noticeable how different Mr Potts' approach was to that of Mr Khan. Gone were the open questions that invited a frank and honest reply from the patient. Mr Potts' approach was much more abrupt.

'You're feeling better,' he might say. Although the slight inflection in the voice suggested that this was a question, the words were actually a statement, and should the patient not be feeling better, they actually had to contradict the consultant to make this known. Mr Khan's approach would have been quite different. 'How have you felt since I saw you last?' he would have asked. There was, in fact, very little communication with the patients at all. Whereas Mr Khan stood face to face with a patient, Mr Potts stood at the foot of the bed, at some distance from its occupant. The conversations that took place largely involved the group of doctors and nurses at the foot of the bed, the subject of the discussion, the patient, rarely being involved. In addition, management decisions were debated in hushed voices, almost suggesting that it was inappropriate for the patient to hear what was being said.

It was also noticeable that Mr Potts encouraged brevity, and placed great trust in the competence of his long serving registrar. Mr Khan might say, *'Yesterday's hernia Sir, no problems at all; probably home on Wednesday.'* Mr Potts would then wave at the patient from the foot of the bed, say *'Good, good,'* and immediately move onto to the next patient. It was easy to see that patients would feel excluded from such consultations which, in some cases, barely lasted fifteen seconds. Even Mr Potts's review of Mr Quigley only lasted a couple of minutes. Mr Khan expressed his concern that the situation was unstable, and Mr Potts agreed that surgery would be indicated in the event of further bleeding. However, his only words to the patient were *'Don't worry, we'll sort you out one way or another.'* In particular, he did not ask to be informed in the event that surgery was required.

Paul realised that as Mr Khan had indicated, an important part of his role as house officer would be to speak up for the patients, and keep them informed of decisions taken about them on the consultant's ward round.

When the round was over, Mr Potts lingered for ten or fifteen minutes, drinking a cup of coffee in the office and chatting about the excellent sailing that was available in the sheltered waters off the west coast of Scotland. Paul was relieved when he departed. He had to arrange the investigations that Mo had identified earlier, and three new admissions needed to be examined in preparation for their surgery the following day.

****

It was during the afternoon when Paul was working on the female ward that his bleep rang with its urgent tone. He dashed to the nearest phone.

'Patient collapsed, Surgical Five Male ward,' the switchboard operator said.

Paul set off down the corridor at a run, his heart in his mouth. This was the first emergency that he had faced, and he was worried. What was the nature of the problem, would he be able to cope? As he dashed onto the male ward, he passed a student nurse carrying some bloodstained sheets. 'It's Mr Quigley,' she said, 'in bed three. Sister's already there.'

Passing through the screens that surrounded the patient's bed, it was immediately apparent that Mr Quigley had suffered another significant bleed. His face was as pale as the sheet upon which he was lying. There was evidence of bloodstained vomit on the floor, and the characteristic odour of melaena hung in the air, the result of altered blood in the stool. Sister Ashbrook was at the bedside, and to Paul's profound relief, it was immediately apparent that she was accustomed to dealing with such situations.

'Hello Dr Lambert,' she said briskly. 'A further major bleed about five minutes ago. Blood pressure is down to seventy-five over thirty-five. We'll need a second drip in the other arm. I've got the drip and cannula available if you would be kind enough to slip it in.'

Happily, Paul was able to pass the cannula successfully into the vein at the first attempt, and very soon blood was running into both arms. Mr Quigley's blood pressure improved a fraction.

'Has Mr Khan been informed?' Paul asked anxiously.

'Yes. He's with a patient in the out-patient department but says he'll be here within ten minutes. I've spoken with the patient's wife as well and asked her to come in.'

Paul relaxed a fraction. Senior advice would be arriving very soon meanwhile, Sister Ashbrook, with her years of experience, had effectively assumed the lead. Paul was delighted she was there, and welcomed the fact that she had taken control. When Mr Khan arrived, he was brisk and business-like.

'We need to take Mr Quigley to theatre as soon as he's stabilised. I'll have to return to the outpatient clinic shortly as there are still some patients waiting to be seen, but these are the things you need to arrange. Book the emergency theatre: it's Monday, that's Surgical Three's admitting day, so we'll have to use their theatre. Tell them that, all being well, we should be ready in about an hour. If they've already got some cases booked, they'll have to postpone them unless their patients are as urgent as ours, which is unlikely. Contact the emergency anaesthetist and make sure he sees the patient before he's taken to theatre. Did you take some extra blood to the lab for cross matching earlier today?'

'I did,' Paul replied.

'Fine, then ring the lab, and make sure they have those four units available as soon as possible. Obtain the patient's consent for *'whatever necessary to stop gastrointestinal bleeding, and to treat the underlying cause'*. Finally, speak with the patient's wife and make sure she understands the gravity of the situation. People believe that nobody should die from haemorrhage on a surgical ward, but regrettably it does happen from time to time. Be sure to warn her of that possibility. I have to go back to the clinic now, but don't hesitate to give me a ring if there is any further deterioration - otherwise, I'll meet you in theatre in about an hour.'

With that he was off, and Paul set about the tasks that he had been given; pleased they had been expressed so clearly. It was impossible not to be impressed by the manner in which both Sister Ashbrook and Mr Khan had reacted to this life-threatening emergency. There had been no sense of panic under pressure; both had been calm, clearheaded and decisive. He wondered whether he would ever become confident and experienced enough to behave in such a fashion.

Paul rang the Surgical Three theatre first to check the availability of the theatre suite. Unfortunately, there were already a couple of surgical urgencies booked by the on-call team of the day; a patient with appendicitis and another who had an abscess which needed to be lanced. These cases were urgent, but not life-threatening. The theatre staff accepted the emergency without hesitation; they would go off duty at eight-thirty to be replaced by the night staff, regardless of what cases were undertaken. Similarly, the anaesthetist accepted the case readily enough, but asked that the patient's clotting studies be undertaken which meant a further sample of blood needed to be taken. Unfortunately, however, the Surgical Three surgeon, a senior registrar, was far from happy when Paul spoke with him on the telephone. It was already 4.30 pm, and he clearly had plans for the evening.

'Damn it,' he said, 'surely your case can wait? It won't take me more than ninety minutes to knock off an appendix and an abscess. Bring your case to theatre after that.'

A senior surgical registrar versus a house officer undertaking his first day's duty was scarcely a fair contest, but Paul knew he had to stick to his guns. He explained the gravity of their patient's condition, stressing that Mr Quigley was actively bleeding, and in an unstable condition.

'Tell me,' said the senior registrar, 'how long is this case going to take? How long am I going to be kept waiting?'

'I really don't know,' Paul replied. 'I guess that depends upon what Mr Khan finds when the abdomen is opened.' He knew in this heart that this was true.

'Is your case really so urgent?'

'The patient's blood pressure is down to seventy-five over thirty-five,' Paul said, 'despite receiving two units of blood in the last three hours. You could discuss the matter with Mr Khan if you wish,' he added, pleased that he could call on his registrar for support.

Fortunately, the force of his clinical argument defeated the senior registrar.

'All right, but just get a move on, don't waste any time,' he snapped as he slammed down the telephone.

Back on the ward Paul took the blood sample requested by the anaesthetist and went, slightly apprehensively, to meet Mrs Quigley. He had no previous experience of speaking to relatives, let alone giving them bad news; such matters had not been part of the medical curriculum. Her attitude surprised him.

'He really is a very stubborn man,' she said. 'He's had this ulcer for years and years, and I've told him so many times that he ought to see the doctor and seek advice. Finally, when he did go, the doctor recommended he go along to see a specialist - but would he go? No. The stubborn man simply said he was far too busy at work to take time off.'

Remembering Mr Khan's words, Paul emphasised to her that her husband really was a very sick man, that he had lost a lot of blood, and that the surgery was not without its risks.

'Is this ulcer due to his smoking? Will he have to stop smoking now? If I've told him once, I've told him a hundred times that he'll smoke himself into an early grave.'

'Ulcers can have lots of causes,' Paul replied. 'Smoking, stress and irregular meals can all play their part, but some people just seem to be prone to them. However, I'm sure it would be wise to give up smoking, provided he pulls through the operation. It will be a major operation, and he is quite ill at the moment.'

Quite suddenly, she reached out and held Paul's hand.

'You mustn't think I'm a hard woman, Doctor. I do care for him; it's just that he's been so stubborn for so long about this ulcer. Will you tell him that I love him and wish him well?'

'Look, why don't you go and tell him yourself? There will be a few minutes before he goes into surgery.'

****

Paul had occasionally scrubbed for theatre cases as a medical student, but always as the second or third assistant, usually holding a retractor at arm's length with aching arms, unable to see what was happening in the depth of the wound. On this occasion though, being the sole assistant, he stood directly opposite Mr Khan as he worked, and was able to see every step of the procedure. When the patient had been anaesthetised and draped, Mr Khan opened the abdomen through a long, midline incision above the umbilicus. He quickly displayed the stomach and duodenum, both of which, at least from the front, looked entirely normal.

'Ulcers may occur on any aspect of the stomach or duodenum,' Mo explained, 'but because the blood vessels run behind the duodenum, its ulcers on the back wall that cause bleeding. You may not see any abnormality looking from the front, but if you feel carefully you can usually detect the firmness of the ulcer on the back wall, which indicates where the problem is. Feel the area in the first part of the duodenum, and you will see what I mean.'

As Paul felt, it was quite clear that the tissue in the area where the stomach joined the duodenum was no longer soft and pliable, but was hard, almost rigid. Mr Khan incised the wall immediately in front of this area, so that the inner lining of the bowel became visible. He put tissue-holding forceps on each edge of the cut and, as Paul held these open, he displayed the ulcer on the back wall of the duodenum. It was about a centimetre in diameter, and was covered with a blood clot. The theatre sister handed Mo some strong catgut mounted on a needle, and he under-ran the ulcer, taking large bites of the surrounding tissue. As he did so the blood clot was disturbed, and a fountain of bright red, arterial blood sprayed six inches upwards into the wound.

'Impressive, hey?' Mo Khan commented to Paul, looking across the theatre table. 'It's no wonder that his blood pressure dropped so fast.'

Just as quickly as the fountain had started it stopped, as Mo tied the sutures over the ulcer. With a minimum of fuss, he closed the incision in the front of the duodenum, and then divided the vagus nerve which stimulates the stomach to produce acid. Without this stimulus, there was every prospect that the ulcer would heal and not recur. He closed the abdomen, put a dressing on the wound, and the two surgeons stood back from the operating table and removed their theatre gowns and masks. Then they retired to the surgeon's room where Mo Khan wrote a record in the patient's notes detailing the operative findings and the procedures that had been undertaken. Paul prescribed the patient's post-operative pain relief, and after consulting Mo, a post-operative fluid regime.

'The anaesthetist has put down a nasogastric tube which will enable the nurses to draw off gastric juices and keep the stomach empty whilst it heals,' Mr Khan said, 'but the patient will be 'nil by mouth' for at least thirty-six hours. He'll need three litres of clear fluid every twenty-four hours via his drip, but he may need some blood as well.'

As he walked back to the ward, Paul was surprised to notice that it had gone dark; the lights were shining brightly from the windows of the wards as he passed. During the operation, he had been totally unaware of time. He had been so engrossed in the surgery that it seemed the operation had taken no more than a couple of minutes, but in fact it had taken almost two hours. No doubt time would have passed much more slowly for the Surgical Three senior registrar who was waiting to perform the two operations that had been deferred.

Mrs Quigley had been waiting on the ward whilst her husband was in theatre, and the evening visitors to the other patients on the ward had long since departed when Paul and Mo found her sitting alone in the visitors' room, with a cup of tea that the nurses had provided for her. She jumped to her feet as they entered, and immediately came across and addressed Paul.

She looked strained and anxious. 'I've been waiting to see you, Dr Lambert. Do tell me how he is; do tell me that he's better!'

Paul introduced her to Mr Khan, explaining that he was the surgeon who had done the operation, and was better placed to tell her the situation. To Paul's surprise, Mo gave a significantly gloomier prognosis than seemed justified. Surely, Paul thought, the bleeding has been stopped; the patient is only middle aged, has previously been healthy and will, as a matter of course, make a full recovery. However, Mr Khan explained to Mrs Quigley that this had been a major operation, that the situation remained volatile, that there were still significant hurdles ahead; they would not know for several days if all would be well.

Subsequently, Paul asked him if he was not being unnecessarily pessimistic about the patient's outlook.

'Perhaps a little,' he admitted, 'but let's be realistic. There's a significant chance that he might rebleed, not least because we have effectively replaced all his own blood with anticoagulated blood from the blood bank. He's had a long anaesthetic with all its attendant risks, and there is always the danger of a pulmonary embolism.'

This was the complication that all surgeons dreaded. All too often, after an otherwise successful operation, a blood clot develops in the veins of the legs, then floats up to the lungs, causing instantaneous death.

Mr Khan continued, 'Rather than being overconfident about the prognosis, and then getting egg on your face if the patient has a major complication or even dies, it's much wiser to make relatives and indeed patients fully aware of the risks, even if this causes a little extra anxiety in the short-term.' He explained that the same philosophy applies on the medical wards when patients have heart attacks. The majority of patients, perhaps eighty percent, will recover without complication, but the remainder may die without any warning. It was an important lesson for Paul to put to one side for future use.

Nine hours had passed since lunch, and Paul was famished. The evening meal was served in the doctor's residency at seven pm, designed to coincide with the visiting time on the wards. Unaware of what arrangements, if any, existed for doctors who missed the evening meal, Paul went to the dining room to investigate. Fortunately, food had been left for latecomers in a heated cabinet. The slices of beef had dried and turned to leather at the edge, the mashed potato had formed a thick skin, and the peas had hardened, but a generous portion of gravy helped to make it digestible. He was half way through his meal when he was bleeped by the staff on the ward, and informed that one of the day's elective admissions was grumbling that he hadn't seen a doctor since he arrived in the hospital at ten that morning. The night staff had also noticed that the tablets he took for his angina hadn't been prescribed. Would Paul please go down to the ward to sort things out?

With all the excitement, and his involvement with Mr Quigley, Paul had completely forgotten that one of the routine admissions remained outstanding, and hadn't been clerked. It also struck him that he hadn't written a word in any of Mr Potts patients' notes all day. He returned to the ward to attend to these duties, which meant it was after midnight before he was able to return to his room and get to bed.

Sleep did not come easily; Paul's mind was too active, and too full of the day's events. What an introduction to life on a surgical ward it had been! He had been on his feet and working virtually non-stop for some sixteen or seventeen hours. It had been a rollercoaster of different experiences and emotions, but the management of the bleeding ulcer had demonstrated to him the attraction, almost seduction, of surgery. Mr Quigley was a man in his mid-forties who, without surgery, would have bled to death, but the operative intervention and the technical skill of the surgeon had completely reversed the situation. All being well, a man's life had been saved. Surely this was the reason why surgery was the most glamorous of hospital specialities, and why surgeons were held in such high regard.

Only Paul's day wasn't yet over. At one in the morning the telephone rang. One of Mr Potts' patients couldn't sleep; would Paul please go to the ward to write up some night sedation? And at four he was roused from sleep to replace one of Mr Quigley's drips that had stopped working!

Thought for the day

Experience is the best teacher and the father of wisdom

16th Century Proverb

Chapter 2   An Embarrassing Mistake

2nd August 1966

Paul's pager sounded its loud, shrill, urgent call; it was the second time in two days, and something that would cause his heart to flutter whenever it happened for many months to come. It was Annie Baker, a technician from the pathology laboratory. She sounded concerned.

'Doctor, you've sent us a blood sample from a man called Walter Franklin. The request card says he had surgery yesterday. I thought you ought to know; his haemoglobin is only twenty percent of normal. I've checked with the blood bank and they've no blood cross-matched for him. I think you ought to get a sample down to them straight away.'

Paul was stunned. He'd seen Mr Franklin not a couple of hours before, and he had looked as right as rain. There had been no suggestion that he was bleeding; he hadn't appeared pale or shocked.

He dashed back to the ward, grabbed a needle and syringe, and ran to Mr Franklin's bedside. But when he got there, the patient was sitting up in his bed, calmly reading his newspaper. He looked pink and perfectly healthy. Furthermore, his observation chart showed a rock-steady pulse and blood pressure. He wanted to know why Paul was in such a rush!

Paul's brain tried desperately to consider the possibilities. Surely his haemoglobin couldn't be so low. He wondered if the samples could have got mixed up in some way. Had he labelled some bottles incorrectly; perhaps put the wrong name on one of the specimens? If so, another of his patients, unbeknown to him, was quietly exsanguinating! He felt another flush of adrenaline as a surge of anxiety swept through his body. Desperately, he tried to be rational. But surely that was unlikely as well; he'd seen all his patients less than two hours ago, and none of them, not even Mr Quigley, had given him any cause for concern. Any patient with a blood count of twenty percent would be extremely ill. Could the laboratory have mixed up the samples at their end?

Paul took a blood sample for repeat haemoglobin estimation, as well as one for cross-match, and sent both specimens urgently to the lab for further analysis. He rang Annie to tell her that the samples were on their way, and asked her to phone him as soon as the result was known. 50 minutes later she rang him back, now sounding much more cheerful.

'The haemoglobin is 95% this time,' she said. 'That's odd, isn't it? So strange, in fact, that I've spoken with the boys next door in the biochemistry laboratory, to see whether they've received a specimen from Mr Franklin this morning.'

'They will have done,' Paul said, 'I sent a specimen for electrolytes as well.'

'Yes, I know, and it seems the patient has virtually no potassium in his blood, and more salt than you'd find in the Dead Sea. According to these results, Mr Franklin ought to be dead! Can I ask you, Doctor, does the patient have a drip up?'

'Yes,' Paul said.

'And is the drip running a sodium chloride solution?' There was now a humorous edge to Annie's voice.

Suddenly the penny dropped as Paul realised exactly what she was saying, and precisely what he had done wrong. The patient had a drip in his forearm, and he'd taken the first blood sample from the crook of Mr Franklin's elbow, about three inches higher up his arm. The initial sample had been a mixture of a little blood, and a lot of the salt solution that was being administered.

'Oh, my God,' he said, simultaneously feeling both relieved and embarrassed, 'I've taken blood from the drip arm, haven't I?'

'It looks like it,' Annie said, 'but not to worry; it does happen from time to time, especially at this time of the year when you newly-qualified doctors join us. May I suggest you take another sample for electrolytes from the other arm just for the record?

It was lesson learned the hard way, but Paul recalled what one of his tutors at medical school had said. 'When delivering healthcare, the occasional mistake is inevitable. To err is to be human. The secret is to acknowledge one's mistakes, learn from them, and ensure they are not repeated.'

Thought for the day

Do you want to speak to the doctor in charge or to the nurse who really knows what's going on?

Origin disputed

Chapter 3   The Patient who was B. I. D.

3rd August 1966

Working overnight as the only doctor in a Casualty Department serving half a million people, would be a major challenge even for an experienced practitioner. For Paul, just three days into his first job as a doctor, it was a nightmare. Certainly, there were more senior, more experienced medical staff available should he need advice, but they were tucked up in their beds, fast asleep in the adjacent building, effectively at a distance of ten minutes. Should there be a major road accident or some disaster in the local coalmine or steelworks, Paul would find himself responsible for the initial management of one, or possibly many, critically-injured patients. It was in those first five to ten minutes, when Paul was on his own, even as the medical cavalry would be charging to his assistance, that lives would be won or lost.

These were the days before emergency medicine emerged as a specialty in its own right; before Accident and Emergency departments had permanent senior medical staff. The initial treatment of the most acutely-ill patients was left in the hands of the most junior medical staff. It was a highly unsatisfactory arrangement; unsafe for doctors and unsafe for their patients. An additional hazard was that the house officers suffered the chronic tiredness that resulted from working excessive hours. They undertook the overnight casualty duty having worked throughout the previous day. Fortunately, though, there were senior and experienced nursing sisters on hand in the Casualty Department to offer support.

It must have been about three in the morning when the telephone rang in the tiny, hot and stuffy bedroom, (according to rumour, it used to be an old broom cupboard), in which a bed was available for Paul to sleep, as and when the flow of patients allowed.

'Sorry to trouble you, Doctor Lambert,' it was Sister Barlow's cheerful voice, 'but I've got a little job for you.'

'I'll be right there, Sister,' Paul replied, immediately fearing that the problem would be beyond his experience.

He slipped into trousers and shirt, pulled his white coat over the top, and within a minute was back in the department, only to discover to his surprise that there were no patients waiting to be seen; all the cubicles were empty. An ambulance man however, was hovering in the corridor. He looked relaxed and had a mug of tea in his hand. The kettle in the casualty department was one of the most frequently used items of equipment.

'Oh, there you are, Doc,' he said. 'I'm sorry to have disturbed your sleep. I've got a B.I.D. for you.'

Doctors use many acronyms and abbreviations, and their use can lead to misunderstandings. To most people the letters PR stand for Pro Rata, or possibly Public Relations, but to a rheumatologist they stand for the debilitating disease Polymyalgia Rheumatica. To an obstetrician they mean Pregnancy Rate, to a cardiologist they represent the interval between the P wave and the R wave on an ECG (that's shorthand for Electro-Cardio-Graph by the way) and to a proctologist they mean a Per Rectal digital examination. The abbreviation B.I.D., however, was not an acronym Paul had heard before!

'You've got a what?' he asked.

'A B.I.D. in the back of the van, if you've got a minute, Doc.'

Embarrassed by his ignorance, Paul stalled.

'I'll be with you in a minute,' he said, and slipped into the office to find Sister.

'What on earth is a B.I.D?' he asked.

'A *Brought in Dead*,' she replied.

Paul was none the wiser.

'And what have I got to do with a *Brought in Dead*?' he asked.

'Well,' she explained, 'it means that the ambulance men have found somebody whom they believed to be dead; possibly someone who has collapsed and died in the street, or somebody who's been the subject of a 999 call, but died before the ambulance managed to reach them.'

'And my role?' Paul asked.

'Well,' Sister explained, 'the ambulance crew aren't qualified to certify death. That's a medical responsibility; so they need a doctor to certify that the patient is indeed dead. If they are *'brought in dead'* obviously, there's nothing the hospital can do for them. So, we don't admit them; indeed, we don't allow them to come through our front door. Instead, they go to the city morgue to be dealt with by the Coroner. He arranges a post-mortem examination to ascertain the cause of death, and to make sure there are no suspicious circumstances. The ambulance crew simply need you to sign the death certificate for them.'

Alarm bells immediately started to ring in Paul's head! He'd spent five long years at Medical School learning to diagnose hundreds of different conditions, but always on the assumption that the patient was alive. He'd been taught the difference between tetanus and tetany; he could diagnose scabies, scarlet fever, syphilis, and syringomyelia; he even knew the life cycle of the schistosomiasis parasite, but no one had ever taught him how to be absolutely certain, certain beyond all reasonable doubt, that someone was dead.

He knew, of course, to feel for a pulse and listen for a heartbeat, but for how long should you listen? Five minutes, ten minutes, half an hour? He'd been a boy scout and learned that if you held a cold mirror in front of the mouth and condensation formed, the patient was alive, but that was scarcely the definitive test of death!

Moreover, it was certainly not a diagnosis he could afford to get wrong. On the third day of his medical career, he didn't want to feature in a *'Local doctor is struck off Medical Register'* newspaper story, or be named in a television *'Patient wakes up in City Morgue'* news headline.

Nervously, he went with the ambulance man into the back of his 'van', as he called it, but he needn't have worried about getting this particular diagnosis wrong. The body was in an advanced stage of decomposition, having been found by a caretaker in the backyard of an office block, known to be frequented by the homeless. The smell was overpowering.

He felt for a pulse, listened for heart sounds, and checked the reflexes in his eyes, much to the amusement of the ambulance man, who clearly regarded such tests as unnecessary.

'Best to be sure, eh Doc,' he said with a wry smile on his face.

Paul duly pronounced the patient dead and signed a death certificate. Fortunately, there was no requirement to make any supposition about the cause of death. All that was necessary was to certify that this decomposing corpse had indeed died, and of that, there was absolutely no doubt.

Paul washed his hands thoroughly and returned to his room, but it took him some time to get to sleep! He resolved that when morning came, there was an important job for him to do; he had to discover the definitive diagnostic test for death. He also wondered how soon it would be before the next great hole in his medical knowledge would be laid bare for all to see. In fact, it was to be the very next day!

Thought for the day

Either he's dead, or my watch has stopped.

Groucho Marx 1890 - 1977

Chapter 4   Mr Quigley's Nasogastric Tube

4th August 1966

Paul hadn't inserted a nasogastric tube before, nor had he been taught how to perform this procedure. This was a task normally undertaken by the nurses, and naively he didn't anticipate that it would be difficult. At any one time, there were half a dozen patients on the ward being treated with these tubes. The nurses never seemed to have any difficulty inserting them, so Paul assumed that popping one into place would be a straight forward procedure; no more than a two-minute job. How wrong he was.

The purpose of the tube is to remove acidic digestive juices from the stomach. It's made of plastic, is about fifty centimetres long, with a diameter approximately that of a drinking straw. It is passed up the nose, through the back of the mouth, and then down the gullet. When in place, one end rests in the stomach, the other dangles from the patient's nose where a syringe can be attached to suck out stomach secretions.

Paul's patient was Raymond Quigley whose bleeding duodenal ulcer had been treated by Mr Khan three days earlier. Taking the tube out of its plastic bag, Paul fed it gently into his left nostril. It went in about half an inch, and then stopped; it appeared to have met an obstruction. Paul withdrew it and tried again, this time pushing a little more firmly, but again the tube came to a halt, suggesting it had reached a fairly solid blockage. Paul wondered whether at some time Mr Quigley had broken his nose, and that the channel up the nostril had been narrowed, or deformed as a result.

'Let's try on the other side,' he suggested.

As on the left, the tube met some resistance, but this time, by pushing a little more firmly, the tube advanced. Paul relaxed feeling he was making good progress when Mr Quigley suddenly winced in obvious discomfort. His hand went to his nose.

Don't worry,' Paul said, using his most soothing voice, and gently guiding his patient's hand back to his side, 'we're making progress now.'

However, as he pushed more of the tube up his nose, Mr Quigley became progressively more alarmed. He became unable to speak and pointed anxiously to his cheeks, both of which were now swollen like hamster's pouches. Then, quite suddenly, in front of Paul's eyes, the tip of the plastic tube emerged like a viper's tongue from between his lips. Mr Quigley opened his mouth, and clearly visible inside, were 20 inches of plastic tube, all coiled, twisted and buckled. Clearly the tube had not been going down the gullet into the stomach at all; it had taken a false turn at the back of the mouth! Paul felt a sudden wave of panic as he realised that retrieving the situation, and the tube, might prove difficult and possibly hazardous.

He was tempted to ask Mr Quigley to spit it out, through his mouth, hoping that the whole tube, including the last few inches that were still dangling from his nose would follow. Unfortunately, however, the tube was much wider at the top, and it seemed highly unlikely that it would pass through his nose. The only alternative was to pull the tube backwards, up through the nose, and hope and pray it didn't tie itself in a knot somewhere at the back of the throat as invariably happened whenever Paul attempted D I Y jobs involving plastic coated electrical cabling or plastic hosepipes. If that happened, it would be impossible to remove the tube either upwards or downwards, and the patient would have to go back to the operating theatre to have it retrieved! Paul felt a cold sweat on the back of his neck.

Deciding that withdrawing it through the nose was probably the better option, he slowly started to pull the tube upwards. To his great relief, the hamster's cheek pouches gradually subsided, the viper's tongue disappeared, and the tube came out without undue difficulty. A wave of relief swept through him as he realised that, although he had caused Mr Quigley some temporary distress, no serious harm had resulted.

Paul apologised, gave Mr Quigley a couple of minutes to recover, then tried again. Gently, Paul eased about four inches into his nose, then stopped and looked in his mouth, and was pleased that the tube was nowhere to be seen. He advanced another inch, re-inspected the mouth, and was delighted there was still no sign of the tube. Now feeling relaxed, certain that the tip of the tube must already be safely in the gullet, he pushed another two inches up the nose, with renewed confidence.

Suddenly, and without any warning, Mr Quigley's hands grasped desperately at this throat as he gasped for breath. He suffered a paroxysm of coughing, and his cheeks took on an ominous purple hue. He tried to speak, but without breath was unable to do so. There was a wild fear in his eyes. Instantly, Paul knew what was amiss; the tube had not gone down the gullet, but instead had gone down 'the wrong way', and was stuck in his windpipe blocking his airway. Immediately, he pulled the entire tube out, but Mr Quigley was now in fear for his life. He gasped for breath, making a high pitched, wheezing sound, his eyes watered, he coughed repeatedly, but fortunately and to Paul's profound relief, over the course of the next five minutes, his breathing gradually returned to normal, and he regained his composure. Putting a reassuring arm around his shoulders, Paul again apologised profusely for causing him so much anxiety and discomfort.

'Don't worry Doctor,' Mr Quigley said, when eventually he regained enough breath to speak, 'It's me that's being a nuisance. You've got your job to do. We'll try again, but for God's sake, give me a moment or two to catch my breath.'

Mr Quigley seemed to think the problem was his fault; clearly, he didn't realise this was the first time Paul had undertaken the procedure. Paul though was certain it was due to his inexperience. He wondered whether this was an appropriate moment to call for assistance. He'd been told repeatedly during his training that if junior doctors met any difficulties, or were uncertain how to proceed, they should call for help. Failing to call for help when it was required, they insisted, was a greater sin than calling unnecessarily. Certainly, Paul was having difficulty but surely passing this wretched tube wasn't such a tricky job. After all, it was something the nurses did, day in and day out. And he was damned if he was going to lose face by asking them for their assistance.

Whilst he was considering what to do, he received some encouragement from Mr Quigley.

'Come on Doctor,' he said, 'let's get it over.'

With the benefit of hindsight, Paul knew he should have called for assistance. The 'retrospectoscope' is the greatest of all medical instruments, but foolishly, he didn't! And so it was that with considerable trepidation he continued. Approximately six inches of tube disappeared up the nose before the disaster happened. Mr Quigley was sitting on the side of his bed with Paul standing about 12 inches away, directly in front of him. Without warning, and accompanied by a loud retching noise, he vomited. A pint and a half of stale blood mixed with yellowy-green bile hit Paul in the middle of his chest. Involuntarily he took a step back. Within a few seconds, a second vomit occurred, this time landing on Paul's shoes and on the floor, but also splashing beyond the confines of the screens that surrounded the bed.

In a flash, the Ward Sister, Jean Ashbrook appeared. She was a slim, dark-haired woman with sharp features and a sharper tongue. She ran her ward with brisk efficiency. She was never one to hide her emotions, whether praising the work of her nurses or, as was occasionally necessary, keeping the junior doctors in order. She assessed the situation instantly; the patient still retching, a pool of blood and bile on the floor, and Paul, looking stupid, still holding the nasogastric tube in his hand, with the patient's vomit down the front of his white coat dripping onto his shoes.

Sister turned to the student nurse who accompanied her. 'Nurse Meredith,' she said, 'please show this doctor the correct way to pass a nasogastric tube, and then clear up this unholy mess.' Was it Paul's imagination, or was there the slightest emphasis on the word *'Doctor'*, and the word *'correct'*? Then 'tutting' loudly, her eyes to the ceiling, and with a sad shake of her head, she turned on her heels and left. Nurse Meredith's first concern was the patient. 'I'm so sorry you've been sick, Mr Quigley,' she said, her voice calm and sympathetic. 'Let's start by rinsing out your mouth.' Within a few minutes she had calmed the patient, washed his face, and put him at his ease. Then it took her less than 60 seconds to pass the tube in a skilful, painless, effortless and totally professional manner.

She busied herself anchoring the tube to the patient's nose then looked across at Paul. For a second their eyes met, and in that moment, Paul saw sympathy and understanding. His heart missed a beat.

'Hello,' she said, a soft smile warming her face. 'Your new on the ward aren't you. I'm pleased to meet you.' Paul was ashamed, humiliated and felt a complete fool.

'Thank you,' he said, 'and thanks for showing me how to pass the tube. I'm afraid we weren't taught how to do that at Medical School.'

Nurse Meredith looked Paul up and down, her eyes passing from his red face, to his soiled white coat then to the vomit on his shoes.

Her eyes twinkled, and again she smiled, now looking slightly amused.

'Now what are we going to do with you?' she asked.

This was a question that was already causing Paul concern. He didn't relish the prospect of walking through the ward in his present state, passing Sister on the way, and then creeping along the hospital corridors to his room, though he was sure that Sister would have enjoyed the sight.

'You stay here for a minute while I slip and get another white coat for you from the linen cupboard,' she advised. 'I need to collect some sheets to freshen up this bed as well.'

When she returned, she had hidden the white coat amongst the sheets and pillowcases she had brought. Behind the patient's screens, Paul changed his coat, and used the old one to wipe his shoes.

'That's made you look a little more respectable, Dr Lambert,' his saviour said, now laughing, 'but you really don't smell too good. You slip away and change your shirt while I tidy up here. I'll get one of the other nurses to help me.'

'Thank you,' Paul said, 'you've been extremely kind to a doctor in distress.'

Severely chastened, he left and managed to escape from the ward and reach his room without attracting too much attention. He realised how foolish he had been, and in his heart knew that his public humiliation was a just reward for his arrogant assumption that as a doctor he knew better than the nurses. And there was an important lesson for him to learn; when you don't know what to do, don't be too proud to ask.

Thought for the day

'We don't just have egg on our face, we have omelette all over our suits.'

Tom Brokaw 1940 –

Chapter 5   Fun with Magic Markers

5th August 1966

Paul had just said 'hello' to a patient newly arrived on the ward, and was explaining that he needed to take her history and examine her, when his bleep sounded yet again. Although he had been delighted to be allocated the pager less than a week before, (it had made him feel like proper doctor, no longer merely a medical student), that initial pride had already evaporated. He now realised how easy it was for others to contact him to add to his workload, and to disrupt his daily schedule.

The switchboard informed him that Sir William Warrender was in the surgeons' changing room in theatre, and wished to speak with him. Paul apologised to his patient, walked briskly to the theatre, and found Sir William together with his nephew Johnny Nolan, who was the other newly-qualified house officer allocated to the unit. They were relaxing over coffee and biscuits.

The Surgical Five unit to which Paul had been appointed consisted of a male ward, a female ward and an operating theatre. The unit was supervised by two consultants; Mr Leslie Potts, who was Paul's boss, and Sir William, for whom Johnny would be working. Sir William was the hospital's senior consultant and its father figure. Paul judged that he was in his early sixties, probably within a few years of retirement. Tall and distinguished with white hair, his face held a kindly expression indicative of his gentle manner. He was always immaculately dressed in a formal suit with a freshly ironed, city shirt accompanied by a sober tie. In the summer months, as a final flourish, he added a rose or a carnation, grown in his own garden, to the buttonhole of his jacket. His manners reflected his appearance; he was invariably courteous and unfailingly polite, whether to nurses, doctors or patients. He had been in post since the inception of the National Health Service in 1948 and was well respected, both inside the hospital, and in the wider medical fraternity. Whereas Mr Potts was distant and brusque with his patients, Sir William was adored for his excellent communication and interpersonal skills. He always found time to reassure patients, to explain to them the nature of their surgery, potential complications and details of their expected convalescence.

Johnny was a likable, quick-witted rogue, whose pranks had provided several memorable moments during their student years. His appointment as a house officer in a prestigious hospital had more to do with his family connections than the marks he achieved in the final medical school examination. It was Johnny who had bricked up the entrance to the Nurse's Home one New Years Eve. He was also responsible for replacing the bust of the hospital's founder and benefactor with a skeleton dressed in a nurse's uniform on the 'open day' when 'A level' students interested in applying to study medicine were invited to look round. Johnny had been Paul's best friend at Medical School, and Paul had been delighted when he learned that they would be working together for the first six months as newly qualified doctors.

'Ah, Lambert,' Sir William said when Paul entered. 'I'm pleased you were free to come and join us.'

It was the custom and practice at this time for consultants to address their house officers by their surnames, and Paul took no offence. By assuming that he was 'free', rather than working with a patient, Sir William had made it sound as if calling him to the theatre was a casual request which Paul could have declined had he so wished, rather than an instruction from his boss which had to be obeyed.

'I'm afraid there's been a little problem with the marking of patients,' Sir William continued. 'Two patients arrived in theatre today whose operation site had not been marked on their skin. I also understand from the theatre staff that one of Mr Potts' varicose veins patients arrived in theatre yesterday, and the marks on the legs were almost invisible.'

At first Paul failed to understand how this affected him. The patients on that morning's list had been clerked by Johnny, and he knew with absolute certainty that all the patients that he had clerked the day before had been marked appropriately. He'd marked them himself.

'But I marked them myself, Sir,' he said, 'very boldly, with a black marker pen.'

'Yes, I do realise that,' said Sir William gently, 'but it appears you used a washable marker pen instead of an indelible one. You need to remember that before patients come to theatre, they are all washed and shaved. I want you both to go down to the stores department and pick up an indelible marker for future use.'

He went on to explain that every year somewhere in the country, a surgeon either operates on the wrong patient, or performs the wrong operation. There were even examples of the wrong limb being amputated.

'Such mistakes,' he said, 'are indefensible and completely preventable. I know we all pay an annual premium for medical negligence insurance, but when these things happen, it's not good for the reputation of the profession, certainly not good for the career of the surgeon concerned and, of course, it's an absolute disaster for the patient.'

He then detailed other ways in which such terrible mistakes could be avoided, such as writing the patient's first name and surname, their hospital number, and the type of operation to be performed in full, both on the patient's consent form and on the operating list. No shorthand or abbreviations should ever be used.

'The side on which surgery is to be performed should be written in capitals,' he instructed, 'so a patient for a hernia operation should be listed as *'RIGHT inguinal hernia repair'*, not as *'RIH'*. Similarly, an amputation must be recorded as *'LEFT mid-thigh amputation'*, not as *'LMTA'*.

He turned to Paul. 'Which is your first finger?' he asked.

Paul held up his index finger.

'Most people in this country would agree with you, but did you know there are parts of the world where the thumb is regarded as the first? The lesson is that their descriptive names – thumb, index, middle, ring and little – should be used.'

He went on to describe other safeguards. 'All the documentation should be checked as the patient leaves the ward, again as they arrive in theatre, and a third time by both anaesthetist and surgeon before any procedure begins. Accidents happen,' he said, 'when these basic procedures are not followed.'

The lesson was an important one, but Paul felt that Sir William, who at times could be somewhat pedantic, was rather labouring the point. He illustrated the matter by telling the two housemen how a surgeon friend of his, who was travelling to give a lecture, ended up in Newcastle-Upon-Tyne when his true destination was Newcastle-under-Lyme. It seemed to be rather a weak example when only the week before the national newspapers had reported that a man whose rupture was to be repaired as the third patient on an operating list, had unfortunately been sterilised; the man scheduled to be number two on the list had decided at the last minute not to proceed with his vasectomy!

Paul was unhappy at being reprimanded, albeit gently and constructively, so soon after his arrival on the unit. In his eyes, Sir William was a gentleman as well as the senior surgeon. Paul held him in high regard and would obviously follow his advice for the benefit of the patients. However, he was also aware that he could have a significant influence on his future career. With his support and a good reference, his prospects would be good. With a bad reference, he might end up as a GP on a far-flung Scottish island, or on a £10 assisted passage to one of the colonies.

The situation for Johnny was quite different; Sir William was his uncle, and his future in his father's medical practice in a leafy Surrey suburb was assured. The relationship though was on his mother's side, giving him a different surname, for which Johnny was grateful. He didn't wish his connection to the hospital's nationally-renowned surgeon to be too obvious. Paul had already noticed that the exchanges between Sir William and Johnny in front of patients or the nursing staff were always appropriately formal. No one would have suspected there was a family connection. Away from patients though, the relationship was more relaxed. Johnny dropped the 'Sir' that he used in public, and Sir William referred to his nephew by his Christian name. Johnny evidently regarded Sir William as a benevolent uncle rather than as a senior consultant.

As the two junior doctors left the surgeons' room, and walked together back to the ward, a smile crept over Johnny's face. It seemed that he had some mischief in mind.

'If we really take him at his word, we could have some fun with this,' he said, with a twinkle in his eye. 'I've got a man coming in next week for a circumcision. I shall draw a bold black arrow all the way down from his umbilicus to the tip of his manhood.'

'You scarcely need to mark a circumcision,' Paul commented. 'He's only got one such appendage to choose from; there really can't be any confusion.'

'Nonetheless,' said Johnny, still smiling, 'we've been told to mark it, and mark it I shall, as prominently as I can! We've also got a man being admitted with piles. I'll draw concentric circles around the area, possibly in different colours, to make it look like an archery target, or a dartboard.'

He paused. 'Did my Uncle Bill say anything about the proper name for different toes? I've a patient coming in for an operation on a toenail. I think it's the middle one, but he didn't tell us the correct anatomical names for toes. Is it called the middle toe, or is it the third toe?'

'Call it the roast beef one,' Paul said.

'What on earth do you mean?'

Paul started to recite the traditional nursery rhyme, so well-known to children.

'This little piggy went to market
this little piggy stayed at home,
this little piggy had roast beef,
this little piggy had none,
and this little piggy went wee, wee, wee all the way home!'

'That's a great idea,' Johnny exclaimed. 'I'll write *'Ingrowing toe nail on the RIGHT roast beef toenail'* on the list that goes to theatre, and also on the consent form. It will keep the nurses amused, and it does accurately describe the nail for surgery. Have you got any suitable cases for marking?' he enquired, looking at Paul.

'With respect, I think you and I are in slightly different situations, Johnny,' Paul said. 'I work for Mr Potts, and he's not the sort to find such behaviour amusing!'

****

A week passed and nothing further was said about marking patients until Sir William, at the end of one of his ward rounds, turned to the two housemen.

'You two, in my office, at the double,' he commanded. His voice was unusually sharp, his face and tone surprisingly severe. Johnny and an apprehensive Paul followed behind his brisk step.

Inside the office, he scowled at the two junior doctors such that Paul became convinced that he must have committed some grave error. He wracked his brains wondering what he had done wrong. What terrible mistake had he made? Sir William enjoyed their discomfort for a full minute, glaring at each of them in turn, before his demeanour changed, and a smile appeared on his face. It became apparent that he was merely getting his own back, having a little joke at their expense.

'You two are full of tricks, aren't you?' he said, now smiling broadly. 'Your marking of operation sites on patients provided good entertainment for the theatre staff recently, particularly the patient with piles, though I confess the theatre sister had to explain to me what was meant by a *'roast beef toe'*. Perhaps if I'd ever married and had children, I would have known! However, I thought that marking my boots 'L' and 'R' was a step too far. I'm not quite so old that I need that sort of assistance.'

Paul looked sharply at Johnny because this was news to him, and it did seem a little unkind.

Sir William continued. 'I suppose medical students and junior doctors have always got up to silly japes. I confess that as a young man I played my fair share of foolish tricks.'

He then embarked on a long and convoluted story that involved him putting earwigs under the door of matron's bedroom when he was a resident doctor. Paul relaxed. Sir William wasn't a bad sort at all; a bit old fashioned maybe, but kindly and benevolent and obviously quick to forgive. He was much liked by all his patients too, no doubt because his bedside manner was superb. It was no wonder that he was so well respected in the hospital.

Thought for the day

C'est double plaisir de tromper le trompeur.   *(It's doubly pleasing to trick the trickster.)*

Jean de la Fontaine 1621 - 1695

Chapter 6   Suppositories

23rd August 1966

Sister Ashbrook stood in the doorway and surveyed the scene. This was her ward, her domain. She smiled to herself; everything was ready, all spick and span. She noted the satisfying symmetry of the metal-framed hospital beds which were equally spaced along the walls, each bed dressed with freshly-laundered linen sheets, their corners neatly folded in the traditional way. The bedside lockers had been cleaned and tidied, wilting flowers having been replaced with fresh blooms. The windows had been cleaned, the linoleum floor was spotless. The visitors, whom she considered noisy and untidy, had departed leaving the ward quiet and calm. The sight pleased her. She was proud of her ward, proud of her nurses and proud of the care they gave to their patients. Her ward was held in high regard by the hospital's formidable matron, and that pleased her as well. All was now ready for the highlight of her week; the ward round by the hospital's senior consultant, the man she respected above all others.

When Sir William arrived, she greeted him with her customary, 'Would you care for a coffee and a biscuit, Sir, before you start your round?'

Equally predictably came his usual reply; 'That's very kind of you Sister, but we must see our patients first.'

With Sister at his side, he led his entourage onto the ward. He was followed by Mr Khan, several medical students wearing their long, white coats, then by the nurses with their stiff, white aprons and starched frilly caps. Bringing up the rear were the two housemen; Johnny pushing the trolley containing the patients' case notes, with Paul at his side. Paul still found it hard to believe that he had actually passed his final medical examination and was now a doctor and a member of this formal medical team. Acutely conscious of his inexperience, he fervently hoped that he would not be found wanting.

The first patient seen on the ward round was Barry Webb, who was recovering from an operation to remove his gall bladder. On his bedside locker, in a glass specimen jar, looking like a collection of small black pebbles, were the gallstones that had caused him months of pain. After a few minutes of polite conversation during which the recent warm weather was discussed in some detail (Sir William always liked to put his patients at ease) the consultant enquired about the wound. With some pride, Barry unbuttoned his pyjamas and revealed his surgical wound. Six inches in length, it was situated in the upper part of his obese and hairy abdomen. Neatly stitched, with no hint of any infection, it was healing beautifully.

'Haven't I got good healing flesh?' Barry remarked, clearly pleased with himself.

Sir William turned to the doctors, nurses and medical students encircling the bed. 'There, you see how it is,' he said. 'If the wound heals well and the patient makes a smooth convalescence, he gives credit to his *'good healing flesh'*. However, if there's a problem with the wound, perhaps an infection, or worse, a wound that fails to heal, it's a case of *'what's gone wrong with your stitches, Doctor?'* It's a bit tough on the surgeon, isn't it? We can't win either way.'

His audience smiled politely, despite this being an adage most of them had heard many times before. Then, turning back to the patient, Sir William asked, 'Have you moved your bowels since the operation, Mr Webb?'

'No, not yet. Earlier, I heard some rumblings in my belly, as if there was some wind rolling round, but no action yet.'

'Aha,' said Sir William, holding up his right hand, his long, bony, index finger pointing to the ceiling. Sister snapped her fingers which prompted a flurry of activity. A junior nurse ran to get the rectal tray, and a second nurse disappeared to fetch a clean towel from the linen cupboard. A fingerstall was produced from the rectal tray, and passed to Sir William. The consultant slowly and carefully rolled the rubber sheath onto his erect index finger, an action that caused a parallel image to enter Paul's mind. He glanced at Johnny, who seemed to have the faintest smile on his face; presumably, the same thought had occurred to him. Paul glanced at the group of young nurses, but their faces showed no reaction. Perhaps they hadn't attended schools where sex education was part of the curriculum.

With the fingerstall in place, Sir William was handed a three-inch square of lint, in the centre of which a slit had been cut. Designed to protect the knuckles from any soiling during the forthcoming examination, this was placed over his index finger, which was still raised aloft.

Sir William turned to Johnny. 'Now, young man, learn from my experience. No one should be too superior or too proud to perform the humble rectal examination. If you don't put your finger in it, sooner or later you'll put your foot in it!'

Mr Webb was turned onto his left side, his knees were drawn up to his chest, his pyjama trousers were lowered, and his buttocks were adjusted so that they were overhanging the edge of the bed. The screens had been pulled around the bed, offering privacy from the other patients on the ward, but not from the doctors and nurses accompanying Sir William. Paul thought it an unnecessary indignity to perform the examination with such a large audience, but this didn't seem to bother Sir William. Again, the surgeon's right index finger was held aloft, and another nurse appeared holding a small glass jar containing the glycerine that was to act as a lubricant. Sir William plunged his finger into the jar and then, with considerable relish, into the anus of the patient who gave an involuntary start, surprised by this sudden rear-end attack.

Sir William pushed his finger to the very hilt, beaming broadly as he did so. 'Sister,' he announced, 'no wonder Mr Webb can feel wind rolling around his belly. It can't escape. He's bunged up. Two suppositories, please.'

These appeared as if by magic, were lubricated, and passed to the consultant who thrust them deftly into the patient's rectum. By this time, yet another nurse was standing at Sir William's side, with a paper bag held open, into which Sir William placed the now offensive rubber sheath and lint. He then marched off to the washbasin situated halfway down the ward, followed by a nurse who had a freshly-laundered towel over her arm, like a waiter at an expensive restaurant. The whole episode had been quite a performance, and the teamwork shown by the nurses had been impressive, suggesting hours of practice.

An impish thought occurred to Paul; perhaps this was an exercise organised by the ward sister in advance, the various nurses being designated different tasks. Nurse One collects the rectal tray, Nurse Two passes the finger stall, Nurse Three passes the lint, Nurse Four produces the lubricant, Nurse Five has the suppositories ready, Nurse Six holds the paper bag open and Nurse Seven accompanies Sir William to the sink with the freshly laundered towel – and all the while, Sister Ashbrook supervises, ensuring that the entire performance proceeds with the precision and discipline that would be demanded by a regimental sergeant major at an army camp.

It was not altogether a surprise to find that the whole pantomime was repeated further down the ward, and then a third time after Sir William had moved to the female ward. Paul wondered whether perhaps the teams of nurses from the two wards had competitions to see who could perform the exercise most efficiently, just as a team from the Royal Artillery used to compete with the Royal Engineers to assemble a field gun in the Royal Albert Hall during the Remembrance Service each November.

Later in the office, the junior doctors reflected on the morning's events.

'It's all very well Uncle Bill taking four hours to see his patients, but we've still got a hundred and one jobs to do. It'll be midnight before we're through,' Johnny complained, exaggerating, but making a valid point.

'Perhaps if he did fewer rectal examinations, we would get around faster,' Paul responded.

'Or inserted fewer suppositories,' Johnny added, remembering the ritual that was enacted each time. 'That would save time as well.'

These remarks earned them a mild reproach from Sister Rutherford, who was the antithesis of Sister Ashbrook on the male ward. Whereas Jean Ashbrook was young, sharp and critical, Gladys Rutherford was warm and caring, a homely woman of mature years. She made young nurses and junior doctors welcome on her ward, and did everything she could to help, guide and support them.

'Sir William has a traditional bedside manner,' she said. 'Some may regard him as being a bit old-fashioned, but he takes a personal interest in his patients. They have great respect for him, and they benefit hugely from the personal attention he gives them.'

'Perhaps if we had a sweepstake to guess how long the round takes,' Johnny suggested, 'you know, as sometimes happens for the best man's speech at a wedding, at least the time would seem to go faster. Or perhaps it would be more fun to estimate how many suppositories he inserts during the course of the round.'

Sister gave him another disapproving look, but said nothing. Perhaps she felt that Johnny, as Sir William's nephew, was allowed to say such things.

'I would have thought that, on average, about eight suppositories are inserted each round, so my money's going on eight.' Johnny continued. Paul suggested four.

However, Mo Khan, who had served as Sir William's assistant for many years, was reluctant to participate. 'I'm not sure that this is such a good idea,' he said. 'What happens if Sir William finds out? I'm sure he would disapprove and I don't want to blot my copybook.'

'Don't be such a spoilsport,' Johnny remarked, in a tone that a houseman would not normally be expected to adopt when addressing a registrar. 'I can assure you that my Uncle Bill is not without a sense of humour. He's not likely to find out, but even if he does, I'm sure he would only regard it as a bit of fun. And it won't do the patients any harm; they're going to have the suppositories inserted whether we count the number or not!'

Reluctantly, Mr Khan agreed to participate, and decided on twelve. It was suggested this was excessive, but the registrar just touched the side of his nose. 'Don't forget, I've worked for Sir William longer than you.'

Sister, however, could not be persuaded to participate. She looked rather prim, and said she preferred not be involved. Without actually saying so, it was clear she didn't approve.

'If you're not joining in, perhaps you would keep the score?' Johnny suggested.

'Certainly not,' she responded crossly.

'I'll keep the score then,' Johnny said. 'I'll start with some investigation cards in my right-hand coat pocket, and I'll transfer one to my left-hand pocket each time a suppository is inserted. I'll be like the cricket umpire counting the six balls of an over.'

It remained to be decided how much the stake should be, and after some deliberation, the sum of sixpence was agreed, none of the juniors having much money to spare.

And so it was that the great suppository game was begun which was to provide hours of harmless entertainment during Sir William's seemingly endless ward rounds.

****

The following week Sir William was, once again, followed onto the ward by his registrar, the two-house officers, Sister and a gaggle of nurses. The patient in the first bed was Freda Farrington who, having had a hernia repaired, was due to be discharged later in the day. Inevitably, having checked her chest and wound for any evidence of infection, Sir William asked about her bowels. Johnny's hand moved expectantly to his white coat pocket, but when Freda assured Sir William they were in good working order, he assumed his normal posture, albeit looking a trifle disappointed. Paul wondered whether the patients ever discussed amongst themselves the experience of having one of Sir William's digital examinations, and if they did, whether it was thought wiser to deny any slight constipation, even if their bowels were a little on the stubborn side.

It was the third patient seen on the round who actually volunteered that since her operation, she hadn't managed to get her bowels working. Presumably she was unaware of the fate that befell anyone bold enough to make such an admission, or perhaps she felt that her bowel problem was sufficiently severe as to justify Sir William's radical therapy, rather than the gentler laxative therapy she would have received had she had a quiet word with Sister Rutherford.

Immediately, Sir William raised his index finger to the heavens, thus summoning the rectal tray, and he reiterated the stock phrases that his staff heard so often. 'No one should be too haughty or too proud to perform the humble rectal examination. Mark my words, sooner or later, if you don't put your finger in, you'll put your foot in it.'

The seven nurses set about their duties with exemplary efficiency; a finger stall was placed on his upheld finger, gauze added to protect his knuckles, lubrication applied and at the completion of the military operation, two suppositories had been inserted into the patient's anus, and Johnny had transferred two cards from his right-hand pocket to the left, a look of satisfaction on his face. The suppository sweepstake had begun. In no way did the game detract from the seriousness with which each consultation was undertaken. Each patient was thoroughly assessed and examined; due consideration being given to an appropriate course of management. The suppository sideshow simply provided a little extra interest.

As on the female ward, the visit by the senior consultant to see his male patients was the highlight of the week and in no time at all, the rectal tray was again in action. Standing across the bed from Sir William, Paul tried to avoid eye contact with the patient to prevent unnecessary embarrassment. Instead, he looked across the top of the patient's bare buttocks as Sir William started to perform his examination. He noticed that one of the junior nurses standing there was Nurse Meredith, his saviour when Mr Quigley had vomited over him during his ill-fated attempt to pass a nasogastric tube. Paul's discrete enquiries had revealed that her name was Kate, and he had been trying to pluck up courage to ask her out. He knew that it should be the most natural thing in the world for him to ask her for a date, but as one of three brothers who had attended a boys' grammar school, he lacked confidence when in the company of the opposite sex.

Since they both worked on the same ward, he had often seen her, and occasionally had spoken to her about their patients, but each time he did so, a subtle change had come over him. He felt anxious, hesitant and ill at ease. He got butterflies in his stomach, and was conscious of his heart thumping in his chest. What was it about her? Paul looked across at her again. In many ways she was quite unremarkable, the sort of girl you could pass in the street, and not really notice. She was of average height, slim, with a neat figure, and mousy brown hair that was held neatly under her nurse's cap. Was it just that she had been kind to him, and come to his rescue when he was struggling with Mr Quigley's nasogastric tube during his first week on the ward? No, there was more to it than that. He admired the way she handled herself on the ward. She moved easily through the sick patients with a smile here, and a kind word there. She seemed at ease with herself, enjoying her work, undertaking her job without any fuss, and certainly not drawing attention to herself in any way.

She had a fresh complexion and blue eyes, but she could not be described as a classic beauty. It was not a face that you would see on the front page of a fashion magazine, but it was one nevertheless that Paul found attractive. Quite suddenly she caught Paul's eye and smiled. Paul realised that he must have been staring at her. He managed half a smile in return before turning and looking away, feeling embarrassed. Again, he was aware of the butterflies and the heartbeat in his chest, and knew that his face had become flushed. He tried to concentrate again on what Sir William was saying, but a moment or two later decided to risk another glance at Kate. She must have been waiting for him to do so, as she immediately caught his eye. She seemed to be amused at his embarrassment, and again favoured him with a gentle smile. It was a beautiful smile, full of warmth and friendship. It struck Paul that she was quite comfortable with the silent communication occurring between them, whereas his heart was thumping so hard that he feared everyone in the vicinity must hear it.

He watched her as Sir William started his usual patter. 'No one should be too superior or proud to perform the humble rectal examination,' he reiterated. 'If you don't put your finger in...'

Kate smiled, and started to mime the phrase she had heard so often, in time with Sir William's words. Paul smiled back, but to his chagrin, Sir William noted his amusement. He had completed his digital assessment of the rectal contents, and was about to insert some suppositories. He withdrew his finger and glared at Paul.

'No, Lambert,' he said, wagging a soiled finger at his unfortunate houseman. Paul saw a small fleck of faeces flick off his finger, and land on the white bed sheet. 'This is no joking matter. I'm absolutely serious about the need to examine patients thoroughly, and that includes a rectal examination. If you omit it, sooner or later you'll miss something important. Many a patient with rectal bleeding has been treated as a simple case of piles, but had they been properly examined, a cancer might have been detected and their lives saved. In medicine, thoroughness must be routine; it's the key to good patient care.'

It was galling for Paul to be reprimanded so publicly, but he was not in a position to say that he hadn't been laughing at Sir William at all.

Further down the ward, Sir William met Dennis Slater. He was a university student who had annoyed Johnny intensely by treating him as he had treated his fag, at the well-known public school he had attended. He had been admitted for observation because it had been unclear whether his obnoxious behaviour was the result of a head injury or alcoholic intoxication. Having been summoned unnecessarily by Dennis on numerous occasions, Johnny's opinion was that Dennis was not in any way ill; he was simply arrogant and rude.

When Sir William reached Dennis, the young man was lounging by his bed reading a magazine, a mug of tea at his elbow. Sir William examined him, reviewed the observation charts which fortunately were entirely satisfactory, and then proceeded to give him a lecture on the dangers of alcohol, and the need for moderation. Dennis listened meekly enough, though it seemed unlikely he would take any notice. Satisfied that Dennis could go home and that his ward round was over, Sir William turned to the door in anticipation of the coffee and biscuits that awaited him in the office. Paul was delighted. His estimate of eight suppositories had proved to be correct. When Sir William departed, he would be declared the winner of the sweepstake, and would collect sixpence from each member of the team.

Johnny, however, had other plans. 'I don't think Dennis has moved his bowels whilst he's been with us, Sir,' he said innocently.

Sir William's response was entirely predictable. He turned back to the patient, raised his index finger, and the rectal examination tray was summoned. As Sir William performed the usual pantomime, words and actions now totally familiar, Johnny's expression registered considerable satisfaction, as the young man who had so annoyed him, suffered the indignity of a rectal examination, performed in the presence of an audience that included young nurses. As Sir William was occupied inserting, first one, and then a second suppository into Dennis' back passage, Johnny, smiling broadly, casually transferred one investigation card and then a second from his right to his left jacket pocket. Not only had he wreaked his revenge on Dennis, but he had also scooped the jackpot. Ten suppositories had been the total he had predicted.

Nothing could be said to him about the incident whilst Sir William drank his coffee in the office, but as soon as he left, Johnny was attacked from all sides.

'A blatant case of cheating.'

'Not in the spirit of the game at all.'

'Unbecoming of a member of an honourable profession.'

Johnny, however, was unrepentant; 'A most satisfying morning's work,' he said.

In the weeks that followed Sir William's ward rounds, although slow and ponderous, continued to provide a mixture of education and amusement, especially when Sister Rutherford finally agreed to participate in the sweepstake. This came as something of a surprise, as previously she had disapproved, feeling that the sweepstake was disrespectful to her favourite consultant. However, when she relented, it gave the green light to the junior nurses to participate, so that on this occasion, the kitty was considerably larger than usual.

Since it was Sister's first involvement in the game, by common consent, she was allowed first selection of the number of suppositories to be inserted.

'Seven,' she said.

This caused some jocularity. She had been Sir William's ward sister for many years and should have known that he usually inserted suppositories two at a time. It was unlikely an odd number would win the jackpot. Nevertheless, Sister was not to be moved.

In due course, Sir William arrived and led his staff onto the ward. It seemed that the theme for this particular round was to be the effect of drugs. He had just read an article in a medical journal which suggested that many 'across the counter' medicines such as cough mixtures had been shown, in scientific studies, not to have any useful therapeutic effect.

'Now we shall have to find other treatments for patients who have nothing wrong with them,' he remarked humorously.

He stopped beside the bed of a lady who had vomited blood due to the aspirin tablets she had taken for her headaches. Although the aspirin had relieved her pain, as a side effect it had eroded the lining of her stomach, causing an ulcer to form.

'You must be aware,' Sir William explained, 'that the drugs you prescribe may affect people in different ways. Take alcohol, for example. That's a drug, after all, and it can have very variable effects in different people.'

He turned to Sister. 'How does alcohol affect you, Sister?'

'I'm afraid it makes me giggly, Sir William.' He turned to his housemen. 'And you, Lambert?'

'That seems to depend on the time of day, Sir. If I take alcohol at lunchtime, it makes me sleepy, but if I drink in the evening, it loosens my tongue and I become rather over-talkative.'

'And what about you, Johnny?'

'I'm teetotal,' Johnny said with a twinkle in his eye.

Sir William smiled; he obviously knew better, but didn't contradict his nephew.

Sir William continued. 'And we know it makes other people aggressive, the results of which we see in the Casualty Department every Saturday night. So you see; one drug, but many different reactions. So be aware that the drugs you prescribe for patients may not always have exactly the effect that's described in the textbook.'

Eventually, the consultant arrived at the last bed, and throughout the entire ward round only four suppositories had been inserted, a surprisingly low number. The only possible winners of the jackpot were Mr Khan, who had selected four and Johnny, on six. Could Johnny be trusted not to cheat again? He'd been given a rough time after the last episode; surely, he wouldn't dare to repeat the same trick again.

The patient in the final bed had undergone an operation on her piles. With a very tender rear end making bowel movements painful, it was inevitable that Sir William would perform an examination, but would he insert any suppositories? Everyone watched with bated breath as the examination proceeded, and sure enough, the index finger was raised, indicating that suppositories were required. Johnny couldn't conceal his delight and took two investigation cards from his pocket in eager anticipation, a triumphant grin on his face. Once again, he was going to win. There was more cash in the kitty than usual, and on this occasion, no-one could possibly accuse him of cheating.

When one suppository had been inserted, Sir William looked up. Sister gave an almost imperceptible nod of the head, and a second suppository was inserted. Again, Sir William looked up.

'I think one further suppository should do the trick,' Sister said.

A final suppository was inserted, the seventh of the round. Without further comment, Sir William walked down the ward. He washed and dried his hands before returning to the group.

'What's your favourite charity, Sister?' he asked on his return, a broad grin on his benevolent face.

Sister thought for a moment. 'I think probably our own ward's amenity fund. There are a number of items that would be appreciated by our patients that the NHS is unable to afford.'

'An excellent choice,' said Sir William. 'Now, shall we go and have that cup of coffee?'

It was clear that the game was up, and the sweepstake that had been providing entertainment for months would have to stop. Fortunately, Sir William didn't appear to have taken any offence; in fact, he was in a buoyant mood during the coffee break in the office. He must have assumed that his nephew was the prime mover in the escapade because, before he left, he turned to Johnny and said, 'After today, I don't suppose you'll ever forget that no-one should be too 'high and mighty' to perform the humble rectal examination, and that if you don't put your finger in.....' he paused expectantly; '....one day you'll put your foot in it' Johnny added.

Thought for the day

If you have a stomach ache, in France you get a suppository, in Germany a health spa, in the United States they cut your stomach open and in Britain they put you on a waiting list.

Phil Hammond 1955 -

Chapter 7   Mrs Ann Brown

3rd September 1996

Mrs Ann Brown presented in the emergency department on a Monday afternoon. She arrived in a state of collapse with a thready pulse, a barely recordable blood pressure, and looking as pale as a ghost. She had passed a stool containing a large volume of fresh, red blood, and was continuing to bleed from her back passage. In view of her extreme condition, the casualty officer called for reinforcements, and since the wards were quiet, Mo Khan and Paul went to offer assistance. At first glance, it was obvious that the patient was critically ill; the first priority therefore, was resuscitation. At this stage in his career, collapse from blood loss was a situation with which Mo Khan had become familiar, and he fell effortlessly into the usual routine. Assisted by Paul, he placed an oxygen mask over Mrs Brown's nose and mouth, used large cannulae to put drips into both arms, then infused fluid whilst blood was being prepared for transfusion. Initially, she was too ill to give any sort of history, but as she responded to treatment, they began to obtain some background information from her.

She was 42 years of age, and had recently come to live with her sister in the local area following a separation from her husband, who still lived with her son and daughter in the family home in Bristol. Initially, the bleeding had been minor and intermittent, but this proved to be the prelude to a dramatic haemorrhage. She had collapsed at her sister's home, and been rushed to the hospital by ambulance. Paul and Mo questioned her closely for clues as to the underlying cause of the bleeding, but none were apparent. She said that prior to this episode she had been perfectly fit and well.

Such dramatic haemorrhages may be due to an abnormality of blood-clotting, such as haemophilia, but Mrs Brown was unaware of any such problem. She had never had any particular difficulty with heavy periods, or with excessive bleeding at the time of dental extractions.

Having denied any recent medical problems, the doctors were surprised to find two fairly fresh abdominal scars, one in the upper abdomen, and one more centrally placed. Mo asked her why she had needed these operations.

'One was for gall stones,' Mrs Brown explained, 'and the other was an exploratory operation because they thought I had appendicitis.'

'And did the surgeons in Bristol experience any particular problems with bleeding when you had those operations?'

'None at all.'

Knowing they would need to review the notes, Mo asked Mrs Brown which hospital she had attended in Bristol.

'It was the Bristol Royal, but there's no need to involve them, it was all very straightforward.'

Mo asked the patient to turn on her left side, and had a look inside her back passage with a short telescope to see if he could discover the cause of the bleeding. The examination was a failure.

'There's still a lot of blood washing around in there,' he said to Mrs Brown, 'I can't see what's going on. I suggest that later this evening we give you a short anaesthetic, and repeat the examination. When you're asleep, we'll be able to wash away the blood, and see what's going on. If we can identify the source of the bleeding, we should be able to stop it.'

He turned to Paul. 'I'll go and organise the theatre and the anaesthetist. I'll leave you to write up the notes, and get written consent for the anaesthetic and examination?'

After Mo had left, Mrs Brown made an unusual request.

'Doctor,' she said, 'under no circumstances do I want my son or my husband to be informed of my medical problem. I don't mind if you talk to my sister, but on no account should anybody speak with my husband or son. Is that quite clear?'

Paul explained that doctors were bound by an ethical code which included confidentiality, and that no information should be given to a third party without the patient's express permission. In saying this though, he was aware that, in practice, this rule was occasionally broken. So, to ensure that everyone was aware of this specific request, he attached a note prominently to the front of her medical records. He was, however, curious to know why this specific request was made.

'My husband and I are getting divorced; we're going our separate ways. Unfortunately, my son has decided to side with my husband. If you were to meet them, they would probably express sympathy for me, but then start asking nosy questions about my illness when in reality, they don't care for me at all. I would prefer to keep the details of my illness to myself; thank you very much.'

She sounded very definite, had clearly decided this in advance, so Paul did not press the matter.

Paul was off duty when Mo took Mrs Brown to theatre, and only heard about the operation the next day. When the blood had been washed away to allow a good view of the bowel, he found a deep ulcer involving a major blood vessel barely an inch inside the back passage. The most common cause of such an ulcer would be a tumour, but apparently, this didn't look cancerous, and unable to be certain of its cause, Mo had taken a sample for analysis. Then with some difficulty, he had closed the ulcer with sutures.

****

Mo's handiwork with needle and thread suturing the ulcer was successful; the bleeding stopped. As a result, Mrs Brown's condition improved, the colour returned to her cheeks, and her observations remained stable allowing her intravenous infusion to be discontinued. Over the next few days, Paul was able to spend more time with her, and got to know her better.

She was a slim lady with a bony, angular frame. Paul wondered if she might have lost weight recently, but she strenuously denied this. Her face, with its prominent cheek and jawbones, crowned with dark hair streaked with grey, carried a pinched, tense, and unsmiling expression. She appeared to carry the worries of the world on her shoulders. It was noticeable that she didn't mix well with the other patients on the ward, being somewhat withdrawn. She was difficult to engage in conversation, and was usually to be found sitting on her own. It seemed to Paul that she was depressed, presumably as a result of the break-up of her marriage, and the difficult relationship with her husband and son.

Unfortunately, on her fifth day in the hospital, the day of her planned discharge, Mrs Brown bled again. On this occasion, the volume of blood lost, although significant, was not life-threatening. Nonetheless, it necessitated a two-pint blood transfusion, and as a result, she made a return trip to the operating theatre. As before, it was Mo Khan who undertook the procedure and again the blood was washed away to enable the lining of the bowel to be visualised. At this second examination, the ulcer looked deeper and more ragged than before, but again there appeared to be no obvious reason why it had developed. The sutures inserted previously had disappeared, presumably dislodged by the act of defecation, so once again, Mo sealed the ulcer with sutures.

Mrs Brown had been admitted under the care of Mr Potts, who was known for his speed and efficiency; he normally conducted his ward rounds in a brisk and business-like fashion. It was unusual for him to spend more than two or three minutes at any patient's bedside, but on his next round, he spent a long time with Mrs Brown.

He interrogated her personally, and in considerable detail. Clearly, the case caused him concern, partly because the volume of blood lost posed a threat to her life, but mainly because of the lack of any obvious diagnosis. How can you offer a rational treatment without knowing the cause of the trouble?

Attempting to solve the mystery, he questioned Mrs Brown about her general health and bowel habit. Finding himself unable to add anything to their existing knowledge, he asked questions that might suggest a rarer cause of the rectal ulcer. Had the patient participated in any unusual sexual activity?

'My husband and I live apart. We're getting divorced.'

'That doesn't quite answer my question, does it?' the consultant said, persisting with his line of enquiry.

'The answer is still no,' snapped Mrs Brown.

'Have you travelled to any tropical countries recently?'

'My husband always put himself and his job before me,' was the angry retort. 'We rarely had any holidays, and now that I have to fend for myself, I scarcely have enough money for the clothes I stand up in, never mind any thoughts of foreign travel.'

Concerned that the patient might have an abnormal bleeding tendency, Mr Potts enquired, as his junior staff had previously, whether there had ever been any excessive bleeding or bruising with minor injuries, but try as he would, he could add nothing to what was already known about the patient.

Later, over a cup of coffee, Mr Potts again raised the puzzling case of Ann Brown.

'You say the ulcer didn't look like a tumour?' he asked the registrar.

'No, it didn't,' Mo replied, 'and we now have the laboratory report of the sample I took for analysis. The pathologist says there's nothing to suggest this is cancer, indeed nothing to suggest any particular diagnosis at all. The changes seen under the microscope were entirely non-specific.'

The consultant turned to Paul. 'Have you run tests to look for abnormalities of blood clotting?'

'Yes, I have twice, and both samples were entirely normal.'

'And have the laboratory looked for abnormal infections?'

'Yes, Sir, they have, and again, everything is totally normal.'

'You say she's had two recent operations. Have you got the notes from the Bristol hospital?'

'Yes,' Paul replied, 'they arrived this morning and they confirm that she's had two operations within the last six months. One was to remove the gall bladder, although it seems that she didn't have gallstones, only some slight inflammation of the wall of the gall bladder. The second operation appears to have been performed because she was getting a lot of abdominal pain. The surgeon didn't really find much wrong when he operated. He removed the appendix but, on analysis, it was said to be normal. On both occasions, she healed up well, and she was discharged from the hospital in standard time. There's no suggestion that she had any abnormal bleeding.'

'Actually,' Paul added, 'she has quite a thick set of notes from Bristol, and as well as her operations, she's had investigations for headaches without a diagnosis being made.'

'Well,' Mr Potts said, 'we don't have a diagnosis to explain this ulcer either, and that's a grave concern when she bleeds so heavily from it. The trouble is that I can't think of any other investigations that will help; we'll just have to hope she doesn't bleed again, and that the ulcer heals. But one thing you might do is to speak with her husband, and see if he can throw any light on the matter.'

'There's a problem there, Sir,' Paul replied. 'As you know, Mr and Mrs Brown are getting divorced, and she has specifically instructed that under no circumstances must we impart any information about her condition to her husband, or to her son.'

'How very odd! Obviously, we have to abide by a code of confidentiality, but it should be possible for you to speak with him, without giving away details of her condition. Simply ask him whether he can shed any light on the matter.'

Sister Rutherford joined in the conversation. 'Mr Brown rang the ward earlier, and said he intended to travel to visit his wife on Saturday. In the circumstances, it may be best if Mrs Brown doesn't see anyone speaking with him.'

She turned to Paul. 'If you like, I'll catch him when he's leaving after visiting time, and you can speak with him in the office.'

****

Mr Brown seemed a pleasant man, perhaps a little older than his wife. He was clearly anxious about her condition, eager to know the cause of her troubles, and the plans for her future care. Paul however had to explain that, unfortunately, he was unable to answer his questions because his wife had specifically instructed that they were not to talk to him about her medical condition.

'I suppose I'm not surprised,' he said, 'it's the sort of thing she would do.'

He went on to confirm that he and his wife were getting divorced, saying that there was no third party involved, but that the love they had once shared had simply melted away over the years.

'We just appear to be drifting apart. I don't seem to be able to do anything to please her. Don't get me wrong,' he said, 'it's not that I hate her. I don't wish her ill, in fact, I'm sorry she's poorly now, but we can't go on as we are. We're simply no longer compatible. That's why we agreed to go our separate ways. Our children are grown up now, they're independent, they can see what has happened to us, and they understand. I was talking it over with my son only this morning, and he thinks I should get on with the divorce straight away, but I don't really feel that I can whilst she's ill; but we'll have to get the divorce finalised one day.'

As Mr Potts had suggested, Paul asked whether Mr Brown could throw any light on his wife's illness, but as he didn't know the nature of the illness, and since Paul was unable to inform him, not surprisingly, he was unable to add anything useful.

Paul had scarcely said goodbye to Mr Brown than he was bleeped again. Mrs Brown had produced another blood-stained stool. He hurried to the ward and confirmed that she was indeed bleeding – very heavily. The pulse and blood pressure chart at the end of the bed indicated she was doomed unless the blood loss could be stopped. Another trip to theatre seemed inevitable. Paul undertook the now familiar steps to resuscitate and transfuse. He called for Mo, who in turn rang Mr Potts at his home, and within the hour, poor Mrs Brown was once again in the operating theatre, this time with Mr Potts in charge of proceedings.

Working through a telescope, Mr Potts attempted to stem the flow of blood, but was unable to do so. The ulcer was wider and deeper than before, it could not be sealed with sutures, and it was with considerable regret that Mr Potts decided that if Mrs Brown's life was to be saved, there was no alternative but to remove the rectum. Showing great surgical skill, he then performed a complex two-hour operation, which involved the removal of Mrs Brown's back passage. This meant forming a colostomy; a permanent opening on the front of her abdomen through which her bowels would function. In future, her stool would be collected in a plastic bag, carried on a belt that she would wear around her waist.

As Paul watched the stoma being fashioned, he was acutely aware that when speaking with Mrs Brown before the operation, he had only obtained her permission for an examination by telescope and suturing of the ulcer. It was true that the standard small print at the bottom of every consent form, gave the surgeon licence to do *'whatever necessary'* but very few patients bothered to read the whole form, indeed most signed the form without reading any of it. Paul often thought that if he were to write *'removal of head and all limbs'* on the form, the majority of patients would happily sign it without a second thought! In this case, with the ongoing bleeding, there was no alternative to creating the stoma, but it was going to come as a devastating shock to Mrs Brown when she learned of it.

****

Fortunately, the first few days after Mrs Brown's operation were free of any complications. Heavily sedated, and confined to bed with her abdomen bandaged, she was blissfully unaware of the nature and complexity of her surgery. The nurses on the ward were caring and compassionate to everyone in their care, but certain patients, in view of their individual circumstances, received especially sympathetic treatment. Mrs Brown was one because of her relative youth, her difficult family circumstances and her unfortunate medical problem. As the days passed, and the need for pain relief and sedation diminished, she became noticeably brighter, and more cheerful than she had been before her operation. She seemed to revel in the care and attention she received, and began to engage more freely with the other patients on the ward.

One day, she spoke with Paul about her plans for the future. She had originally trained as a teacher, and although she hadn't worked since her marriage twenty years before, she was now considering returning to that profession, possibly in a part-time capacity. She thought that since she was effectively starting her life again as a single woman, teaching would raise her status, give her independence, and offer financial security. At no stage in the conversation, did she make any mention of her colostomy, or the effect that a stoma might have on her plans, and this caused Paul some disquiet. Afterward, he went to discuss the matter with Sister Rutherford to seek her advice and guidance.

'Sister, Mrs Brown has just been speaking to me of her plans for the future, but she never once mentioned her colostomy. In fact, she doesn't seem to realise that she has one. I presume she hasn't been told yet.'

'No, she hasn't, and it's been worrying me too. The fact that she has a stoma doesn't preclude any of her plans of course, and most folk, especially the younger ones, adapt to the new situation really well; indeed, the vast majority lead full, active lives.'

'I appreciate that,' Paul said, 'although there will be plenty of hurdles for her to overcome. So what do you suggest? Do we just wait until the colostomy starts to function? Surely that would come as an awful shock to her. Wouldn't it be better for us to make the first move; to inform her, and prepare her in advance?'

'Undoubtedly, and frankly the sooner she's told, the better. At the moment, she's more cheerful and positive than she was before her operation; that will certainly help when she's told. Are you free now?'

Together, they walked down the ward, pulled the screens round Mrs Brown's bed, and drew up two chairs. As they sat there, Paul glanced across at Sister, and she looked back at him. Neither of them had thought who was going to open the conversation, and there was a momentary pause. Mrs Brown looked anxiously at each of them in turn, wondering why they had come to see her, sensing there was some bad news to relate.

Hesitantly, Paul explained that when she had been taken to theatre for the third time, the intention had been to stop the bleeding by stitching the ulcer in the manner that had been successful on the previous occasions. He told her that unfortunately, this had proved impossible. The heavy bleeding had continued, it would have resulted in her death had it been allowed to carry on, and for that reason, a length of bowel including her back passage had been removed. He then explained that since her back passage had been removed, it had been necessary to allow the stool to exit the body by another route, in other words, to perform a colostomy. He paused, uncertain if she understood what a colostomy was, but she had obviously heard of this operation.

'That's the 'bag' operation isn't it, Doctor?'

'Yes,' Paul said, grateful she already had some understanding of a stoma. 'The bowel now ends on your tummy wall. Your motions will appear there, and will be collected in a small plastic bag. You will need to wear a belt around your waist to support the bag.'

To his surprise, Mrs Brown's anxious expression melted away, and she began to look more relaxed.

'Obviously, you will be with us for a week or so yet,' Sister added, 'so there will be plenty of time for us to tell you more about it. We'll show you the bags and the belt, and explain how they work. We won't let you go home until you've got the hang of it.'

'So that means I'll have to come back into hospital for another operation, doesn't it?' Mrs Brown still seemed relaxed about the situation, even managing a smile, apparently unruffled by the thought of yet more surgery.

With a shock, Paul realised he hadn't made the situation completely clear.

'No,' he said. 'We're not planning any more surgery.'

'So the plumbing just goes back to normal on its own, does it? That's very clever.'

'No,' Paul explained, as gently as he could. 'I'm afraid that you don't have a back passage anymore. It isn't possible to return the plumbing to normal. I'm afraid the colostomy, the artificial opening, is permanent.'

Such a possibility had clearly never entered Mrs Brown's head, and the revelation shocked her. A look of horror crossed her face, initially disbelieving, then frightened and angry.

'But why? Why have you done that to me?' her voice, previously composed, now halting and strained.

Sister moved from her chair, sat on the bed beside Mrs Brown and put an arm around her shoulders, whilst Paul emphasised this had been the only way to stop the bleeding which, without treatment, would have led to her death. He stressed that such a step would not have been taken unless it had been absolutely necessary. Mrs Brown though didn't hear a single word that was being said, as she cried inconsolably.

For a while, no one spoke while Sister continued to comfort the patient. Paul knew there was little further he could usefully do or say, yet was conscious that it would be awkward to walk away and leave her in such distress.

Sister seemed to understand his dilemma. 'I'll stay here with Mrs Brown for a moment. Would you please ask one of the nurses to come and join me?'

Gratefully, Paul slipped away confident that Sister and her team would do their very best to comfort and console the patient, aware they were much better equipped for the job than he was.

****

After this episode, Mrs Brown's mood changed radically. She became sullen and uncommunicative, and showed a deep resentment towards both the medical and nursing staff. Her conversations with Paul were monosyllabic, and there were embarrassing moments on Mr Potts' ward rounds when she refused to speak to him. She wouldn't look at him, declining even to acknowledge his presence. Worse still, she refused to acknowledge the existence of her stoma. She ignored the nurses when they tried to demonstrate the belt and bag to her, and refused to change the bag herself. She simply called the nurses for assistance whenever the colostomy needed any attention, as it frequently did.

Her physical recovery, however, continued to progress satisfactorily such that, within a further week, she would have been discharged had she not continued to refuse to have anything to do with her stoma. She wouldn't even look at it, let alone handle it.

Then the story took another twist. Sister Rutherford rang Paul, concern in her voice.

'Ann Brown is bleeding again. I'm not sure, but I think it's coming from her front passage.'

'Probably just her period, Sister,' Paul said remembering she was only in her early 40's.

'I don't think so, Paul. It doesn't look like menstrual loss, and it's not her time of the month. Perhaps you could come and have a look when you have a minute.'

Paul wasn't particularly worried; this was likely to be menstrual flow or possibly some seepage from the wound where the rectum had been. Sister joined him at the bedside and showed him some blood on Mrs Brown's nightdress; undeniably it looked pure and fresh. Paul looked at the wound but found it to be almost healed; it seemed unlikely to be the source of the blood. Perhaps the bleeding was coming from the vagina after all.

Sister suggested that Mrs Brown should insert a tampon, and wear a separate pad over the wound so that, should there be any more bleeding, they would know where it was coming from.

Half an hour later, Sister was on the phone again.

'Paul,' she said, 'there's no blood on the pad, but there's a lot more fresh blood on the tampon. The bleeding is undoubtedly coming from the vagina.'

It was time to seek more senior advice, so Paul discussed the situation with Mo Khan on the phone.

'I just do not accept that this can be explained by an abnormality of her clotting system,' Mo said, speaking quite slowly as he considered how this latest development should be handled. 'She's had major surgery, and the blood clotted normally throughout the operation, but to make absolutely sure, you'd better get another sample to the lab. Also, see if you can get one of the gynaecologists to see her. If Mrs Brown now has a gynaecological problem, we're going to need their specialist advice. I presume you've organised the observations, the drip, and the blood?'

'Of course, I have' Paul said, slightly irritated Mo had felt it necessary to mention it.

Mo rang off with a request that he be informed if there were any significant changes in Mrs Brown's condition.

Later that afternoon, Paul happened to be in the ward office when Mr Phillips, a consultant gynaecologist, entered after he had seen Mrs Brown.

'May I have a word with you and Sister?' he asked, 'in private if I may.' he added, looking meaningfully at two student nurses who had been working at the desk. Sister took the hint and asked them to leave. Mr Phillips crossed the room, and closed the door.

'As you know, Mrs Brown is bleeding from the vagina,' he said, 'and when I took a look inside, it's fairly obvious why. There are numerous scratch marks on the lining of the vagina.'

'Scratch marks?'

'Yes, multiple scratch marks, some of them quite deep; it's as if somebody has been playing noughts and crosses in there.'

'And how have they got there?'

'I think that's fairly obvious, but we need to make sure. I've told Mrs Brown that I need to examine her more thoroughly, so I've asked her to come to my clinic in the morning. While I'm examining her, the clinic staff will search everything she brings with her. It would be helpful if she travelled light. Whilst she's away from this ward, I suggest you make an exhaustive search of her bed, her locker, and all her belongings. If I'm right with my diagnosis, she doesn't need a gynaecologist, she needs a psychiatrist.'

The next day the plan was put into action. Sister waited until Mrs Brown had departed, and then began a thorough search of her bed and locker. It took twenty minutes, and she was about to give up when she found it. It was a four-inch metal nail file, whose end had been sharpened to a point. It had been concealed by being taped to the underside of one of the metal bars of the bed. Paul rang Mr Phillips to tell him of their discovery, and learned that the staff in the gynaecology clinic had found an identical object concealed in the lining of her handbag. Finally, the picture had become crystal clear. She had inflicted the vaginal wounds on herself; so presumably, the rectal ulcer had also been self-inflicted. No wonder the sutures that Mo had placed in the ulcer had come adrift, and with hindsight, not surprising that the laboratory could find no sign of disease when examining samples taken from the ulcer.

Paul asked Mr Phillips if he had ever seen such a case before.

'Only once,' he said, 'in a young woman who did something similar when newly-married. As a result of the scratches, she bled every time she had intercourse, which alarmed her husband. She used it as a device to avoid intimacy.'

Then Paul had a moment of enlightenment, and a cold sweat swept over him. He suddenly realised he knew exactly why she had harmed herself, and that all along he had held the key that could have unlocked this mystery. He just hadn't had the sense to realise it. All too clearly, he now recalled what her husband had said. *'I really don't feel I can divorce her whilst she's ill'*. He was unwilling to finalise the divorce until his wife was restored to health. That was why she had done it. She was trading on his good nature. As long as she was ill, she could cling onto the marriage. Paul cursed himself for not appreciating the significance of the information he'd been given. Perhaps if he'd shared this knowledge with Mr Potts, the colostomy operation might have been avoided.

He rang Mo to tell him the puzzle had been solved, and sought guidance as to whether they should inform Mr Potts of the latest developments at this stage, or wait and tell him on the next ward round.

'We don't need his medical advice at the moment, so I think we'll leave it until the morning. She's made a fool of all of us. The boss is not going to be best pleased.'

There was always a slight tension in the air when Mr Potts was on the ward. It wasn't simply that he was brusque; it was that there was a sharp edge to his tongue. Any error, real or perceived, on the part of a junior doctor earned a brisk reprimand, delivered in front of patients and nursing staff alike. Mo was concerned how the consultant would react when told that Mrs Brown had been self-harming. He decided it would be wise to inform him of the latest developments in the office, knowing it would be difficult to tell the full story at the beside in Mrs Brown's presence. Rather cautiously, Mo raised the subject.

'Sir, since you were here last, we've made some progress in the case of Mrs Brown and now have a much clearer understanding of her problem.'

Fairly briefly, he explained about the episodes of vaginal bleeding, the deep scratches the gynaecologist had discovered, and the subsequent discovery of the sharpened nail files.

When he finished, there was a long pause, finally broken by the consultant.

'Damn her! She's taken us all for a ride, and made a complete fool of me. I've taken away her rectum, given her a colostomy, and she's nothing but a bloody nut case.'

'But she's still ill, Mr Potts,' Sister Rutherford said, rather tartly.

Mr Potts echoed the sentiment that had been expressed by the gynaecologist. 'Maybe she is, Sister, but she needs a psychiatrist, not a surgeon.'

Paul knew he had a confession to make, and thought that the sooner he got it off his chest the better.

'I'm afraid, Sir, that all the while, I've had a bit of information about Mrs Brown that I didn't mention because I didn't appreciate its relevance. But I believe that had I informed you, the problem might have been solved earlier. You see, during a conversation I had with Mr Brown, he mentioned that he was unwilling to proceed with the divorce whilst his wife was ill. Presumably, that's why she has been harming herself. Whilst she was ill, she felt confident that he wouldn't divorce her. I'm sorry I didn't mention it earlier.'

The boss looked thoughtful, and there was another long pause. It was a relief to Paul when he spoke again.

'Don't worry; perhaps there was a clue there, albeit a tiny one. I'm afraid that I've missed some much more obvious ones.'

Paul looked up, surprised. Mr Potts explained.

'A middle-aged lady is going through a difficult separation and divorce, estranged from her son. She's had two operations in Bristol within the last year, without any definite pathology being found. There were multiple attendances with headaches, but always with negative investigations, and a set of notes four inches thick for a patient who is basically healthy. The signs were there if only I had thought about them.'

He stopped and paused. 'Have you told her that we now know what she's been up to?'

'No, Sir,' Paul said, 'but since both nail files have been removed, I'm sure she will have realised.'

'You say she's in a side ward now? You'd better keep her there until she's discharged, and since she's made a monkey of me, you'd better keep her out of my way too. Get the psychiatrist to see her, and to take her to his ward. If I ever see her again, I shall probably say something I shall regret.'

Mr Potts then undertook his ward round, but didn't go anywhere near the side ward.

There remained the problem of Mrs Brown's attitude to her stoma. Clearly the subject ought to be raised with the boss, but equally, it was obvious he had washed his hands of her. It was a problem that Sister, Mo and Paul would have to sort out later.

Thought for the day

The truth is rarely pure and never simple.

Oscar Wilde 1854 - 1900

Chapter 8   The Medical Detective

24th September 1966

Sir William laid aside the journal he was reading, and looked at the clock on the wall of his office. It was two minutes before ten o'clock. He smiled; he had a surprise planned for the new group of students who were waiting for him on the ward. He eased himself from his chair, stretched his back, and then set off down the corridor.

It was the beginning of a new University year, and he vowed, as he always did on these occasions, not only to teach them to be good doctors, but to impart to them, the common sense and good manners that he believed should be the hallmark of all who practised in the caring professions.

'Good morning,' he said, as he entered the room.

The students stood up, respectfully. 'Good morning, Sir,' they responded.

There were eight students in the group, six young men and two girls. Mr Solanki and Mr Patel had been educated in India, the rest had attended English schools.

'Now let's start at the very beginning,' Sir William said, having learned the names of the students.

'Being a doctor is like being a detective. A crime is solved by interrogating suspects, by examining the crime scene looking for evidence, and if necessary, by undertaking some forensic tests.

To make a diagnosis, a doctor follows the same three steps. Firstly, we take the patient's medical history; in other words, we ask them to describe their symptoms. Then we undertake a physical examination, and finally we perform some tests, perhaps blood tests, maybe x-rays or scans. Of the three, listening to the patient's story is by far the most important. You should be able to make a working diagnosis in 70% of patients from the history alone. Your clinical examination will solve the problem in perhaps 20% of cases, and various investigations will give you the answer in a further 5%.

He paused and waited for the inevitable question.

'And the last 5%, Sir?'

'In the last 5%, you will never find out,' Sir William responded with a smile. 'Most will simply get better on their own, though just occasionally you may need the pathologist to solve the mystery for you with a post-mortem.

Now,' he continued, as a nurse wheeled a lady of about fifty into the room, 'your very first patient.'

The patient, a bright-eyed, homely-looking woman was wearing a pink dressing gown over her nightdress, and wore white slippers on her feet.

'I want you to meet Mrs Bradshaw, a lady who has been with us for some time.'

He invited the patient to transfer from her wheelchair to the examination couch; he made sure she was sitting comfortably, before thanking her for agreeing to meet the students. Sir William was a gentleman who led by example.

'In a moment, we're going to take Mrs Bradshaw's history, but before we start, I wonder if any of you have already made any observations about her? I'm sure you would normally be too polite to voice them in her presence, but Mrs Bradshaw has assured me she doesn't mind.'

His enquiry was met with silence. 'Well, did any of you notice how she walked?'

After a pause, one of the girls volunteered hesitantly. 'As she left the wheelchair, I thought perhaps she moved with a slight limp, Sir.'

'Well done, Miss Seddon; she does indeed walk with a limp, and I'm sure Mrs Bradshaw won't mind telling us why.'

'Aye, I suffered with polio as a bairn,' Mrs Bradshaw responded. 'Ma bonny wee sister died of it, poor mite. I was luckier. I dinna die, but it left me with this weakness in ma leg.'

'Any other observations?' Sir William asked.

'I think Mrs Bradshaw is Scottish,' Mr Morris offered having heard her strong accent.

'Indeed I am, young man. I'm from Glasgow,' the patient confirmed with a smile.

'Anything else?' Sir William wanted to know.

There was silence, so the surgeon prompted them again. 'Mr Solanki, would you care to look at Mrs Bradshaw's hands.'

The student walked to the front, and examined her hands. 'I think she does much work,' he volunteered.

At this, Mrs Bradshaw smiled broadly. 'Aye, indeed I do,' she confirmed.

'What kind of work do you think?'

Mr Solanki looked at Mrs Bradshaw's hands again, turning each one over in turn. 'Physical work,' he suggested, 'probably many hours spent with her hands in water.'

'Well done Mr Solanki, anything else?'

'I think she smokes many cigarettes.'

'Right again, well done. Mrs Bradshaw has some nicotine staining on her fingers, doesn't she, and I think we can detect the faint whiff of her last cigarette on her dressing gown. She also has the face of a chronic smoker. Note those many deep facial skin creases. Now, has anyone made any observations of her general demeanour? What about you, Miss Croft?'

Miss Croft was tall and blond with an attractive figure not disguised by the utilitarian white coat she wore; a young lady who was likely to catch the roving eye of Mr Potts!

'Well,' the student began cautiously, 'Mrs Bradshaw seems to be quite relaxed and confident sitting talking to us. It's almost as if she's enjoying it. She's not fazed at all. If it were me, I'd be worried to bits. It's as if she's used to being in hospital.'

'Excellent work, young lady. That's a very astute observation, and one that's spot on. Mrs Bradshaw has indeed been with us for quite a long time.

Now it's time for us to take our first history. Our patient suffers from a pain in her abdomen; it's under her ribs on the right-hand side.'

The senior surgeon looked around and at the back of the group he spotted a slightly-built, brown-haired student, who seemed to be attempting to make himself invisible.

'Mr Booth, I'd like you to come to the front, and ask Mrs Bradshaw a few questions. To begin with, we need to discover how severe the pain is.'

Reluctantly the student dragged himself to the front. 'Is the pain severe?' he asked, in a voice that was barely audible.

'Severe doctor? Aye, it's terribly severe! Cuts me like a knife it does, and it's with me all the time.'

Mr Booth took a step back, satisfied he had elicited the required information, and eager to return to his place.

'Well, Mr Booth, how bad is the pain?'

'It's very severe, Sir.'

'Well, let's just tease that out a bit, shall we?' Sir William said. He turned back to the patient. 'Tell me Mrs Bradshaw, what do you do when you get the pain? Suppose you were at work when the pain came on?'

'I just have to keep working, don't I? You don't get paid if you don't work, do you? I just take my pain-killers and crack on.'

'And what pain-killers do you normally take?'

'Maybe an aspirin or two, but I'm not really a tablet-taker; as often as not, I just struggle on.'

'I believe you've had a baby or two,' Sir William said, 'is it as bad as labour pains?'

Mrs Bradshaw laughed. 'One or two, Doctor? I've actually had five bairns, but no, it's nothing like as bad as labour pains. They're in quite a different league.'

'So, Mr Booth, how severe is the pain?'

The young student looked annoyed. 'But she said it was severe, and quite obviously, it isn't!' he protested.

The consultant smiled patiently. 'Yes, that is indeed what Mrs Bradshaw said.' He emphasised the words *Mrs Bradshaw* to indicate that he wished patients to be formally addressed and not referred to as *'she'*. Then he turned to the rest of the group.

'Let that be your first lesson,' he said. 'You can't always take the things patients say at face value. If you're to understand their symptoms, you have to probe a little deeper. You see, some patients are tougher than others; some are stoical and minimise their symptoms, whilst others exaggerate their problems, eager for them to be taken seriously. You probably recognise from your own experience that some people take a few days off work several times a year with what they call *'flu'*, whilst others, with the same infection, simply call it *'a bit of a cold'*, and carry-on working.'

And so it went on, Sir William demonstrating to the students how to elicit the precise site of the pain, its character, severity, and duration; all the while impressing on them, the need to treat their patients gently and courteously.

'Before you go though,' Sir William concluded, 'we must thank Mrs Bradshaw for helping us today. I think, Miss Croft, you observed that she looked at home on the ward. Full marks to you; Mrs Bradshaw is actually the domestic on this ward. You will see a lot of her in the weeks to come. She was kind enough to agree to act as our patient this morning. And Mr Solanki, you were quite right too; she does indeed work extremely hard, keeping the ward so beautifully clean and tidy. We'd be lost without her.'

Mrs Bradshaw left the room delighted to have helped the consultant whom she and the rest of the staff admired and respected, and glowing with the praise he had heaped upon her.

Thought for the day

I am putting old heads on young shoulders

Muriel Spark 1918 - 2006

Chapter 9   Sue Weston

26th September 1966

As the weeks passed, Paul gradually gained in confidence, and with the experience he gained and with his increasing familiarity of hospital routines, he was able undertake his duties with greater efficiency. The majority of his time was spent on the ward, but it was the time spent in the operating theatre that he found most interesting.

Many buildings have a unique atmosphere, whether the awe-inspiring grandeur of an English cathedral, the close, friendly warmth of a busy, country pub, or the gloomy oppression of a funeral parlour; and so it is with an operating theatre. Even when not in use, the marble floor, the tiled walls, the theatre table in the centre with its overhead lamp a yard across, waiting expectantly to illuminate the next operation, combine to create an aura of their own. This is a place of drama, excitement and suspense; a place where lives are won and lost. Entering the theatre makes the senses quicken, even for the experienced surgeon. This is where knowledge and skill are put to the test, a place where the surgeon's technical ability, or lack of it, will dramatically affect the lives of those who have entrusted themselves to his care.

For many reasons, Paul enjoyed his visits to theatre. There was the academic interest as the anatomy learned at medical school was brought to life, and the fascination of actually seeing the organ that has been causing the patient's symptoms, and the disease, possibly infection or malignancy, within it. Finally, there was the satisfaction of watching the surgeon correct the problem, maybe relieving a blockage, possibly repairing injured tissue, or most dramatic of all, arresting haemorrhage. There was also the sense of teamwork. The surgeon, the anaesthetist, and the scrub nurse, supported by assistants, runners, and theatre technicians, all working together as one unit with a common purpose; that of helping the patients who had, quite literally, put their life in the hands of the team.

Paul discovered that assisting in the theatre was a pleasant and interesting change from the more routine and sometimes repetitive work on the ward. It was very instructive to assess a patient's surgical condition before their operation, then to witness the surgical intervention, and later to follow the patient's postoperative recovery. The disadvantage was that whilst assisting at operations, Paul's work on the ward did not go away; it simply remained for him to do later. It meant that time spent in theatre always resulted in an exceptionally long working day. There were, however, potential hazards for a young male house officer in theatre, as Paul was to discover when Mr Potts required two assistants to help him perform an operation to remove a cancer of the rectum.

The patient was an elderly man whose tumour was situated about three inches above the anus. Mr Potts' objective was to divide the bowel above and below the cancer, remove the length of bowel containing the tumour, and then anastomose the bowel by suturing the two open ends together to restore the continuity of the intestinal tube. Theatre clothing was unisex; both the surgeons, who at this time were almost invariably male, and the nurses, almost invariably female, wore thin, green, cotton pyjama-style trousers and a green cotton smock. The only difference between the sexes was that the surgeons tended to wear rubber boots whilst the nurses, who were a little further away from the wound and anything that might spill from it, preferred slip-on wooden clogs or pumps.

Mo Khan and Paul had already changed into their theatre clothes, and were having a drink and a chat in the sister's office, when a telephone message came through from Mr Potts to say he would be a few minutes late. He instructed that Mr Khan should start the operation by opening the abdomen on his behalf. Mo went to find the anaesthetist Dr Tom Lester, a consultant, who was reading a newspaper in the surgeon's room whilst awaiting the arrival of the consultant surgeon. Dr Lester was a small, slightly built, quietly spoken man, who had a rather downtrodden air; he looked as if he carried the cares of the world on his shoulders. He had a reputation for being economical with words, only using the minimum number that any particular situation demanded. When Mr Khan announced that he would be starting the operation before Mr Potts arrived, Dr Lester's single response was 'Right'.

Mo Khan and Paul started to scrub up, while Dr Lester went to the anaesthetic room, and began to anaesthetise the patient. In due course, the patient was wheeled into the theatre and transferred to the operating table. The diathermy leads were attached to the patient's thigh, the abdomen was exposed, an antiseptic iodine solution was painted on the skin from the level of the nipples to mid-thigh, and sterile drapes were laid around the operation area.

During the months Paul had been in post he had seen Mr Khan operate regularly, and had come to admire his careful surgical technique. Nothing was hurried, bleeding was kept to a minimum, visualisation of the anatomy was good, every step of each operation being completed with meticulous attention to detail, and yet the operations were completed in good time. He was always calm and quietly spoken. Instruments were requested, never demanded, from the scrub nurse, with a polite 'Please' and 'Thank you'.

When everything was prepared, Mo made a long vertical incision in the patient's lower abdomen, then dissected through the skin, the subcutaneous fat and the various muscle layers, until the inner lining of the abdominal cavity, the peritoneum, was exposed. Division of this thin membrane allowed access to the abdominal cavity, and a first view of the abdominal contents. It was educational and helpful to his juniors that Mo had a habit of thinking aloud during the surgery.

'The first thing to do,' he mused, 'is to see if there's any evidence that this cancer has spread from the rectum to the glands or liver.' He asked Paul to pull the upper end of the wound towards the patient's chest with a retractor while he inspected the liver before sweeping a hand over its entire outer surface.

'So far so good; no sign of any spread there. Now, we must look for any glands. If they are involved, we should find them along the vessels that carry blood away from the rectum.'

Fortunately, there was no evidence of spread to the glands which meant that, provided the rectal tumour itself had not grown directly into the tissues adjacent to the rectum, there was a good chance of a successful cure for this patient's cancer. Sadly, the absence of visible spread of a cancer to glands or to the liver did not automatically mean that the patient would be cured, since if a few cells (microscopic in size, and certainly too small for the surgeon to see or feel) should float away in the blood stream and lodge in a distant site, the patient would, at a later date, get a recurrence.

It was at this moment that Mr Potts strode into the theatre.

'Good morning all,' he breezed. 'I'm glad to see that you've started without me. That will save us a bit of time.'

He walked over to the theatre table, and looked over Mr Khan's shoulder. Again, in his booming voice, he said, 'That incision isn't long enough, Khan; let's have another inch at either end, right down to the pubic bone at the bottom end. This is a low tumour, and we will need good exposure to get it out. There's nothing to be gained from struggling through a small incision.' Then, turning to Paul, he added, 'We'll also need a strong assistant on the retractor at the lower end. I hope you've had a good breakfast, Lambert.'

Without waiting for a reply, he walked to the sink unit to scrub up. It was noticeable that when Mr Potts entered, the atmosphere in the theatre underwent a subtle change. Prior to his arrival, the theatre team had been undertaking their work seriously and conscientiously, but in an atmosphere that was calm and relaxed. With Mr Potts in the theatre, there was a certain tension discernible in the air. The relaxed atmosphere had somehow melted away. Paul expected that his consultant would adopt the same theatre gear as everybody else, but this was not the case. When he came to the table, he saw that Mr Potts had tied a length of white crepe bandage round his forehead, to form a sweatband. He was also wearing a surgical headlamp. This was a relatively new development, essentially a modification of the original miner's headlamp, which focused a strong beam of light to illuminate the area at which the surgeon's head was pointing. In operations such as this, where the dissection was to be carried out deep in the pelvis, it was much easier to illuminate the scene using the head torch than by requiring the theatre technicians to manhandle the large overhead theatre lamp.

'Right,' said Mr Potts, 'all change.'

He replaced Mr Khan, who had been at the patient's right side, and who now went to stand directly opposite Mr Potts to act as first assistant. Mr Potts indicated that Paul should stand at his right elbow, in anticipation of the work that was expected of him holding the pelvic retractor. The scrub nurse for this major procedure was the senior theatre sister who stood alongside Mr Khan, across the table from Paul and Mr Potts.

'Right, let's have those theatre lights down,' said Mr Potts.

All the theatre lights were dimmed, leaving just the surgical wound, and the surrounding area brilliantly illuminated. This was 'theatre' in the traditional sense of the word, and Mr Potts was clearly planning to be the star performer.

'Now, where are you up to, Khan? Has this tumour spread anywhere?'

'No Sir, it all looks completely clean.'

'Right, I'll take your word for that; let's crack on.'

He spoke to the theatre technician. 'Tip the patient's head down, Harry.'

The operating table was tipped head down to allow the coils of moist, slippery intestines to slither into the upper abdomen, thereby giving a better view of the pelvis and upper rectum. These coils of bowel were then held in place with swabs. Mr Potts operated faster than Mr Khan, dissecting sometimes with a scalpel, sometimes with scissors, stopping the bleeding with diathermy or with artery forceps as he went. At each stage of the procedure the scrub sister seemed to know instinctively exactly which instrument was required, and usually had it to hand. Occasionally Mr Potts would say 'Come, come, Sister – seven-inch Spencer Wells next', and she would have them there in a flash. Mr Potts kept up a running commentary throughout; he seemed to be in his element, and thoroughly enjoying himself. He appeared to be more at ease in theatre than on the wards, where he was brusque and, unlike Sir William, ill at ease talking to his patients. He turned to the anaesthetist.

'We had a good game of golf yesterday, didn't we, Tom? Fine weather; a little breezy maybe, but not enough to affect decent golfers. We played at the Stretton Heath Golf Club,' he continued to the theatre staff in general, 'and a close match it was too. Anaesthetist versus Surgeon. Cut and thrust right to the end. It was only settled on the eighteenth green. Now, Lambert, if you look into the wound, you'll see no trace of this rectal tumour at all. That's because it's not in the abdominal cavity; it's deep down in the pelvis, at the level of the prostate and bladder, but we'll soon dig it out. Pass me the self-retaining retractor, will you, Sister dear?'

The retractor was placed in the edges of the wound, and using its ratchet, the two blades were separated, thus keeping the wound edges widely apart, and allowing good vision and access. It freed up the first assistant, so that he could help in other ways, such as cutting sutures close to the knot after they had been tied, or mopping away any blood that might obscure the surgeon's view. Paul couldn't actually see how the operation was progressing or confirm that the tumour wasn't yet visible because to do so, he would have had to move two feet to the left and put his head where Mr Potts' head was, but Mr Khan had a look and agreed.

Mr Potts returned to his account of the previous day's golf. 'Tom had a lucky shot on the ninth. Chipped up from the semi rough thirty yards from the green and, blow me, the ball went straight into the hole!

It really was a complete fluke, but it put him one up at the turn. It meant that I had to concentrate hard and attack the course on the back nine. Now, here we go, we pull the sigmoid loop of colon up, and find the space between the rectum in front and the hollow of the sacrum behind. As we develop the plane of dissection, we have to be very careful that we don't disturb the tumour, since we don't want to spread any cancer cells. Nor do we want any bleeding from the juicy veins on the front of the sacrum. This is where the skill of the surgeon really comes in.

Surgery is one hundred percent interesting, Lambert, not like anaesthetics; that's ninety nine percent boredom.' He shot a glance at Dr Lester that the anaesthetist, who was busy reading The Times newspaper, studiously ignored. He was referring to the old adage that the life of an anaesthetist, like that of an airline pilot, is ninety-nine percent boredom and one percent blind panic.

'It was nip and tuck all the way to the fifteenth, but I had a glorious shot to the green on the sixteenth. A six iron from 150 yards; it went as straight as a die. The ball finished five feet from the pin, I had a single putt, got the birdie, and we were all square again.'

Paul was hanging on to the pelvic retractor, quite unable to see what was going on in the wound, but listening to the account of the golf. He made a private bet with himself that the tale would conclude with a victory for the surgeon and he wasn't to be disappointed. He looked to see what reaction the story was having on Dr Lester, but his nose was still in his newspaper. It appeared that the crossword was of more interest to him, and he certainly wasn't going to rise to the jibe that anaesthetics was boring.

'It was still anybody's game as we stood on the eighteenth tee. Lambert, you've got that retractor in the wrong place again. How can I dissect around the prostate gland if you keep hiding it from me? Let me adjust it for you. Now there it is; hang on to it and keep it still, boy. Now the eighteenth is almost 400 yards long, and there's a pond just in front of the green. We both had good tee shots but Tom decided to lay up short of the water; that's the sort of thing an anaesthetist would do. It left him with a fifty-yard wedge shot into the target. Surgeons are said to have hearts like lions though, aren't they? I decided to go for it. Took a three wood off the fairway, and banged the ball right into the heart of the green. Two putts and the match was mine. Victory to the surgeon, 'eh Tom?'

Dr Lester didn't reply, but Mr Potts seemed not to notice or, indeed, to mind. Then, addressing the world in general, he continued. 'I've always enjoyed sport; athletics, rugby and now golf. I had a lesson from the club professional the other day. He adjusted my grip a fraction, to correct the slight fade that I'd developed.'

To Sister's annoyance, he helped himself to a pair of long handled forceps from her tray, took half a step backwards, and demonstrated his new grip and swing, narrowly missing the large theatre lamp above the table as he did so.

Sister scowled. 'Perhaps you would be kind enough to hand that instrument back to me,' she said, unable to keep the tone of reproof from her voice.

Mr Potts winked at the anaesthetist. 'Come, come, Sister,' he said. 'Relax. Just having a bit of fun,' then, returning to the table, and to his original theme, he added, 'fortunately, I seem to be a natural sportsman and I do keep myself fairly fit.'

Not true, Paul thought. Although of stocky build, he might well have been quite athletic as a young man, but Paul had observed him in the changing room. Mr Potts had clearly put on an inch or two around his waist in recent years.

'I used to play cricket as well to a good amateur standard. I was always a clean striker of the ball.' Paul saw Sister place both her hands protectively across her surgical tray, obviously afraid that Mr Potts was about to demonstrate his prowess with another of the instruments. 'By the end of the season, I was usually top of the batting averages. In the good old days, when I was training in London, there was a 'Juniors versus Consultants' cricket match every summer. I always managed to score plenty of runs. It was great fun, and the nurses used to enjoy watching their heroes at play. I bowled quite well too; took the wicket of my consultant chief once. As I remember, it was a fast, straight ball that knocked his middle stump right out of the ground. He didn't like that at all. The following year, I thought it wise to bowl him some gentle deliveries to feed him a few soft runs before I took his wicket.' He laughed heartily at the memory. His junior staff smiled politely behind their masks.

The germ of an idea entered Paul's head.

'Do you think the consultants here could raise a team, Sir?' he asked.

'You mean a match against the residents? That sounds like a challenge. What an excellent idea.' Mr Potts thought for a moment. 'I suspect we could raise six or seven, and we could rope in a few of the local GPs to make up the numbers. But certainly, if you arrange it, we'll take you on. We'll be far too strong for you of course. But we'll happily give you a quick thrashing to keep you in your places,' he added with a grin.

Suddenly, Mr Potts was shouting. 'There's a bleeder, down there, in the hollow of the sacrum. Khan, apply pressure. Sister, more swabs. Lambert, keep that retractor in place, for God's sake. Harry, get me the suction machine at once. Tom, we may need some blood for transfusion very soon.'

All at once there was real tension in the air, and Mr Potts became terse and anxious. His movements were hurried and tremulous. Despite the headband, there were beads of sweat on his brow running down towards his eyes.

Sister turned to one of the theatre runners. 'Swab for the surgeon's brow please, nurse.'

Mr Potts turned away from the theatre table for a moment and one of the junior nurses mopped his brow. It took a good five minutes to control the bleeding, and for calm to return, but in this time at least a pint of blood had collected in the suction bottle. Meanwhile Dr Lester had laid aside his newspaper, and replaced the infusion of saline with blood. The operation continued, and slowly Mr Potts regained his composure. With Paul's inexperience, and from the position that he occupied at the table, he couldn't see what had caused the bleeding, nor indeed how it had been controlled, but he did wonder whether it would have happened had Mr Potts been concentrating on the surgery, rather than reflecting on his past sporting achievements. It seemed that surgery as well as anaesthetics could be one percent blind panic, at least in Mr Potts' hands.

Sister had been waiting for calm to return before she asked Mr Potts a question. 'Mr Potts, we have a staff nurse with us today who has come to theatre for the first time. Would you mind if she came to the table to watch the operation? It will be a good experience for her.'

'No, no,' said Mr Potts, 'the more the merrier. Come to see the maestro at work, has she? I hope she's not the delicate sort that's likely to faint at the sight of a drop of blood.'

The new nurse was already gowned and scrubbed, and she came and stood at Paul's right-hand side. She spoke to Mr Potts in a surprisingly confident manner.

'Let me introduce myself, Mr Potts. I'm Staff Nurse Weston and no, I certainly won't faint. I've just worked for three months in the Casualty department, and we see plenty of blood there. I will be fine, thank you.'

Paul recognised the name; it had cropped up several times during gossip in the doctor's residency. She had a considerable reputation as a flirt. As Johnny had once remarked to Paul, 'Sue Weston eats nice, quiet lads like you for breakfast, Paul. My advice is to stay well away!'

Mr Potts resumed his description of the operation. 'We've separated the tumour so that it's free from the sacrum at the back, and from the bladder and prostate at the front. Now we're ready to remove the cancer that you can see in this length of bowel that I've mobilised.'

The operation continued. It was helpful for Paul to have the running commentary to know how the procedure was progressing since, from his position, the view was limited to the entrance of the wound, the lower part of which he was pulling down with his retractor to give Mr Potts as much space as possible in which to work. His arms were beginning to cramp, so from time to time, he shifted the retractor from one hand to the other. He had been standing on one spot for over an hour by this time and his legs were beginning to ache as well. Suddenly, he was aware of another sensation on his leg. Something was touching his right calf; it was warm, soft and tickled slightly. Before he could work out what it was, it stopped, and he thought he must have imagined it. But it returned a few minutes later. There was a definite gentle stroking of the skin above the level of his surgical boot. Whatever it was had found the gap between the top of the boot and the bottom of his trouser leg. He looked down, and to his horror, saw that Sue Weston had slipped her foot out of her wooden clog, and was using her stockinged toes to gently stroke his calf. He frowned at her, but her eyes simply laughed back at him. He turned around, hoping that there would be somebody in the theatre behind them whose presence might inhibit Sue's antics, but there was nobody there. He tried to move his leg away but was limited by the table in front, and the solid frame of Mr Potts to his left. Wherever he tried to go, the stockinged toes followed him, tickling and sending his senses racing.

Mr Potts was continuing his commentary. 'Pass me those cross clamps, Sister. We're going to clamp the bowel above and below the tumour, but we have to be careful not to spill any of the content of the bowel into the operating field. If we can avoid contaminating the wound, we shall avoid getting an infection. Tom, this would be a good time to give some antibiotics.'

The soft stroking of Paul's calf continued. He couldn't deny that it was a pleasant sensation, but he was angry and embarrassed, and very afraid that someone would see. Again, he tried to edge to his left, and for a short time Sue kept her toes to herself. Thank goodness, Paul thought, she's realised that he didn't welcome her attentions. However, this proved incorrect as he became aware of a new, and altogether far more distracting, stimulus. She had moved her whole body closer to him, and he felt the warmth of her thigh against his. Then her hip met Paul's, and started an almost imperceptible gyratory movement.

Paul suddenly had a brainwave; perhaps he could get Sue moved to another position round the table.

'Mr Potts,' he said, 'I don't think Nurse Weston can see the various stages of this operation from where she is standing. She would probably see more if she were to move to the top end of the table.'

Before Mr Potts could reply, Sister spoke. 'She's here to understand the duties of the scrub nurse, so she is fine where she is.'

The thigh and hip contact continued but, in addition, something warm and soft was now touching Paul's right upper arm as Sue pretended to get a better view of the proceedings. Paul knew instantly what it was; Sue was gently rubbing the outer side of her breast against him. Surely Sister must notice he thought, but no, all her concentration was focused on her tray of instruments, and on anticipating the requirements of the surgeon. Instinctively Paul moved to the left, but immediately came into contact with Mr Potts.

'Don't crowd me, Lambert,' he said. 'You're allowed to stand at the right hand of God, but God in this case is right-handed, and I can't work if you're cramping my style.'

Reluctantly, Paul resumed his previous position, ever more conscious of the warmth and softness of Sue's body against his arm and hip. He looked across at Mr Khan. It was clear that, unlike Sister, he was acutely aware of what was happening. Paul was certain that he was annoyed but, equally, felt unable to intervene. Afterwards, Johnny said that he would just have relaxed and enjoyed it. There was no doubt that it was a pleasant sensation, but Paul was terrified that Mr Potts, or Sister, would see what was happening, and be furious. However, both were concentrating on their jobs, and were completely unaware of Sue's behaviour.

With a triumphant gesture, like a magician lifting a rabbit from a hat, Mr Potts raised the diseased length of bowel out of the wound, held it aloft, and then placed it in a metal kidney dish provided by Sister. He turned to Harry, the theatre orderly.

'Now, Harry, take that into the sluice, remove the clamps, cut it open, clean it up, and let's see what we've got. We need to be sure that we've removed the whole tumour.'

Harry disappeared into the sluice with the specimen, while the surgical team, including the Theatre Sister, stood back from the table for a minute or two, giving Paul the opportunity to rest his aching arms, and with a great sense of relief, to put some distance between Nurse Weston and himself. Harry soon returned with the specimen that he had cut along its length and opened, so that the inner lining was exposed. In the centre was a craggy ulcer perhaps an inch across, with a hard raised edge. The centre was covered in a dirty grey slough. It was a typical cancer. Mr Potts was delighted.

'That's fine. We've got a healthy margin of at least an inch above and below that tumour, so there is every prospect of a cure here. All we've got to do now is to join the two ends together and we're through. Almost time to put the kettle on.'

Everyone resumed their places at the table, and Paul was handed his retractor again but, as before, while Sister was concentrating on the next stage of the operation, and anticipating the instruments that Mr Potts would require, Sue Weston started her tricks. She half turned to her left and strained forward, as if trying to see what was going on in the operation. It was impossible for Paul not to appreciate that she was a well-endowed young lady, but he was trapped. He couldn't move his arm because he was required to hold the retractor, and he couldn't move bodily to the left because 'God' was standing there, suturing together the two ends of bowel, completely unaware of the little drama that was going on at his side. With his eyes he appealed to Mr Khan, who clearly was aware of Sue's antics, and who now looked very angry, but who was unable to intervene.

Mr Potts continued to describe the procedure. 'That's good. We have got two layers of stitches in place to join the bowel together so in a minute I'll leave you, Khan, to stitch up. You made this incision so it's only fair that you should close it.'

Paul's body started to respond to Sue's sensual stimulation. Theatre trousers are only thin, and he needed to press forward against the operating theatre table to make sure his emotions didn't show.

'Distract yourself,' he said to himself, 'think of something else. Who scored the goals in the World Cup final? Too easy! In what order were they scored? Again, too easy! Who passed the ball to the scorer for each of the four goals?'

But he couldn't think. Finally, Paul decided the situation had become intolerable, and that he had to put an end to it, so suddenly and forcibly he used his right shoulder to push Sue away.

The sudden movement attracted Sister's attention. She saw Paul's arm against Sue's chest, and looked at him with undisguised fury, completely misunderstanding the situation. She turned to Sue and in her sharpest voice said 'Nurse Weston, leave the table at once. Go and take your lunch break immediately.'

Sue left the theatre, closely followed by Mr Potts, leaving Mr Khan to close the abdomen. The theatre lights were raised, the atmosphere in theatre relaxed, and the operation was completed without further incident. The whole procedure had taken over two hours, and it was a relief for Paul to take off hat, mask, gloves and gown, stretch his arms and legs, and then sit down in the surgeons' room. A cup of coffee was produced whilst Mr Khan was writing up the operation notes, and Paul was writing out postoperative instructions, wondering how soon it would be before there were repercussions. He didn't have long to wait.

Sister burst in, red in the face, slamming the door behind her. 'Dr Lambert,' she shouted, 'I will not have arrogant young doctors molesting my nurses in theatre, indeed, right under my very eyes. In all the time that I've been in nursing, I have never seen behaviour like it. I shall be reporting this matter immediately to....'

Mr Khan interrupted in a voice that was quiet yet firm. 'Sister, I saw exactly what went on; indeed, I had been aware of the situation for fifteen minutes or so before you noticed. I can assure you that Dr Lambert was not responsible; he was entirely the innocent party.'

Sister looked at him doubtfully. 'Are you absolutely sure?'

'Absolutely, positively 100% sure Sister, without any shadow of a doubt at all. Dr Lambert was actually trying to distance himself from the girl. Do you not remember that he suggested that the nurse should be moved to another position round the table so that she could observe the surgery, but that you said that she should stay where she was? Remember also that Dr Lambert was actually reprimanded by Mr Potts for 'interfering with God's right arm' when he tried to move away from that nurse? She had been making a nuisance of herself whenever your back was turned. There is no doubt at all that the guilty party has gone to lunch. She is the one to whom you need to speak, not Dr Lambert.'

Sister still looked uncertain. 'Yes, but I saw Dr Lambert rubbing up against Nurse Weston.'

'No, Sister. You saw Dr Lambert push Nurse Weston away.'

Fortunately, Sister was reassured, and accepted Mo Khan's explanation. She left the room, no doubt, in search of her new staff nurse.

'Thank you,' Paul said to Mo. 'Thank you very much indeed.

'My pleasure,' Mo replied.' I should keep clear of that girl in future; she's trouble. There are much nicer nurses for you to get to know on the ward.'

Paul looked at his registrar in surprise. Did he know that he had had feelings for Kate, or was in just a casual remark?

Thoughts for the day

Not tonight Josephine.

Attributed to Napoleon 1769 – 1821

Sexual intercourse began, in ninety sixty-three,

Between the end of the Chatterley ban and the Beatles first LP

Philip Larkin 1922 - 1985

Chapter 10   A Humble Hero

30th September 1966

'Lambert,' Sir William said, 'I've a little job for you. I'm in the outpatient clinic, and there's an interesting chap here who needs to be admitted as a matter of urgency. He has a gland in his axilla. I rather fear it's something sinister.'

'And his name, sir?'

Paul heard Sir William's rich chuckle at the other end of the phone. 'He's Polish, and his name is quite unpronounceable, but everybody seems to call him 'Tom'. Shall I send him up to the ward?'

'Just give me a couple of minutes, Sir. I need to check we have an available bed. All being well, I'll ring to confirm in a minute or two.'

Later that morning, Paul walked down the ward, to see the new patient, and to arrange some preliminary investigations. It was easy to understand why he was known as 'Tom'. According to his records, his full name was Aleksander Tomasz Szczepanski. The notes recorded that he was 57 years of age, and had been born in Zerkow in Poland. His appearance was quite shocking, indeed distressing. Slightly built and short of stature, he would have been quite nondescript, but for the appearance of his head, face and neck. These features were grossly deformed. It was clear that at some time in his life, he had been most terribly burned. His mouth was dragged over to one side by unyielding scar tissue, his left eye reduced to a narrow slit. The tip of his nose was missing, resulting in one nostril being twice the size of the other. He wore a close-fitting, grey woollen cap that was pulled low over his forehead, and a sweater with a high-roll neck. Only when he undressed to be examined, did Paul see the full extent of his injuries; the ugly, livid scarring extended over most of his neck and scalp. All that remained of his left ear was a blunt stub.

Hoping that his expression did not reveal the distress he felt at seeing such terrible injuries, Paul attempted a light-hearted comment.

'You have been in the wars, haven't you?'

'Yes, Doctor, I have. I'm afraid I'm not a pretty sight.'

The words were spoken with a strong East European accent.

'Hello,' Paul said, holding out his hand. 'My name is Paul Lambert. I've come to ask you a few questions, and to take a look at the lump you have in your armpit.'

The new patient grasped Paul's hand readily in a firm grip. 'Hello, Doctor. I am Aleksander Szczepanski, but it is perhaps easier if you call me 'Tom'. That is what most people do.' He spoke slowly, quietly and with dignity, enunciating the words with difficulty through his twisted lips, his phrases punctuated with short pauses.

'Then, if that really is alright with you, I will call you 'Tom' as well.'

Paul enquired about the swelling that had developed in his armpit, and Tom explained he had noticed it about two months earlier. Initially, he had thought little of it, because it had not caused him any pain. Subsequently, because it became larger, he went to see his general practitioner, who referred him to the hospital. There was little else of note in his story. When Paul came to examine him, he had no difficulty in locating the gland. It was the size of a large acorn, situated just beneath the skin. Unfortunately, it was ominously hard and craggy.

****

Sir William was accompanied by a group of medical students when he reviewed Tom on his ward round, a couple of days later. The results of the blood tests and x-rays that Paul had arranged were now available.

'I'm sorry to say that the tests we've done so far, haven't told us exactly what the problem is,' the consultant said. Then, choosing his words carefully, he continued, 'I think the best way to get to the root of your trouble, would be to winkle out that little lump of yours, and have a look at it under the microscope. That will help us to understand what's going on.'

'And when will that be done, Doctor?'

'Hopefully tomorrow. Then it will take a couple of days to analyse the specimen. I suggest you stay with us until then,' replied Sir William. He already had a fair idea of the diagnosis, and knew that a decision on further management would be required at that stage.

'That's fine with me, thank you, Doctor. Is it a big operation?'

'Not at all, in fact, we can do it for you under local anaesthetic.'

Sir William led his team on to the next bed, that of William Sugden, and invited one of the students to present the patient's details to him. The student he selected was a bright but somewhat anxious young man called Malcolm Chapman.

Malcolm began, nervously. 'This elderly gentleman was admitted last Tuesday, Sir. For the last four months, he has....'

'Did you say elderly?' Sir William asked innocently.

'Yes, Sir,' Malcolm replied.

'And precisely how old is this *'elderly'* gentleman, Chapman?'

Malcolm glanced at the patient's notes. 'He's 59, Sir. In fact, he'll be 60 in two months time.'

'I see. Just two years younger than I am then.'

Smiling broadly, Sir William put his hand on Mr Sugden's shoulder. 'Hello, old timer,' he said, jovially, 'it's good to meet you.'

'And you, old fellow,' Mr Sugden responded in kind, fully aware that the consultant was only teasing.

Malcolm was mortified and turned bright red. 'I'm so s -sorry, Sir,' he stuttered, 'I truly didn't mean any offence.'

'And none taken, young man, none taken,' Sir William replied, his eyes twinkling. He turned to the rest of his team.

'What you consider to be *'young'* or *'old'* depends entirely on where you're standing. But perhaps we can agree that 59 is late middle-age! Mind you, children always want to be older than they are, don't they? How often do you hear a child say *'I'm nearly seven'*, when they're really only six and a half? And the very elderly, people older than 59,' he added, with a sideways glance at Malcolm, 'are often proud of their advanced years. They're also prepared to add a bit on! You will often hear an octogenarian say *'I'll be 85 next birthday, you know!'*

Anyway, we had better move on. Chapman, you were telling me about Mr Sugden.'

Back in the office at the end of the round, Sir William, a mug of tea in his hand, put Tom's chest x-ray on the viewing box.

'All Tom's blood tests are normal. What can you see on his chest x-ray?' he asked Malcolm.

The student hadn't seen many chest x-rays before, so the consultant put a normal x-ray on an adjacent screen, so that he could compare them. Malcolm quickly spotted the abnormality; there was a large shadow in the lung. In the question-and-answer session that followed,

Sir William suggested that the most likely diagnosis was a tumour of the lung. If the gland in the armpit proved to consist of cancer cells which had spread from the lung, then regrettably, the disease would be beyond the reach of any form of treatment. The outlook for Tom would be extremely poor.

Sir William thanked his team for their support, as he always did at the end of his round, and as he was leaving, commented to Paul, 'You should ask Tom how he was so badly burned and how he came to live in the UK. Did you know that many Poles walked halfway across Europe to get here? I feel sure he'll have an interesting tale to tell.'

Paul didn't know but resolved to find out.

****

Experienced surgeons do not mind whether their patients are awake, or asleep whilst performing surgery. Many patients though, express a preference to be fully anaesthetised. They are concerned that if they are conscious, they may experience pain, or perhaps move at an unfortunate moment whilst the surgeon is working. Often though, as with Tom's gland, the nature of the procedure does not justify a general anaesthetic. In such cases, one of the nurses is often asked to sit and chat with the patient, thus distracting them from the surgical procedure.

Another way of distracting patients is to invite them to listen to music of their choice. From the surgeon's point of view, music with a soft beat and gentle lyrics is most suitable; heavy rock music is best avoided! On one occasion, a patient insisted on hearing Frank Sinatra singing Mac the Knife, but Sir William decreed that this was unsuitable, and instructed that the music be turned off! In modern times, of course, the advent of music downloaded onto mobile phones has eliminated the problem.

Sir William asked Mo to remove Tom's gland, a procedure that was expected to take less than thirty minutes to complete; Paul acted as his assistant. Tom seemed relaxed as he lay on the table with his arm out at right angles, supported by a board. The skin of the armpit was shaved, washed with an antiseptic solution, and then towelled. Mo injected lignocaine into the area, then waited for the anaesthetic to take effect, before making an incision. He had no difficulty in locating the lymph node in the fatty layer immediately beneath the skin. Fortunately, it wasn't close to any important structures, and after dividing the blood vessel that supplied it with oxygen, it slipped out easily.

Mo looked carefully at the gland, then took a fresh blade, and cut it across. Having seen cancerous glands previously, he immediately feared the worst. It looked sinister. If the pathologist subsequently confirmed that it contained cancer cells that had spread from the lung, then the condition would be incurable. For Tom, this would be a death sentence. Without a word, he showed it to Paul then handed it to the scrub nurse, who placed it into a jar filled with preservative, ready for it to be transported to the laboratory for analysis.

'All finished now,' Mo said to Tom, 'I hope that wasn't too painful for you.'

'Just a little uncomfortable, Doctor; not the worst pain I've had in my life,' Tom replied with a wry smile.

Paul pulled off his gloves and tossed his gown into the laundry skip as Tom was returned to the ward.

'What a lovely man,' said the nurse who had been sitting chatting to him. 'He was so polite and dignified.'

'What did you talk about?' Paul asked.

'You were there, weren't you listening?'

Paul confessed he had been completely unaware of their conversation, engrossed as he was, assisting at the operation.

'He was telling me about village life in Poland when he was a child. It sounded idyllic. I wonder why he left.'

'Did he tell you how he came to be so badly burned?' Paul asked.

'No, he didn't, and I didn't like to ask.'

On the ward, it was noticeable that Tom did not mix easily with his fellow patients. Most were confined to bed, but those patients who were ambulant chatted in small groups, watched television, or sat and read in the smoky haze of the restroom. Tom was rarely with them. Paul wondered whether this isolation resulted from his different nationality, his appallingly disfigured face, or possibly from his own personality and reticence.

One day, as he walked down the ward, he overheard laughter.

'Did you ever see such an ugly mug?' one patient asked of another. 'He could easily get a part as an alien in a horror movie; he certainly wouldn't need any makeup.'

'He looks like a Polish gargoyle, if you ask me,' responded another, 'I've seen prettier faces on the monkeys at the zoo.'

Paul ignored the remarks, but later reproached himself for not intervening. Maybe Tom's decision to keep his own company resulted from overhearing such cruel comments. Thereafter, as a point of principle, he made a point of chatting to Tom whenever he was passing. It was usually no more than a superficial conversation about the weather, or the hospital food, but he hoped it made Tom feel he had at least one friend on the ward.

Life on the ward was generally less hectic in the late evening than during the day. When it was his turn to be on duty through the night, it was the time Paul used to enjoy most. By eleven o'clock or midnight, the ward was quiet, and a sense of peace and calm prevailed. The main lights would be off, leaving most of the ward in darkness. One of the night nurses would be sitting at a small table in the centre of the ward, reading or writing under a single overhead light. Most of the patients would be resting quietly or sleeping, though one or two might still be reading using the night light on the wall above their bedhead. After a day spent dashing to and fro, working against the clock, Paul found it soothing to arrive, and survey the scene from the ward doors. At this hour, it was possible to take a leisurely stroll around the ward, checking each patient in turn, without feeling rushed; having time for a chat with any patient who was awake or anxious.

It was at such a time, whilst Tom remained on the ward waiting for the laboratory report on his gland, that Paul recalled Sir William's remark about there being *'an interesting story about the burns'*. He plucked up the courage to ask.

'It all happened a long time ago....' Tom began and then paused.

Paul prompted him to say more. 'You mean in the war in Poland?'

'No, no. It happened in England.'

'In the blitz, in London or Liverpool?'

'No, I was in the air force. I had a crash.'

'You mean in the RAF?' Paul said, surprised. He couldn't imagine how a Pole could come to fly with the RAF, and felt somewhat ashamed of his ignorance. Slowly, he persuaded Tom to tell the whole story.

'I was born in a small village near Zerkow in Poland. My father was the headmaster of the local school which my sister and I attended. She was two years younger than me. When I was old enough, I joined the Polish Air Force. I was young and adventurous, and probably a little foolish. I learned to fly, and in 1936, I joined a squadron flying fighter planes. Then, in 1939, our whole world changed; Germany attacked Poland with overwhelming force.'

He spoke slowly, quietly, and as the theatre nurse had remarked, with great dignity. There were long pauses as he shared with Paul the events that had devastated his life; the memories still raw a quarter of a century later.

'It was a David versus Goliath contest,' Tom continued, 'Germany was far too strong. There was no warning, no declaration of war; the attack took us completely by surprise. Many of our planes were destroyed before they had time to leave the ground. Others, including my own, got into the air. We managed to shoot down one or two enemy planes, but in reality, we never stood a chance. In the end, a few of us managed to fly to Romania. I wanted to fight on, but our planes were stolen by the Romanians.'

'But how on earth did you get from Romania to England, with Germany in between?' Paul asked.

Tom's lips twisting into an awkward smile. 'Very slowly,' he replied. 'I went through Yugoslavia, then into Italy, and eventually reached France.'

'And how long did the journey take?' Paul asked.

'Five or six months,' Tom replied. 'I walked a lot of the way. At one stage, I stole a bicycle and cycled a bit; I completed the journey by train. When I reached England, I thought I would be welcomed into the RAF with open arms. I had combat experience; I'd already shot down a German bomber, but they didn't want me. Eventually, they saw sense and created a Polish Squadron.'

Again, there was his crooked smile. 'I was in 302 squadron flying Hurricanes. We fought alongside the RAF. We hated the Germans, and we were angry, young, and reckless. We were successful though; we shot down plenty of enemy planes. I did too, until the day my luck ran out, and I crashed. I spent the next two years in and out of hospital.'

One might imagine that he would speak of pride in his achievements, but the words were spoken with sadness. The events still lay heavy on his mind.

'You took part in the Battle of Britain then?'

'Yes, I did. That's when I was shot down.'

'I didn't know that Polish airmen fought in the Battle of Britain.' Paul admitted.

'I sometimes feel that people here don't want to know about Poland's contribution to the defeat of Germany.' There was now a hint of bitterness in his voice.

Paul waited, sensing that he wanted to say more. Then when he continued, his voice was no more than a whisper.

'Few people realise how badly Poland suffered. My homeland was invaded from two sides; by Germany from the West, and by Russia from the East. The people suffered horrendously.'

'You must have been about 24 at the time,' Paul asked, 'were you married?'

Tom paused, and Paul wondered if his question had been too personal. But he continued. 'Yes, I was, to Zofia. She and I came from the same town, Zerkow. Zofia was a teacher at my father's school. That's where we met. We married just before the war began, but I lost her. I was away in the air force when the Germans swept through. They captured her. They were picking up most of the educated people: teachers, lawyers, priests and doctors. I learned later that she had been taken away with others in a truck. She simply disappeared as did thousands more. I still don't know what happened to Zofia though I presume she must have been killed.'

It was an horrendous story.

'You went looking for your wife?'

'Yes, yes, of course. But I'd left Poland in 1939, and it wasn't possible to go back at the end of the war. When the war was over,' he explained, 'we Poles expected to be free to return home; after all, we'd fought alongside the British from 1940 onwards. But Poland was annexed by the Soviet Union. Your Mr Churchill and the Americans allowed Poland to be ruled by Stalin. It was many years before I was able to return to try to find Zofia. I went back to Zerkow of course, but learned very little; simply that she had been taken away, along with my father and my sister. Nobody knew where they'd gone, no messages were ever received, and none of them ever returned. Presumably, Zofia was killed along with many others. But how, or where, or what happened to her, I shall never know. I just pray that she didn't suffer too much before she died.'

'Did you and Zofia have any children?'

'No. We had only been married for six months when Poland was invaded. I had a letter from her just before the war started. She said she'd missed a monthly period, and to this day I still wonder if perhaps....' His voice gave out and tears filled his eyes. Quietly, Paul rose and pulled the screens around the bed. He gave Tom a few moments to recover.

'I'm sorry,' Tom said. 'It's been a long time since I spoke like this of those terrible days.'

'And so you returned to England?'

'There was no future for me at home; Poles were second-class citizens in their own country. So yes, I returned to England, but found that Poles were not welcome here either.'

Again, there was bitterness in his voice. 'It took me a long time to find a job. My appearance put people off, of course, and there were British servicemen coming home who were also looking for work. I've been a night watchman ever since, on my own, and out of sight.'

Paul heard laughter coming from the day room, where other patients were playing cards, despite the lateness of the hour.

'And apart here as well it seems.'

'Maybe, but I really don't mind; I've grown used to my own company.'

'Look,' Paul said, 'I think there are only three playing; it would be far easier with four. Do you want to join them?'

'No,' he said firmly. 'If they want me to join them, they will ask.'

He clearly had his pride, and was not prepared to beg.

For the last thirty minutes, Paul had been asking him questions, not because it was necessary as part of Tom's medical history, but out of interest, and for his own education. It struck him, and not for the first time, that medical staff ought to know much more about the background of their patients, especially the elderly in nursing homes and residential accommodation. Doctors and nurses enquire about their patient's medical symptoms, but they really know very little of the lives they have led in the past, or to which they will return when discharged from hospital. Too often they are just known as Ben or Betty in bed No 11 or 12. How much better it would be, and how much more respect they might receive, if they wore a name badge saying *'Ben, retired teacher', 'Betty, retired telephonist,' or 'Tom, Battle of Britain Fighter Pilot'.*

Tom had told his story quietly, but now he looked Paul in the eye and spoke forcibly.

'Are you married, Dr Lambert?'

Normally, Paul would have ducked such a question, preferring to keep his personal life private, but this man had opened his heart to him, and deserved honesty in return.

'No, I'm not.'

'Perhaps you have a sweetheart; one of the nurses maybe?'

'There's a girl who I would love to be able to call my sweetheart, and yes, she is a nurse; she's called Kate.'

'Does she work on this ward?'

'No, she used to be on this ward. This is where we met, but now she works on the female ward.'

For a second, Tom put his hand on Paul's in a simple gesture of friendship.

'Well, Doctor Lambert, you make sure you look after her, and live for the present. You can never tell what the future might hold, or when happiness may be snatched away from you.'

****

During a quiet moment on Paul's next night on duty, he went to have another chat with Tom, only to find that he wasn't by his bed. Nor was he in the group of patients who were playing cards in the restroom. He asked if they knew where he was.

He was answered by a bearded man with a strong Mancunian accent. 'You mean the ugly Polak, Doc? No, I don't know where he is, and I can't say I am particularly fussed.'

Slightly shocked, Paul glanced to see what reaction his remarks had engendered in the rest of the group.

The only one who seemed to show any surprise commented. 'He tends to keep to himself, Doctor. Sometimes he leaves the ward, and has a wander around the hospital.'

'Perhaps he would like a bit of company, and enjoy a game of cards,' Paul ventured.

The bearded man replied. 'He wouldn't be welcome here. We don't owe the Poles anything. They're an ungrateful lot.'

Paul asked him to explain.

'Well, Doc, I served in the war. Served for four years, I did. There wouldn't have been a war but for Poland. The Germans rolled them over in a couple of weeks. They just turned and ran. And when it was all over, what did they do? They poured into our country looking for sympathy, and taking jobs away from true Brits.'

Paul knew it would not be appropriate for him as a doctor to have a dispute with his patients. He was also conscious though, that the Polish war experience had been a closed book to him until Tom had so recently opened his eyes, but he didn't feel able to allow such a remark to pass unchallenged.

'I don't think your facts are completely correct,' he suggested.

'Maybe they are, maybe they aren't, but I don't want to see his ugly mug here. It would stop me concentrating on my cards!'

'Where did you serve in the war?' Paul asked, wondering if it was appropriate to reveal how Tom came by his appalling injuries.

'I was in the Royal Army Catering Corp,' he replied. 'I wanted to see active service but failed the medical. I've got flat feet.'

It was as well that Paul's pager sounded at that moment, for had he not been required to return to the office to answer it, he might well have said something that he would have regretted!

****

Two days later, the pathology report of the gland removed from Tom's armpit became available. Paul read it apprehensively:

Name: *Aleksander Szezepanski*
Dob: *18-10-16*
Hosp no: *37846*
Consultant: *Sir WW*
Ward: *S5M*
Clinical information: *Lymph gland from L. axilla*
Macroscopic appearance: *The specimen comprises a previously bisected lymph gland 2cms in diameter. The cut surface has an irregular, grey appearance.*
Microscopic appearance: *The lymphoid tissue is entirely replaced by malignant cells showing abnormally large and irregular nuclei and multiple mitoses.*
Histological diagnosis: *Lymph gland infiltrated by undifferentiated cancer cells, compatible with a secondary spread from the lung.*
Signed: *Dr G Farmer, Consultant Pathologist.*

Paul groaned. It was exactly what had been expected, but it was still distressing to have the diagnosis confirmed. If the tumour had been confined to the lung, then surgical removal might have offered the chance of a cure, albeit a small one, but the presence of cancer cells in the armpit indicated that the cancer had spread beyond the reach of any treatment. Regrettably, Tom had only a few months to live. The situation was discussed in the ward office, before Sir William's next ward round.

'Sir,' Mo Khan began, 'do you feel Tom should be treated with one of the new cytotoxic drugs? I've read reports recently suggesting that the latest drugs might extend Tom's life for a month or more.'

'A doctor's priority,' the consultant replied, 'is not to keep the patient alive as long as possible, but to consider the quality of their life. At present, Tom is weak and he's tired, but he has no pain. He's able to walk around, and enjoy his food. If we start him on chemotherapy, he'll spend what little time remains vomiting. It's sometimes better to help the patient to accept that their life is drawing to a close, and to concentrate on relieving pain and anxiety. There really ought to be an eleventh commandment, you know; *Thou shalt not strive officiously to keep alive.*'

'Then we must think about the support Tom will need for his remaining days,' Mo said. 'Ideally, he would be nursed at home in the midst of a caring family, but Tom has no living relatives, and his next of kin apparently is a neighbour.'

'Then I suggest Tom is allowed to go home now, provided he feels able to do so,' Sir William remarked, 'but understands he may return to us when the time comes.'

But Tom didn't make it home. His condition rapidly deteriorated, though fortunately, he remained free of pain. He wasn't confined to bed, and occasionally was able to visit the hospital shop, though the distance he was able to walk, reduced daily. He accepted the inevitability of his fate with quiet dignity, and unlike many patients, was not afraid to ask how his illness was likely to progress. His various questions were answered with total honesty. It was a surprise therefore, when Paul found him in tears one evening, as he happened to be passing. Quietly, he pulled the screens around his bed.

'Hey, Tom, this isn't like you.'

'I'm sorry. I'm letting myself down,' he said, pulling a handkerchief from under the pillow and wiping his eyes.

'Is there a problem? Are you in pain?'

'No, Doctor, it's just silly thoughts going through my head. I'll be alright in a minute.'

'Is there anything I can do to help?' Paul asked, 'I've got time for a chat.'

'I'm suddenly overwhelmed with sadness,' Tom confessed.

'We all have to die sometime,' Paul said gently. 'The clock ticks for us all.'

'I know. But you see, I'm not sad that I'm going to die; I'm not afraid of dying. I know you kind people are here to help me. I'm sad that no one will remember me. I lost all those who were dear to me many years ago. When I'm gone, no one will even know I've been here.'

Paul was lost for words. He felt her eyes watering. Here was a man whose entire family had been snatched away from him, who had searched in vain for years to find out what had become of them and then, having accepted that they must all be dead, had lived in the shadows, isolated by his dreadful disfigurement. Slowly, he composed himself and put his hand on Tom's.

'Perhaps only a few will remember you as an individual, as Aleksander Szczepanski,' he said softly, 'but millions will be grateful to you for the service you rendered in the war. Every time they stand in silence on Remembrance Sunday, they will be honouring you and your comrades. And you've made a great impression on all the staff here. You can be sure we will remember you.'

Tom allowed himself a weak smile. 'It seems funny to hear you call me Aleksander,' he said, 'after all these years being known as 'Tom'. My Zofia used to call me Aleks. You've no idea how much I've missed her over the years. My life would have been so very different had she been at my side.'

Paul felt himself welling up again; he didn't trust herself to speak. Tom put his hand on Paul's arm and added 'perhaps it will not be long before I see her again,' he said.

****

A couple of days later, Johnny Nolan, Paul's fellow houseman, was working in the accident department, when the nursing sister dashed in.

'Dr Nolan, do you know a man called Szczepanski; a man with scars on his face from old burns?'

'Certainly, I do. He's one of the patients on our ward. Why do you ask?'

'He's been found collapsed on the main corridor of the hospital. Apparently, he was having an epileptic fit so he was brought here.

He's wearing pyjamas and a dressing gown, and his hospital bracelet says he's one of your patients.'

'And you say he was fitting? He doesn't have a history of epilepsy.'

'Yes. Apparently, he was seen having a major fit. He's now unconscious. Dr Makin is looking after him. He thought you might be able to give him some background information.'

Johnny joined Bill Makin, and found that Tom was indeed deeply unconscious. Bill had been considering all the various causes of fits and coma, but when told of Tom's diagnosis, he accepted that the fits meant the tumour had now spread to the brain. Tom was transferred back to the surgical ward, was given large doses of sedatives to prevent further fits, but he remained deeply unconscious. The staff felt it was a blessing when he slipped away the next morning.

It was Sister's responsibility to empty Tom's bedside locker. She found some dirty socks, underpants and handkerchiefs, a book of crossword puzzles, a watch, and a few coins but, in addition, there was a brown envelope addressed to Sir William, and a small box made of stiff cardboard. Originally it had been white, but was now grey and scuffed, as if from frequent handling. The box contained a bronze medal in the shape of a cross. The cross was two inches wide; its horizontal bar represented aircraft wings, whilst the vertical bar depicted propellers. Hanging from the medal was a ribbon with purple and white diagonal stripes. It was accompanied by a slip of card on which was typed *'Distinguished Flying Cross. Awarded to Aleksander Tomasz Szczepanski 1942'*.

'May I borrow that for a moment?' Paul asked when Sister showed it to him.

He took the medal and walked down the ward. The bearded Mancunian was lounging in the patients' restroom, smoking and watching television.

'I thought you might be interested to see this,' he said, fixing him with his eye and showing him the medal.

'What is it, Doc?'

'It's the Distinguished Flying Cross,' he said. 'It was awarded to Tom, the ugly Polak. I guess you didn't know he served in the RAF, and fought in the Battle of Britain. He got those terrible burns when he crashed defending this country.'

'Well, bugger me,' commented the Mancunian, 'would you believe it?'

Sir William brought Tom's letter with him, when he came for his next ward round. 'I thought you would be interested to know what Tom wrote,' he said. He read the letter out loud.

'Dear Doctor,
Please thank your doctors and nurses for their kindness to me. I do not think I shall have time to write a proper will, so respectfully ask you to decide these matters for me. Do give my things to old soldiers, if you think that best.
May God bless you all,
Aleksander Szczepanski 'Tom'

There was silence as everyone reflected on Tom's courage, and the quiet dignity he had shown throughout his illness. His homeland had been overrun in war, his wife captured and killed. Then after an arduous and dangerous journey across Europe, he had joined the Polish arm of the Royal Air force. He had served with great bravery and distinction before being so terribly injured. Yet when the war was won, he found his own country subjugated, and when he settled in England, had never been made welcome by those who ought to have been grateful to him. For thirty years, he had been forced to work as a night watchman, out of sight and out of mind.

****

Some two months later, Sir William came to the ward, a smile on his face and a parcel under his arm.
'Now,' he said, 'I have some news to share with you.'
He unwrapped the parcel.
'Paul, you said Tom's one great sadness was that he feared that no-one would remember him when he was gone; that no-one would ever know he existed.'
He revealed a polished oak plaque, into which Tom's medal had been inlaid. Beneath the medal, on a small brass plate, were inscribed the words:
In memory of 'Tom' Szczepanski DFC who served with distinction in the Polish arm of the Royal Air Force.

'I am pleased to say the hospital authorities have agreed that the side ward in which he died is to be dedicated to him,' Sir William concluded.

Thought for the day

The first test of a truly great man is his humility

John Ruskin 1819 - 1900

Chapter 11 Cash or Conscience

15th October 1966

'We're so sorry to disturb you, Doctor. We really don't like to trouble you at this time of the night. We know your job is to deal with major accidents and emergencies, but the instructions from our doctor said to come here.'

These apologetic words were spoken by John Collins, a man of about 30. He was accompanied by his wife. Unsurprisingly, they had realised that Paul had been called from his bed; he had stubble on his chin, looked bleary-eyed, and had simply thrown a white coat over his pyjamas.

John went on to explain. 'I've been troubled with indigestion for a week or so; I've been treating myself with milk, bicarbonate of soda and such like. But it's got worse, so earlier this evening, I tried to see my own doctor. The surgery is at his house you know, but there was a note on the door saying there was no service until ten tomorrow morning. It said that anyone with a problem should come here.

At the time,' John continued, 'I didn't feel ill enough to come to the hospital, but during the night, the indigestion got quite severe, and I couldn't sleep. I took more milk, but it didn't help. And unfortunately, we've run out of the bicarbonate. That's why I've come here. All I need is some indigestion tablets, or a white bottle. I'd no idea you would be in bed. I thought there would be a duty doctor working a night shift.'

'There is,' Paul growled. 'It's me. I was working on the wards all day yesterday, and I'll be 'on duty' here until nine in the morning!'

Paul knew it was wrong to be angry with the patient; it wasn't his fault, but he was furious.

'And who is this doctor who gives such an excellent service?' he asked sarcastically.

'It's Dr Clark in Chepstow Street.'

Paul prescribed an alkaline mixture, and Mr Collins and his wife went happily on their way, but Paul felt abused. He remonstrated with Sister.

'Why the hell should I have to see Dr Clark's patients in the middle of the night, simply because he's too bone-idle to arrange a roster with his colleagues? Damn it, he's supposed to offer a 24-hour service, but he absolves himself from all responsibility by sticking a note on the surgery door telling patients to come here. It saves him the cost of arranging cover, I suppose.'

Sister tried to assuage Paul's anger. 'It's no good getting het up about it, Paul. It happens all the time. Dr Clark is notorious, and he gets away with it because his surgery is just round the corner. He couldn't do it if his practice was five miles away.'

'So he gets paid for giving a 24 hour service, never does any night calls, and we pick up pieces, is that it?'

'That's about the size of it.'

Paul was livid. It was already 4.30 in the morning, and he'd had virtually no sleep at all.

'Right,' he said to Sister. 'We'll see about that. What's his telephone number?'

'I'm not sure, but Bob on the switchboard will get it for you from Directory Enquires.'

Two minutes later, Paul was on the phone. The phone rang and rang and rang before eventually a sleepy female voice answered.

'Hello,' Paul said. 'Is that Mrs Clark?'

'Yes, it is. Who on earth is that?'

'This is Dr Lambert, from the City General Hospital. May I speak with Dr Clark please?'

'Dr Clark isn't on duty. He's not taking calls tonight.'

'So I believe. I'm sorry to disturb him,' Paul lied, 'but I've just seen one of his patients as an emergency in the Casualty department. I'd like to speak with him about his management.'

There were shuffling noises and gruff curses at the other end of the line, before finally a male voice answered.

'Hello, Dr Clark here. Who's that?'

'This is Dr Lambert from the hospital. I'm ringing to let you know I've just treated a patient of yours, a man called John Collins. He's suffering from mild indigestion. I've given him an antacid mixture, which should solve the problem. He saw the notice on your surgery door, and attended Casualty as instructed. I thought you ought to know, so that you'll be able to continue his treatment.'

There was a long pause, so long in fact that Paul thought he wasn't going to answer. Finally, he spoke.

'You impudent young pup. A letter in the morning would have sufficed.' Then the telephone receiver was slammed down.

With the savage satisfaction of knowing he wasn't the only one whose beauty sleep had been disturbed, Paul retired to the hot and stuffy cubby hole that served as his bedroom, but too angry to sleep, he tossed and turned until morning.

****

The next afternoon, Paul and Mo Khan were assisting Mr Potts in the operating theatre.

'We're nearly finished here,' the consultant said, 'you put the last few stitches in, Khan. I need to have a word with Lambert. In the surgeon's room now, Lambert!'

Conscious that the angry tone of the consultant's voice had caused the theatre staff to stare at him, Paul slipped off his gown and gloves. It was obvious he was in trouble, but he couldn't imagine why. He wasn't aware he'd done anything wrong.

Mr Potts was waiting for him in the surgeon's room. He came straight to the point.

'Lambert, I've had Dr Clark on the phone. He says you rang him last night, and were extremely rude to him.'

'Certainly, I rang him, Sir,' Paul protested. 'But I was definitely not rude. In fact, I was at great pains to be formal and polite.'

'But you rang him in the middle of the night. What possible justification was there for that?'

Paul told him the whole story, confidently expecting Mr Potts' understanding and support. Everyone knew that the Casualty Department was for genuine accidents and real emergencies. It was not there for patients whose problems were minor, and certainly not there to allow a lazy GP to use the hospital to deputise for him, free of charge, without prior notice. Paul however, was sadly mistaken.

'I'm deeply disappointed in you, Lambert. You should have known better. Surely you understand that it's important to foster good relationships with our colleagues in general practice. Dr Clark is a senior practitioner; you are young and inexperienced. There was no justification for ringing him in the night, especially about a patient whose condition was not urgent. If you were unhappy about an aspect of Dr Clark's work, you should have shared your concerns with me, rather than taking the matter into your own hands.'

'But Sir, I....'

'No, Lambert. I expect you to show a great deal more maturity in future. You need to stay calm, and consider things carefully before you act in such an ill-considered manner. You're not going to get very far in surgery, if you take such impulsive actions.' A threat was clearly implicit in the consultant's words.

Unable to understand why Mr Potts should support a GP who so blatantly abused the system, Paul was amazed at the attitude his boss had adopted. To be criticised in these circumstances seemed grossly unfair, but he bit his tongue. He knew better than to argue with the consultant.

Mr Potts looked at him expectantly, perhaps waiting for an apology, but if indeed that was the case, he was destined to be disappointed. After working through the night, Paul felt weary, obstinate and bloody-minded. There was a long pause.

'Well, Lambert. What have you got to say for yourself?'

'Nothing, sir.'

Mr Potts glared at his trainee, but Paul was damned if he was going to apologise. He was right, Dr Clark was wrong. And so was Mr Potts for supporting him.

There was a prolonged silence. The consultant looked as if he was about to continue the tirade but he didn't.

'All right, Lambert. This time we'll leave it at that, but don't let it happen again.'

'No, sir.'

And with a final, 'That will be all, Lambert.' Paul was dismissed.

Afterwards, Paul spoke with Mo Khan. He simply couldn't understand why Mr Potts had sided with Dr Clark. Mo listened quietly, as he always did, and then offered a simple explanation.

'Hospital consultants need to keep the local doctors happy. It's the GPs who send them patients, not just to their NHS clinics, but also to their private rooms. That's where the money is. Popular surgeons can easily double their NHS salaries if they can attract a steady stream of private patients.'

'So,' Paul said bitterly, 'Mr Potts turns his back on blatant abuse of his junior doctors, simply to keep the general practitioners sweet, and to line his back pocket.'

Mo smiled sympathetically. 'That's about it, Paul. That's the way the system works. I know it's not fair, but be warned; it doesn't pay to buck the system. The system has been in place for many years, and it's not likely to change in the near future. You have to accept it, because if you try to change it, you'll end up being frustrated and disappointed.... and if you complain too loudly, you might end up being thrown out on your ear. There are plenty of young doctors eager to have surgical training waiting to take your place.'

Paul remained bitter about the reprimand he had received, but was simply too tired to argue.

Mo put a sympathetic hand on his shoulder. 'Cheer up Paul; I'll make you a cup of coffee. You look as if you need one.'

Thought for the day

The love of money is the source of all evil

I Timothy ch 6 v 10

Chapter 12   The Biter gets Bit

30th October 1966

They had reached the patient in the third bed when the sound of laughter emanated from the entrance to the ward. Freddie Ginks was strolling towards them; he was wearing a classic, dark-grey suit, complete with waistcoat and black bow tie, with Sir William's trademark red rose in his lapel. He had even laced his hair with talc to make it grey, and had mimicked the consultant's tousled hairstyle. Freddie was a locum registrar, deputising for Mo Khan who had taken a month's leave to visit his family in India. He was reputed to be a good diagnostician and a capable surgeon, but his progress up the surgical career ladder had stalled, some saying that the medical establishment disapproved of his extrovert personality which they felt to be unbecoming of a consultant surgeon.

'What is the justification for all this jocularity?' Freddie asked, using a passable impersonation of Sir William's deep melodic voice, when the laughter had finally died away.

'I'm very sorry, Sir,' Paul said, in his most deferential voice, 'just a little private joke.'

'Ward rounds are no place for jokes.' Freddie replied his voice stern, his expression severe, and still playing the part of the senior consultant. 'Our patients expect us to be serious and focussed at all times. We must maintain our concentration and devote ourselves exclusively to their well-being. You would do well to remember that, Lambert.'

'As I say, I do apologise, Sir,' Paul said with mock respect.

'Apology accepted, Lambert, but let's have less of this untoward levity.'

Unless the unit was 'on take' for emergency admissions, the pace of work slackened at the weekend. Most consultants could be relied upon to stay away from the hospital unless one of their patients was particularly unwell. By and large, this was welcomed by the junior doctors, as it enabled them to complete their duties quickly, leaving time for some well-earned rest and relaxation. The exception was the gentlemanly and benevolent Sir William, who frequently made an appearance on a Saturday morning, and regrettably on a Sunday morning as well if inclement weather kept him from his garden. This was generally regarded by the nursing and medical staff as a hindrance, since unless there was a medical problem that required his advice, it simply interrupted the morning's routine, and delayed the time by which the work was completed.

In theory, Sir William came to see any seriously ill patients who required his advice, but in practice it was mainly for a coffee and a chat. He was a bachelor. He lived in a nearby cottage that had once served as the lodge to the manor house which, many years before, had been demolished to make way for the hospital. Had he been asked, he would probably have agreed that he regarded it largely as a social visit.

On this particular Saturday morning, the real Sir William was attending a surgical meeting in Birmingham. This was welcome news, and the junior doctors planned a quick ward round to review the patients, a midmorning coffee, then some much-deserved R and R for the rest of the day.

Earlier, they had congregated in the office waiting for Freddie to arrive. Ten minutes had passed, and when he'd still failed to put in an appearance, they had embarked on the round without him. They were accompanied by Sister and a couple of student nurses and as the most junior member of the team, Paul pushed the notes trolley in time-honoured fashion. It was soon after they had started that Sir William's lookalike arrived.

'We've wasted far too much time already, so let's get on with this ward round,' Freddie continued tersely. 'This is Mrs Enstone, isn't it, whose gallstones we removed last week. Tell me how things have been since my last round, Lambert.'

It was evident that Freddie intended to maintain the charade for the rest of the morning, so the juniors followed his lead.

'She's made excellent progress, Sir,' Paul responded, despite finding it difficult to keep a straight face. 'All being well, she'll be going home in the morning.'

'That's good,' Freddie said, still miming Sir William's voice. He turned to the patient, 'Well done, Mrs Enstone.' he said, 'you've made an excellent recovery. We'll see you in the clinic in a month's time.'

And so it went on, the patients obviously accepting that a little tomfoolery was permissible. Joining in the charade, one elderly lady took his hand, enquired after his health, and offered to lend him her Saga magazine, which caused great amusement. It must be said that the fun they were having in no way detracted from the care given to the patients. All were managed just as carefully as if the boss had really been present, despite Freddie insisting that he be treated in a manner which befitted the most senior consultant in the hospital. Freddie said later that he had been tempted to perform Sir William's suppositories routine, but felt this would have been a step too far.

They were halfway around the ward when the inevitable happened. The real Sir William strolled through the door!

On this occasion though, he wasn't smartly dressed; he'd come straight from his garden. His surgical meeting had been cancelled; he'd spent a couple of hours weeding, and then popped into the hospital for a drink and a chat. He was wearing a pair of old corduroy trousers and an open-necked, checked shirt, and for once in his life, he wasn't wearing a tie. He had heavy brogue shoes on his feet.

For a moment or so, Freddie was oblivious to Sir William's advancing presence, but then he looked up and saw him. Instinctively his hand went to his lapel, and he tore off the rose. He tried to tidy his tousled hair, but only succeeded in creating a shower of talcum powder that settled like dandruff on his shoulders. He froze, dumbstruck with horror. There was no escape; he had been caught red-handed, ridiculing his consultant. His heart sank; surely this would be the end of his career in surgery.

When he saw Freddie, Sir William stopped midstride. He too was lost for words.

For some time, the real Sir William and his caricature stood five yards apart, staring at each other. You could have heard a pin drop. Paul waited for the consultant to explode. But he didn't. The slightest smile crossed his face, and then he turned on his heels without saying a word, and went back to the office.

'Oh my God! What have I done?' Freddie muttered. 'I really am in trouble now.'

Sister, her nurses and Paul were too shocked to respond; they just stood, open-mouthed and appalled. Freddie was right, there would be all hell to pay for such insolence.

Within a minute, Sir William was back, now wearing a junior doctor's white coat.

'Would you mind if I joined you for the rest of your round, Sir,' he said to Freddie, his voice light, no hint of anger in the voice, 'I'm sure there's much I shall be able to learn from you.'

Freddie was too confused to reply, but he sensed Sir William was expecting him to continue the round in the role of consultant.

'You want me to continue?' he managed to stutter.

'You've started, and since you believe that you are as experienced as I, it's only right that you should continue,' Sir William affirmed.

And that is what happened. At every bed, and at every opportunity, Sir William asked Freddie the most searching questions, seeking out the gaps in his knowledge, laying them bare mercilessly in front of Sister and the rest of the team. In truth, Freddie was so shell-shocked that he failed to do himself justice. He stuttered and stalled, making numerous schoolboy errors, as Sir William clearly and painfully demonstrated to him the extent of his ignorance of surgical matters. Although he was dressed as a consultant, it was obvious to all that he did not have a consultant's wisdom, knowledge or experience.

At the end of the round, everyone, including Sir William, went to have the usual coffee and biscuits in the ward office. Inevitably, the atmosphere was strained as everyone waited for the reprimand which was bound to come. But it didn't, and slowly Freddie regained a semblance of composure.

'Sir William,' he began, 'I really must apologise. Truly, it was only meant to be a bit of fun. I didn't mean any offence. And we didn't let it affect patient care, honestly, we didn't. We examined each and every patient just as carefully as if you'd been here.'

'I'm sure you did,' Sir William, replied, 'and no offence taken. I think you've probably learned your lesson, so we'll say no more about it.'

And, true to his word, Sir William said nothing further about it, and Freddie's career prospects were not harmed. Indeed, several years later, he was appointed as a consultant surgeon, albeit in a different hospital. However, that did not prevent the story adding to Sir William's reputation as a benevolent gentleman. It became folklore within the hospital, becoming embellished over the years, as indeed it has been as retold today!

Thought for the day

I've taken my fun where I've found it   And now I must pay

Rudyard Kipling 1865 – 1936

Chapter 13   A Life Changing Decision

12th November 1966

David Entwistle attended the casualty department of the City General Hospital one evening during the second week of November. Although Paul didn't realise it at the time, he was a patient who was to change the course of his medical career. Nineteen years of age, David was a tall, extremely slim, sociology student from the local university. In the days when he had been a college student, Paul had envied undergraduates studying subjects such as sociology, politics, or English literature. Unlike those studying medicine, they only had eight or so hours of formal tuition a week, which left them ample time to participate in the wide variety of extracurricular activities that comprise a full university experience. It also gave them the opportunity to undertake part-time jobs, which supplied the funds needed to support the hectic social life that appeared to be their main preoccupation.

David's medical story was classical. Approximately 24 hours before, he had experienced a vague discomfort in the middle of his abdomen. At the time, he had thought little of it, presuming he'd simply overindulged the night before. However, during the course of the day, the pain had got progressively more severe, and had settled in the lower-right corner of his belly. Apart from his abdominal problem, he was a fit and healthy young man, albeit built like a beanpole.

When he arrived at the hospital, the tenderness in his lower abdomen was extreme; he nearly jumped off the bed when Paul put a hand on his abdomen. This was undoubtedly a case of appendicitis. It was equally clear that he needed to be admitted, so Paul phoned Mo Khan, and gained his permission to transfer David to the ward with a view to surgery.

Paul had little doubt that his diagnosis would be confirmed and that later in the evening he would assist in theatre whilst the registrar removed the appendix. Since the illness was of short duration, and the patient was young and slim, it promised to be a quick and straightforward operation. Little did he realise how wrong this assumption was to be.

Just as Paul had anticipated, at eleven-thirty David was being anaesthetised whilst Mo and he changed into their green theatre outfits, scrubbed up and donned surgical gowns and gloves. The patient, endotracheal tube in his throat and intravenous drip in his arm, was wheeled through from the anaesthetic room, and lifted gently onto the operating table. The abdomen was widely exposed and Mo painted the skin with an antiseptic solution and placed surgical drapes around the operation site in the usual fashion. Everything was now ready for the operation to begin.

It was at this moment that Mo spoke to the theatre sister who was standing opposite him, her tray of surgical instruments, needles and swabs at the ready.

'It seems very quiet tonight Sister, do you have any other cases booked?'

Sister did not appreciate the significance of this innocent-sounding question, nor indeed did Paul realise that her answer would change the course of his life.

'No.' she replied, 'I'm pleased to say this is the only case.'

Mo looked up over his mask. 'Paul,' he said, 'come and change places with me.'

Paul looked back across the table, not understanding the reason for his request, before suddenly realising what was being suggested.

'Are you sure?' he said, 'I haven't done one before you know.'

'I know,' Mo replied, 'but you've assisted at a dozen or more.'

The theatre sister and the anaesthetist exchanged a meaningful glance. They had seen that the patient was young and slim, knew Mr Khan to be a skilled and experienced surgeon, and had expected the operation would be completed within 30 to 40 minutes. This was not going to be such a quick procedure after all. For the theatre staff, this only meant a longer operation, and the possibility of being late for the one a.m. meal provided for night staff. But for the anaesthetist, it meant getting to bed late and missing sleep. He made no comment but a frown crossed his face.

Mr Khan, who had seen the exchange, clearly understood what was going through their minds.

'We've all got to learn,' he said, 'there's a first time for everything, whether it's our first appendix, our first solo anaesthetic, or our first case as a scrub nurse.'

With considerable trepidation, Paul changed places, and Sister passed him the scalpel. He could feel his heart banging in his chest. It was true that he'd assisted at a number of appendix operations, but seeing one and doing one are totally different things. There had been no time to prepare mentally for the test that was imminent, though he suspected that had been Mr Khan's intention. He would have been far more nervous had he had time to think about it. Looking at the area of virgin skin in front of him, Paul felt the sweat forming on his brow.

He knew exactly where to make the incision. It would be two inches long, and centred on McBurney's point in the right iliac fossa. Holding the scalpel in his right hand, he made the initial incision, drawing the knife carefully along the skin. Lifting the blade away, he saw that he'd created the faintest scratch, no more than a red line on the skin, scarcely causing any bleeding at all. Mr Khan started a running commentary that he was to continue throughout the procedure.

'Use your left thumb and forefinger to tense the skin,' he said, 'so that the skin won't move away from the blade. You're bound to be tentative at first; you just need to apply a little more pressure.'

Paul made a second cut, and again lifted the scalpel away. Whilst the skin was cut completely through in the centre of the wound, it had not completely parted at either end. The pressure he'd exerted hadn't been uniform along the length of the incision.

'You'll need the full-length of the incision,' Mr Khan said, 'so make sure you're through the skin at both ends. That's better. Now deepen the wound through the fatty layer, remembering that this patient is only quite thin, and you will soon be down to muscles. Some patients have a fatty layer two or more inches thick, but in this young man, it won't be more than a quarter of an inch.'

Slowly, nervously and hesitantly, but with intense concentration, Paul followed his instructions.

'Fine. Now you'll see that there's quite a lot of bleeding from those small vessels in the fatty layer. Place a swab over your side of the wound to compress the bleeding points whilst I do the same over mine. There. That temporarily stops the bleeding for us. Now, as I take my swab away little by little, it exposes the bleeding points one by one, and you can cauterise them using the diathermy machine.'

This was the first time Paul had used the diathermy machine. It involved grasping the bleeding vessel in the points of the electric forceps, and pressing the pedal on the floor with his foot. One or two of the bleeding vessels were too large to be coagulated, so these were clipped with forceps. They now needed to be tied in a reef knot with thread, something Paul had learned how to do when he was a Boy Scout. He did this two-handed. Left over right and under, then right over left and under, pulling the two half hitches up in opposite directions, just like tying up a Christmas parcel with string. On numerous occasions, he'd seen the consultants and Mr Khan tie knots effortlessly, one-handed, taking only a second or two; he was conscious that his efforts were slow and clumsy in the extreme.

'If we're going to make a surgeon of you,' Mr Khan commented, 'you'll need to learn how to tie knots left-handed.'

This was true; a right-handed surgeon, ties knots with his left hand, never letting go of the end of the thread at any time. Some surgeons have particularly difficult knot skills to acquire. The ear, nose and throat surgeon, when removing tonsils, has to tie knots in the confined space at the back of the throat. A surgeon performing keyhole surgery ties knots inside the abdomen, with his hands outside the abdomen, whilst only able to see what he is doing by watching the television monitor. And when knots are tied to control large bleeding arteries, it is vitally important that they do not come undone!

Beneath the fatty layer, the abdomen has three layers of muscles, but in this thin patient, these layers were not well-developed, which was presumably why Mr Khan had decided this was a suitable patient for Paul to perform his first operation. By this time, Paul had ceased to feel nervous. His entire concentration was devoted to following Mr Khan's instructions. Nor was he conscious of the other people in the theatre; he wasn't even aware of the theatre sister, even though she was standing opposite him, handing him surgical instruments, as and when they were needed.

Slowly, he dissected his way through the muscles and reached the glistening peritoneal layer that forms the inner lining of the abdomen. Mr Khan pointed out that in the deepest part of the wound, he'd only exposed half an inch of peritoneum, whereas his skin incision was two inches long.

'Your incision has got shelving edges,' he said. 'The edges need to be vertical; otherwise, you won't have enough room in which to operate when we actually get inside the belly.'

He supervised whilst Paul increased the length of the incision at the level of the fat and muscles layers until it met with his approval.

'Don't be fooled into believing that the best surgeon is the one who works through the smallest hole and leaves the shortest scar,' he said. 'The best surgeon is the one who operates safely; and it isn't safe to struggle to complete an operation through an inadequate incision.

Now, I want you to open the peritoneum and then, if you don't mind, I'll put a finger into the abdomen, and we'll find out exactly where this young man's appendix is situated.'

Paul knew that the position of the appendix was very variable. Sometimes it would be found sitting exactly where the incision had been made, but often it was tucked behind part of the large bowel.

Typically, in a case of appendicitis, a fatty apron called the omentum moves to the inflamed area, and wraps itself around the inflamed appendix, limiting the spread of infection. Indeed, when Paul looked into the wound, all he could see was the omentum obliterating everything else. Mr Khan, from his side of the table, probed within the abdomen with his index finger. Using only his sense of touch and previous experience, he located the appendix, and identified the structures to which it was adherent. He withdrew his finger.

'Pop a couple of fingers into the abdomen, and you'll find that the omentum is stuck to the inner aspect of the muscles. I want you to slide a finger gently between the muscle wall and the omentum. I've started it off, so you should be able to feel the plane that I want you to separate. It's like separating two segments of an orange with your eyes closed. Just slide your finger gently up and down the cleft, and you'll feel the omentum peeling away from the muscles.'

Tentatively, and again conscious of moisture on his brow, Paul separated the two a little, then asked Mr Khan to check that he was progressing satisfactorily.

'Yes, absolutely,' he said, 'you're in exactly the right place. Just continue along that line.'

Reassured, Paul continued to work between omentum and muscle, and soon the two sides were apart.

'Now, if you put your finger in again,' Mr Khan continued, 'you'll feel the appendix. It's about the size and shape of a chocolate finger biscuit. We're in luck today because nothing else is stuck to it. Identify it, and then gently hook your index finger around it, and flick it into the wound.'

As before, it was nerve-wracking for Paul to be working, unable to see exactly where his finger was, unsure how much pressure to apply, and unable to be certain that he was not damaging any neighbouring structures. He felt a cold trickle of sweat run down the small of his back, and afraid to continue with the manoeuvre, he again asked Mr Khan to check things were progressing satisfactorily. Then, yet again having been reassured, he coaxed the appendix very gently into the wound. It was red, angry, and inflamed.

His next task was to divide the arteries that were supplying blood to the appendix, and apply ties to them. Applying forceps to the blood vessels and cutting them with scissors was easy, but he was concerned about applying the ligatures. The blood vessels were friable, engorged, and carrying far more blood than was usual because the appendix was so inflamed. It was vitally important that these ligatures were secure.

'It's probably worth putting an extra half-hitch on them for security,' Mr Khan said. 'Those vessels will bleed very freely if the ties come adrift.'

This was a remark that stuck in Paul's brain, and which came back to haunt him later that night.

Laboriously, he tied his Christmas parcel knots to the vessels, applying a third and then a fourth half-hitch for good measure. Mr Khan then showed him how to detach the appendix, and seal the resulting hole in the bowel. He also had to take a specimen, so that they would know which antibiotic to use if the patient subsequently developed an infection.

They were now ready to close the abdomen, and Sister passed Paul the suture used to close the peritoneum. Mr Khan, however, ordered him to stop.

'Now,' he asked, 'what have you forgotten?'

Paul was flummoxed, and could think of nothing that he'd overlooked, although the truth was that during the operation, he'd not been thinking for himself at all. His entire concentration had been given to following Mr Khan's instructions to the best of his ability.

'What are you going to ask Sister to do?'

It was the request from surgeon to scrub nurse that Paul had heard during every operation he'd ever witnessed. Suddenly, the penny dropped!

'Sister, please may we count the swabs and instruments to make sure they're all present and correct.'

'That's right,' said Mr Khan, 'too often it's left to the nursing staff to do the check, but it's the surgeon's responsibility. That means an examination of the operation area, concentrating particularly on the space within the abdomen, and two counts, conducted jointly by the surgeon and the scrub nurse. It's sad but true that every year, some surgeon in the U.K. manages to leave a swab or an instrument inside a patient.'

Paul checked the wound and abdomen, then counted aloud whilst Sister identified the swabs they had used, most of which were now hanging on the swab rack against the theatre wall.

Then Mr Khan guided Paul, step by step, as the abdomen was closed. The edges of the three muscle layers were sutured together, and they checked there was no further bleeding in any part of the wound. Then Paul closed the fatty layer and finally sutured the skin. Again, he was conscious of his clumsy knot-tying technique, but the wound, the only part of his handiwork the patient would see, looked reasonably respectable when it was finally closed.

Sister handed him a dressing, which he applied to the wound, and his first ever surgical operation was complete.

Paul stripped off his hat, mask, gloves, and gown, feeling completely drained. Looking at the clock, he found it was one-thirty in the morning. The operation had taken nearly two hours, but during the procedure, he hadn't been conscious of the time at all.

'Thank you, Sister,' he said, 'for being so patient,' and then turning to the anaesthetist, 'and you too. I know Mr Khan would have done the operation in half the time.'

'Probably less,' Sister commented, 'but as he said, we all have to learn. That really wasn't too bad for a first attempt.'

The words were not spoken unkindly, indeed might have been taken as a compliment. Suddenly, with the completion of the operation and the lifting of the tension, Paul felt exhilarated. He could have laughed aloud. He'd been working non-stop since 8.30 in the morning, but didn't feel in the least bit tired. He had performed his first proper operation; he'd removed an inflamed appendix, and Sister had implied that he'd done all right; that it had been a reasonable effort. He felt good and was proud of himself. It was at that moment; he decided that he wanted to be a surgeon.

They went back into the restroom for a cup of coffee and a biscuit.

'If we're going to make a surgeon of you,' Mr Khan reiterated, 'you're going to have to learn to tie left-handed knots. In most situations in surgery, there simply isn't enough space in the wound for you to be tying knots with two hands. Let me show you how.'

He went out of the room, and returning with a length of suture material then gave an impressive demonstration of how it was done. He was able to tie a secure reef knot, one-handed, in five seconds. He passed the thread to Paul then laughed at his first ungainly attempts.

'It takes practice,' he said. 'Take some suture material away with you, and practice in your own time.'

'I will, and thank you for your patience this evening. My first proper operation, I can't believe I've actually removed an appendix. If you will excuse me now, I'll take a quick walk around the wards to check that things are tidy before I go to bed.'

'Oh, no, you won't,' Mo said with his quiet smile, 'you've not finished here yet. You need to write an account of the operation in the patient's notes, and record the procedure in the theatre logbook. Then there are the post-operative instructions for the nurses to be written, not to mention the patient's postoperative medication for pain relief and the fluid balance chart.'

In his buoyant mood, the adrenalin still pumping through his veins, Paul had forgotten that he was still the houseman, the most junior member of the team. Paperwork was the house officer's responsibility, and this was Mr Khan's way of bringing him down to earth.

****

As he lay in bed, Mr Khan's remark *'making a surgeon of you'* came into Paul's mind. He hadn't previously considered surgery as a career, merely as a necessary stepping-stone to becoming a fully-registered doctor. Nonetheless, something had been awakened within him. The operation he had performed had been the turning point that had changed the course of this young student's illness. Had it been left undiagnosed and untreated, it might have proved fatal, and the surgical intervention he had performed, albeit with an enormous amount of help from Mr Khan, had been the event which had eliminated the disease, and would return the patient to health. Although performing this operation had made Paul want to pursue a career in surgery it, had also demonstrated to him just how much knowledge he would have to assimilate, and how much technical skill he would need to acquire.

Sometime later, he woke in a cold sweat, gripped with sudden fear. The euphoria he'd experienced on completing the surgery had been replaced with an acute attack of anxiety and self-doubt. Had he tied the arteries taking blood to the appendix properly? Could the ligatures have slipped, and the patient be quietly bleeding to death on the ward? Suppose he died, a bright young man in his first term at university. Paul tried to be rational. Surely, Mr Khan would have intervened had he not been happy with any part of the operation. But then again, could he tell, simply by watching, just how tight those ligatures were?

He tried to get back to sleep but couldn't. There was a devil in his head, stoking his self-doubt that simply would not be silenced.

He tried to be logical. The instructions he'd written for the nurses were that observations of pulse and blood pressure should be taken through the night. Surely the nurses would ring him if the patient showed signs of bleeding. But then he remembered that the observations had only been requested every two hours; that was the routine after an appendix operation. But was this often enough? If the ligature on a blood vessel came adrift immediately after they'd taken a set of observations, it might be another two hours before the nurses noticed that the patient was quietly bleeding to death. Finally, agonising over the situation, unable to sleep, envisaging all manner of calamities that might have occurred, he could bear it no longer. He rang the ward to speak with the staff nurse. He tried not to sound concerned.

'Hello,' he said, 'I'm sorry to trouble you, but will you please tell me how David Entwistle is? He's the lad who had his appendix removed earlier?'

Staff nurse sounded surprised at the question. 'Yes, he's fine,' she said, 'he's come out of his anaesthetic. He asked for a drink a little while ago, but the instructions were that he should have nothing by mouth, so we've just given him a mouthwash.'

'Are his observations alright?' Paul asked anxiously.

'Yes, absolutely fine,' she said.

Reassured, he settled back into the bed. Now, he thought, I'll be able to get some sleep. But sleep wouldn't come. He tossed and turned and fretted. Common sense told him there was nothing to worry about, but a lingering doubt at the back of his mind wouldn't allow him to relax. An hour passed, and then another, and finally, unable to stand it anymore, he decided to go to the ward to check on the patient himself.

'Hello,' said the staff nurse, surprised at Paul's sudden appearance, 'we weren't expecting you. Is there a problem?'

'I've just come to check on David Entwistle,' he said.

'He's absolutely fine, no problems at all.'

Nonetheless, they went together to see how he was. He was fast asleep, appeared to be in no discomfort, and his observations were indeed absolutely normal.

The nurse was clearly puzzled that Paul should have left his bed to visit the ward at five in the morning, to see a patient who was causing no concern whatsoever.

'Was it a difficult operation? Are you expecting some troubles? Do you want us to do some extra observations?'

'No,' he said, 'it wasn't difficult, but it was my first appendicectomy.'

'Ah, now, I understand. Well, he's absolutely fine. You go back to bed, and I promise I'll ring you if there are any problems. But as you can see, he's absolutely fine.'

One thing was very obvious to Paul; there would be no point in attempting a career in surgery unless he was able to carry the responsibility and pressure that went with it.

He did return to bed, and finally got some sleep; but David was the first patient he went to see in the morning.

Thought for the day

To be a successful surgeon, you must have the eyes of a hawk, the heart of a lion and the hands of a lady.

       Richard Gordon (Gordon Benton) 1921 - 2014

Chapter 14   Paul gains Sister's respect

30th November 1966

Ever since Paul's first week on the ward when Sister Ashbrook had witnessed his embarrassment when Mr Quigley had vomited blood and bile down the front of his clean white coat and shirt, he had been aware that the ward sister regarded him as something of a liability, the weak link in the team, someone to be carefully watched and supervised. Paul recognised, of course, that on that occasion he had indeed acted unwisely, continuing with repeated attempts to pass the tube into Mr Quigley's stomach, when the sensible thing would have been to seek advice. Sir William regularly preached that the ward sisters had a wealth of knowledge and experience available to newly qualified doctors, and after that first humiliation Paul had often asked for guidance. Unfortunately, however, he had not found Sister Ashbrook particularly helpful either to him or to other house officers who sought her advice; her responses were usually curt and accompanied by remarks such as '*do they teach you young doctors nothing at medical school these days.*'

As a result, if Paul was uncertain about a medical matter, he would have a chat with Mo Khan. However, should he need advice concerning ward procedure or protocol, he would speak with Sister Rutherford on the female ward, or with Kate Meredith, the young nurse who had rescued the 'Quigley situation', of whom he was very fond. Throughout September and October, he had admired her from afar, but subsequently, managing to overcome his shy personality and natural inhibition, he had taken her to the pictures on a couple of occasions, and they had also enjoyed a party in the doctor's residency.

As it happened, the arrival on the ward of a young Glaswegian called Jimmy McMillan was destined to significantly redress Paul's relationship with Sister Ashbrook. Jimmy was the archetypical Scot, wiry of stature with a good head of red hair, who had been admitted to have a rupture in his groin repaired. One's initial impression was of an extremely fit man; he worked as a milkman, and the combination of his physical job and the time he spent working out in the gym, accounted for his fresh complexion and muscular frame. These looks though were misleading, since he had a major health problem. He had a severe form of diabetes, a condition in which blood sugar levels are raised due to the body's inability to produce the hormone insulin. Diabetes is a common ailment, the vast majority of sufferers having a mild form which develops over the age of fifty. Treated with tablets and diet, it rarely causes major problems.

The more severe form develops in children and young adults and requires injections of insulin. Such patients are at risk of serious complications, notably loss of consciousness should their blood sugar level rise too high or fall too low. Jimmy had a particularly unstable form of diabetes and needed to inject himself with large doses of insulin twice a day.

It was two days after Jimmy's operation, during which time his diabetes had been carefully monitored and controlled, that Paul's pager sounded with its urgent tone. At the time, Paul was in the residency enjoying his lunch. A patient had collapsed on the male ward, would he attend immediately. All sort of thoughts flashed through Paul's mind as he raced to the ward. *Which patient has collapsed? Will it be someone I already know or a patient I've never seen before? What has caused the collapse? Will I be able to diagnose the problem and know what action to take?* Worse still, the troubling thought *'could I in some way, through my inexperience, have been responsible for the problem?'* also flashed through his mind! Paul wondered whether all doctors were afflicted with such moments of self-doubt, or was it just those who were naturally introspective. It was a constant source of amazement to him that so few doctors develop stress induced stomach ulcers.

Arriving breathless on the scene two minutes later, Paul saw that the drama was unfolding adjacent to a bed half way down the ward on the left-hand side. It was Jimmy's bed, and it was Jimmy who had collapsed. In full view of all the other patients, he was laying on his back, on the floor, cold and lifeless, his pyjama jacket wide open. Sister Ashbrook was on her knees, bouncing on Jimmy's chest, administering cardiac massage. A senior staff nurse, also on her knees, was undertaking mouth-to-mouth respiration. A student nurse had a collection of heart monitor leads in her hand, and was struggling to apply these to Jimmy's chest, though hampered by Sisters' ongoing cardiac massage.

Emergency resuscitation was an exercise practiced regularly by both junior doctors and nurses, and Sister Ashbrook had matters organized exactly as described in the official manual. The patient was on a hard surface, in this case on the floor, so that compression on the chest squeezed the heart and forced blood to circulate round the body. Had the patient still been lying on a soft mattress in bed, cardiac massage would have been ineffective, since pressure on the chest simply pushes the patient bodily into the mattress. The whole patient then bounces back in a rather alarming manner, and no compression of the heart results. Sister Ashbrook, in exemplary fashion, had both hands, left on top of right, over Jimmy's breast bone, and was pumping rhythmically twice every second. Periodically, she paused to allow the staff nurse, her mouth on Jimmy's, to blow twice to inflate his lungs. Another nurse rushed up with the emergency drugs trolley, and was promptly dispatched by Sister to get the defibrillator and to call for the anaesthetist. All the while, the scene was being witnessed in shocked silence by the other patients, every one of them horrified at what had happened to this lively and likeable young man. He had looked fit and well until a few moments earlier, indeed he was due to be discharged from the hospital that afternoon, and had been cheerfully bidding farewell to his new found friends.

Sister spoke to Paul as soon as he arrived.

'Jimmy's had a heart attack, Dr Lambert. Take over the cardiac massage from me. I need to apply these ECG leads, and see what the heart tracing is doing.' Her instructions to the junior house officer were crisp, clear and authoritative. There was no doubt that despite the arrival of a doctor she had assumed the senior role.

'We may need to defibrillate him,' she continued, 'I've called for the anaesthetist, so that we can intubate him and ensure the airway.'

All the while Jimmy remained ominously still. He was pale and bathed in sweat.

Paul though felt uneasy; something was wrong. It would be most unusual for a slim man in his early 30's to suffer a massive heart attack, even if he were diabetic. An alternative explanation would be that a blood clot had formed in his legs during his operation, and then travelled to his lungs, but again this seemed unlikely. Although comatosed, Jimmy was sweating, and neither of these diagnoses caused that. He bent down and felt carefully at Jimmy's neck.

'Stop everything you're doing for a second,' he said.

'No, no,' Sister countermanded, 'keep going.'

As carefully as he could, despite the ongoing resuscitation, Paul felt for the carotid pulse in the neck, and was fairly certain it was present.

'Hold everything,' Paul repeated, 'I want no movement at all.'

This time Sister did stop chest compression and looked up angrily, but it gave Paul a moment's opportunity to examine again, and he was now certain that there was a pulse. It was faint, but it was definitely there. This wasn't a cardiac arrest at all. There was a pulse; therefore, the heart had not stopped. What was it that Sir William was always drumming into his staff? *'Common things occur commonly.'*

'Stop everything that you're doing,' Paul instructed. 'You're making the situation worse; no more cardiac massage, no more ventilation.'

He dashed to the treatment room, grabbed the largest syringe he could find, and filled it to the brim with the solution that he wanted. A couple of minutes later, he was back at Jimmy's side, to find that Sister had recommenced cardiac massage and her staff nurse was again giving mouth-to-mouth resuscitation. He needed to find a vein, and he needed to find it fast. If this wasn't possible in one of the veins in the arm, then an injection would have to be made directly into the large femoral vein in the groin. He held his breath, slid the needle through the skin, and fortunately, despite Jimmy's collapsed condition, found a vein at the first attempt. He injected the entire content of the syringe as quickly as possible. All the while Sister was kneeling over Jimmy, pummelling his chest and staff nurse, her lips on Jimmy's, was blowing into his lungs.

The effect of the injection was dramatic. Within thirty seconds, Jimmy was semi-conscious and thrashing violently with both arms and legs. One wild, uncoordinated swing of his right arm caught Sister Ashbrook full on the chest, and knocked her over backwards. She lay helpless, like a tortoise on its back, arms and legs flailing in the air; staff nurse, who was performing the artificial ventilation, fared little better. She got a mouthful of spittle, followed by a tirade of foul-mouthed abuse, before being tossed bodily to one side, joining Sister on the floor. As she fell, she collided with the resuscitation trolley which tumbled on top of her, scattering oxygen masks and tubes, syringes and needles, drugs and dressings over a wide area. The student nurse, believing that Jimmy had come back from the dead, ran screaming from the ward, adding to the pandemonium. Within a minute, Jimmy was sitting up, conscious but confused, shouting abuse at the top of his voice at Sister, her nurses, indeed at the entire English population. Language was heard that had never been heard on the ward before, all in the broadest of Glaswegian accents.

Paul stood up, well pleased with the result of his actions. He admired the scene laid out before him. Jimmy was in the centre, conscious if a little befuddled, berating everything and everybody around him. Sister and her staff nurse lay in heaps, struggling to regain their feet, not to mention their dignity and composure. The entire contents of the emergency trolley lay scattered around on the floor. Two student nurses, who had been watching the resuscitation from the sidelines, stood shocked and bewildered by the events that had unfolded before them, events that, without doubt, would be the talk of the Nurses Home for many weeks to come. Paul wasn't altogether unhappy that every patient on the ward had witnessed the episode. In fact, he felt rather smug. He realized of course, that this was not a particularly honourable emotion, but in the circumstances, he considered it to be justified!

Slowly Sister Ashbrook sat up, and then rose unsteadily to her feet, taking a few seconds to straighten her dress and her crumpled apron. She retrieved her cap, which had ended up on the floor a couple of yards away. She placed it on her head and secured it in position.

There was a long pause.

'What was in that syringe?' she asked.

Paul shouldn't have smiled, it was wrong of him to do so, but he simply couldn't resist it.

'A strong sugar solution,' he said. 'Jimmy's diabetic. He was in a diabetic coma. If you recall, he's just resumed his insulin injections. He probably hasn't started to eat as much as normal yet, so his blood sugar will have fallen.'

He was on the verge of saying *'as Sir William regularly reminds us, common things occur commonly'* but thought better of it.

Sister Ashbrook looked steadily at him for a moment or two, and then said quietly, 'Thank you, Dr Lambert......' there was a pause, '.....and well done.'

They were words Paul never thought he would hear from the Sister who had rarely missed an opportunity to belittle him.

Then Sister Ashbrook turned away and was her normal self again. She began firing instructions at her nurses in her usual brisk fashion.

'Get Mr McMillan back into bed. Give him a hot sweet drink and something to eat.' She turned to another of her nurses. 'Tidy up this mess on the floor.' To a third, 'Ring the anaesthetist, and tell him that he's no longer needed.'

Once again., she was the sister in charge of her ward. She had regained her composure, and was acting as if nothing untoward had happened.

Undoubtedly, Sister Ashbrook had suffered an embarrassing setback in the battle for supremacy that she waged with the junior doctors. For Paul it was a significant milestone, for although she never mentioned this incident or Jimmy McMillan again, it did change his relationship with her in a subtle way. No longer did he feel any need to justify his actions to her. He recalled what Mo Khan had once said of his relationship with her, *'I can't say that we like each other, but we do have a respect for each other.'*

That summed it up rather nicely, Paul thought, and he felt that he too had won Sister's respect.

Thought for the day

There can be no surgeon who is not also a physician.

Theophrastus Paracelsus 1493 - 1541

Chapter 15   Rosie

12th December 1966

A couple of weeks before Christmas, Rosemary Roberts was admitted to hospital. She was known to her many friends and family as 'Rosie'. It is of course totally inappropriate for a doctor to find his patient attractive, but it was impossible for Paul not to fall for Rosie. She was absolutely gorgeous both in appearance and personality. Her eyes were bright and sparkled, reflecting her zest for life, her full mouth had a ready smile which caused cute dimples to pucker her cheeks, and the blonde curls that framed her face were enchanting. Her beauty was enhanced by her complexion; her skin was smooth, strikingly pale almost opalescent, as if moulded from the finest bone china, but sadly this was the result of the two congenital abnormalities from which she suffered. The first was a narrowing of the veins that drained blood away from her liver and stomach; the second was that her kidneys contained many cysts. The narrow veins restricted the flow of blood and caused back pressure which resulted in blood pooling in the lining of the stomach. This then leaked into the lumen of the stomach and was lost. Consequently, Rosie was invariably pale and anaemic. There was a real concern that one day she might have a major haemorrhage.

The renal cysts affected the function of her kidneys such that toxic substances which would normally have been excreted in the urine, built up in her body. It was the combination of the anaemia, a tinge of yellow jaundice from her liver troubles and kidney failure that gave her the pale 'bone china' complexion.

Sadly, her whole life had been spent in and out of hospital, having a variety of treatments, multiple blood transfusions and more recently renal dialysis. Despite this, nothing seemed to dampen her bubbly personality and her eternal optimism. She also had a tendency to burst into fits of giggles, which Paul found irresistible. He was attracted to her from the moment he first saw her. For a doctor this would have been unforgivable, but for the fact that Rosie was just six years old!

It was unsatisfactory for her to be nursed on an adult ward, but she had been transferred from The Children's Hospital to have an operation to create a by-pass of the narrow vessels, and the only surgeon in the city with the experience to perform such an operation was Mr Potts. If successful, this would take the pressure off the stomach veins, and reduce the chance of bleeding.

Rosie was given her own side ward, a room which normally held two patients. This enabled her parents to visit outside normal visiting hours, and occasionally to stay overnight to keep Rosie company. It had its own washbasin, but Rosie had to walk the length of the ward to use the other facilities. Wise beyond her years and familiar with hospitals and hospital routine, she was quite at home talking to the other ladies as she walked past their beds. Inevitably, she quickly became a firm favourite, and other patients would often pop in to chat with her as they passed her room. Sister Rutherford, the ward sister, had grandchildren of the same age; she simply treated Rosie as one of her own in a kindly but not overly sentimental fashion, and certainly tried not to spoil her. However, others were unaware that their visits tired Rosie, and eventually, to give Rosie time to rest, it proved necessary to keep the door closed with a sign stating that Sister's permission had to be sought before Rosie was disturbed.

Before Paul went to admit her, he sat in the office and read the notes that had accompanied her. They were five inches thick, and chronicled her care from birth to the present day. In the first months of her life, she had been seriously ill, but a diagnosis had proved elusive and it had taken a long time to discover where her problem lay. Thereafter, there had been numerous admissions to correct her anaemia and to treat the renal failure that she subsequently developed. Initially, this had been managed with a special diet, but she now required dialysis with the expectation that she would soon require a kidney transplant. It was however the bleeding from the stomach that was currently the major cause of concern, and the reason for her admission for surgery.

Armed with the huge set of notes, Paul put his head round the door of her side ward.

'Hello,' he said.

'Hello, who are you?'

Rosie didn't seem in the least perturbed that a stranger had come to see her.

Paul was about to say Dr Lambert, but realised this would sound a bit formal to a six year old.

'Paul,' he said.

'Are you a doctor?'

'Yes, I am.'

'Dr Paul,' she said, a quizzical look on her face. She repeated it again. 'Yes, I like that. I shall call you Dr Paul. Are you going to look after me?'

'Well, Mr Potts is going to look after you, but I'm going to try to help him.'

'Mr Potts is my new consultant, isn't he?'

'That's right. He's a very clever man.'

Paul heard her giggle. It was the first of many times he was to do so, and a sound he came to love.

'I call him Mr Potty.'

'You mean the thing that babies sit on, to have a wee?'

'No silly, Potty, you know, potty meaning silly.'

The juxtaposition of the words amused her and she giggled again. It was impossible for Paul not to laugh with her.

'Why do you call him Mr Potty?'

'Because he talks in riddles; he says things that I don't understand.'

Paul could well believe that!

'He talks to Mummy and Daddy and uses long words.'

'Don't let him catch you calling him Mr Potty.'

'Oh no, I won't. He's going to do an operation to make me better, so I'm going to be especially nice to him.'

'Now,' Paul said, 'I've got to ask you lots and lots of questions, so can I sit down here by the bed?' He drew up a chair.

'You're going to *'admit'* me, aren't you?'

Paul smiled. She was obviously well and truly hospitalised.

'Yes,' he confirmed, 'I'm going to *'admit'* you.'

'Well,' she said, 'I'm very special. I was born with stenosis of my hepatic veins and multiple renal cysts.' She spoke the words very slowly and carefully, but got them all absolutely correct. 'It means I've got portal hypertension. It's called the Budd Chiari Syndrome. Lots of doctors have never heard of it. Dr Portly says its 'small print stuff''.

'And who might Dr Portly be?'

'Dr Portman, my doctor in the children's hospital, but he's ever so fat, so I call him Dr Portly. I have made up names for all my doctors.'

'I'd better behave myself then, or you might end up calling me Dr Grumpy or Dr Dopey. Am I allowed to have a name for you?'

'Yes, as long as it's nice?'

'What about Miss Cheeky.'

'No, that's not nice enough.'

'What about 'Sunshine'?'

She thought for a minute. 'Yes, I like that. You can be Dr Paul and I will be Sunshine.'

When it came time for Paul to examine her, she asked to feel his hands.

'Why?' he asked.

'I want to check that they're warm.'

They met with her satisfaction, and Paul examined her in the usual way.

'You're better at it than Mr Potty' she said.

'How so?'

'He digs his fingers in, and he's got very sharp finger nails.' Again, it was impossible for Paul not to laugh.

When the clinical examination was over, Paul left the room with a smile on his face. He had been charmed by Rosie's innocence and vulnerability, and determined that he would do everything in his power to help her through the challenges that faced her in the days ahead.

Later Paul was to meet Mr and Mrs Roberts, Rosie's parents who both seemed very young, probably little older than he was, possibly 26 or 27 years of age. They had a second daughter called Claire, who was four. They lived 40 or so miles away, but fortunately had a car, both drove, and one or other of them visited each evening; both of them if they could find a baby sitter for Claire. At weekends, Paul would see all four of them together as a family, and was impressed how well they were coping despite the anxiety and stress of Rosie's illness. Sometimes the family would play card games or board games, and the parents would show no favouritism to either of their daughters, both of whom were able to lose with good grace and without tears. At other times, the parents would read or chat between themselves, leaving Rosie and Claire to play together as might have happened had they been in their own home.

As the days went by, and Christmas came closer, Rosie's room slowly filled with soft toys, gifts from other patients and from the staff; far more than she would ever want or need. The walls became covered with paintings and drawings, some of which were Rosie's handiwork, others the artistic efforts of her younger sister Claire. One particularly large drawing was of a man with lop-sided eyes, gaps in his teeth and spiky hair, which she insisted was a portrait of Paul. She also started to make a paper chain as a Christmas decoration for her room, and never short of willing volunteers to assist, the chain lay on the floor coiled like a snake, growing rapidly with every passing day.

At Sister Rutherford's suggestion, Rosie created a nativity scene on a small table in the corner of her room. She made the stable out of cereal boxes, of which there was no shortage of supply on the ward, and she fashioned the characters and animals out of plasticine. Inevitably many of the other patients came to help, some of their models being exceptionally lifelike, but Rosie would allow only her own, or Claire's creations to be added to the scene. Paul was at a loss to know why the lambs were green until Rosie explained, with her infectious giggle, that they had been playing 'roly-poly' on the grass. He asked what a small pig like creature was, that was lying on the floor and was told with much indignation, 'that's the baby Jesus of course.' Was it any wonder that all the staff on the unit now addressed her by the nickname of 'Sunshine'?

Thanks to her prolonged periods in hospital, Rosie had been absent from school a great deal. Despite appearing self-assured and mature for her age, she was behind with her school work, so a tutor taught her for an hour each weekday morning. The tutor was particularly concerned about her reading ability, and asked the staff to encourage Rosie to read to them should they have any spare time. Often, if it was quiet in the evening, Paul would try to persuade her to read to him, but she wasn't at all keen. She would happily look at the pictures but struggled with even the simplest words, and found it difficult to concentrate. The only way she would agree to read a few pages was for Paul to promise to a read a story to her afterwards.

Perhaps because Paul was something of a 'soft touch' where Rosie was concerned, it frequently happened that she would read to him for five minutes, then he to her for twenty minutes. She was particularly keen on a book which contained 'Princess stories'; the stories of Cinderella, Snow White and Sleeping Beauty, but she had heard these so often and knew them so well, that she would ask Paul to tell her a new princess story, so if he had the time, particularly on his evenings off duty he would oblige. Together, they invented a beautiful princess who had the most marvellous adventures. She sailed to distant lands, met inhabitants of strange countries, and talked to animals, goblins and fairies. Whilst on her travels, their princess, whom Rosie decided should be called Priscilla, concocted magic potions from flowers and ferns, visited dangerous precipitous mountains, dark caves and mysterious forests, and frequently found herself in frightening situations. Inevitably there was a handsome prince to rescue her from all danger.

Sometimes Rosie would fall asleep before the story had ended, but more often Night Sister would come in and say, 'Enough Paul, time for six year olds to go to sleep.'

Mr Potts' objective was to get Rosie fit for the major surgery she faced. The operation, designed to divert excess blood away from the stomach to reduce the chance of a catastrophic haemorrhage, was relatively new and had rarely been undertaken in children. The chance of a successful outcome was therefore unknown, but even in adults the procedure was known to carry a high mortality. However, the risk of death from an uncontrollable bleed was much greater if the condition was left untreated, and so it was agreed that surgery was justified.

Initially a date of the 18th December was pencilled in for the procedure, and an entire morning's theatre session reserved for the operation, but unfortunately these arrangements had to be cancelled when Rosie developed a cough and cold. Her condition was again improving at the beginning of Christmas week, but after chatting with her parents, Mr Potts suggested it would be kinder to let her enjoy Christmas and have the operation between Christmas and the New Year.

Christmas Eve arrived and fortunately Paul was not required to be on duty until the 27th. He had the chance of a couple of nights rest and relaxation after weeks of long hours and hard work. He could have gone to his parent's home at lunchtime, but was eager to experience Christmas in the hospital, not least because Kate was on duty until nine a.m. on Christmas Day. Paul delighted in Kate's company. In his eyes, she was not only beautiful, but kind, caring and compassionate; he adored her.

Although Paul had done most of his Christmas shopping there were still one or two small gifts that he wanted to buy. He also wished to find a little present for Rosie, not that there was any shortage of presents already waiting for her to open on Christmas morning. Knowing that her room was overflowing with teddy bears, dolls and all manner of stuffed animals, he bought a simple silver bracelet with a single charm on it; a miniature silver princess.

In the evening, he joined the congregation for the traditional Christmas Eve carol service that was held in the hospital chapel. Although christened as a child, he was not a religious person finding that the concept of a virgin birth didn't sit easily alongside his medical training. Nevertheless, he found comfort in hearing the Christmas message, and had always enjoyed singing the carols with their familiar words and tunes. Walking through the door, he was welcomed warmly by Father Patrick Doherty, the hospital padre, and took a seat near the back as the chapel gradually filled. The congregation numbered some 40 or 50 people, mainly hospital staff. About a dozen patients were there, each accompanied by a nurse, some in wheelchairs in the centre aisle, others wrapped in blankets sitting in the pews. Rosie and Claire arrived with their parents. They walked to the front of the chapel and admired the Christmas tree, adding a present to those already placed under the tree that would later be distributed amongst orphaned children in the city. Rosie spotted Paul and waved merrily before the family took seats near the front, where the children would get a better view during the nativity service.

Just before the service began, the chapel lights were dimmed, and the first verse of 'Once in Royal David's City' was heard, sung by a clear, solo, soprano voice, which floated in through the open chapel doors. As the second verse commenced, the nurses' choir entered. The nurses walked in pairs, each wearing their formal hospital cape; the nurses in navy blue, the sisters in maroon, crisp, white, starched caps on their heads. Each carried a candle-lit lantern held high upon a long shepherd's crook. The light from the candles cast flickering shadows on the walls of the chapel. The nurses took their places at the front of the chapel, and the service began.

The Christmas story was told in readings and carols as, no doubt, it was being told in thousands of churches up and down the country, but this service had an extra warmth, a certain intimacy. This was the hospital coming together as family; dedicated, caring people who shared a common ideal, who not only worked together but also worshipped together.

When the service was over, the nurses' choir led the congregation out of the chapel, again walking two by two as they embarked on their tour of the hospital wards. Paul spoke with various members of staff, received a seasonal greeting from Matron, and chatted with Rosie and her parents. Later, he went to his surgical ward to await the appearance of the choir. For the patients lying in their beds, it was a memorable experience. Without warning, the lights on the ward were dimmed, the sound of carols reaching their ears before the choir could be seen. As in the chapel, the choir entered two by two, lanterns ablaze. They walked to the centre of the ward, and then formed a semicircle around the tree in the candlelight. Regrettably, there was only time for them to sing a couple of carols before they had to move on, but it was sufficient to bring tears to the eyes of many of the patients. How sad it is that time does not allow these wonderful traditions to continue in modern hospital life.

Later, Paul returned to the doctor's residency where there was warmth, music and laughter. Very few of the junior doctors had been able to go home for Christmas, but all were determined to enjoy the festivities as far as their clinical duties would allow. Paul stayed for about an hour having a beer and a chat, then slipped back to the ward for five minutes to steal a kiss from Kate, and wish her a quiet Christmas night. This was to be her last night on duty, her father having arranged to pick her up in the morning to spend the rest of the Christmas period with her family. Whilst on the ward, Paul popped into the sideward to see Rosie hoping that she might still be awake, but she was fast asleep, blond curls spread on the pillow, and a huge red stocking tied to the foot of the bed. No doubt she was dreaming of Father Christmas and the presents that he would deliver during the night.

****

Paul was up early on Christmas morning, planning to give Rosie her present before breakfast. Relaxed after a good night's sleep, he was at ease with the world as he walked along the hospital corridors, exchanging greetings with everyone he passed; nurses with tinsel trimmings on their dresses, cleaners in fancy dress, and porters wearing Father Christmas hats as they pushed the breakfast trolleys to the wards. Turning onto his own ward, he found the office door was closed, but as he walked past, he waved cheerfully to the nurses through the glass partition; Sister Rutherford waved in return. Paul wanted to see his little ray of sunshine, his lovely princess first; there would be plenty of time to spend with the nursing staff later in the day.

In buoyant mood, he hurried towards Rosie's room, eager to see the smile on her face and to wish her a Happy Christmas. He knew the nursing staff would have filled her stocking with her 'Father Christmas' presents when she was asleep. He understood the joy the sight of a stocking full of presents, mysteriously delivered during the night, could bring to a small child.

Cheerfully he knocked on the door, and walked straight in. To his surprise, the room was empty. No tree, no decorations, no pictures, no nativity scene, no fairy lights. He guessed that in his enthusiasm he must have entered the wrong side room. He looked again but no, he was in the right room, and yet there was no sign of Rosie, or indeed any evidence that she had ever been there; just a big bed with freshly laundered linen sheets, neatly folded ready to receive the next patient. For a moment he stood there bewildered, confused, without understanding, then suddenly was overcome with a terrible fear as it dawned on him what it meant, what must have happened.

In an instant, Sister Rutherford was at his side.

'Oh, Paul, I'm so sorry, we weren't expecting you so early. I tried to stop you as you passed the office door.'

Paul gazed at her blankly.

'It all happened so quickly, just after midnight, a sudden haemorrhage. She slipped away in just a few minutes; there was nothing anyone could do.'

She ran through the usual platitudes at which doctors and nurses are so good, and so practised. 'It was very quick, she didn't have any pain, and she really didn't suffer.'

But Paul wasn't listening, his mind was numb. He simply could not believe that such a lovely, innocent child could be so cruelly snatched away. What had she done to deserve this; such a cheerful little girl who radiated happiness to those around her? She had suffered ill health from the day she was born, tolerated long periods in hospital with scarcely a tear, had endured unpleasant diets and painful injections, months of dialysis then, just when there was the possibility that her health might be improved, she had died.

Scarcely aware of what was happening, Sister Rutherford guided him to the office, her arm around his shoulder. Both the day staff and the night staff were there, and the communal grief was profound. Kate and two of the other nurses were in tears. A shocked and sombre atmosphere filled the room. Mugs of tea were dotted around but nobody was drinking. Everyone sat in silence, lost in their own thoughts, devastated that such a precious, beautiful and brave little child should die.

Eventually the night staff explained what had happened. Before they had turned out the lights, Kate had read her a story; then Rosie went to sleep as normal. She had not stirred when the nurses filled her Christmas stocking with the presents that her parents had left for safe keeping in the office. At 1 a.m. when routine observations were taken, the nurses had noticed that Rosie's blood pressure had fallen. Johnny Nolan had been called but just as he reached the ward, Rosie had vomited a vast amount of fresh blood, and collapsed. Before a blood transfusion could be commenced, there was a further huge vomit and Rosie had slipped away. Her parents were phoned, had rushed to the hospital, but unfortunately had not arrived until it was too late.

The night staff, deeply traumatised by what had happened, then had the thankless job of trying to console Rosie's parents, and undertaking all the dreadful tasks that are required when a patient dies, and the body has to be 'laid out'.

When the story was finished there was a prolonged silence; no one wanting to be the first to speak.

Slowly, hesitantly, comments were made.

'Poor little mite.'

'So beautiful, so innocent.'

'She had suffered all her life, and for it all to come to this.'

'And her poor parents, what must they be thinking?

Sister Rutherford allowed comments to be made in this desultory fashion for some time as the staff, combined in their grief, consoled each other. Then she cleared her throat and addressed her nurses a firm voice.

'I know how much you all came to love Rosie, and how well you nursed and cared for her. It's a tragedy that she should die; that all our efforts should have been in vain. Yet I'm sure you also realise, that all the other patients on the ward also knew and loved Rosie, just as we did. They're bound to be equally upset, perhaps more so, since we are more familiar with death. They will need our help and support. Today will be a difficult day for us all, but we have to remember that it's Christmas morning. It's going to be a busy day; there will be lots of visitors on the ward, and plenty of work for us to do. So let's attend to our duties professionally. Staff nurse, I want you to start the drug round, the other nurses and I will sort out breakfast.'

Then she turned and addressed the night staff.

'I'm sorry this has been such a dreadful night for you, but we all knew that a massive bleed was possible; that's why Rosie was in hospital and why she was to have her surgery. I also know you did everything humanly possible to try to save her. But there's nothing to be gained by sitting here brooding. It's time for you to go off duty. Go to bed and try to get some sleep.'

Slowly, almost reluctantly, the nurses stood up and went their various ways; the day staff to attend to their duties on the ward, the night staff to their beds. Sister Rutherford took Paul to one side and spoke quietly to him.

'Paul, Kate is the most junior nurse here by some margin, and this is the first time that she's seen anything like this. Understandably she's very upset. I have to stay here on the ward. Will you see her safely back to the Nurses' Home for me please?'

Sister had noticed, as indeed Paul had, that although the other nurses had left, Kate was still sitting quietly in the corner, not crying now but stunned by the events she had witnessed during the night. Paul took her by the hand and they walked slowly, heads down, along the hospital corridors, then onto the link corridor that led to the Nurses' Home. There Paul held Kate in his arms, her head on his shoulder, her cheeks still wet with tears. It was not the passionate embrace of two young lovers, simply two people offering comfort to each other at a time of great sadness. Later in the day, Kate's father would come to pick her up to take her home for a family Christmas, but reluctant to leave Kate on her own, Paul spoke with the Home Sister who agreed to look after Kate until her father arrived.

****

After the nurses had served Christmas lunch to the patients, and then eaten their own lunch in a sombre silence, Paul took his leave of them and returned to the residency. It was a lovely crisp winter's day; cold but sunny, and there was still a hard frost on the ground. He had an hour to kill before going to catch the train that would take him home for his second turkey dinner of the day, so he wandered into the municipal park adjacent to the hospital where others had gathered to walk off the excesses of their Christmas lunches. A child was riding a brand-new bicycle, another sported new roller skates, no doubt gifts from Santa delivered during the night. Couples, old and young, were simply strolling, enjoying the last hours of sunshine before night fell.

Paul sat on one of the park benches, and thought about Rosie. He closed his eyes and saw her face, her blond curls, the dimples which appeared whenever she laughed, which she did so often. He heard the infectious giggle that he had come to love; he remembered the funny names she coined for the various members of staff, and her perpetual cheerfulness in the face of adversity. She had been such a beautiful, innocent child, so very special; someone he would never forget. What a tragedy that she had to die.

Opening his eyes, he noticed two figures walking slowly down the path towards him, hand in hand, their heads bowed. It was Rosie's parents. As soon as he saw them, he felt the tears welling up in his eyes. He stood when they reached him. They looked gaunt and drawn, grief etched on their faces, but both dry eyed.

Rosie's father spoke first.

'Hello, Dr Paul.'

'Hello, Mr Roberts, look I'm so very sorry,' Paul mumbled, uncertain what to say.

'Yes, it's very sad. A terrible day for us, but we were warned this might happen one day. We've lived with that knowledge for the last six years, throughout Rosie's life, in fact.'

He was talking quietly, calmly, his emotions apparently under control. Perhaps talking about it dulled the pain that he must surely be feeling.

'For the first year of Rosie's life, nobody had any idea what was the matter with her. She was clearly very ill, but the doctors couldn't be certain of the diagnosis. All sorts of treatments were tried in an attempt to improve her health, but all to no avail. Finally, when Rosie was about two, they got to the root of the problem; they worked out exactly where the problem lay. We were warned that most children born with Rosie's condition died before they reached the age of ten. We've always lived with that knowledge and slowly became reconciled to it. We learned to live day by day, and we've valued every moment we've spent with her, but always knowing that this day might come. Of course, when we heard about this new operation, we hoped and prayed that the inevitable might be avoided, but sadly it was not to be.'

A hundred thoughts flashed through Paul's mind. How could Rosie's parents be so calm, so contained, at a moment like this? For six years, this bubbly, effervescent, beautiful child had graced their family, lit up their lives with her giggles and her laughter, and now she was gone, snatched away so cruelly in the middle of the night, impossible to replace. They would grieve for her every day for the rest of their lives. And Christmas time for them, when everyone around was celebrating, would always be a time of the greatest sadness. And what on earth would they say to Claire? How could you possibly explain to a four year old that her big sister had gone forever? Suddenly, Paul became aware that Rosie's mother was speaking.

'Paul, I want to thank you for caring for Rosie. You weren't just her doctor, you became her friend. She liked you a lot, spoke of you often, and we appreciate you went out of your way to help her. We know you spent time with her when you could have been off-duty. We've all heard about Princess Priscilla and her adventures.'

Paul remembered the tiny packet he had in his pocket.

'Look, I had a small gift for her. I'd like you to have it.'

'That's very kind of you Paul, but we wouldn't know what to do with it. Please put it with the other presents in the chapel.'

Then she turned to her husband. 'I think we ought to go; we have to pick up Claire from my mothers, and then somehow we've got to explain to her what has happened.'

Paul watched as they walked slowly back across the park. They say the pain of bereavement eases with time but for them, life would never be the same. They would have their memories and photographs of course, but would never again hear that infectious giggle, or see the smile that brought sunshine to their lives. They faced a future without their beloved child; a future forever tinged with sadness.

Thought for the day

I love thee with the breath, smiles and tears of all my life,

And if God chooses, I shall but love thee better after death.

Elizabeth Barrett Browning 1806 - 1861

Part 2

The City General Hospital 1970

Chapter 16   Mr Mills' Stomach Ulcer

5th August 1970

When Paul had completed his period of residency as a house officer, he undertook a series of posts in different hospitals which offered experience in a variety of surgical specialties, such as casualty, urology and orthopaedics. By studying hard, he gained a detailed knowledge of anatomy and of surgical disease which enabled him to pass the two-stage examination, each with a pass rate of just 30%, and thus he became a Fellow of the Royal College of Surgeons. Henceforth he would be addressed as Mr Lambert, no longer as Dr Lambert.

During this time, four years in all, he slowly overcame his shyness, courted the lovely Nurse Kate Meredith, and eventually, after overcoming many difficulties and misunderstandings, he asked for her hand in marriage, an invitation that she gladly accepted. The full story of their romance is told in the Doctor Paul – Nurse Kate series of novels. They were married in the Hospital Chapel, and it was therefore as a married man and a more experienced surgeon that he returned to be Sir William's registrar at The City General Hospital, the post previously held by Mohammed Khan.

Mo's promotion to the grade of senior registrar had been long overdue, but happily, he had now reached the penultimate step on the surgical ladder. After three or four years in his new post, he would be eligible to apply to be a consultant, though this would almost certainly be in a district general hospital. The appointment of an 'overseas' surgeon to a teaching or university hospital at this time was as unlikely as snow in the Sahara in summer. Paul was convinced that Mo would make an excellent consultant. He was a sound clinician, a good teacher and when operating, he was the best technical surgeon that Paul had seen.

In view of his greater experience, Sir William now allowed Paul to see newly referred out-patients, and it was when he was busy working in the clinic that the call came through which signalled the onset of a major problem.

'It's Dr Webb on the phone wanting to speak with you. She says there's a patient on the male ward who's bleeding, and she insists she needs immediate help. She sounds to be in a bit of a flap, but it does sound urgent.'

'All right,' Paul said to the nurse, who had taken the message, 'tell her I'm on my way.'

Dr Elizabeth Webb and Dr Richard Jennings were the newly qualified house officers who had joined the unit the week before.

Unfortunately, Liz had made a poor start and the nursing staff had already raised concerns about her performance.

Paul excused himself from the patient he was seeing in the clinic, then dashed up the stairs, and ran along the corridor to the surgical unit. Dr Webb was waiting for him at the entrance to the ward. He made a mental note to speak with her about that later. If a patient was bleeding, she should be at the bedside commencing resuscitation, organizing a blood transfusion, and inserting an intravenous line. This was an example of the deficiencies of medical school training. Students gained an excellent theoretical knowledge enabling them to pass their examinations, but often lacked an understanding of the priorities of medical management.

Liz looked terrified. 'It's Mr Mills,' she said. 'He's pouring blood from his back passage.'

The name meant nothing to Paul. 'Who is Mr Mills?'

'He's a patient who came in today; he's only in his fifties. He's known to have a stomach ulcer.'

'But it's not our day to be on call to admit emergencies. Why have we admitted a patient with a bleeding ulcer?'

'No,' Liz replied, the anxiety clearly evident in her voice. 'He's not come in as an emergency. He was admitted from the waiting list. I was checking he was fit enough for his operation tomorrow. I did a rectal examination, and found he was bleeding profusely.'

Arriving at Mr Mills' bedside, Paul expected to find the patient collapsed on the bed, pale, cold and sweating, gasping for breath, with a racing pulse and a desperately low blood pressure. In fact, he looked to be a perfectly healthy, middle-aged gentleman.

'He doesn't look as if he's lost a lot of blood,' he said, sounding puzzled.

'What's his blood pressure?'

'Oh, I haven't taken that yet.' Liz replied.

Inwardly Paul groaned. It was easy to see why the nurses had raised concerns about her. It wasn't just her superior attitude towards them; they would quickly have realized that she wasn't a competent doctor.

If Mr Mills was bleeding, monitoring his pulse and blood pressure was basic medicine. Every nurse knew that within a week of arriving at the hospital. This was an omission that could not be ignored.

'Don't you think you should have taken the blood pressure?' Paul observed, perhaps a little too severely. Immediately, he regretted his comment, as tears welled up in Liz's eyes.

'All right, let's set that aside for the time being. Perhaps you would like to take Mr Mills' pulse and blood pressure now. He appears to be pink and comfortable. He really doesn't look as if he's lost a lot of blood.'

These investigations proved to be entirely normal. Feeling the need to rebuild Liz's confidence, Paul invited her to relate the patient's clinical story.

'Mr Mills has had indigestion for many years,' she said. 'It tends to come and go, but recently it's been present most of the time. It's caused him to lose a lot of time from work. He's tried all the usual bland diets and medicines, but nothing seems to help, and he's now started to vomit. That's why he's come into hospital. His operation is planned for tomorrow.'

'But has he had any bleeding from the ulcer before?' Paul asked.

'No.'

'But you say he's bleeding now.'

'Yes, he is – heavily.'

Paul frowned. This just didn't fit. Heavy bleeding would inevitably result in shock. The patient should be cold, pale, and sweaty.

'Is this just a splash of blood on the surface of the stool, or is the blood mixed throughout?' he asked, knowing that a little surface blood probably just meant that Mr Mills had piles.

'No,' she said. 'The whole stool is bright red.'

To Paul, this statement seemed incompatible with the pink, healthy man who was sitting, looking relaxed, in the bed in front of him, but who was now wondering what all the fuss was about. The rectal tray was still sitting on the bedside locker, and the obvious way to resolve the mystery was for Paul to inspect the stool himself. Mr Mills didn't look particularly pleased with the prospect of a further examination, but turned on to his side in preparation without complaint.

A minute later, as Paul withdrew his finger, he was able to inspect the stool on the plastic glove. Immediately, he relaxed and smiled. This was not the characteristic red of fresh blood, it was subtly different. It was as if a red dye had perfused through the stool. He knew exactly what it was, not due to any academic brilliance, but simply because he had seen it before. It was an appearance that every experienced surgeon recognizes, but something rarely recorded in surgical textbooks.

'That's certainly red, but it's not blood,' he said to Liz. 'Ask him what he ate for his dinner last night.'

'Lamb, potatoes and vegetables,' Mr Mills said in response to Liz's enquiry. 'My wife cooked a lovely shoulder of lamb. She said it might be the last good meal I had for a week or two, with me having an operation.'

Paul needed to prompt him. 'And the vegetables that you ate were.....?'

'Beetroots, Doctor.'

'Beetroots fresh from your own garden?' Paul suggested.

'Well, from the allotment actually, Doctor. I never have much luck with carrots or peas. The carrots get infested with flies, and the mice eat all the peas, but the beets always do well. My wife serves them with a tasty white sauce. They're always delicious; they're tender and sweet. I can't resist them.'

Liz looked tearful again. 'So it's not blood then,' she said. 'Look, Paul, I'm sorry to have troubled you....'

'Don't worry, it's an easy mistake to make, and I only know because I've seen it before. You're not the first to make that mistake, and you won't be the last. You were right to seek advice. If you're worried about a patient, you should never hesitate to seek help. It's better to ask for assistance unnecessarily than to fail to ask for it, when it's needed. But when we've got a little more time, we do need to have a chat about the way to respond if a patient really is bleeding heavily.'

There was much for Paul to ponder as he returned to the outpatient clinic. Liz had not seen a stool discoloured by beetroot before, so it was reasonable for her to be concerned if she believed the patient was bleeding. And she had sought advice, which was good. However, not to have taken the patient's pulse and blood pressure, and not to be starting resuscitation whilst waiting for him to arrive, was inexcusable. It was clear that she would need close supervision in the weeks and months ahead. Theoretically, this was Mr Potts' responsibility. He was her consultant, the person who, in due course, would be asked to state whether she was sufficiently competent to be registered with the General Medical Council, and allowed to work unsupervised as a doctor. But in practice, as her immediate superior, it fell to Paul to cover her back. It appeared though, that if he were to be overcritical, or perhaps merely honest about her performance, she would burst into tears.

After lunch, the team congregated in the office, waiting for Mr Potts to arrive for his twice-weekly ward round.

Fortunately, on this occasion, he was in one of his more congenial moods. He greeted the team with a smile, and then complimented Liz on her appearance. She did indeed look smart and attractive, with her shoulder length hair, and wearing a grey pencil mini skirt and high heels, but her attire was scarcely practical, or appropriate in the circumstances. Paul thought that she ought to follow the example set by Victoria Kent, who had joined the team as the Senior Registrar at the same time that Paul had rejoined as the registrar. Victoria's hair was cut short in a sensible fashion and her clothes and shoes were practical, comfortable and discrete. As such, she was accepted without question by the nursing staff.

A couple of days before, Paul had taken Liz on one side and suggested that, because the nurses had to wear uniforms strictly in accordance with Matron's rules, they wouldn't take kindly to Liz wearing miniskirts, high heels and low necklines.

He'd been reticent about offering advice but knew it had to be said.

'But I'm a doctor, not a nurse, and I like to look nice,' she had protested. 'I want to be smart when I'm working, and it does seem to be appreciated by the men on the ward.'

In response, Paul had suggested that whilst this was probably true, and that no doubt it raised the men's blood pressures as well as their spirits, it was likely to be resented by the nurses. He'd advised her to dress more soberly. He'd also added that if she wore flat heels during the day, she'd probably find that her feet would be more comfortable at 11 o'clock at night.

Offering this advice had made Paul feel positively middle-aged. It amused him to think how his mother, always traditional in her views, would have laughed if she could have heard him.

Liz, though, had looked unconvinced, and had offered no response. Paul tried to give the message gently and constructively, hoping it would be taken in the right spirit, but it was obvious that it had not been heeded.

Liz smiled sweetly in response to the consultant's compliment, and said a polite, 'Why, thank you, Mr Potts' but in the background, Paul saw Sister Ashbrook's face harden.

The first patient they saw when the ward round began had a simple hernia which presented no risk to the young man's life, although it did cause him some pain and interfered with his job.

'Suppose a man has discomfort walking,' asked Mr Potts, looking at Liz, 'perhaps from a rupture such as this, or maybe from arthritis of the hip, at what stage would you offer him surgery?'

'Perhaps when he was only able to walk a mile or so,' she replied, tentatively.

'A very reasonable suggestion, my dear, but not quite what I was looking for.' Mr Potts turned to Paul, raising an eyebrow.

'Well, Sir,' he responded, 'you have to accept that surgery and anaesthetics are not without risk, and that operations are not always 100% successful, so perhaps a couple of hundred yards.'

Mr Potts said nothing though it was obvious from his slight frown that he did not agree with this answer. He turned to Victoria.

'There isn't a precise answer, Sir. It depends upon his lifestyle,' she said.

'Exactly,' said Mr. Potts. 'It depends entirely upon his lifestyle. A retired seventy-year-old, who drives a car, and spends his evenings relaxing in the pub, perhaps playing darts or dominoes, doesn't need to walk very far. He wouldn't need surgery, even if he could only walk fifty yards. However, it would be justifiable to operate on a postman who could still walk several miles since, without an operation, he wouldn't be able to do his job. But you are right when you say that not all operations are successful. Sometimes, I think we surgeons are the victims of our own success. Results from surgery are getting better all the time, and patients are beginning to expect complete relief from all their symptoms, and a guaranteed cure for every disease. It's important for them to understand that's not the case. No surgical procedure is uniformly successful. The reality is that some patients will be worse off after their operation than they were before. And, of course, some operations result in the patient's death. This should always be discussed before any surgery is performed. Too often, though, doctors avoid telling patients unpalatable truths.

And that applies to nurses too,' he said, turning to Sister Ashbrook, a smile on his face, 'how often do you hear a nurse with a large syringe and needle in her hand, say to a patient *'just a little scratch, it won't hurt'*? Whenever I've had an injection, it's hurt like hell.

Mind you,' he continued, changing tack, 'patients don't always remember everything you tell them. A little while ago, Sister Jenkins and I ran a little experiment in the outpatient clinic. At the end of every consultation, I told each patient three facts about their condition. I then arranged for Sister to interview them as they left the hospital a few minutes later. Believe it or not, on average, patients only remembered one of the three things I'd mentioned to them. The study was published in the College Journal,' he added proudly. 'The lesson is that information for patients should always be written down, so that they may refresh their memory at home when they are less stressed.'

'That really is interesting, Mr Potts,' volunteered Liz, somewhat unnecessarily, and earning herself another glare from Sister Ashbrook.

'You're welcome, Liz,' replied her boss with a smile and the touch of his hand on her shoulder.

They had been at the patient's bedside for ten minutes or more, but Liz was right. The exchange between Mr Potts and his staff had been interesting and educational. Junior hospital doctors received little formal teaching. Theirs was a traditional apprenticeship. They worked alongside the consultants, watching, listening and learning whilst on duty. 'Surgical wisdom' such as this, was not to be found in surgical textbooks. It could only be gained with experience, by working alongside the consultants on the wards, in the outpatient clinics, and in the theatre.

In due course, they arrived at Mr Mills' bed, the patient who had been admitted for an operation on his stomach ulcer. To Paul's surprise, he saw that intravenous fluid was running through a drip into his arm. He couldn't understand why. Surely Liz had believed him when he had reassured her that the discoloration of the stool was simply due to beetroot?

Liz introduced the patient to Mr Potts, describing Mr Mills' symptoms, detailing the length and severity of his indigestion, adding that he had recently started to vomit and lose time from work. Mr Potts nodded to the patient, and said that his operation was planned for the following morning. He was about to move to the next bed when Sister Ashbrook interrupted.

'Mr Potts, Dr Webb has omitted to tell you an extremely important bit of information. Mr Mills is actually bleeding from his ulcer at the moment. I did inform Dr Webb about it earlier, but it seems she decided that she knew best. She has ignored me and chosen not to take any action. So I took it upon myself to put up the drip as a sensible precaution.'

She looked hard at Liz, a self-righteous look on her face, and then added, perhaps a little unnecessarily, 'I do think it unfortunate when a newly-qualified doctor cannot listen to her experienced ward sister.'

This last remark seemed needlessly barbed, but if Sister Ashbrook had indeed informed Liz that she thought the patient was bleeding, Liz, in turn, had clearly not told her ward sister that the discolouration of the stool was due to beetroot, and not to blood. The antagonism between houseman and nursing sister was getting unpleasant and unfortunately, had impinged on patient care. A drip had been placed, quite unnecessarily, in Mr Mills' arm. A bit of friendly rivalry between doctors and nurses was not a bad thing; indeed, it made for a good relationship, but there was a danger that this confrontation might get out of hand. Paul expected that Liz would immediately counter by saying that Mr Mills was not bleeding, but, for a moment, she hesitated and looked uncertain. She glanced at Paul enquiringly, as if needing reassurance, and confirmation about the beetroot.

Paul was about to explain the situation to Mr Potts, hoping to defuse the tension that had arisen, when Liz suddenly regained her confidence.

'That's because it isn't blood, it's staining from beetroot,' she blurted. 'Mr Mills has an allotment, and ate home-grown beetroot last night. He doesn't need a drip.'

Her face was stern, her voice sharp, and the words were aimed like bullets at Sister Ashbrook. Mr Potts glanced at the two women, who were now glaring at each other, two cats, hackles raised, bristling for a fight. He seemed to find the situation amusing.

'Well, I wonder who's right,' he said with a smile. 'There's only one way to find out. Sister, would you please ask one of your charming nurses to fetch the rectal tray.'

Mr Mills, however, looked far from happy. 'Not again,' he protested. 'It's not pleasant having someone's finger thrust up your backside. And it's been done twice today already!'

'Just relax. This won't be in the least bit uncomfortable,' Mr Potts replied, ignoring the advice he himself had given not five minutes before, about telling little white lies to patients.

He donned an examination glove, and conducted the third rectal examination that the patient had endured that day. Withdrawing his finger, he looked carefully at the colour of the stool. Then, holding the soiled glove on high, his forefinger raised like an umpire confirming a batsman's fate, he glanced in turn at each of the warring women. He paused, deliberately prolonging the tension, enjoying holding the two antagonists in suspense.

With a huge grin on his face, he delivered his verdict. 'Definitely beetroot,' he announced. 'Well done, Liz, well done indeed.'

Liz's features relaxed into a triumphant smile. Sister Ashbrook looked furious.

'Thank you, Sir,' Liz said. Then, without so much as a glance in Paul's direction, she added, 'I knew it wasn't blood. That's why I saw no need for a drip.'

Paul was incensed. It was outrageous that Liz should claim to have made the correct diagnosis. She, too, had believed Mr Mills was bleeding and, worse, had panicked at the prospect. He tried to catch her eye to convey his feelings to her, but she studiously avoided his gaze.

Then Mr. Potts proceeded to add to Sister Ashbrook's fury, and to make the situation even worse, by declaring, 'I'm sorry about the examinations Mr Mills, but we've sorted it out now, and it's nice to know that we have a bright, young doctor working for us. Not only bright, but pretty as well. Congratulations, Liz, I can see you'll make an excellent house officer. Better luck next time, Sister,' he added over his shoulder, already walking down the ward to see the next patient.

The whole episode had amused Mr Potts greatly, and he remained in an effervescent mood for the rest of the round, but Paul was far from happy. Liz's attitude toward Sister Ashbrook was worrying. It had been wrong for her to take the credit for realising that the cause of the coloured stool, but more importantly, she had deliberately embarrassed her ward sister in front of her own nurses. Sister Ashbrook was not one to take such humiliation lying down. Without a doubt, she would want her revenge, and there would be ample opportunity for her to obtain it. She was an experienced ward sister. She had been in charge of the ward for at least ten years; she knew every trick in the book, and a few more besides. Liz had been qualified for just one week, and was a complete novice. She had been exceedingly foolish to make such a powerful enemy.

Paul sighed. Regrettably, it appeared that life on Ward Five was not going to be as harmonious in the future as it had been in the past.

Thought for the day

Those who in quarrels interpose

Must often wipe a bloody nose

John Gay 1685 - 1732

Chapter 17   Dr Elizabeth Webb

7th August 1970

The patient brought by ambulance to the casualty department was a pleasant 26-year-old woman called Helen Seddon. She was in severe pain, and it was obvious from the moment that Paul entered the cubicle that she was extremely ill. She had a classical story of bowel obstruction, the symptoms of which may easily be imagined by considering the result of a blockage of any other sewage pipe. Nothing comes out of the bottom end, and the pipe then 'backs up' until it overflows at the top. Her constipation and foul vomiting were accompanied by severe griping pains and loud gurgling noises; the result of spasms of her bowel as it attempted to squeeze faeces passed the blockage. As a result of the vomiting, Helen was severely dehydrated. She needed fluid replacement by intravenous infusion as a matter of urgency. Her appendix had been removed six months previously by the Surgical Five team, so the most likely cause of her obstruction was internal scar tissue, though this would only be confirmed by a surgical exploration. It was unlikely to be due to anything sinister in such a young woman.

Paul explained to Helen that although an x-ray would be needed to confirm the diagnosis, she would almost certainly require an operation later in the day.

'Are you sure it's necessary for me to stay in hospital?' she asked.

'Yes, it is. And you will need to remain with us for at least a week after the surgery.'

On hearing this news, Helen's first thoughts were not for herself, but for her husband and her children.

'We are not a wealthy family,' she explained. 'My husband works in the market. He starts very early in the morning. I do part time cleaning work in the evenings to make ends meet. It will be very difficult for my husband to stay at home with the children. It's the summer holidays now so they're not going to school.'

Since there were no family members, or neighbours available to take care of the children, Paul spoke with the almoner to arrange some domestic help, then phoned the female ward to ask them to prepare a bed for the new admission.

That afternoon, he was scheduled to work in the out-patient clinic, but during the course of the session, he slipped away to review Helen, and to look at her x-rays. Sister Gladys Rutherford met him with open arms and a welcoming smile. In her mid-50's, motherly and plump, she was everything that Sister Ashbrook was not. Warm, friendly and caring, she was a superb ward sister, loved by her patients, appreciated by her nurses, and respected by the consultants. The junior doctors thought she was perfect. Always helpful, particularly to new house officers, she guided them through their early difficult months, and was always prepared to revive them when they were weary, with mugs of hot tea and words of encouragement. Whereas there was always a degree of tension in the air on Sister Ashbrook's male ward, here the atmosphere was peaceful and calm. Yet despite the relaxed ambience, discipline was strict, and the nursing care was of a high standard. No one sought to take advantage of her good nature.

She gave Paul a big hug, and planted a kiss on his cheek.

'I heard a rumour that you were coming back. It's lovely to see you again.'

'It's great to be back. Just like old times.'

'How long has it been?'

'Nearly four years, but Sister, I'm afraid I must keep moving though. I've just slipped out of the clinic to see Helen, the young woman with a bowel obstruction.'

By chance, they were joined at that moment by the newly appointed senior registrar, Victoria Kent, and together they went to review their patient. Fortunately, Helen now looked a little more comfortable, thanks to some fluid replacement, and a generous dose of morphine. The x-rays confirmed the diagnosis of bowel obstruction, but the blood tests indicated that Helen remained dehydrated. Victoria decided it would be wise to give more fluid before an operation was undertaken, so her surgery was deferred until later in the day.

It was not Surgical Five's day to admit emergencies. Paul and Victoria had only become involved with Helen because she had previously been a patient of Mr Potts. They would have been perfectly entitled to ask the 'on call team of the day' to operate on her, but that was not the way things were done on their unit. They felt an ongoing responsibility for their patients; Victoria would perform the operation, Paul happily agreed to assist.

'Do you think Dr Webb would like to come along and watch?' he asked Victoria as they left the ward.

'It wouldn't be a bad idea to ask her. It will be helpful for her to scrub up and assist us, before she's faced with the challenge of assisting Mr Potts.'

That evening, Paul joined the crowd of newly qualified house officers as they ate in the doctor's 'mess', the residency that would be their home for the next six months. They sat around the large communal dining table chatting nervously, reflecting on their first few days as practising doctors. Paul felt a considerable sympathy for them. At this early stage, they had yet to realise just how arduous their jobs would be, how difficult it was to make the transition from medical student to doctor, or how jaded they would become as they tried to cope with the never-ending stream of tasks which would be delegated to them. Spotting Liz Webb and Richard Jennings, the two new Surgical Five house officers, sitting together, he suggested to Liz that she might be interested to join Victoria in the theatre to witness Helen's operation. She immediately looked dismayed.

'We're planning to go out this evening for a drink; we want to celebrate having survived our first week as doctors,' she said, looking to Richard, her fellow house officer for support.

Her response indicated that she completely failed to understand the responsibilities of her job.

'I'm afraid that won't be possible,' Paul said. 'As Surgical Five house officers, one of you is required to be in the hospital, available to the patents on our wards, at all times. One of you can leave the hospital if you like, but not both of you at the same time.'

'But we thought we would hand over our patients to the Surgical Three team for the evening; surely they are 'on call' tonight,' she protested, shocked at what she had just heard.

'They are indeed 'on-call' until tomorrow morning; therefore, both of their house officers need to remain in the hospital. Together with the Surgical Three registrar, they will be responsible for the surgical emergencies that arrive through the night, but I'm afraid that we can't hand our Surgical Five patients to them. They simply couldn't cope if they had to cover the patients on our wards, as well as staffing casualty, covering their own wards, and caring for new admissions. Didn't you realise that?'

There was a long pause during which neither Liz nor Richard replied.

'I'm sorry to be the bearer of bad news,' Paul added.

'No,' Liz said finally. 'We didn't realise that.'

Paul was amazed at this response, as were many of the other newly qualified doctors around the table, who obviously understood better than Liz what was expected of a house officer.

'You don't need to come to the theatre tonight if you don't want to. It's entirely up to you. Victoria and I can manage perfectly well on our own. But we thought you might be interested to watch. I presume you've 'scrubbed up' in theatre before?'

'No,' she said. 'I haven't.'

This was another astonishing admission. How could she possibly have studied for five years at medical school, and never have 'scrubbed' for an operation?

'In that case,' Paul said emphatically, 'it will definitely be to your advantage to come to theatre and practice 'scrubbing up', before you have to 'scrub' to assist Mr Potts. He will expect you to be familiar with theatre routine.' He thought it best not to add that he had a short fuse, and didn't suffer fools gladly!

He was dismayed at the way the conversation had developed. Liz, their glamorous new house officer, clearly had no idea of what was required of her. Although Paul was quite prepared to show her the ropes whilst she settled in, and was certain that Victoria would also be generous with her time and advice, just as Mo had helped Paul when he was newly qualified, it was obvious that Liz faced a steep learning curve. Unless she tackled this with enthusiasm and determination, the job would quickly overwhelm her.

Paul kept these thoughts to himself, but hoped that Liz would take the opportunity to assist at Helen's operation later that evening. 'Scrubbing up' required practice and attention to detail. The theatre staff would happily instruct medical students and student nurses how to do it, but they wouldn't expect to have to teach a qualified doctor.

The exchange left Paul deeply concerned; he feared Liz would struggle to cope with life as a junior hospital doctor and, as it transpired, these fears were quickly confirmed.

****

At eight o'clock that evening, cheerful and relaxed, Paul walked to the theatre to assist Victoria as she performed Helen's operation. Although a number of the theatre nurses were new, the theatre sister and senior staff nurse remembered Paul from his previous time at the

City General, and greeted him like a long-lost friend. The operating theatre, old fashioned even by the standards of the 1970s, was just as he remembered it. The theatre itself was quite small, but it had four large alcoves, each having a different function. On one side was the 'preparation' area, where trays of sterile instruments were stored on Formica shelves, each tray specific for a particular operation and individually labelled. Adjacent to it was the 'scrub up' area with its long metal, waist-high trough, surmounted by three pairs of elbow taps. On the opposite side of the theatre were the 'sluice area' where dirty instruments were washed, and the alcove occupied by the two autoclaves. The larger autoclave, used to sterilise several trays of instruments at a time, was a polished steel cylinder six feet long and three feet across with a circular pressurised door at one end, akin to the door on a submarine's torpedo tube. The smaller autoclave, a quarter the size of its neighbour, was used to sterilise small individual items, such as instruments inadvertently dropped, or very occasionally thrown by an irascible surgeon. Whenever opened, the autoclaves belched clouds of steam making the working environment hot, humid and oppressive.

Maintaining a pleasant temperature during surgery was further compromised by the theatre's position, situated as it was on a south-facing balcony. A major part of the theatre roof and its end wall consisted of glass, effectively turning half of the room into a conservatory. At the height of summer, the temperature frequently rose above eighty degrees, despite attempts to reduce it by 'white washing' the glass on the inside, and hosing cold water across the outer surface. In winter, the problem was to keep the room sufficiently warm. Many a patient, having lain virtually naked on the operating table for an hour or two, was returned to the ward shivering from the cold.

Paul was looking forward to assisting Victoria at Helen's operation. He had worked alongside her for twelve months in a previous job, and held her in high regard. She was battling against a well-established prejudice. 50 years previously, the medical staff at the City General had been exclusively male, as the portraits of past consultants on the walls of the main corridor bore testament. Women still comprised only a tiny proportion of consultants in the NHS. Some had made the grade in peripheral hospitals in less competitive specialties, such as radiology and anaesthetics, but there were no female consultant surgeons in any of the hospitals in the city. It was suggested that surgical training was too demanding for women. Certainly, the training was exacting and arduous. Few achieved consultant status under the age of 40. The need to work long and unpredictable hours, and the requirement to live in the hospital periodically, made a social or family life outside the hospital difficult. Yet academically, women were just as capable as men. They were equally dexterous, and just as able to undertake technical surgical procedures. In general, they were probably better communicators than their male counterparts, and certainly more caring and sympathetic.

Paul would have been loath to admit that he had any sexual prejudice, but in truth, before meeting Victoria, he had wondered if she might be a tough, hirsute 'hockey type', with a flat chest and a booming voice. Such irreverent thoughts however, were quickly dispelled when he met her. Of average height, she had a natural fresh complexion, devoid of any makeup, which made her look younger than her 28 years. She had warm, brown eyes and an engaging smile that quickly put her patients at ease. The more Paul saw of her as he worked alongside her, the more he liked and admired her. Unassuming, without any airs or graces, she was thoughtful and quietly spoken, yet her words were chosen with care. On the ward, she was thorough, and never gave the impression of being hurried or in a rush. In the theatre, she took great care with every procedure. She handled the tissues gently and avoiding excessive bleeding or bruising. As on the ward, she worked quietly without any fuss, bother or histrionics.

Paul was also happy to be back in the theatre where he had started his surgical career. Had he been in a strange theatre, or working alongside a new surgeon, he might have felt anxious, fearful of creating a poor first impression, but back in these familiar surroundings, he was completely at ease. He looked around to see whether Dr Webb had followed his advice and come to 'scrub', but it seemed that she hadn't.

Dressed in their 'theatre greens', Victoria and Paul scrubbed their hands from fingertips to elbows, then donned their gowns and surgical gloves. The abdominal skin was prepared in the usual fashion, and Victoria made her initial incision. As soon as the abdomen was opened, the obstructed loops of bowel, bloated to three times their normal size, their walls tense, pink and moist, mushroomed up through the wound like an over-inflated bicycle tyre's inner tube. Victoria immediately asked Sister for warm damp flannel swabs to cover and protect them for the duration of the operation.

It was at this moment that the theatre door opened, and Liz appeared, still wearing her mini skirt, short white coat and stiletto heels. Sister immediately spotted this inappropriately attired intruder. Scrubbed at the table, unable to deal with the situation herself, she turned to her staff nurse.

"Staff nurse, go and …."

But she needed to say no more, for the staff nurse had also seen Liz, and was already shepherding her back through the door, to prevent any further contamination of the theatre environment.

'Who on earth was that?' Sister asked.

'That's our new house officer, Dr Elizabeth Webb,' Paul replied.

'Oh, is that so?' Sister responded.

'I'm afraid she hasn't visited an operating theatre before,' he added. 'I think it would be helpful if she were to scrub up, and join us at the table. There might be some unfortunate consequences if her first experience was when Mr Potts was operating.'

With a surgical cap covering her forehead, and a mask concealing her nose and mouth, little was visible of Sister's face, but the frown lines that appeared around her eyes suggested that she wasn't overly happy with this proposal. However, she voiced no objection.

Victoria's initial objective was to identify the site of the obstruction, and this proved difficult. As soon as one 'balloon like' loop of bowel was laid to one side, another sprang out of the abdomen obscuring the view. The loops wriggled like an angry snake as the bowel spasms continued their attempt to overcome the blockage. And extreme caution was required. The wall of the gut was stretched, thin and under tension such that it could easily have been ruptured had it been handled roughly. Such an event would have been a disaster, since highly toxic bowel content would have spilled within the abdomen, dramatically increasing the chance of severe sepsis and death. Victoria however, handled the bowel with great care, and as more and more loops were lifted out through the wound, it became possible to see some collapsed empty gut beyond the point of obstruction.

Out of the corner of his eye, Paul saw Liz re-enter the theatre accompanied by Staff Nurse. She was now wearing a standard, utilitarian theatre smock, a garment designed to be both shapeless and sexless. Her blond hair had been bunched beneath a theatre cap, though odd strands hung down untidily around her neck. On her feet she wore white rubber boots which appeared to be a couple of sizes too large. Loose on her feet, the heels dragged noisily along the floor as she walked. She looked significantly less glamorous than she did when working on the ward!

Victoria looked up and spoke quietly to Sister.

'Sister, would you mind if Dr Webb were to scrub and come to the table? It will be good practice for her, but I'm sure she will need to be closely supervised.'

'No, I don't mind, provided of course, that she scrubs correctly.'

Victoria called across to Liz. 'Dr Webb, I suggest that you scrub up and join us. Then you'll be able to observe exactly what we're doing. If you watch as the operation is performed, it will give you a good appreciation of the symptoms Helen has suffered this last week. It will also help you to understand how her post-operative care should be handled.' Paul noted that she had failed to mention the main reason for getting Liz to scrub up; which was to learn how to do it correctly, before she had to do it with Mr Potts watching!

Sister turned to her Staff Nurse.

'Dr Webb is going to join us at the table. Supervise!' Her voice was stern. 'And supervise carefully,' she added. 'This will be the first time she's scrubbed. Keep a very close eye on her and make sure that she does it properly. We must not compromise the sterility of this procedure.' There was a strong emphasis on the words *'very close eye'*.

'I will,' Staff Nurse replied, smiling as she spoke, and there was something about the smile that suggested that she was going to enjoy her task of supervision.

As Victoria worked, over her shoulder, Paul was able to watch events in the scrub up area. Liz was scrubbing her hands with antiseptic soap, using a hard-bristled brush, for the requisite three minutes, under the eagle eye of the Staff Nurse. She was instructed to scrub carefully under her long, manicured nails, and to concentrate particularly on the sides of her fingers and the web space between one finger and the next. Paul noticed however, that Liz was not scrubbing her forearms, and was still wearing a watch. Sister noticed this too, caught Staff Nurse's eye, then silently tapped her left wrist with her right index finger. In response Staff Nurse nodded and smiled, but said nothing either to Sister or to Liz.

When all the distended bowel loops had been laid to one side, the cause of the obstruction was identified. There was a strong cord of scar tissue, looking like a short length of thick white string, lying across the bowel, compressing it and completely blocking it. A quick snip of the scissors was all that was required to release this band, and relieve the obstruction. Immediately, gas and liquid stool poured from the distended loops through into the collapsed bowel beyond. However, the short length of bowel that had been lying directly beneath the scar tissue was deep purple in colour, and considerably bruised.

Across in the scrub up area, Liz had decided that the statutory three minutes of scrubbing had elapsed, and she turned to pick up a theatre gown. It was at this point that Staff Nurse informed her that she ought to have removed her watch. Liz looked daggers at her, but had no option but to remove the offending article, thereby contaminating her clean hands. Scowling, she began the scrub up process again. Perhaps Staff Nurse's behaviour had not been above reproach, but Liz's error had been absolutely basic. It was born out of ignorance, and the Staff Nurse knew that all medical students had opportunities to visit theatre as part of their training, long before they qualified as doctors.

Victoria looked at the damaged bowel thoughtfully.

'We have to decide whether it's safe to leave this tiny length of crushed bowel, or whether it would be wiser to remove it. It's been compressed so tightly, and for so long that I'm not sure that it's still viable. We'll wait and watch it for a few minutes, to see if it recovers.'

Although she had said *'wait and watch'*, she carefully wrapped the damaged bowel in warm moist swabs, then crossed her arms across her chest, and started to chat, asking Paul of his experience whilst working away from the City General in his previous job. She was particularly interested to know how much practical surgery he had been allowed to perform.

'I was pleased at the amount I was able to do, and happy with the supervision and training I was given.'

In fact, Paul had performed quite a variety of surgical procedures, including operations for ruptures, varicose veins and piles, and had also assisted at numerous major operations. Staffing levels were thinner in the peripheral hospitals than they were at the City General, and as a consequence, trainees gained more practical experience.

As they were chatting, Liz completed the second scrubbing of her hands, this time including her wrists and forearms, which she then dried quite correctly on the sterile paper towel provided. Staff Nurse showed her the bin into which the towel was discarded, and then indicated that she should step forward to pick up a gown. Unfolding and donning a surgical gown is difficult and requires practice. The surgeon is required to remove the gown from its sterile wrapper, and then unfold it, all the while holding it away from their body, to prevent it coming into contact with any non-sterile surface. It is necessary to wriggle into the gown's arms, then to stand still, whilst an assistant pulls the gown up over the shoulders, and ties a series of cords at the back, from the neck down to the level of the buttocks.

At this time, the surgeon was usually male, the nurse typically female, and the manner in which this task was performed has been known to convey many a silent message from nurse to surgeon, unseen by any other member of the theatre staff. A rough tug of the gown on to the shoulders with no contact between female hand and male skin has a totally different significance to the lightest, faintest, featherlike caress of finger tips on the nape of the neck, a sensation that Paul had experienced more than once in his bachelor days!

Liz's first attempt to don a gown had to be abandoned as she allowed its outer sterile surface to touch her cotton shift, and on her second attempt, after the gown had been safely tied at the rear, she inadvertently allowed its cuff to touch the shelf as she reached for a packet of surgical gloves. On each occasion, she was instructed to remove her gown, and in doing so she inevitably desterilised her hands. She was therefore again directed back to the scrub up unit for a three-minute scrub! It was like watching a game of snakes and ladders in which every snake leads right back to the starting square. Liz's face, or as much as one could see of it behind her mask, was a picture of suppressed fury. Paul felt sympathy for her, but knew that she was learning two important lessons. Firstly, how to scrub up proficiently for a surgical procedure, and secondly, that nurses knew a great deal more about practical procedures than she did.

Meanwhile, Victoria was taking a second look at the area of bowel that had been crushed. She had waited another five minutes to see if it would recover, but even so, it still looked distinctly unhealthy, and she therefore informed Sister of her intention to remove it. With no undue haste, and without spilling even the slightest drop of bowel content, she removed the damaged length of bowel, and then sutured the open ends together, thereby restoring the continuity of the intestine. She checked that all swabs and instruments had been removed from the abdomen, and started to close the wound.

By this time, Liz had successfully re-scrubbed, re-gowned, and her final task was to put on her gloves. She didn't know what size of gloves would fit her, so Staff Nurse opened a packet sized seven and a half, realising that gloves that were a little on the large side would slip over the fingers more easily than gloves that were too small. She also demonstrated to Liz how to dust her hands with the drying powder before attempting to don the gloves. Unfortunately, Liz spilled most of the powder on the floor, and as anyone who has attempted to apply Marigold gloves when washing the dishes knows, it is almost impossible to put rubber gloves on to damp hands. As a result, Liz struggled to get her fingers into the gloves, the empty tips of which fell over in flaps like rabbit's ears. Eventually, after battling with each finger in turn, and muttering barely audible curses under her breath, she achieved her objective. Victoria was just inserting the last suture into the skin, and preparing to apply a surgical dressing to the wound, when Liz, now successfully gowned and gloved, tentatively approached the operating theatre table. As she did so, the final disaster occurred. Her mask slipped down off her nose, and without thinking, she committed the most elementary of mistakes; she pushed it back into place with her sterile gloved hand. In doing so, she slid down the longest snake on the board, and was dumped once again at the starting point. For a moment she looked as if she about to cry, but instead she turned venomously on her tormentor.

'Damn you,' she shouted at the Staff Nurse. 'You've done all that out of spite.' Then she added, 'I need a drink. Make me a cup of coffee.'

For a moment, there was silence, tension like static electricity in the air. A sudden flash of fire lit up in Staff Nurse's eyes, and there was movement behind her mask as her mouth opened to respond. But Paul intervened.

'I'll make the coffee,' he said quickly. 'Do you want one too Sister, and how about you Staff Nurse?'

'Yes, I'll have a coffee,' Victoria said out loud. 'Milk, but no sugar, please.'

Then quietly she added, as an aside to Paul, 'Quite the diplomat, aren't we? Clearly Dr Webb needs a little advice, but don't worry, I'll have a quiet word with her when I've finished here. You go and make the coffee.'

When Helen had been safely returned to the ward, the nurses, no doubt because of Liz's outburst, declined to join the surgeons for a drink. They chose instead to remain in the theatre, to tidy away the dirty gowns and instruments, wash down the table and prepare for the next day's operations. As Liz drank her coffee in sullen silence, Victoria and Paul attended to the necessary paperwork before Victoria addressed Paul.

'Would you mind slipping to the ward to check that Helen is alright while I have a word with Dr Webb?'

Paul took the hint and left Victoria alone with Liz. She proceeded to tell the new house officer, in the quiet and constructive fashion that was typical of her, that nurses were vital members of the team, and had a great deal of practical experience that she had yet to acquire. They should not be considered subordinate to the medical staff, particularly by newly qualified doctors fresh out of medical school. She hoped that Liz would heed the lesson, knowing that her life on the unit would become exceedingly difficult if she continued to regard the nurses as doctors' hand maidens.

As Paul left the hospital that evening, he reflected on the events of the day. Liz was an obvious concern. His first impressions were that she was totally unsuited for life on a surgical unit. The house officer was a key member of any surgical team. He or she was the doctor who spent most time with the patients. The houseman was the one who made sure that all the prescriptions were written, that all the blood samples had been taken, that the results of the investigations were available for ward rounds, and that all the drips were running smoothly. The houseman had to ensure that the *'consent for operation'* forms were signed, that the operation lists were prepared and circulated to the wards, that blood was available for those who needed transfusion, and that relatives were kept informed of the progress of their loved ones. There were a thousand and one jobs for them to do, and in truth, scarcely enough hours in the day in which to do them. The house officer was the lubricant that kept the surgical unit going, and a good relationship with the nursing staff was vital. A successful house officer needed to be cheerful and hard-working, to be well organised, and to be a good communicator. But he or she also needed to be humble enough to act occasionally as a nurse, a porter or a domestic, or to make the coffee or tea. Paul did not think that Liz had these attributes, and doubted that she would acquire them in the weeks to come. Perhaps her intelligence, combined with a pretty face and pleasing figure had enabled her to rise above such menial tasks in the past, but a haughty attitude would cut no ice with the nurses on the ward, or in the theatre. If Liz was to survive, she had to accept that she was the most junior member of the medical team, and had to recognise that she had much to learn from the nursing staff. Relations between the doctors and nurses on Surgical Five had always been excellent. That was one of the factors that made working there so pleasant; the last thing the unit needed was a doctor-nurse confrontation. But Paul was also concerned for himself. As the next most senior doctor, it would fall to him to cover her tracks, to correct any errors or omissions that she made. A reliable and conscientious house officer could make Paul's job significantly easier, but a house officer who was a liability, would add significantly to his workload.

****

At nine p.m. the following evening, Liz arrived in the Accident Department to begin her first casualty duty. Paul was in the office writing up a patient's notes, but Liz did not immediately go to join him. Instead, she attracted the attention of Richard, her fellow house officer whose shift was coming to an end. She took him by the arm, and led him into an empty patient cubicle. There they engaged in a long and earnest conversation; Liz looking wide-eyed and agitated, Richard seemed to be doing his best to calm her. Ten minutes elapsed before Liz, looking very apprehensive, joined Paul.

Although he knew that Liz had made a poor start to her medical career, Paul was not totally unsympathetic to her situation. Having been qualified as a doctor for only one week, she was about to be first *'on call'* through the night for accidents and surgical emergencies for a population of approximately half a million people. Paul would work alongside her until the waiting room had been cleared, usually about two in the morning, but because there was only one bed in the department, he would then go to his room in the residency, leaving Liz on her own. If the flow of patients allowed, she would grab some sleep as and when she could. Paul would be able to join her within five minutes if she needed assistance, but she faced a daunting, challenging night. She would, of course, be supported by some long-standing and extremely competent nurses who were accustomed to working alongside inexperienced house officers, and who were always willing to advise and offer practical help. However, the Casualty Sisters did not relish the first few weeks in August. Supervising the new recruits involved them in additional work, and required extra vigilance.

'Hi, Liz,' Paul greeted her in a manner that was somewhat more cheerful than he felt. 'It's good to see you. I take it you gained some familiarity with the casualty department when you were a student?'

There was a long pause. 'No, I didn't.'

Yet another disappointment, but since she had not bothered to learn how to scrub up in theatre either, Paul was not altogether surprised.

'Surely you were attached to one of the surgical units during your training?'

'Yes, I was; Surgical Three.'

'Did you never come to casualty when it was Surgical Three's admitting day?'

'No, I didn't know we had to.'

Paul was angry. As a student she had obviously been both lazy and foolish. Medical students, during their training, were attached to one of the surgical units for two, ten-week periods. Each unit was responsible for staffing the casualty department every fourth day. Attendance records were not kept, but since students were training to become house officers, they were expected not merely turn up for the short formal teaching sessions that were held in office hours on weekdays, but to take the opportunity to see all aspects of a houseman's work, and that included casualty and theatre duties. Liz's failure to familiarise herself with life in casualty meant extra pressure for her, and additional work for Paul.

'In that case,' he said, barely managing to hide the irritation that he felt, 'we'll start by seeing the first few cases together. It will give you a chance to meet the staff, to become familiar with the department, and hopefully it will help you to settle in.'

In his heart however, he knew that this was wildly optimistic. With her lack of preparation, her innate ability to upset the nursing staff, and her nervous disposition, it was inevitable that she would find casualty duties extremely tough. She had a long and difficult night ahead of her.

For the next two hours, Liz followed Paul round like a lost sheep. As they saw each patient, Paul took the history, performed an examination, then explained how the patient was to be managed. Liz's only contribution was to record the consultation on the patient's casualty card. Frequently he invited her to ask questions, but none were forthcoming. She was content simply to act as a scribe. One patient had a minor skin laceration needing a couple of stitches, and Liz was forced to admit that she had never inserted a skin suture during her training. Later in the evening, Paul suggested that she saw some patients on her own, but in every case, having recorded the history and examined the patient, she expected him to make the diagnosis and decide on management. Her lack of knowledge and her inexperience worried him intensely. It was clear that despite having passed the final medical school examination, she was simply not equipped for the task that lay before her. Partly Paul's concern was selfish. As the next senior officer, he recognised that many nights of lost sleep awaited him as he covered her deficiencies.

When the surgical cubicles and the waiting room were finally empty, Liz and Paul sat with the nursing staff in the office, having a well-earned cup of tea and some hot buttered toast; the usual 'pick-me-up' for weary hospital staff when matron was not around. Although tired, Paul was pleased that the evening shift had produced some interesting cases. Liz though was tense and anxious. They both knew that the time had come for Paul to depart, leaving Liz on her own to care for any patients who presented during the remaining hours of the night. A bed was available for her in the department, but Paul knew it was unlikely that she would sleep well. When he had been a house officer, he had found it extremely difficult to relax when on duty in casualty. Unless absolutely exhausted, he would lie awake worrying whether he could cope with whatever emergency might arise. Then later, having attended to a patient, he would still find it impossible to sleep, his mind reflecting on his diagnosis and treatment, concerned that he might have made some catastrophic mistake and that the patient would suffer, even die, as a result. Paul often thought that if he had more self-confidence, he would have greater peace of mind. But would that make him a better doctor? Perhaps the patient is better served by a doctor troubled by a degree of self-doubt.

He reassured Liz that the nursing staff were very experienced, and would offer her every possible assistance. He also stressed that if she had any problems, she should call him; that it was better to call too often, than not to call when help was needed. With that he left her, walked through the empty corridors to the doctor's mess, and bedded down in his own room, dreading to think how many times she would disturb him during the night. She would probably need advice about every single patient that attended!

It seemed that he had hardly got to sleep when the telephone rang, though the clock on his bedside cabinet told him that ninety minutes had elapsed since he'd left the department. Logic suggested that it would be Liz, but it wasn't. It was the casualty sister, sounding concerned.

'Do you happen to know where Dr Webb is?' she asked.

'No, I don't. I'm tucked up in bed, and she's certainly not with me! Isn't she in casualty?'

'No, she's not. She seems to have disappeared.'

'I suppose it's possible that she's been called to one of the wards, though the staff there should know that if they need a doctor tonight, they should call Richard.'

'I've rung both the male and female wards, and she's not there.'

'Have you tried theatre?' Paul asked, though he knew full well that there was no earthly reason why she should be there.

'Yes, and I've tried her room as well, but there's no reply. Switchboard has tried her bleep, but no one seems to know where she is.'

'Have you got a doctor in casualty?'

'No, we haven't and obviously we must have one.'

Paul groaned. Life on a surgical unit was tough enough when everyone was present and pulling their weight, but it would become a nightmare if members of the team went absent without leave.

'In that case, I suppose I'll have to come down, but please do keep bleeping Liz. She must be somewhere in the hospital.'

Arriving in casualty, Paul asked how Liz had seemed in the short time that she had been on her own.

'Well, we didn't see much of her. When you left, there were no patients waiting to be seen, so Dr Webb announced that she was going to go to sleep in the duty room. Shortly afterwards, when a patient arrived with a twisted ankle, we called her, but she wasn't there. And the bed hasn't been slept in either. She must have slipped out of the department without anybody noticing. Goodness knows where she is now.'

This was totally unacceptable. There were circumstances when it was justifiable to leave the department when on duty, but to disappear without informing anybody was unforgivable. Paul realised with dismay that the only available solution was for him to complete the night shift on Liz's behalf. Quickly, he arranged for the patient with the ankle injury to be strapped, told him to return in the morning for an x-ray, and then, furious with Liz, he bedded down in the hot and airless room that was allocated for the casualty doctor. As it happened, he slept reasonably well, only being disturbed once to see a drunk with a head injury who felt the sharp edge of his tongue. He merely required observation by the nurses until he could be properly assessed, when the effects of the alcohol had worn off.

The next morning, after a refreshing shower and a quick breakfast, Paul hurried to the ward in time for Mr Potts' round. Victoria had already completed her own review of the patients, checking to ensure that their progress was satisfactory, and that there had been no change in their condition during the night.

At 9.30 the medical team were waiting for Mr Potts to arrive when Liz walked in. This was a different house officer to the one they had known previously. Gone were the bright lipstick, eye shadow, and the rose-tinted cheeks. Gone too, Paul noticed with some satisfaction, were her high-heeled shoes. Without any of her usual make up, and with her hair seemingly unbrushed, she no longer looked the glamorous young model. She looked tired and worn. Polite greetings were exchanged, and then Paul waited, expecting an explanation for Liz's absence from casualty the night before, but none was forthcoming. It became obvious that Paul would need to broach the subject himself.

'The Casualty Sister contacted me last night, Liz, because you disappeared from the department. She was left without any medical staff, and had no idea where you were.'

'Yes. I'm sorry about that Paul, but I was taken ill. I developed a migraine.'

'But Sister rang your room, and there was no reply. She also bleeped you. She couldn't find you anywhere.'

'I'm afraid I was too ill to answer the phone.'

This was outrageous. If a member of staff, for whatever reason, was unable to perform their duties, they had a responsibility to arrange cover, or if that wasn't possible, to let somebody know of the problem. Paul looked to Victoria for support and guidance.

'Look Dr Webb,' Victoria said gently but firmly. 'I'm sorry if you were unwell, I trust you are now recovered, but if for any reason, any reason at all, you need to go off duty, you must let someone know. It's a question of patient safety.'

'But I was genuinely ill,' protested Liz.

'Maybe you were, but I doubt that you were too ill to inform Sister, or to make a single telephone call to Paul,' countered Victoria. Liz looked sullen but did not reply.

Paul remained furious; he didn't believe for one moment that Liz had suddenly been taken ill; she had taken fright and run away to hide. But there was no time for him to add to Victoria's comments as Mr Potts walked through the door. It was obvious that Liz was not coping, and he vowed to inform Mr Potts of her behaviour at the end of the round.

Sir William's rounds usually lasted three or more hours, but Mr Potts managed to review all his patients and was ready to leave within fifty minutes, during which time Paul contributed little; he was preparing himself to broach the subject of Liz's dereliction of duty with his boss. He had decided to do this in her presence over the customary post-round drink. On this occasion though, Mr Potts did not enter the office, but remained in the corridor outside.

'Aren't you coming in for a cup of tea or a biscuit, Mr Potts?' Sister asked.

'Not today, thank you, Sister.' he replied. Then turning to Liz, he said, 'My secretary says that you want to have a word with me.'

'Yes, please, Mr Potts, if that's convenient.'

'Of course, it is, my dear. I have to say you do look a little tired. I hope Miss Kent and Lambert haven't been working you too hard.'

'I confess I do feel very tired, Sir. Indeed, that is what I'd like to talk to you about,' she replied, with a 'please come to my rescue – I'm a helpless female' look on her face.

'Well come and have a coffee with me in my office, and we'll see what can be arranged to make life a little easier for you.'

With that, he put his arm across Liz's shoulder, and guided her down the corridor. Victoria and Paul exchanged glances, wondering what the outcome of their meeting would be. It was obvious that Liz wasn't coping with the workload and needed some support. But would she admit that she had deserted the casualty department in the middle of the night? Probably not. Would Mr Potts offer her guidance and advice as to how to manage the workload better? Possibly. Would he appoint an extra pair of hands to give her some assistance? Highly unlikely. Or would Victoria, Richard and Paul be expected to undertake extra duties? Almost certainly.

As it transpired though, it was none of these possibilities, and Paul's concern that their work load would increase as they carried a passenger were not realised. Two days later, Liz abruptly resigned her post. She was informed that as a result of her decision not to complete her probationary year, she could not be registered with the General Medical Council, nor be qualified to treat patients; but she said that this didn't worry her. She had decided to seek employment, either in a research laboratory, or with a pharmaceutical company where life was more civilised, and folk only worked on weekdays from nine 'til five. On reflection, Victoria and Paul had no doubt that this was a sensible career choice for her to make.

Thought for the day

If at first you don't succeed, try, try and try again

Then quit. No good being a damn fool about it.

W. C. Fields 1880 - 1946

Chapter 18   The International Soccer Star

17ᵗʰ August 1970

Mickey McGovern was a good-looking, cocky, 23-years-old professional footballer who had just moved to the city's first division club for a record fee. His photograph had been prominent in both local and national newspapers while the transfer deal was being negotiated. Although highly talented, and already an established international player, there had been considerable speculation about the wisdom of signing him. He had been in trouble with the police on several occasions, usually in connection with late-night drinking, pretty girls, or fast motor cars. It was feared that he might prove to be a bad influence on the younger players of the club. The club's manager however, had been quick to reassure supporters that he was no more than 'a bit of a lad', and that with hard work and firm discipline administered under his close supervision, there wouldn't be any problems.

   A groin hernia had been diagnosed at the medical examination that was part of the transfer arrangements, so Mickey was admitted to the City General Hospital to have it repaired. Inevitably, his arrival on the ward, unannounced and unexpected, caused a stir. As he walked jauntily to the bed to which he had been allocated, accompanied by one of the nurses, there was urgent and excited whispering amongst the other patients.

   'Hey, isn't that Mickey McGovern?'

   'It certainly looks like him.'

   'If it isn't, it's his spitting image.'

   The moment that Mickey had changed into his pyjamas and the screens had been drawn back, his neighbour plucked up courage, and asked the question that was on everyone's lips.

   'You're Mickey McGovern, aren't you, the lad who's just been signed to play for the Rovers?'

   'Aye, that's me, Grandad. Recognised me, did you? Here – pass me that newspaper, the one with my photo in it. I'll let you have my autograph.'

Although his neighbour was old enough to be Mickey's father, rather than his grandfather, he declined to take offence. He would gain considerable kudos from being able to chat with this young star.

'Thanks, Mickey,' he said, genuinely pleased. 'I'll give it to my boy. He's football mad, and a great fan of yours. He'll be green with envy when he hears you're in the bed next to me. He'll probably visit me every night now.'

Quietly, he decided to milk some information from Mickey. He might hear some juicy titbits that could earn him an easy fiver if he passed them to the local newspaper.

'Tell me, what made you decide to come to the Rovers when other clubs wanted you to play for them?' he asked innocently.

Sure enough, Mickey was pleased to sit and chat, and was cheerfully sharing football gossip with his neighbour when Janet Smith, Mr Potts' new house officer, came to examine him. She was armed with Mickey's notes, a blood pressure machine, and various other items of medical equipment.

Liz's sudden departure had left the unit short staffed, but credit to Mr Potts; a replacement had been appointed within the week in the shape of another tall and attractive girl, called Janet Smith. She was Australian, had qualified in Sydney, but chosen to do her house jobs in Britain to be with her fiancé, a British engineer. They planned to marry and set up home in Australia when her husband's contract ended.

Janet though was not quite in the usual Leslie Potts mould. She was indeed strikingly pretty, but her hair, though blond, was unfashionably short and tousled. It could have been her crowning glory, but no attempt had been made to make it look attractive. With her clear complexion and high cheekbones, she could have graced the cover of any fashion magazine, but her face was devoid of make-up, and was unsmiling. It was her eyes, though, that were her most notable feature. They were strikingly blue, and had a directness that challenged those who met her gaze. And her clothes were severe. She was wearing an elegantly-tailored, pinstriped, grey suit, a plain white blouse sealed with a brooch at the neck, and well-polished black, flat-heeled leather shoes.

Blatantly, Mickey examined Janet's figure from head to toe, his gaze lingering on her chest and legs. He was impressed by what he saw. In his mind, he allocated girls to one of four categories, *'slags'*, *'tarts'*, *'regular birds'*, and *'high-class totty'*. He didn't consider any of them to be beyond his reach. Janet definitely belonged in the top category, and given half a chance, he decided he would chat her up. What a tale he could tell his new teammates if he managed to score with this young doctor.

All went smoothly as Janet asked Mickey about his rupture. She learned that his groin ached when he played football, and there had been occasions when he had been forced to miss training. Once, he had been unable to join England's under-21 squad for an international match, which had been a huge disappointment to him.

Having recorded Mickey's story in the notes, Janet needed to examine his rupture. She pulled the screens around the bed, and asked him to lie down and lower his pyjama pants. Whilst she was conducting the examination with cool, clinical efficiency, probing his groin with her long elegant fingers and carefully manicured nails, Mickey was acutely conscious of the closeness of her attractive figure. Desperately he tried to prevent his emotions from becoming aroused but with limited success. Janet, observing the effect her examination was having on her patient, quickly marked the rupture with an indelible pen then instructed him, in a voice as cold as ice, to pull up his pyjama trousers. She now needed to check that Mickey was fit for an anaesthetic.

'Take your top off please, I need to examine your chest,' she ordered.

'I'll let you examine my chest, if you let me examine yours,' Mickey responded in a flash, a cheeky grin on his face.

For a second, there was silence then Janet raised her arm, and slapped him hard across the face. Taken by surprise, Mickey fell back on to the pillows. For a second, he looked angry then began laughing out loud. 'You're a frisky young minx, aren't you? Come here, girl, give me a kiss, and we'll call it quits!' He sat up and made a grab for her waist.

Immediately, Janet realised that her spontaneous reaction, justified as it may have been, was entirely inappropriate. Had she slapped a spirited boyfriend who had made a suggestive remark, there wouldn't be a problem; but she was a doctor, and Mickey was her patient. And she had hit him with force. One side of his face already looked red and painful. Horrified at what she had done, she fled from the scene.

Sister Ashbrook found her two minutes later, sobbing quietly in a corner of the office.

'What on earth's the matter, Janet?'

Janet blurted out the whole story, confessing that she had struck Mickey as hard as she could across the face. She was certain that she would be sacked.

'I've only been a doctor for three weeks,' she sobbed. 'No one will employ me after this. My career is ruined, and I've spent five long years at Medical School to get where I am. What on earth can I do?'

'If I were you, I should go immediately and speak to Mr Potts,' she suggested. 'I'm sure he will manage to sort things out. Meanwhile,' she added, a grim and determined look on her face, 'you can leave Mickey McGovern in my hands. He's going to be with us for at least three days. I'll make sure he has good cause to remember his stay with us.' She already knew exactly how Mickey was to be rewarded for his insolence.

Unfortunately, when Janet spoke with Mr Potts' secretary, she learned that the consultant was away at a surgical conference, and wasn't expected back until the next morning. Miserably, she returned to the ward, and tried to concentrate on her duties. She was later to spend a long and sleepless night convinced that her medical career was over before it had really begun.

Meanwhile, back on the ward, Mickey's neighbour, who had overheard the exchange, slipped quietly to the corridor where the trolley phone used by patients was stored. His opportunity to earn a little extra beer money had arisen somewhat sooner than he had anticipated.

****

It was a pale and anxious houseman who went to see Mr Potts the next morning. Janet approached his office with the apprehension she had once felt as a school girl when sent to see the headmistress.

'Mr Potts,' Janet began, her voice high pitched and trembling, 'I've a terrible confession to make. I've struck one of your patients.'

'You've done what?' the consultant asked, incredulously.

'I'm terribly sorry, Sir. I hit one of your patients. I tried to tell you yesterday, but you weren't in the hospital.'

'Who on earth did you hit?'

'Mickey McGovern, Sir, the young footballer.'

'And where did you hit him?'

'He was in his bed, Sir, in the middle of the ward.'

'No, I didn't mean where was he at the time. I meant which bit of his anatomy did you attack?'

'I slapped his face, Sir.'

Mr Potts motioned her to a chair. 'Then I think you'd better sit down and tell me all about it.'

Quietly, Janet recounted the events of the previous afternoon.

As he listened, a smile crossed Mr Potts' face. 'And did you hit him hard, my dear?'

'As hard as I possibly could, Sir,' Janet admitted. 'But I didn't do it deliberately. Honestly, I didn't. It was sort of instinctive. It just happened before I had time to think.'

'So now you've come to make a clean breast of it, have you?' Mr Potts said, now laughing out loud, and emphasising the noun in the middle of his sentence. 'Well, it sounds as if he deserved it. I think we'd better go right away, and sort it out, hadn't we? Is he still on the ward?'

'Yes, Sir, he's having his operation this afternoon.'

'Right then, you come with me.'

Mr Potts strode purposefully to the male ward, Janet following two paces behind. The consultant marched straight to Mickey's bed. The young man looked up in surprise. Brusquely, Mr Potts drew the screens and stood over his patient, bearing down on him, his face stern, hands on his hips.

'I believe you were extremely rude to this young doctor yesterday,' he declared. 'You made a highly inappropriate and sexist remark.' His voice was loud and authoritative.

'Y…. yes, I'm afraid I did, but it was only in fun. I… I didn't mean any harm,' the young man stuttered, his normal self-confidence having deserted him.

'And what would happen to your reputation if such behaviour were to come to the ears of the press or your club manager?'

Mickey looked horrified. 'Please, you can't let that happen, Doctor. I can't afford any more bad news stories. You see, I've been a bit of a bad lad in the past; I've had a spot of bother with the law. My contract with the Rovers has a clause in it about my behaviour. They can kick me out if I get into any more trouble – and I'm on good wages. I really am very sorry.'

He turned to Janet. 'I do apologise, Miss. I wasn't thinking. It was just a flip remark. I truly didn't mean what I said.'

He turned back to face Mr Potts. 'Please, Doctor, can we let it pass?'

Mr Potts addressed Janet. 'Are you prepared to let the matter drop if he apologises to you?'

'Yes, Sir, I am, and I ought to apologise to him for striking him.'

'Not at all, my dear, you were entirely justified. Such behaviour is not to be tolerated. Now, young man, let's hear what you have to say for yourself.'

Mickey duly obliged with a grovelling apology which Janet received with great relief.

'There you are, my dear,' Mr Potts said to his young house officer as they walked back to the office, 'I don't think we'll hear any more about the matter. But you really ought not to be so sensitive, you know. A good-looking girl like you is bound to get the odd suggestive remark, and occasional wolf whistle. You really ought to be flattered.' He patted her bottom. 'Now off you go and get on with your work, and we'll say no more about it.'

Janet seethed with anger. Her new boss was not as direct with his sexist behaviour as Mickey, but he was just as bad. It was all she could do to stop herself from slapping his face as he smiled at her before turning back towards his office.

Mr Potts had suggested that would be the end of the matter, but he was wrong. Mickey's neighbour was again on his way to the telephone in the corridor.

****

A couple of hours later, a seedy-looking man in a shiny suit knocked on the door of the office as Janet was writing up some notes, and Sister Ashbrook was struggling with the following week's staffing roster.

Sister looked up. 'Yes, what is it?' she said, irritated at being disturbed.

'I've come to have a word with Mickey McGovern,' the young man said.

'May I ask who you are, and what you want to speak with him about?' Sister asked. 'It's not visiting time, you know.'

'I'm from the National Recorder', the young man said. 'I believe he's propositioned a female member of staff, and had his face slapped for his trouble. It'll make a great exclusive. I just need to verify the story.'

Janet looked up in alarm. 'How on earth did you hear about that?' she blurted out, without thinking.

'So it is true, that's great,' the reporter commented, suddenly excited. 'So who hit him, and what had he done to deserve it?'

'It was....' Janet began, red-faced and flustered.

Sister, though, interrupted, and took control of a situation that was rapidly spiralling out of control.

'It's time for you to leave,' she said firmly, rising from her seat.

However, the reporter recognised that a great story was within his grasp.

He turned to Janet, knowingly. He saw how attractive she was. 'It was you, wasn't it? So what did he do to you? Did he try to lay his hands on you, or kiss you?'

Janet was appalled. After her chat with Mr Potts, she had believed the matter was closed. Now she could see her name being splashed all over the national newspapers, her reputation in tatters, her career ruined.

When Janet didn't reply, the reporter added. 'He's done it before you know. You're not the first girl he's molested. You'll be doing everyone a favour if you make an example of him.'

Janet said nothing, but the reporter wasn't going to turn his back on an exclusive.

'I can make it worth your while, Doctor. There are big bucks to be made out of a story like this. I can see the headline now; '*Soccer star's sex assault on hospital doctor*'. If you would give me an interview, and perhaps we could have a photo of you, maybe wearing something a little more.....'

'Out, out,' Sister shouted as she ushered the reporter from the room, but not before he had noted the name badge on the lapel of Janet's white coat.

The reporter's next stop was the hospital canteen where, over a cup of tea and a biscuit, he had no difficulty in finding a group of student nurses with whom to chat. They unwittingly confirmed the story that had already become the hottest bit of gossip on the hospital's grapevine for many months. It had indeed been the tall and attractive Dr Janet Smith who had slapped Mickey McGovern's face after the young footballer had made unwelcome advances whilst wearing nothing more than his pyjama bottoms. The reporter located the public phone in the hospital's main corridor, and spoke with his editor, who promptly changed the headline on the paper's front page.

Back in the office, Janet was inconsolable, and again in tears. Sister was furious with Mickey for being the root cause of the problem, and she felt desperately sorry for Janet. She determined to do her utmost to support the houseman whom she respected for standing up for her sex. She felt it would be grossly unfair if her name were to be splashed all over the national newspapers. Tight-lipped, she went in search of Mr Potts.

Half an hour later, Mr Potts rang the offices of the Recorder, and asked to be put through to the editor.

'Oh, hello Charlie,' Mr Potts began, 'I was at the golf club this weekend, and I see you've managed to reduce your handicap. We must have a game sometime, and then I can see how good you really are.'

Charlie smiled to himself, not fooled by these introductory pleasantries. He knew that Leslie Potts was a busy man, and wouldn't ring in the middle of the day simply to have a chat about golf.

'Come on, Leslie,' he said, 'I know what's on your mind. It's to do with Mickey McGovern and that lovely lady doctor you have working for you, isn't it? I'm told she's an absolute stunner. You always did have an eye for a pretty face and a shapely figure.'

'I've just rung to let you know that nothing at all happened. It seems the young man said something that was misunderstood; then the rumour mill embellished it. The story has got completely out of hand.'

'That's not what I heard, Leslie. I heard that young Mickey got fresh with the young lady, and had his face slapped good and hard.'

'No, Charlie, I assure you it's simply a rumour that's got out of hand. It wouldn't be wise for you to publish it. If you took the trouble to come to speak with the lad, or my doctor, or indeed the ward sister, you'd find they all flatly denied that anything significant happened.'

'Come on, Leslie, I can understand you want to keep a lid on things, but we both know that Mickey tried it on with that doctor.'

'Just a rumour, Charlie, just like the rumour I heard that you turned up in our Casualty Department recently somewhat the worse for wear after Rovers' cup win over United.'

For a minute there was silence at the other end of the phone. 'You wouldn't, Leslie, not to an old friend.'

'Yes, Charlie, I would. Indeed, if any word of this gets into the newspapers, I will. Airing dirty washing in public works both ways.'

Charlie took a moment or two to consider his options. 'OK', he said finally, 'you win, but it's a shame. It would have made a great news story.'

'So would Newspaper Chief in a drunken brawl with boyfriend.'

****

As always, everything on the ward was spick and span in anticipation of Sir William's arrival. All the patients had been instructed to stay in their beds, preferably sitting smartly to attention. For Sister Ashbrook, his rounds were the highlight of the week. To show respect, patients were expected to remain silent. Most were happy to oblige, but as Sir William entered the ward, Sister spotted one of Mr Potts' patients sitting on the side of his bed with his legs dangling down. He had one slipper on and one slipper off, and his pyjama jacket was unbuttoned, revealing an obese belly and a hairy chest. He was reading the Racing Times. As Sir William and his team drew ever closer to this errant man, Sister despatched a nurse to insist that he tidy himself up.

In a voice that echoed round the ward, and was certainly loud enough to reach Sir William's ears, he remarked, 'An important person you say; is the Queen to visit us today?'

When the hospital's senior consultant arrived at his bed, the punter lowered his newspaper an inch or two, smiled sweetly, said a polite 'Good Morning' to Sir William, and then calmly resumed his racing selections.

Paul rather hoped that he would add to the drama of the situation by asking Sir William for a tip for the 2.15 at Kempton Park, but unfortunately, he didn't. Furious at this perceived insolence, Sister glared at him whilst Sir William fixed him with a beady eye for a second or two as he passed. He 'tutted', and then marched on without comment. Later the wayward patient was to feel the sharp edge of Sister's tongue, and he subsequently came to suspect that the needles used for his daily antibiotic injections were significantly larger and somewhat blunter than they had been before.

Then a further incident enlivened the ward round. Sir William was in mid-sentence explaining to a builder how long he should be off work following his stomach operation, when a loud and indignant voice was heard from the opposite side of the ward. The voice was unmistakably female.

'Stop that. Remove your hands at once!'

The voice came from behind the screens which were drawn round Mickey McGovern's bed. Sister was the first to react. Without a word of apology to Sir William, she dashed to investigate, fiercely protective of her young nurses. If Mickey was up to his tricks again, molesting her staff, she would throw him onto the street, no matter what the consequences. It took her no more than five seconds to reach Mickey's bed.

'What on earth is going on here?' she demanded, as she flung the screens open.

Mickey was lying on the bed, a tanned, muscular, athletic figure wearing only a pair of white football shorts. A pretty young physiotherapist was sitting beside him. Both looked up in surprise at Sister's sudden appearance.

'Nothing, nothing at all.' the physio replied, sounding puzzled. 'Why, Sister, what did you think was going on?'

'Is Mr McGovern being a nuisance? Has he made a pass at you? Did he put his hands on you?'

'Why no, Sister, not at all,' the therapist replied, whilst thinking that perhaps she wouldn't have minded too much if he had.

'Well, what was all that shouting about 'keeping your hands off'?'

'He didn't have his hands on me, Sister. I'm trying to get him to do his exercises, trying to mobilise him after his operation. He's supposed to lift his legs off the bed using only his leg muscles, but he keeps using his hands to take the weight.'

'Are you sure?' Sister demanded, still deeply suspicious.

'Yes, Sister, quite sure.'

'That's just as well then. I'll leave you to get on.'

She shot a fierce glance at Mickey. 'I'm watching you, young man. You misbehave, and I'll have you out of here so fast your feet won't touch the ground.'

'Now I wonder what Sister thought I was doing,' Mickey commented suggestively, grinning at the physio, the minute Sister's back was turned. 'Would you shout out if I showed you?'

The physio smiled back at him. 'Yes, I would, and you might find that your exercises suddenly became ten times more painful. Now get that leg in the air, and let's have less cheating!'

In due course, Sir William, with his entourage of doctors, nurses and medical students reached Mickey's bed. Since he was a patient of Mr

Potts, it was to be expected that Sir William would walk straight past, but Sister had other ideas.

Would you mind advising on a little problem with one of Mr Potts' patients, Sir William?' she asked innocently. 'Mr Potts is on leave at the moment.'

Sir William looked to Paul to be told the nature of the problem to which Sister had referred, but Paul was not aware that there was a problem. Nevertheless, he told Sir William of Mickey's occupation and his hernia operation, all the while hoping that Sister would interrupt and disclose her concerns. True to form, Sir William then spent ten minutes telling Mickey how to minimise the chance of the rupture recurring. He was only to undertake light training for the first month, and not to expect to be match-fit for at least two months. Having forgotten there was said to be a 'problem', he was about to move on when Sister decided the moment was ripe for Mickey to be taught a lesson that would forever remind him of his stay on her ward.

'I don't think Mr McGovern has moved his bowels since his operation, Sir William,' Sister Ashbrook said.

True to form, Sir William responded as she knew he would. He raised his index finger in the air, as if summoning a waiter in a high-class restaurant. It was a signal the nurses knew all too well. They were to pass him the rectal tray.

'Just turn onto your side', instructed Sir William.

Obediently, Mickey complied, not realising what fate held in store for him. 'Now drop your shorts,' Sir William continued.

As he placed an examination glove on his hand, and applied a generous portion of lubricating gel to his index finger, Mickey suddenly realised what was about to happen.

'What, with all these people around?' he protested, suddenly alarmed.

'Don't worry, they're all doctors or nurses, they've seen it all before,' Sir William reassured. 'Now draw up your knees and try to relax.'

But Mickey was far from relaxed; he was mortified. With a dozen people crowded within the screens, his cheeks reddened with embarrassment, and he covered his face to hide his humiliation.

'Everyone should be prepared to perform the humblest of jobs on a surgical unit,' Sir William commented, repeating one of his favourite sayings, as he performed a rectal examination.

'Well done, Sister, you were quite right. He's really bunged up. But I'm sure a couple of suppositories will do the trick!'

Two glycerine suppositories were peeled out of their plastic wrappers, dropped into his hand, and then thrust into Mickey's anus by Sir William's chunky finger.

'There you are, young man,' he said as he wiped the young footballer's bottom with a dry swab. Give those suppositories half an hour to work, and then slip down to the toilet. When you've moved your bowels, you can go home.'

Mickey pulled up his shorts, muttering something unprintable under his breath, though not loud enough for the nurses to hear – which was perhaps as well.

Sister returned to the office quietly satisfied.

Thought for the day

An editor; A person employed by a newspaper, whose business it is to separate the wheat from the chaff, and to see that the chaff is printed.

Elbert Hubbard 1859 - 1915

Chapter 19   Harry Grimshaw M.P.

30th September 1970

Leslie Potts was not a man to hide his light under a bushel. The polished brass plate beside the impressive front door announced in bold block capitals that the owner of this substantial Georgian property was Mr Leslie Potts, MB ChB, PhD, FRCS(Eng). Consultant Surgeon. The man in question was sitting behind his polished mahogany desk in his private consulting suite. His secretary, a pretty young brunette with a ready smile and a cheerful disposition, popped her head around the door. Whereas most surgeons when appointing doctors to work for them selected the best applicant for the job, irrespective of their age, sex or appearance, Mr Potts always chose the prettiest of the girls! He adopted the same principle when appointing secretaries.

'I'm sorry to disturb you Mr Potts,' she said, 'but I have a gentleman on the phone who wants to know if you would see him today. He says he's a very busy man, and that his problem is painful and urgent. Do you have time to squeeze him in?'

'Yes, that's fine. Arrange for him to come as my last patient,' the consultant replied.

He had no objection at all. Private practice was lucrative, and at least two of the patients he'd already seen that afternoon required surgery, which would add significantly to his income.

'The more the merrier,' he added cheerfully, 'and by the way Samantha, do please call me Leslie; Mr Potts sounds far too formal.'

When the extra patient arrived, Mr Potts recognised him at once. He was the local MP, Harry Grimshaw, whose photograph regularly featured in both regional and national newspapers.

'Thank you so much for seeing me here, and not at the City General,' Harry said, as he shook Mr Potts firmly by the hand. He laughed. 'I'm sure you appreciate that had I been seen in the hospital, I should undoubtedly have been recognised. Within two minutes, the press would be speculating about my health, and wondering if there was soon to be a vacancy in the cabinet. But please treat me just as you would any other Health Service patient.

In other words, you don't expect to be sent a bill, thought Mr Potts!

Fifteen minutes later, when the consultation was over, and an infected toenail had been diagnosed, Harry was again up to his tricks.

'You say it only requires a minor operation,' he said, 'however, I do have to shoehorn it into a very busy schedule. There's never a good time for me to be away from Westminster.'

He took out his diary, and flicked through the pages frowning.

'I had hoped to be back in London later today to attend a function at Transport House,' he said, thinking aloud, 'but it's already too late for that. In any case, this damned toe is so painful it's interfering with my work; I'd better get it sorted out at the earliest opportunity. Is there any chance that my operation could be done in the next couple of days? Tomorrow would be best if you could fit me in. Of course, in the hospital I wouldn't expect any special favours.'

This rankled with Mr Potts. Harry Grimshaw was an MP, indeed a cabinet minister in a Labour Government that was hell-bent on eliminating the private practice that provided him with his lucrative income. Yet, here he was, asking to by-pass the waiting list, and also dictate the date of his operation. He clearly expected all the benefits of private medicine on the NHS.

Mr Potts paused before replying, wondering how best to respond. He could decline to co-operate. He could point out that the waiting time for non-urgent surgery was six months, that the opportunity to choose a convenient time to fit in with work commitments was important to many businessmen and professional people, not just to politicians. Did Harry not understand that anyone with a family, or with a holiday booked, would also like to choose the date of their surgery? He looked Harry in the eye, still undecided what to say. The politician seemed to read his mind.

'I know I'm asking for a little favour,' he said smoothly, 'but as you can imagine, I am quite influential. I'm sure that I'll be able to return the favour in the not-too-distant future.'

You scratch my back, I'll scratch yours, thought Mr Potts.

'All right,' he said reluctantly. 'Take a seat in the waiting room, and I'll see what I can do.'

As Harry left the room, he reached for the phone. He dialled the hospital then waited for a couple of minutes, drumming his fingers impatiently on the desk, whilst the switchboard located Paul Lambert, his trainee.

Paul was working in the outpatient clinic when the call came through. He heard his consultant's familiar voice.

'Lambert, I have a patient with me at the moment who needs to come into the hospital.'

Paul presumed, correctly as it transpired, that the consultant was speaking from his private consulting rooms.

'He's something of a VIP,' Mr Potts continued. 'It's Harry Grimshaw. I presume you know who he is?'

Paul thought quickly. 'You mean the politician, Sir?'

'Yes, that's right. He's got an in-growing toenail. Put him on tomorrow morning's operating list as the first case. He'll need to be clerked in as usual of course, but just treat him as a routine patient. Oh, and by the way, you'd better get Sister to organise a side room for him.'

'I presume he'll be a private patient then, Sir.'

The consultant laughed. 'You must be joking, Lambert! With the Labour Party determined to abolish all the pay beds in the NHS, he couldn't possibly risk the press finding him in a private bed. They would hound him out of office for being such a hypocrite. No, he'll be an ordinary NHS patient.'

Although an 'ordinary NHS patient' with an in-growing toenail would never be treated in a side room, Paul knew better than to comment. He was a junior doctor; it wasn't wise to upset one's consultant.

'That's fine, Sir,' Paul replied, 'I'll pass the message on to the houseman.'

'Actually, Lambert, it would be better if you admitted him and managed his care yourself. He's rather a forceful character. The houseman might find him a bit overpowering. Besides, he's very influential; it's important we create a good impression. Who knows, there may come a time when we need his support.'

'And when will he be arriving, Sir?'

'In about thirty minutes.'

'Do you happen to know which toe it is?' Paul asked. This was important information. The site of surgery needed to be marked on the patient's skin with an indelible pen, and detailed in capital letters on the typed list which would guide the theatre staff the next day. Failure to follow these basic routines could lead to catastrophic errors which were a disaster for the patient, expensive for the medical insurance company, and highly damaging to the surgeon's reputation!

'It's one of the big toes,' Mr Potts replied, 'I can't remember which side. It will be obvious when he arrives. I'll leave the matter in your hands then.'

Despite having said 'just treat him as a routine patient', it was clear Mr Potts intended that Harry Grimshaw should have special treatment. Non-urgent NHS admissions were normally notified to the ward a week in advance by the administrative staff, not by the consultant immediately prior to their arrival.

Paul phoned Sister Ashbrook who was in the office on the ward. She was working on the nurses' duty rota, a weekly chore that she detested. She found it impossible to staff the ward appropriately without denying her nurses the time 'off-duty' they had requested.

When Paul mentioned that Mr Grimshaw was to be nursed in a side ward, she became angry. All three side wards were already occupied; the patients in them needing privacy for sound medical reasons. One had an infection, and required to be isolated to prevent it spreading to other patients. The second was receiving terminal care, and only that morning, she had placed an elderly man in the third side room, where he was receiving more intensive nursing care than was possible on the main ward.

'But that's ridiculous,' Sister exclaimed, when told that Mr Grimshaw merely had an in-growing toenail. 'How can I possibly justify moving a sick patient out of a side ward for such a trivial condition?'

'I'm sorry, Sister, but I'm afraid that's what I've been instructed to arrange. Perhaps a cabinet minister's toenail is more important than yours or mine! And Sister,' Paul added, 'would you mind giving me a bleep when he arrives? I've been invited to give him my personal attention. He's to go first on tomorrow's list, so I won't have much time to check him in, and organise any tests that may be necessary.'

'And you say he'll arrive in thirty minutes? That doesn't give me much time to move a patient who actually needs a side ward onto the main ward, does it?' Sister replied pointedly. Then she posed the question that Paul had asked only a few moments earlier.

'I suppose he's a private patient then?'

'No, Sister. It seems he's a politician who wants the perks of private care on the NHS.'

There was a pause before Sister replied. 'Oh, does he now? Well, we'll see about that, won't we?'

Paul smiled at the curious inflection in her voice. Perhaps she was a Tory voter. He wondered what she had in mind. She would no doubt ensure his nursing care was up to the high standard she delivered for all her patients, but he doubted that Harry would receive the choice of menu, the silver service or linen serviette, those little extras that private patients enjoyed.

When Paul was informed that Harry Grimshaw had arrived on the ward, he saw the final patient in the clinic, then had a cup of tea and a chat with the clinic staff, before going to see the 'Very Important Politician'. There was no reason for him to hurry as the nurses required thirty minutes or so to settle a new patient onto the ward.

As he entered the office to pick up Harry Grimshaw's notes, Paul was met by Sister Ashbrook. She was now even more irritated than she had been when Paul had spoken with her on the phone.

'He's arrived without any records at all,' she fumed, 'not even a piece of paper with his name on it. And what's more, he hasn't allowed us to do any part of the admissions procedure.'

'On what grounds, Sister?'

'He says he's busy. He's working with what he chooses to call his secretary.'

'Well, he's going to have to allow me to clerk him in,' Paul said, picking up the blood pressure machine and some foolscap sheets which would later be incorporated into Mr Grimshaw's notes. 'If he doesn't, he won't be on tomorrow's operating list.'

Paul knocked politely on the door, entered the side ward, and found Harry Grimshaw slouched in an armchair, fully dressed, a cigarette dangling from the corner of his mouth. There were already two cigarette butts in a saucer at his elbow, and a generous scattering of ash on the chair and on the floor. Paul knew that Harry Grimshaw had started life as a miner, then become a Trade Union Official before going into politics. He therefore expected he would have a muscular frame, but if that had once been the case, he had now gone to seed. His obese belly hung generously over the top of his low-slung trousers, no doubt the result of too many formal dinners. He had a double chin; his neck lost in rolls of fat. His eyebrows were thick and bushy, and met in an untidy fashion above the bridge of his nose, mirroring the shaggy moustache he wore on his upper lip, except that the latter was nicotine-stained. It was, however, his nose that was his most striking facial feature. Large and red, nasal hair mingling freely with his moustache, its coarse skin was covered in spidery red blood vessels, suggesting a lifetime of alcohol abuse, evidence of long evenings spent in working men's clubs and Westminster bars.

It was immediately apparent why Sister had laid heavy emphasis on the word 'secretary'. The girl sitting on the bed opposite Mr Grimshaw could not have been more than 20 years old. A dyed blonde, she wore a low-cut blouse that revealed a generous cleavage and a mini skirt that was little more than a pelmet. She lounged on the bed, her knees at Harry's eye level, as he relaxed in the armchair.

Paul began to introduce himself, but was immediately interrupted.

'Don't you know who I am?'

Subconsciously, Paul's brain snapped into 'judgement mode'. He had only been in Mr Grimshaw's presence for a few seconds, but already knew this was a person he could never come to like or respect. Over the years, he had found that when meeting someone for the first time, he formed a judgement of them very quickly and once made, this opinion rarely changed.

'Yes,' he said, 'you're Harry Grimshaw; Cabinet Minister with responsibility for Industry and Commerce. Mr Potts rang me to say that you were coming.'

Paul began to explain the need to examine Harry in preparation for his operation, but was interrupted for a second time.

'For Heaven's sake, Doctor, can't you see I'm busy? Come back later.' The voice was brusque and authoritative; clearly, this was a man accustomed to being obeyed promptly and without question.

Neither Mr Grimshaw nor his 'secretary' looked busy. There were no papers, pencils, or notepads to suggest feverish activity, but it was clear that Paul would not be allowed to undertake an examination at this time. Deflated, he muttered an apology and left the room, annoyed that he would need to return to do the job later.

Paul pencilled in Harry Grimshaw's name on the operating list that had already been drafted for the next day, stating Harry would have surgery for an in-growing toenail on one of his big toes. *'Side not known at this time'*, he wrote, not wishing to be criticised for omitting this information. He then busied himself with other tasks, returning to Mr Grimshaw's side ward a couple of hours later. By this time, the nurses had assembled a patient case file, but the only information it contained was Harry's name in capital letters on the front cover. Every sheet in the folder remained blank; Mr Grimshaw had still not allowed the nurses to undertake the admissions process! Sister informed Paul that although the MP's secretary had left, her place had been taken by his wife.

Once again, Paul knocked on the door, this time waiting for an invitation to enter, before turning the handle. The contrast in appearance between Mrs Grimshaw and the secretary could not have been greater. There was however, a distinct similarity between Harry and his wife. Both were short, fat and rather hairy! She was wearing an old woollen cardigan, a tweed skirt, and brogue shoes. As before, Harry insisted that he was not to be disturbed, but this time Paul was more persistent.

'Sir, there are a number of jobs that the nurses and I must perform if you're to be ready for your surgery tomorrow. It's getting late, and we need to get on with them. I need to check you're fit for an anaesthetic. We also need your signature on the *'consent for surgery'* form.'

Once again, Mr Grimshaw's reply was uncompromising. 'Damn it, Doctor; you really shouldn't interrupt at a time like this. Can't you see I have my wife visiting? I'm a busy man. Thanks to my important role in government, we're not able to spend a lot of time together. Surely, if I'm to have a major operation in the morning, I'm entitled to some peace and quiet with my family this evening.'

Paul was sorely tempted to retort that surgery on a toenail could scarcely be described as the most major of operations. He contented himself however, by remarking that for his own safety, certain basic checks needed to be undertaken before his surgery could be performed. Whether the MP believed Paul or not, it made no difference to his decision. He wasn't going to waste time on nurses' paperwork, nor would he submit to a physical examination, and that was the end of the matter. Reluctantly, Paul left the room empty-handed, and for a second time cursed this selfish, egotistical individual.

He rang the anaesthetist to inform him there was a 'special' patient on the list in the morning, but explained that he hadn't been able to make any assessment of his fitness for surgery.

'Then perhaps you could phone me when you've managed to give him the once-over,' the anaesthetist suggested, 'and let me know if there are any problems. If there are, I'll visit early in the morning, and take a look at him. Otherwise, I'll see him when he arrives in theatre. You'd better place him last on the list; then if there are any worries about his chest or heart, he can have an x-ray and an ECG before he comes to theatre.'

'I'm afraid Mr Potts specified he should go first on the list.'

'But that can't be right,' the anaesthetist protested. 'His toenail is infected. We don't want the theatre contaminated by the first case of the day. It isn't fair on the patients who are to follow. It puts them at risk of developing a wound infection.'

'I know that, and obviously Mr Potts knows it as well. But those are my instructions.'

'If that's what the mighty man wants, I guess that's what the mighty man will get,' the anaesthetist replied in a resigned tone, 'but it flies in the face of good surgical practice.'

Harry Grimshaw's intransigence left Paul extremely angry. Junior doctors worked long hours. Their job demanded sacrifices, both of them and of their families. Time off duty was precious, and this evening he should be at home relaxing, not wasting time hanging around the hospital waiting to examine Mr Grimshaw. He rang Kate, his wife, to explain the situation to her.

'Hi Kate, I'm sorry, but I'm going to be late home. Mr Potts has insisted that I have to admit our local MP. I think it would be easier if I ate in the hospital canteen, and came home when I've sorted him out.'

'But Paul, I've already cooked our evening meal. You promised faithfully you wouldn't be late tonight. Please don't let me down again.'

'OK, I'll come home, and we'll eat together. Your cooking beats anything that the hospital has to offer, but I'm afraid I shall have to go back later.'

When he got home, he found Kate in a fractious mood. She demanded to know why Paul had to be the one to admit Mr Grimshaw.

'It's not your job to examine new admissions,' she said. 'The house officer should be doing it.'

'I'm sorry, Kate. You're quite right, but Mr Potts insists that I do it. I think he wants to create a good impression.'

'You really should stand up for yourself, Paul. You could have told him it was your night off; that we were going out and that you weren't available.'

'But we're not going out, are we? In any case, if your consultant specifically instructs you to do something, you don't ask questions, you just get on and do it.' Paul's day had been long and tiring, he still had work to do, and he wasn't in the mood for a lecture.

Later that evening, long after the patients' visitors had left the ward, Paul returned to the MP's side room, passing one of the night nurses coming in the opposite direction. Mr Grimshaw's notes were tucked under her arm. She was grim-faced and looked distressed.

'I'll take the notes,' Paul said, 'if you've finished with them.'

'Yes, I've finished with them, and you're welcome to them – and to him,' she added. 'He's the rudest man I've had to deal with. He'll not be getting my vote, come the next election! I'd rather vote for Screaming Lord Sutch of the Monster Raving Loony Party. Good luck. You'll certainly need it!'

As before, Paul knocked, waited for an invitation to enter, and then again explained why he needed to examine him.

'Look, can we get this over as quickly as possible? I've numerous important telephone calls to make. Incidentally, there isn't a phone in here. You'll have to get me one.'

Paul didn't regard himself as a stubborn man although he accepted that as his mother often said, when the mood took him, he could become somewhat pedantic! Faced with this objectionable man, he felt more than pedantic; he felt possessed of a bloody-minded determination that Mr Harry Grimshaw would be thoroughly examined, whether he liked it or not. He would overcome whatever objections the man raised, even if it took until midnight. It was, after all, in his best interests.

Obtaining details of the infected toenail was straightforward. It had been troublesome for about a year, the in-growing edge digging into his flesh, causing pain when he walked. However, Harry's humour changed when Paul enquired after his general health; had he experienced any symptoms to suggest problems with his heart, such as breathlessness, or pain in the chest when walking? Was he able to sleep flat in bed at night? Did he get any swelling of his ankles?

'Are these damn silly questions really necessary?' the MP demanded to know.

'Yes, Sir, of course, they are. If you're to have an anaesthetic, they're essential. In any case, there's a lot to be said for having a full medical assessment from time to time. If any problems come to light, they can be nipped in the bud.'

Questions about his waterworks and bowels were barely tolerated, but enquiry about his social habits, the number of cigarettes he smoked, and the amount of alcohol he consumed, proved a step too far. Mr Grimshaw's patience was exhausted.

'I've had enough of this bloody silly interrogation. It's time for you to leave,' he shouted.

'But I need to examine your toe, and mark it for the operation tomorrow.'

'Potts examined me, surely that's enough. And it's bloody obvious which toe it is! It's twice the size of the other one; it's as red as a ripe tomato, and bloody painful! Now get out.'

'Did Mr Potts listen to your chest, take your blood pressure or examine your heart?' Paul asked. He knew exactly what the answer would be, but was determined to make the point.

'Of course not,' Harry roared, 'I've come for an operation on this bloody toe, not my chest. Now for God's sake, get out and leave me in peace.'

It was clear that Paul would make no further progress, so reluctantly he left the room. Mr Grimshaw's heart and lungs had not been examined, nor had his toe. Further, formal written consent for surgery had not been obtained.

The night nurse was in the office when Paul returned to record these events in the medical case notes. She looked concerned.

'Paul, I'm worried. I haven't been able to take his blood pressure, or fill in the nursing charts, and he refused point-blank to provide a sample of urine for me to test. I don't know what to write in the nursing notes. He's an important person. Sister's bound to check his records tomorrow. You know what she's like; I'm going to be in trouble if they're incomplete.'

'In his medical file, I'm simply going to state that he wouldn't co-operate. Then I'll list the formalities I've had to omit. I can only suggest you do the same. By the way, is there a socket for the telephone in his side room? He wants one for his personal use.'

'Yes, there is. The phone is supposed to be available for all the patients, but in the circumstances, for the sake of a quiet life, I'll wheel it down and leave it for him.'

'If he were a child that would be regarded as a reward for bad behaviour!' Paul commented, as he replaced the records in the notes trolley.

The nurse smiled. 'Maybe it would, but I regard it simply as a case of taking the line of least resistance. Anyway, if he were a child, I would spank his bottom good and hard!'

'I'm sure you'd enjoy doing that,' Paul commented. 'I suspect he would too, but that really would get you into trouble with Sister!'

Since the night staff were just putting the kettle on, Paul joined them for a hot drink, the first of their long night shift.

Later, Janet Smith, Mr Potts' new house officer arrived, and together with the night nurse, they embarked on the routine evening round to check that the drips were running, and that the patients had sedation available to them should it be needed during the night. Nothing was more irritating for a doctor than to be woken in the night, and have to leave a nice warm bed to prescribe a sleeping pill for a patient especially if, with forethought, the sedation could have been prescribed before the doctor retired.

They were just completing the round when Matron's dark shadow fell across the ward entrance.

'Matron must have heard that we have a distinguished visitor on the ward,' staff nurse whispered. 'We're not usually honoured by one of her visits when we're on night duty, especially as late as this. Thank goodness she didn't arrive twenty minutes ago when we had the kettle on!'

She went to meet Matron who asked to be introduced to Mr Grimshaw, but she was back in double quick time. Paul asked what sort of a reception Matron had received.

'Mr Grimshaw was very short with her,' she said. 'He made it abundantly clear after two minutes that the interview was at an end. But at least he was formal and polite, far more so than he was with me!'

Paul looked at his watch, and was immediately struck by a guilty pang. It was eleven-fifteen. He had stayed on the ward far longer than was necessary. He could have gone home as soon as he'd finished with Mr Grimshaw; Janet could have undertaken the evening ward round on her own. Why on earth hadn't he done so? Kate would be annoyed, and rightly so. He turned to leave then, remembering Mr Potts' instructions, reluctantly told the nurse that if Mr Grimshaw needed attention during the night, he was to be called, rather than the house officer. Then he walked the short distance to their hospital flat to find that Kate was already in bed and fast asleep. He crept in besides her, managing not to disturb her, which was just as well; she was on the early shift in the morning.

Unfortunately, at one in the morning, Paul's slumber was interrupted when the bedside phone rang, not as he would have expected by the ward nurse, but by the senior night sister. She sounded apologetic.

'I'm so sorry to trouble you, Dr Lambert, but I've just been called to see Mr Grimshaw. He says he hasn't been able to sleep, and has requested some night sedation. He's also complaining quite forcibly that his blood pressure tablets haven't been prescribed for him, and that he's missed his evening dose. As you know, the nursing staff can't dispense any drugs without a prescription signed by a doctor. Would you mind coming to the ward to do the necessary paperwork?'

Paul was furious. 'Yes, I do mind, Sister; I mind a great deal!' he replied coldly. 'His medication hasn't been prescribed because he wouldn't let me complete my clinical assessment. Perhaps you would be kind enough to explain to him that in such circumstances, the law does not permit me to prescribe for him. Then you can ask him whether he's now prepared to answer my questions, and let me examine him. If he is, then I will prescribe for him, though you might also tell him that I'm not actually in the hospital at the moment.' Paul was at his pedantic best!

'If you would hold the line, Dr Lambert, I'll go and ask him.'

A few moments later, Sister was back on the phone.

'Mr Grimshaw didn't look particularly pleased; in fact, I'd say he's more in need of his blood pressure tablets now than he was before. But he has agreed.'

'In that case Sister, I'll be with you in five minutes.'

'What was that all about?' a sleepy voice at his side asked.

'It's our local MP behaving intolerably badly, Kate,' Paul replied. 'I've got to go back to the ward to sort him out. You go to sleep. I'll try not to be too long.'

Kate gave him a kiss, and then turned away, and promptly fell back to sleep.

Arriving in the side ward, Paul subjected Mr Grimshaw to a searching interrogation. He obtained and recorded details of all his previous illnesses, and questioned him in detail about his drinking and smoking habits. There was a certain bloody-mindedness in the thoroughness of his assessment, as he gained a satisfying revenge for being disturbed from sleep. It all confirmed that Harry Grimshaw did not lead a healthy lifestyle.

When listening to Harry's chest, Paul found an area where the breath sounds were unusually coarse, suggesting some underlying disease. An x-ray would be needed to discover the nature of the problem, but given that Mr Grimshaw had been a heavy smoker for fifty years; it was likely to be something rather unpleasant.

When examining his abdomen, Paul was sorely tempted to subject the cabinet minister to the ignominy of a rectal examination, but he relented. In truth, it would have been difficult to justify in a man who didn't have any bowel symptoms, and who had simply been admitted with an in-growing toenail! Paul completed the admission procedure by marking the offending toenail with an indelible marker, and obtaining written consent for the operation that was planned for the next day.

By the time he had finished, Mr Grimshaw's face registered unconcealed fury. As Sister had hinted, he was at risk of bursting a blood vessel at any moment. Paul prescribed blood pressure tablets as well as night sedation, but instructed they be withheld until the patient had also allowed the nursing documentation to be completed.

The anaesthetist had asked to be contacted if the examination revealed any problems, but Paul felt unable to disturb him at two in the morning. Instead, he attached a note conspicuously to the front of the patient records warning about the chest problem then, quietly satisfied with the night's work, returned to his bed.

The next morning, the MP was indeed placed first on the theatre list, despite the fact that his toenail was infected. Only essential staff members were allowed into the theatre to witness the operation. Paul heard later that the anaesthetist had declined to administer a general anaesthetic, agreeing that there was a problem in Harry's chest. The operation was therefore performed under local anaesthetic.

Normally, at the end of a theatre session, Mr Potts went to enjoy his lunch with his colleagues in the consultants' dining room. On this occasion though, he went to see Harry Grimshaw, and decided that the MP was fit to go home without delay. However, to everyone's surprise, Harry asked if he could remain in the hospital until five pm. After all the fuss he had made, it was assumed he would wish to escape as quickly as possible.

'My political adviser has arranged for a short press conference to be held on the front steps of the hospital as I leave,' he explained. 'It will be good publicity for the hospital, and it will give me an opportunity to express my thanks to you and your excellent staff. I do hope that will be alright, Mr Potts?'

And a chance for you to have a bit of free publicity in an election year, Mr Potts thought.

The consultant raised an eyebrow in Sister Ashbrook's direction. Sister forced herself to smile sweetly, and despite wishing to give the side ward back to the seriously sick man who had been ejected from it the evening before, she stated that this wouldn't present a problem. Paul completed the necessary paperwork to facilitate the discharge, and prescribed some pain killers for him to take home. He then grabbed a bite to eat, and busied himself with his afternoon's duties, content in the knowledge that his involvement with this disagreeable patient was at an end.

Unfortunately, this optimism was misplaced. At about 4.30 pm, he received a telephone call from Dr Digby, the consultant radiologist.

'Hello, Dr Lambert, I'm sorry to trouble you. I know how busy you junior doctors are, but I have the x-rays of a Mr Harry Grimshaw on the screen in front of me; x-rays that you requested. I take it this is Harry Grimshaw, the politician?'

'Yes, it is, Sir.'

'I thought it must be. On the request card, you suggested there might be a problem on the left side of the chest, and I'm not surprised. There's an ominous shadow at the root of the lung. It doesn't look too good, I'm afraid. I'm sure Mr Potts will want to know about it. Do you happen to know where he is?'

'I think you'll find him in his private consulting room, or if by chance he's finished there, he'll be on his way home.'

'That's fine. I'll try and reach him on the telephone. Mr Grimshaw will need some further investigations as a matter of urgency, but you'd better not mention anything to him until I've spoken to Mr Potts.'

Within a few minutes, Paul was bleeped again. This time it was Mr Potts.

'Lambert,' he said, 'I've had Dr Digby on the phone. I gather he's already spoken to you about Harry Grimshaw's x-ray. I'm afraid I'm tied up at the moment, and not free to come. Ask him to remain in hospital. Tell him I'll come and speak with him in about an hour. It sounds as if we may have to pop a telescope down to see what's going on.'

Paul looked at his watch. It was five minutes before five o'clock. He went straight to the ward only to find that Mr Grimshaw had already left.

'Sister and Matron are escorting him to the main entrance, so he can make his grand departure,' he was told.

Paul raced to the front of the hospital, and discovered that that the press conference had just begun. A well-known BBC reporter was standing, microphone in hand, on the wide flight of steps that led down from the hospital's main entrance. He was linked by wire to his cameraman who was standing a few yards to one side. Mr Grimshaw was stationed on the top step, cunningly positioned such that the reporter was forced to stand one step lower down. To his left, a number of members of staff waited in line, each one step below the next; firstly, one of the nurses from the ward, then Sister, and finally, Matron. Down on the pavement, a chauffeur stood, tall and erect, wearing the traditional black uniform and peaked hat. He was holding the Bentley door open in readiness for the great man's departure. A spotlight held aloft by the cameraman's assistant illuminated the scene.

One might have expected that someone who had simply had a toenail removed, would be able to walk unaided from the hospital in open-toed sandals, with a small sticking plaster covering the wound, but Harry Grimshaw was clearly no ordinary patient! He was using two crutches for support, and his lower limb was impressively swathed in bandages which reached to the level of his knee. Surreptitiously, Paul slipped down the steps, and placed himself in the line between Matron and the chauffeur.

Mr Grimshaw was an impressive orator. He told his television audience how privileged he felt to have received care from the wonderful National Health Service; a service he used whenever he needed medical treatment. He went on to thank the staff for the exceptional care he had received during his stay, and for continuing the excellent work that was the hallmark of all NHS hospitals. He then proceeded to argue that with such an excellent service available, there was no possible justification for private medicine. Why, he asked, should some beds be reserved for the rich? Surely, they should be available to all?

Paul listened to the speech with astonishment. The hypocrisy astounded him. The MP had bypassed the waiting list, coming into hospital at a time of his choosing. He had been placed first on the operating list, been nursed in a side ward, and had benefitted from the personal attention of his consultant. He had enjoyed all the perks of private medicine without it costing him a penny; and all because he was an influential politician! Paul stopped listening. It was clearly a party-political speech, designed for a television audience in an election year. He needed to think what he should say to Mr Grimshaw before he departed.

Eventually, smiling bravely, the MP limped down the steps like a wounded war hero, shaking hands and exchanging pleasantries with each member of staff in turn. Finally, he found himself standing directly in front of Paul.

'I'm surprised to see you here, young man. I hoped I'd seen the last of you last night.' As he spoke, the television smile never left his lips, although there was a cold edge to his voice.

'I know I shouldn't be here, Sir, but I have a message for you from Mr Potts. He wishes to have another word with you before you go home.'

'And what does Potts wish to speak to me about?'

'It's about the chest x-ray that was taken earlier today. There's an abnormality on it.'

The MP's face never flickered; the smile for the camera maintained.

'Do you know what sort of abnormality?'

'Not exactly, Sir, but apparently there's a shadow on the lung, and the radiologist feels some further investigations are required; possibly a look into the lung with a telescope. Mr Potts asked me to catch you before you left. I think he wants you stay in the hospital for a few more days to have the tests arranged.'

There was a slight pause as Harry Grimshaw's nimble brain digested this information, and considered his options.

'Is there a back entrance to the hospital, and if so, how do we reach it?' he asked.

'Yes, there is. The service entrance is round the back. You simply keep turning left, going round the block, until you get there.'

'Meet me there in two minutes.'

The conversation was at an end.

Still smiling, still looking relaxed, though the implications of a *'shadow on the lung'* in a lifelong smoker must have been known to him, he gave one last cheerful wave for the camera, and hobbled to the car. The chauffeur assisted him into the back seat, relieved him of his crutches, and then walked round to the driver's door, before easing the car into the rush hour traffic. It had been an impressive display of quick thinking, combined with a faultless acting performance.

There was a striking contrast between the MP's departure from the front of the hospital, and his return a few moments later to the service area at the rear. The limousine looked incongruous in the hospital's backyard, parked alongside the vans and lorries that were delivering food and medical supplies, and removing rubbish. Mr Grimshaw similarly looked out of place amongst the porters, deliverymen, and refuse collectors who stared at him in surprise. The brief journey to the hospital's back entrance also resulted in a significant change in the politician's demeanour. As Paul escorted him back to the ward through the service corridors normally unseen by hospital patients, a stern face and a stony silence replaced the smile and pleasantries. Paul left him in the side ward that he had so recently vacated. He received neither recognition, nor thanks for identifying the MP's significant health problem, simply a stern, 'tell Potts that I don't expect to be kept waiting.'

Mr Potts duly saw Harry Grimshaw within the hour. Paul was not a party to the discussion that followed, but by the time the night staff came on duty, the side ward was once again occupied by the elderly gentleman who needed specialist nursing care. Mr Grimshaw had been transferred to the private wing of the hospital for his further investigations.

A week later, Paul saw an announcement in the newspapers to the effect that Mr Harry Grimshaw had resigned from the cabinet on the grounds of ill health. The same papers recorded his obituary precisely three months later; the MP had died after *'a short illness bravely born'.*

Thoughts for the day

'Death the Leveller'

Poem by James Shirley 1596 – 1666

The glories of our blood and state
Are shadows, not substantial things;
There is no armour against fate;
Death lays its icy hand on kings:
Sceptre and Crown
Must tumble down,
And in the dust be equal made
With the crooked scythe and spade.

The conduct of public affairs for private advantage. A strife of interests masquerading as a contest of principles.

Ambrose Bierce   1842 - 1914

Chapter 20   Queenie

3rd October 1970

Sir William was wearing a comfortable, loose-fitting sports jacket and a pair of old corduroy trousers, and was at the wheel of his dirty and dilapidated Morris Oxford motor car. It had rusting bodywork, worn tyres and defective lights. Sleeping on the back seat of the car on an old, malodorous, tartan rug, oblivious to the crashing gears and kangaroo hops caused by Sir William's erratic driving, was an equally old and malodorous, golden Labrador with greying whiskers. Paul was sitting apprehensively in the front passenger seat. At the request of one of the local GPs, they were on their way to see a lady who lived in a gypsy encampment.

'Seeing patients in their own homes is both fascinating and instructive, Lambert,' Sir William said, 'and I think you'll find this trip particularly interesting. Have you been in a gypsy caravan before?'

Paul confessed that he hadn't.

'The gypsies are a tight-knit community. Generally, they don't welcome strangers, but Kieran O'Connor, he's one of our local GP's, has their confidence. He's arranged to accompany us. Otherwise, I doubt we would be allowed on to their site.'

The gypsy encampment was enclosed by a canal and a railway shunting yard on one side, and on the other, by two huge, red brick mills whose chimneys stretched high into the grey sky. The mills, now deserted and decaying, had fallen victim to the lower wages paid in the Far East. Dr O'Connor was waiting for them at the site entrance. Fat, bearded, unkempt and wearing a dirty, old overcoat and a battered trilby hat, his square face was pock-marked by the ravages of teenage acne. He might easily have passed for a gypsy himself, but for the old leather Gladstone medical bag he was holding. He greeted Sir William warmly.

'Why, hello, Bill. It's a real pleasure to see you again,' he said, taking the consultant's hand and shaking it vigorously, 'and who might this fine-looking, young man be that you've brought with you today?'

'This is Paul Lambert, my Registrar.'

'And a top of the morning to you too,' Dr O'Connor said. 'My old friend, Bill, is showing you the ropes, is he? Well, I hope the old rogue is treating you well. If he isn't, just let me know, and I'll tell you a few stories of the things he and I got up to when we were students together.' He laughed. 'Well, come along then, I've a fascinating case for you to see.'

A tall, burly-looking man, of about Paul's age, strode to meet them, wearing little more than a string vest and faded jeans. He was swarthy and heavily tattooed, his dark matted hair tied into a ponytail. His misshapen nose and scarred forehead suggested he was familiar with the rougher side of life. Two Alsatian dogs snapped at his heels, snarling and baring their teeth at the visitors.

'They won't harm you whilst you're with me,' the man assured them, 'but you'd better leave that Lab of yours in the car,' he added. 'These two haven't been fed for a day or two. They make better guard dogs if we keep them hungry.'

'Hello again, Mick,' Dr O'Connor said, 'let me introduce you to Sir William Warrender. Without doubt, he's one of the finest surgeons in the land.'

Mick led the way across the site, the doctors followed, very conscious of the two Alsatian dogs circling their ankles looking eager to break their fast. Groups of children, all dirty and undernourished, stopped their games, and observed them with wary, watchful eyes as they passed.

If Paul had been expecting a traditionally-painted, wooden, horse-drawn caravan, he was to be disappointed. Mick's van was a huge metal affair covered with brightly polished chrome strips. A large and apparently new Mercedes saloon stood alongside. The caravan proved to be remarkably spacious, and was equipped with a fridge, television, and brightly coloured curtains and furniture. Numerous Toby jugs and equine brass fittings were displayed on the many shelves. Mick's mother was resting in a large double bed that occupied one end of the van. If the surroundings did not look typically Romany, she certainly did. Wearing a multi-coloured, woollen shawl around her shoulders and with large rings in her ears, she had long, black hair, dark eyes and the same dusky complexion as her son. Assessing her through medical eyes, Paul noticed that she looked drawn, and appeared to be in some discomfort. She was dehydrated and the whites of her eyes were discoloured; he was in no doubt that she had jaundice.

'Hello again, Queenie,' Dr O'Connor said. 'Still in pain, I see. Don't you worry; I've brought along an expert to sort you out.'

He introduced Sir William and Paul, adding, 'For once, Queenie's potions and gypsy charms seem to have let her down.'

Queenie's story was of slight lack of appetite, considerable loss of weight, and in the last few weeks, she had become jaundiced. When Sir William came to examine her, he found a hard swelling in her upper abdomen. His assessment complete, he stood back and addressed his patient.

'I understand that you're not keen to come into hospital, Queenie, but I think that you're going to need a spot of surgery if we're to sort you out.'

Queenie looked doubtful. 'I don't like them places,' she said. 'Would I be in for long, d'you reckon?'

'Until we've made you better,' Sir William replied, unwilling to commit himself at this early stage; 'probably the best part of a fortnight.'

'Is it the big C, Doctor? I want you to tell me if it is. Better knowing than wondering, I always say.'

Sir William was not afraid to meet Queenie's gaze. 'That's certainly a possibility, but we shan't know until we've run a few tests; and it's probably going to mean an operation.'

Queenie's eyes turned to her son, looking for guidance.

'It's for the best, Mammy,' he said, 'and I'll make damn sure they treat you right,' he added grimly, with a sideways glance at Paul, who felt somewhat threatened by the remark.

'Okay, that's settled then,' Sir William concluded. 'Mick, bring your mother in first thing on Monday morning.'

'Well, what did you make of that?' Sir William asked Paul on the journey back to the hospital.

'Must be a tumour in the pancreas, Sir, blocking the flow of bile to the gut, though I suppose it's just possible that her jaundice might be due to gall stones.'

'Agreed,' the consultant replied, 'and I'm sure it will come to an operation. I don't think her general health is too good, though. When she's admitted, I'd like you to go over her thoroughly, particularly to check that her heart and lungs will stand up to a major operation.'

****

'Hello,' Staff Nurse Kate Meredith said. 'Welcome to the ward. In a moment, I'll show you round, but first I need to ask you a few routine questions. I see your Christian name is Rose; are you happy if we call you Rose, or do you prefer Mrs O'Hannagan?'

''Tis a long time since anyone called me Rose, and no-one's ever thought me posh enough to be called Missus. I've always been known as Queenie,' the new patient said with a smile. 'It would sound right queer to be called something else. You'd best call me Queenie.'

'Now, your date of birth, Queenie?'

'You know, I'm truly not sure, dearie. I have my birthday in October, on the 18th, but whether I'm 53 or 54, I don't rightly know. You see, I don't have a birth certificate. There may have been one once, but if there was, it was lost long ago.'

'And I see that you've been widowed.'

'Yes, my Pat had an accident. It happened long ago.'

'I'm sorry to hear that,' Kate murmured.

'Not to worry, I manage very well without him,' Queenie responded, surprisingly cheerfully. 'If you can find yourself a good man, Nurse, you hang on to him, but if he's nothing but trouble like my Pat, it's no bad thing if he's stupid enough to get himself killed in a fight.'

'Who should I put down as your next of kin?'

Queenie thought for a moment before answering. 'I suppose you'd better put down Mick. He's my eldest.'

'Do you have other children?'

'Yes, my daughter, Young Rose, and then there's my youngest, Brendan, though I don't see much of him; I'm afraid we had a falling out.'

Kate completed the admissions process by undertaking some routine observations. She found that Queenie's blood pressure was raised, and that there was sugar in her urine, suggesting she might be diabetic. She also noticed how short of breath she became when she walked down the ward to be shown the day room and toilet facilities. Sir William was obviously right to be concerned that Queenie's general health would need to be improved before she would be fit enough to face an anaesthetic.

'Are you normally as breathless as this when you walk?' Kate asked, after she had suggested that the doctors would want to do some tests before they considered an operation.

'Yes, I am. I was consumptive as a child. I've had a bad chest ever since.'

'Well, I'll leave you now to make friends with the other patients. The doctors will be round later to examine you.'

Then the smile on Queenie's face melted away. 'Before you go, Nurse, would you be knowing what they think I've got? I'm sure that old doctor who came to see me believes it's something nasty. He had such a long face on him when he said I had to come in, and he didn't put me on a waiting list; he gave me the date there and then. Surely that's a bad sign. I'm sure it must be cancer.'

'I'm afraid I don't know what Sir William thinks is the matter with you.' Kate explained gently. 'But he's ever so nice, and he always explains to his patients what's going on.'

Queenie glanced at Kate's name badge then looked her straight in the eye. 'Kate,' she said, 'I want you to make me a promise that you'll always be honest with me – and I mean completely honest; no half-truths, no little white lies to make me feel better. Will you do that? Will you make me that promise?'

Kate looked at Queenie's earnest expression, then paused. 'If that's what you really want, yes, I promise,' she said.

Queenie quickly established herself as a firm favourite on the ward. Permanently cheerful, she chatted freely with the other patients, exchanging banter with the nurses and amusing them by giving nicknames to all the doctors. Sir William was 'The Professor', and Mr Potts became 'Old Grumpy'. Apparently, she had a nickname for Paul as well; though Kate wouldn't tell him what it was, saying it would only make him big-headed. Queenie even started reading the palms of the nursing and ancillary staff, but Sister Rutherford stopped her from forecasting the future of the patients. A patient's prognosis was surely the responsibility of the doctors, she insisted.

Queenie's surgery was deferred whilst her sugar levels were brought under control, but unfortunately there was then a further delay. A shadow was found on her chest x-ray, and her operation was again postponed until it became clear that the shadow was no more than a scar from the tuberculosis she had as a child. All the while, Queenie's jaundice became more obvious, an ominous development.

Queenie sought another quiet word with Kate.

'The doctors do think I've got cancer, don't they?'

Kate, conscious of the promise she had made, was obliged to confirm that this was indeed considered to be the most likely diagnosis.

'Then why would they be wanting to operate on me?'

'Because they need to be certain. You see, there are many different causes of jaundice. It might be due to gall stones; that can produce a similar picture. And even if the problem is cancer, the surgeons can by-pass the blockage, and that will get rid of your jaundice.'

'Sweet Mother Mary, I wish they'd get on with it. I'm looking more like a Belisha beacon every day! Sure, if it goes on much longer, they won't be needing electric lights here at night; they'll just stand me in the middle of the ward!'

She reached out and took hold of Kate's hand. She spoke quietly and earnestly.

'Kate, if I haven't got much time left, there's something I need to do before I go; something I have to put right unless I'm to die with a terrible guilty conscience.

You see, many years ago, when my Pat was alive; there was a dreadful rift in our family. Mick and his younger brother, Brendan, had a terrible row. We were in the London area at the time, selling pegs, working the local fairs, scratching a living as best we could. Brendan fell for a girl. Head over heels he went, and I wasn't surprised, a right pretty little thing she was. But she wasn't our type. She came from a posh family; you know well-to-do people. Her dad was a banker or some such sort; worked in the city he did, and drove a flashy car, but worse than that, they were Protestant. Brendan said he was going to marry her. Mick and Pat were furious, and I spoke against it as well. I was sure it wouldn't last; as different as chalk and cheese they were. She'd been brought up to be a young lady, not the sort to roll her sleeves up and get her hands dirty; she was never going to adapt to the gypsy way of life. And Brendan was a free spirit, a wild fox he was, far too young and restless to be tamed and trapped within four walls like a rabbit in a hutch.

Then the girl fell pregnant, and her family insisted that they got married before it showed too much, though I'm sure they disapproved of the match as much as we did. So Brendan walked out on us. He bought a suit and a tie, and started to work as a clerk in an office. It all ended in pain and tears, of course, as I knew it would. They came from different worlds, and they broke up soon after the baby was born, a little boy it was too. I haven't seen Brendan from that day to this, though I know he does sometimes keep in touch with our Rose.'

There were tears in her eyes as she continued. 'Kate, I have to make my peace with him before I go. I need to apologise. Even though I knew it wouldn't last, I was wrong to criticise. He was my son, he was a grown man, I should have given him a mother's love and support, and I didn't. To be sure, 'tis a burden I've carried in my heart ever since.'

She handed Kate an envelope. 'I want you to post this to him. I need his forgiveness before I go, and I'll pray that he doesn't turn me down. Oh, and Kate,' she added, 'it would be best if Mick didn't get to hear of this. He wouldn't be best pleased.'

At 8 pm, Kate rang the hand bell to indicate that the time had come for the visitors to leave. As the chairs were tidied away, and goodbyes were being said, Kate was approached by a woman whom she thought must be Young Rose, Queenie's daughter. She had the same long, black hair, dark eyes, high cheekbones and dusky complexion. At her side was a rough-looking character whom Kate assumed was Mick, the older of Queenie's two sons.

'May we have a word with you please, Nurse,' Rose began.

Kate led them to the office and offered them a seat.

'What can you tell us about our Mam?'

'She's got jaundice as you can see, but at the moment we can't be certain what's causing it. It seems likely that it will take an exploratory operation to get to the root of the problem, and to do something about it.'

Mick butted in. 'Is she going to die?' he demanded bluntly. 'It's important that we know if she is.'

Alarm bells began to ring in Kate's head. She didn't know the reason behind the question, but she had her suspicions. She went on the defensive.

'Gracious, what a question! I suppose we're all going to die sometime. Why do you ask?'

There was a pause. 'We're just concerned that's all,' he replied sheepishly, but Kate recognised it as a lie.

Then Mick spoke again, this time forcibly. 'Look, Nurse, our Mam's just let slip that she's sent a letter to our Brendan, though only the Devil knows why after the way he's treated her. It's possible that he might try to visit. If he does, he's not to be allowed to go anywhere near her. And he's not to be given any information on her either. Is that clear?'

Kate was taken aback by Mick's glaring eyes, fierce expression, and by the ferocity of the words. 'Look,' she stammered, 'we can't control who visits. It's up to the patient, up to your mother who she sees.'

Mick's fist crashed onto the desk. 'Now you listen to me,' he shouted, his face only inches from Kate's, 'if you know what's good for....'

But Rose restrained him before he could issue his threat. 'Holy Mother Mary,' she cried, 'd'you want half the world to hear you, Mick?'

She turned to Kate. 'It's just that her youngest, Brendan is a nasty piece of work. He's no good for our Mam. He's caused her no end of grief over the years. He'll only upset her and make her condition worse. When you find out what's the matter with her, it would be best if you only spoke to Mick or me about her. You can do that for us, can't you, Nurse?'

Kate's formal training came to her rescue as she remembered the hospital's official policy. 'When it comes to a question of confidential medical information,' she said, 'every patient has a right to privacy. The doctors and nurses are only allowed to divulge personal medical details if the patient has given them permission to do so.'

'But, Nurse,' Rose whined, 'in the circumstances, surely you can....'

'No,' Kate said firmly, 'Your mother will be the one who decides whom she sees, and what they are told. Is that clear?'

Soon after the couple had left, disgruntled that they hadn't got their way, Kate went to see Queenie. She related the gist of her conversation with Rose and Mick.

Queenie crossed herself. 'Jesus give me strength. Will my family ever learn to live in peace?' She sighed. 'I'm sorry they pestered you like that, but I'm pleased you didn't discuss my condition with them. When I've had my operation, I want to be the one who's told what's causing this wretched jaundice, and how long I've got. Then I'll be the one to tell them what I think they need to know. That's fair isn't it?'

'Quite fair,' Kate agreed.

'Is that a promise then?'

Kate drew a finger across her heart and smiled.

'Certainly, it is.'

'Money's a terrible thing, you know, Kate. I wish we could live without it, but I suppose we can't.' She thought for a moment. 'You know, I think I'm going to have to write something down, or they'll be fighting while I'm lying in my coffin. But I wouldn't know how to go about it.'

'Then you'll need to write a will,' Kate replied, 'and if your family are likely to fight over it, perhaps it would be best to get a solicitor to advise you, so you can be sure it's watertight.'

'Can you arrange that for me?'

This was a question Kate hadn't met before. 'I'm not sure, but I can make some enquiries if you'd like.'

The whole episode left Kate much disturbed. Mick had frightened her with his aggressive attitude and threatening behaviour. She didn't like to think that Queenie had to contend with such difficult family problems as well as having what was almost certainly an incurable cancer of the pancreas. Kate knew she had suffered a hard life; she admired her spirit, and was coming to regard her as a friend. But again, she remembered her training; *'Nurses mustn't get emotionally involved with their patients,'* she had been taught, *'to be professional, they have to remain detached.'*

Paul performed Queenie's operation whilst Sir William was away on leave, but to everyone's surprise and delight, he discovered that her jaundice was not due to an incurable tumour, but to gall stones which Paul was able to remove without any great difficulty.

The nurses were overjoyed when Queenie was returned safely to the ward a couple of hours later. During the time she had been a patient, she had become a firm favourite, and the news that her condition had been curable delighted them. She still had to recover from her surgery, of course, but there was now the prospect that she would be restored to health, and be able to return to her old lifestyle.

By the following afternoon, Queenie had recovered from her anaesthetic, though she remained heavily sedated in the side room she had been allocated after her operation. Kate offered her a sip of water to moisten her lips, which she gratefully accepted.

'Thanks, Nurse,' she said. 'I needed that. My mouth was as dry as old leather.'

Kate turned and looked up as she heard the door being opened. Mike and Young Rose had arrived to visit.

'You have visitors,' Kate whispered as the pair approached, but as she glanced at her patient, she noticed that Queenie's eyes were now closed.

You're feigning, she thought. *You sly old thing; you don't want any hassle, do you?*

'How is she?' Rose asked, concern obvious in her voice.

'I'm pleased to say, she's doing fine,' Kate replied.

'It was cancer, wasn't it? How long has she got?' Mike demanded to know.

'I'm afraid we haven't had a chance to talk to your mother about her operation yet.'

'But you can tell us, we're family.'

'I'm sorry, but I'm afraid that I can't. You see, before she went to the theatre, we discussed with her who should, and who should not, be given medical information. Your mother decided it would be best if she were told first.'

'Jesus Christ, Nurse,' Mike exploded, 'I'm her son; I live with her. I've got a right to know!'

'I'm sorry, but your mother was quite definite. She expressly stated that we were not to give any medical information either to you, or to anyone else. No doubt, in due course, she will tell you herself, but in the meantime, we will keep our promise to your mother.'

Although Kate had spoken slowly and firmly, her heart quickened when she saw Mick's reaction. His face reddened and his fists clenched. He strode towards Kate until he could have reached out and touched her. He glared down at her. 'Now you look here, Nurse, you tell me straight what that surgeon found. I've not come here today to....'

Then he stopped, and looked past her as the door to the room opened again. It was Brendan. Like his older brother, he too was a big man, broad across the shoulders with the same dark features, but whereas Mick was wearing faded jeans with a loose-fitting jacket thrown over his vest, Brendan wore a smart grey suit, a collared shirt and tie, and polished black leather shoes.

'What the fuck!' Mick exclaimed. 'Just look what the cat's dragged in. You get the hell out of here.'

But Brendan continued to advance towards them, walking slowly, palms raised in a gesture of reconciliation. 'Hello Mick, hello Young Rose,' he said, now with his right arm extended offering a handshake. 'No hard feelings. Surely with our Mum so ill, this is a time to put old differences to one side.' The words were spoken quietly, the voice cultured, all trace of an Irish accent gone.

'I might have known Bren that you'd turn up when our Mam's on her death bed.' Mick snarled. 'Got the sniff of money, did you? Well, you won't be getting a penny, I'll see to that. Now fuck off, or I'll beat you with my bare fists, just as I did when you decided you were too good for the likes of us. Me and Rose will look after her 'til she's gone.'

'I came because Mum wrote asking me to come; she wanted to see me,' Brendan replied, speaking quietly. 'She thinks it's time we made up, and so do I. It's nothing to do with inheritance.'

As the brothers faced each other, hatred burning in Mick's eyes, Rose intervened, speaking scornfully to Brendan.

'Just look at you standing there, all smug and righteous, with your fancy clothes and posh talk. You burned your boats when you took up with that fancy-talking Proddy tart. Mammy made it quite clear that she wanted nothing to do with you, so piss off and leave Mam alone. We'll be the ones to sort out her affairs.'

Kate, certain that Queenie was not only awake, but aware of what was being said, intervened sternly. 'This is neither the time nor the place to have such a conversation,' she said. 'You should all leave, and if you must have an argument, have it elsewhere.'

For a moment there was silence, and then Brendan spoke. 'You're quite right, Nurse. I'll go and wait outside. I'll pop back later when Mum is on her own.'

Kate looked at Queenie, whose eyes remained firmly closed. She turned to Mick and Rose. 'Your mother needs to rest, so I think it would be best if you left as well.'

Alone once more with her patient, Kate took hold of Queenie's hand. 'They've all gone now, Queenie,' she said softly. 'You are awake, aren't you?'

Slowly, Queenie opened her eyes, which were moist with tears.

'Yes, Nurse, I am. You told them, didn't you? You broke your promise.'

Even though the words were slurred, the accusatory tone of her voice was unmistakable.

Kate was puzzled, not understanding what she had done wrong. 'Told them what?' she asked.

'Told them that I had cancer and was dying.'

'Queenie, I told them no such thing. They're jumping to conclusions. And what's more, they've jumped to completely the wrong conclusion. The doctors were expecting to find cancer, but they didn't. The jaundice was due to a big gall stone. There was no cancer at all. There's no reason why you shouldn't make a full recovery. Everyone's delighted for you. We've saved the stone for you to have as a keepsake. It's in your locker if you want to see it.'

'Well, what do you know? May the Saints be praised,' Queenie said. 'And there was I, busy tying up the loose ends of my life. Now tell me; that was Brendan come to see me, wasn't it? I didn't dream that, did I?'

'Yes, it was. That's what you wanted, wasn't it?' Kate suggested.

Queenie had closed her eyes, but the contented expression on her face told Kate all that she needed to know.

****

Paul dashed to the phone as his pager's shrill call sounded in emergency mode.

'Cardiac arrest, Surgical Five female ward,' the switchboard operator said.

Arriving at the ward doors, his heart thumping, he looked in vain for the screened bed, which normally shielded the collapsed patient from curious eyes, as the nurses commenced resuscitation.

'In the toilets, Doctor,' one of the nurses said breathlessly, as she dashed passed him on her way to get the emergency trolley.

As Paul ran down the length of the ward, he noticed that Queenie's bed was empty. His worst fears were soon confirmed. Queenie was lying face down, half in and half out of one of the toilet cubicles. Sister was there with two of her nurses. They were desperately trying to drag her into the open where they could start resuscitation. The cubicle door was ajar, and Queenie was wedged, face down, knickers round her ankles, with her legs either side of the toilet bowl, and her arms lodged behind the cubicle door. She appeared to have fallen forward from the toilet seat. Paul had to climb over her, and pull her back into the cubicle to free her arms before it was possible to drag her into the more spacious washroom. He noticed that one of her legs was swollen. It was almost twice the size of its neighbour. Queenie was ominously still, her face and hands dark blue. There was a deep cut on her forehead. She wasn't breathing, and Paul quickly established that there was no pulse.

Within seconds, the duty anaesthetist arrived, quickly followed by the nurse with the resuscitation trolley. Cardiac massage was started. A tube was passed into her windpipe, and oxygen forced into her lungs. The anaesthetist then checked her pupils, and found both to be fully dilated. They failed to react when challenged by a bright light. He caught Paul's eye and grimaced. Paul understood his unspoken words. It was almost certainly too late for successful resuscitation.

'I'm afraid that things don't look good,' Paul commented, knowing that as well as doing the right thing for Queenie, he had to manage the feelings and expectations of the nurses who were present, some of whom were quite junior, and very fond of their patient. 'Perhaps someone would fetch an ophthalmoscope so that I can look into her eyes. However, we must continue with cardiac massage until we're sure.'

The swelling of her leg had not been present when he had examined Queenie earlier in the day. The implication was that a blood clot had formed in the veins in her leg, and then broken free and floated in the bloodstream up to her chest where it had completely blocked the circulation in her lungs. At this time, such an event, known as a pulmonary embolus, was both unpredictable and unpreventable.

Two minutes later, Paul's examination confirmed that the blood in the vessels of the eyes had clotted indicating that Queenie had indeed passed away. He turned to the anaesthetist. 'Can I just ask you to confirm?' he asked, not because he was unsure of his diagnosis, but for the benefit of the nurses. He wanted them to realise that no stone had been left unturned.

'Sadly, you're right,' the anaesthetist said a moment or two later. 'I'm afraid there's no point in carrying on. There is nothing more that we can usefully do.'

Gently he withdrew the tube form Queenie's throat, and then laid a hand on the arm of the nurse who was continuing the cardiac compression.

****

'Mr Lambert, an outside call for you.' It was Dave on the hospital switchboard. Paul groaned, irritated that someone was interrupting him in the middle of Mr Potts' outpatient clinic. Friends and family knew not to call during the day unless it was urgent, and staff members who needed to speak with him came through on the internal phone.

'Hello, Paul Lambert speaking,' he said, his tone abrupt.

'Good afternoon, Dr Lambert. This is the Coroner's Officer speaking. I have Mr Frobisher, the Coroner, for you. I'll put you through.'

Paul's heart skipped a beat. What on earth did the Coroner wish to speak with him about?

'Ah, Dr Lambert, I hope I haven't called you at an inopportune moment, but I need to speak with you about one of your patients, a Mrs Rose O'Hannagan. You will recall you reported her death to me a week or so ago.' Mr Frobisher's voice was cultured, clear, and precise. Paul presumed that he was a lawyer rather than a doctor. What was the correct way to address a Coroner, he wondered?

'Yes, Sir,' he said, opting for safety and respect, 'I remember her well. She was with us on the ward for some time. I presume you've received the report I wrote for you?'

'Yes, I have, thank you, and I also have reports written by your consultant, Sir William and by Dr Higgs who performed the autopsy. He confirmed that the cause of death was a pulmonary embolus, as you suspected. It seems that a blood clot formed in one of her legs then floated free to block the blood flow through her lungs. It all seemed to be very straightforward, but now a complication has arisen, which obliges me to hold a formal inquest into the death. You see, I've received a letter from a member of the family. He's alleging malpractice, and specifically, it is certain aspects of your involvement that concern him.'

Paul was stunned. What on earth had he done that the family could possibly complain about? The operation had gone smoothly, there had been no complications attributable to it, and her death was essentially an act of God; something which regrettably happened from time to time, an event that was unforeseeable and, if major, as Queenie's undoubtedly had been, untreatable and fatal. He tried to think what aspect of her treatment the family might be concerned about, but his mind was numb.

'Hello, Mr Lambert, are you still there?'

'Yes, Sir, I am. May I ask which member of the family has complained?'

'It's the son, the one who's a solicitor in the South of England.'

Oh my God, a solicitor; that makes it worse, thought Paul. 'That would be Brendan, the younger son. I didn't know he was legally trained,' he said. 'Does he say what he's concerned about?'

'No,' the Coroner replied. 'That's one of the reasons I wanted to speak with you. I wondered whether you could shed any light on the matter, and if you can, whether perhaps you feel the need to write a supplementary report.'

'Sir, it was very unfortunate that the patient should collapse and die like that, but I can think of nothing that could be the reason for a malpractice complaint. The only contentious issue that arose was that Queenie, that's Mrs O'Hannagan, asked that she be the one to give news of her medical condition to the family. She made us promise not to speak with them about her condition.'

'Fair enough. Well, we'll leave it there, but should you think of anything, do let me know. My staff will be in touch when the date of the inquest is agreed.'

As Paul put the phone down, he was visibly shaken. 'Are you all right?' the clinic nurse asked as she came to see what had delayed him so long.

'Yes, thanks,' he muttered, as he returned to the patient whom he had abandoned mid-consultation.

For the rest of the day, Paul couldn't settle. He wracked his brains, trying to think of any justification for criticism, but could think of nothing.

Then his mood changed from one of anxiety and concern, to one of anger. Damn it, he worked long hours, and he did a responsible job to the very best of his ability. He was always putting his patients first, and now he was being hauled up in court for no reason. As a man with a conscience, he would suffer sleepless nights worrying about it.

For days, Paul silently fretted, keeping his anxiety to himself, but then he remembered Queenie had confided in Kate.

'I suspect there's more to this than meets the eye,' Kate added when he discussed his concerns with her. 'It will be to do with money, with their inheritance. Queenie said as much to me.

Mick is the eldest of her three children, but Queenie, when she thought she was dying, wanted to make up with Brendan. She'd decided to write a will, but if you remember, she died before she had time to write one. That leaves Mick, as her next of kin. There was no love lost between the two sons; Mick hated Brendan. Maybe Mick will inherit and Brendan will miss out. Perhaps that's why he's upset.'

Paul considered Kate's theory. 'You're probably right, Kate. When Sir William took me to the gypsy camp, he did comment that theirs was a rich family. The caravan was enormous, and had all mod cons. It wasn't the old wooden van that you see on picture postcards, and there was a very expensive car outside. But how does having a go at me improve his chance s of inheriting.'

'I'm not sure Paul, but I bet that's at the bottom of it.'

****

Since Sir William had also been called as a witness to the inquest, he suggested that he drive Paul to the Coroner's Court. Sensing Paul's anxiety, the consultant sought to put him at his ease.

'I understand that this is the first time you've given evidence at an inquest,' Sir William commented, 'but there's no need for you to be concerned. I've appeared before several Coroners in my time, but old Mr Frobisher is the best by far. Maybe he's a bit old-fashioned, but he does things strictly by the book, and he's always scrupulously fair. Furthermore, he accepts that medicine is not an exact science, and that outcomes aren't always predictable. He also believes that, in general, doctors and nurses are caring people who do a difficult job, and he supports them whenever he can.'

As they entered the courtroom, Paul was surprised to see how few people were present. He recognised Mick and Young Rose sitting on the public benches. Apart from them, only two other people were present, the first, wearing a crumpled suit, and holding a pen and notepad in his hand, was a slightly-built man barely out of his teens, still sporting his adolescent acne, whom Paul presumed was the reporter for the local newspaper. He looked and felt bored, unhappy to be required to sit every week in the Coroner's Court where nothing ever happened to allow him to demonstrate his literary ability. How he longed to attend the inquest involving a major rail disaster, a juicy murder, or perhaps the death of a local celebrity in embarrassing circumstances. Mind you, he thought, if such a case arose, no doubt the senior reporter would be told to attend.

The only other person in the public area was smartly dressed in a city suit, shirt, and tie; it was Brendan O'Hannagan, his accuser. For a second, their eyes met. Although Paul quickly turned away, he continued to feel Brendan's gaze burning on his face.

If Paul expected the Coroner to be wearing a wig and gown, he was to be disappointed. Mr Frobisher was casually dressed; Paul gauged him to be aged about sixty. He had bushy eyebrows, and a mop of unruly white hair. In his introductory remarks, he stated that the purpose of the inquest was to investigate the circumstances surrounding the sad demise of Mrs Rose O'Hannagan. He emphasised this was not a criminal court, the proceedings were not adversarial, and therefore there was no requirement for the witnesses to be represented by lawyers.

Dr Higgs, the pathologist who had conducted the autopsy, was then sworn in, and invited to read his report to the court. Since Paul had been present at the post-mortem, Dr Higgs' evidence yielded no surprises.

When he had finished, Mr Frobisher asked whether a pulmonary embolus was accepted to be a random and unpredictable event.

'Yes, it is,' Dr Higgs replied.

'And can anything be done to prevent it from happening?' the Coroner wanted to know.

'Sadly, no,' came the reply. 'It's something that can happen to the very best surgeons in the finest hospitals in the land.'

'When you were performing your post-mortem, I take it you examined the area from which the gall stone had been removed. Were you able to make any assessment of the adequacy of the surgery that had been performed?'

'The operation site was free of infection, the tissues were healing satisfactorily, and the surgery seemed to have been performed in a skilful and competent fashion.'

The words were like manna from heaven to Paul. Surely Dr Higgs' testimony put him beyond reproach.

The report that Sir William then read to the court was detailed and delivered, as Paul would have expected, in a clear and confident fashion. Again, his evidence held no surprises for Paul who, in preparation for this moment, had relived every minute of his involvement with Queenie.

'Sir William,' Mr Frobisher asked, 'I understand you were on leave when Mrs O'Hannagan's operation was undertaken. Did you ask Mr Lambert to perform it in your absence?'

'I did.'

'And, in doing so, did you feel that the procedure was within his competence.'

Sir William frowned a little. 'Of course, I did, Sir, otherwise I would not have asked him to undertake it.'

Paul knew that it was his turn next, and that within the next few minutes, he would find out exactly what aspect of his care Brendan O'Hannagan considered to be negligent.

Paul was sworn in, and was expecting to be asked to read the report that he had prepared.

'Mr Lambert,' the Coroner began. We have heard Sir William's account of the care that Mrs O'Hannagan received prior to her operation, and we have Dr Higgs report that the surgery that you performed was more than satisfactory. Rather than ask you to read the whole of your report, may I ask you simply to tell us about her care from the day of her surgery to the day of her death?'

'Essentially, she was making a completely unremarkable recovery, Sir. We were very pleased with her progress.'

'Was there anything, anything at all, to suggest that she might be at risk of having a blood clot in her leg which could float to her lungs, and cause such a catastrophe?'

'Nothing at all, Sir. The notes record that her legs were examined on the morning of her death, and there was no sign of swelling or thrombosis at that time.'

'Thank you, Mr Lambert. Now I understand that there are members of the family who wish to clarify some aspects of their mother's care, and this is their opportunity to do so.'

Brendan raised his hand.

'Perhaps I could ask you to stand, and identify yourself before you put your question,' Mr Frobisher said.

'Of course. I am Brendan O'Hannagan, son of the deceased. I should like to ask Mr Lambert if he is aware that it is not just operations that lead to blood clots in the legs but prolonged hospitalisation?'

Stay cool and calm, Paul said to himself, though his heart was racing. You know far more about medical matters than he does.

'Yes, I do know that,' he replied. 'It's a problem that can afflict anyone who is confined to bed for a long time.'

'Why then,' Brendan demanded in an accusatory tone, 'was my mother kept in bed for two and a half weeks before the operation was performed?'

Paul felt a surge of relief. If this was what was worrying Brendan, his criticism would be deflected easily with medical facts and logic.

'Well,' he replied, 'it is true that your mother was in the hospital for many days before her operation, but during that period, she was ambulant on the ward. She was not confined to bed. She was restless, indeed on many occasions she helped the nurses by serving meals to bed-bound patients, and clearing away the dishes afterwards.'

'But why was the surgery so delayed? All the while you were dithering and delaying, my mother's jaundice was getting deeper, and her general condition was deteriorating.'

'I agree that ideally the operation would have been performed sooner, but we discovered that your mother was diabetic, and that there was also an abnormality on her chest x-ray. There was a delay whilst these problems were sorted out. In consultation with the anaesthetist, we were trying to pick the safest possible moment for her surgery.'

'Does that answer your question?' the Coroner intervened.

Somewhat reluctantly, Brendan agreed that it did. 'But there is another matter that I wish to raise with Mr Lambert,' he added.

Inwardly Paul groaned, and he felt sweat on his forehead. What was he to be accused of now?

'And that is?' the Coroner prompted, sounding a little impatient.

'Why did Mr Lambert give my mother injections of vitamin K? My enquiries inform me that this vitamin actually encourages blood to clot. Surely this was the very last thing my poor mother should have been given.' Brendan's voice had a triumphant ring to it, now certain that he could prove negligence. The junior reporter sat up, and licked the end of his pencil in anticipation of a good story.

But Paul could have laughed out loud he felt so relieved. His accuser was dabbling in things of which he was wholly ignorant. It was on the tip of his tongue to tell him in sarcastic fashion that he didn't know what the hell he was talking about, but he thought better of it. He was in a public court; he would deliver the 'coup de grace' with dignity.

'You're quite correct,' he explained patiently, 'vitamin K is needed to make blood clot. The trouble is that jaundice, such as that suffered by your mother, depletes the body of this vitamin. It means that had she not been given vitamin K, she would have bled uncontrollably during her operation. All we were doing was replacing something that was missing.'

Brendan looked deflated but was not finished yet. 'But how do you know that you didn't give too much thereby making the blood clot too readily.'

'Because we monitored the situation with a regular blood test, and I can assure you the blood test was satisfactory on the day of the operation.'

'Do you have any more questions, Mr O'Hannagan?' Mr Frobisher asked.

'No, thank you.'

Disappointed, the reporter returned his pencil and note pad to his pocket. He would have enjoyed writing a good *'local doctor causes gypsy's death'* story. He had endured another frustrating morning.

'In that case, you may stand down, Mr Lambert.'

'Now it's time for me to sum up the evidence that we have heard,' Mr Frobisher said, 'but before I do, I feel I should read the final paragraph of the statement that Mr Lambert provided for me.' He paused and then cleared his throat in a theatrical fashion.

'In the weeks that Mrs O'Hannagan was on the ward,' he read, *'or Queenie, as she insisted everyone should call her, she greatly impressed the staff with her good humour, cheerful personality, and positive attitude. She was quite a character and a real tonic for the other patients. All the staff who became acquainted with her were deeply saddened at her passing, and asked for their condolences to be passed to her family.'*

The Coroner then paused, and for a few moments, there was silence in the room. Then he replaced Paul's statement on his desk, looked up, and addressed the Court.

'Having read the reports that have been submitted to me, and having heard the various witness statements today, it is clear that Mrs O'Hannagan's death, albeit sudden and unexpected, was due to an unfortunate complication that could neither be anticipated nor prevented. No fault can be attributed to the medical or nursing staff, who clearly did everything in their power to minimise the risks associated with her operation. The verdict is one of death due to natural causes.'

Mick's reaction was immediate. He raised himself to his feet, and with a broad grin on his face embraced Young Rose. Then he turned towards his younger brother. 'There I told you so, you stupid bugger,' he shouted. 'Now piss off back to London, and stay out of our lives.'

The Coroner was about to issue a stern rebuke, but Mick had already turned his back and was making for the exit. Startled, the young reporter reached for his pencil and started scribbling; perhaps he could interest his editor with a *'brothers in a slanging match in court'* story.

As Paul was leaving, the court assistant stopped him. 'Before you go,' he said, 'Mr Frobisher would like a word with you.'

What now? thought Paul, but he had no need to worry, the Coroner was kindness itself.

'I'm sorry I had to ask you to appear in court, and allow Mrs O'Hannagan's son to harangue you in that fashion,' he said, 'but I thought it was the best way to clear the air. From the letters he wrote to me, it was obvious he was intent on pursuing a formal claim of negligence against you, which undoubtedly would have been far more stressful than today's hearing. It would also have been more expensive, and would have dragged on for many months when there was clearly no justification for complaint. As it is, I shall make it clear in my written account that the medical care was beyond reproach, and that will be the end of the matter.'

Paul smiled his thanks then accompanied Sir William back to his battered old Morris Oxford. His boss had left his faithful old Labrador at home, and Paul, in buoyant mood, cheerfully tolerated the smell of the malodorous tartan rug that remained on the back seat.

Author's note: Since the days in which this story is set, preventative measures have been developed that significantly reduce, though not entirely eliminate, the risk of post-operative pulmonary embolism.

Thoughts for the day

Saving is a very fine thing, especially when your parents do it for you.

Winston Churchill 1874 – 1965

When a feller says. 'it ain't the money, but the principle of the thing,' it's the money.

Frank McKinney Hubbard 1868 - 1930

Chapter 21   Mrs Twigg

17th November 1970

'Thank you, Sister but I won't stop for a coffee today,' Mr Potts remarked. 'I've been asked to see a patient on one of the medical wards. I've a referral letter here,' he continued, waving a piece of paper in the air for his medical team to see, 'about a patient the physicians are worried about. Apparently, she's losing weight, and they can't understand why. It seems they've run every test in the book, and still haven't worked out what her problem is. That's typical of physicians of course, they're always so indecisive! I suppose we'll have to go and sort things out for them.'

Mr Potts sounded pleased to have the chance to play one-upmanship with his medical colleagues. Paul was well aware of the rivalry which existed between physicians and surgeons, a rivalry which dates back to the days of the *'barber surgeons'*. In those times, surgeons were not qualified as *'doctors'*, and therefore not entitled to be addressed as such. They weren't regarded as being members of a reputable profession. They were usually barbers who offered 'extras', such as extracting teeth, straightening broken bones, lancing boils and stitching wounds. They were classed as tradesmen, and considered a 'rough lot' by the physicians who pointedly referred to them as *'mister'* in a derogatory fashion. Meanwhile the physicians were cheerfully applying bloodsucking leeches to patients with anaemia, and treating syphilis with purgatives, all the while considering themselves to be superior by virtue of their medical training and qualification.

In modern times, surgeons are required to obtain a full medical degree to become *'doctors'* before they subsequently train to be surgeons. Paul had been pleased to complete his basic medical training to become *'Doctor Lambert'*, but had been even prouder and more delighted when he passed the exam to become a Fellow of the Royal College of Surgeons and was then addressed as *'Mister Lambert'*! With time, the enmity between physicians and surgeons has become little more than friendly competition, akin to the rivalry between the residents of Glasgow and Edinburgh, or between Manchester and

Liverpool. None the less, it offers an opportunity to practise one-upmanship, and nothing pleases surgeons more than to cure a patient by performing an operation when medical treatment has failed.

When Mr Potts had said *'we'll have to go'*, it wasn't clear to whom he was referring. No-one was bold enough to ask for clarification, so the whole team felt obliged to follow as he stalked off down the corridor. Although these consultations on other wards took Paul away from his regular duties, he found them interesting and educational. Whatever the nature of the patient's problem, it was rarely straightforward. It broadened his experience, and was a good opportunity for learning.

Striding purposefully along the main hospital corridor, they chanced to pass the administrative block, which prompted Mr Potts to tell a story about an incompetent manager with whom he had recently crossed swords. Paul presumed that had he heard the same story told by the manager, the emphasis and outcome would have been different! The consultant then turned into the medical corridor which, with its peeling paint and dog-eared posters was just as drab as the surgical corridor they had just left. Reaching the female medical ward, he burst into Sister's office without knocking, the surgical team hot on his heels, like the cavalry in full charge lead by its 'devil may care' officer.

Sister, who had been working quietly at her desk, looked up sharply, a frown on her face and a reprimand on her lips, but recognising the consultant surgeon, quickly held her tongue.

'Ahh, Mr Potts, you took me by surprise,' she said, her voice failing to mask the irritation she felt at the manner of Mr Potts' entrance. 'You will have come to see Mrs Twigg, I suppose'

'I'm not sure of the lady's name, Sister dear,' Mr Potts replied, oblivious to Sister's displeasure. 'It's the woman who's losing weight; the one who's got Dr Longfleet foxed. I gather he hasn't a clue what's the matter with her, and needs the wisdom and experience of a surgeon to sort things out for him.'

Pleased with his quick response, he looked round to his surgical entourage for approval. His manner was jovial, but there was arrogance in the words. It is sometimes said that hospital consultants can be categorised according to their personality; surgeons haughty and self-confident, physicians indecisive and insecure, psychiatrists distant and preoccupied, their heads in the clouds. Pathologists are said only to be confident of a diagnosis when the patient is dead. These caricatures are exemplified by a popular medical joke. It concerns doctors from different specialities who are on a duck shooting expedition. As the first two ducks fly overhead, the physician, with his reputation for procrastination, raises his gun to his shoulder but then hesitates, unable to decide which duck to shoot first, thereby allowing both ducks to fly to safety. When it's the psychiatrists turn, the same thing happens, the psychiatrist explaining; *'I didn't shoot because I wasn't sure whether the ducks were real, or a figment of my imagination.'* Finally, it's the turn of the surgeon. As the birds fly over, two shots ring out in quick succession, and both ducks fall to the ground. The surgeon turns to the pathologist and says; *'Well, tell me what they died of then.'*

The beauty of the story is that it can be varied according to the audience. The one favoured by junior doctors being the one in which the surgeon, having shot the ducks, turns to his lowly house officer and shouts; *'Well don't just stand there dithering, boy. Go and fetch them.'*

In the ward office, Sister reached for the phone. 'If you'll excuse me for a minute Mr Potts, I'll call the house officer. Mrs Twigg has been with us for many weeks now. She's had a great many investigations. He will be able to tell you all about them.'

'That's fine, Sister dear,' replied the consultant. 'You call him by all means, but I'm a busy man. I haven't time to wait for the houseman. I'll make a start without him.'

With that, he exited the office, turned left, and marched onto the main ward, his army of junior doctors and medical students following obediently in his wake. Victoria turned to Mr Potts' houseman, and whispered urgently; 'Get the notes Janet, we're going to need them.'

Sister replaced the telephone, quietly indicating to her staff nurse that she should call the house officer. She followed a few steps behind the visiting team, but stopped outside the office door. She watched, a smile on her face, as the surgical cavalry hesitated then came to a halt halfway down the ward, uncertain of the location of its target.

Coughing politely, she said primly; 'Perhaps you would allow me to show you the way, Mr Potts.' before turning to the right, away from the main ward. She knocked on the door of one of the side rooms.

She just had time to say, 'Mrs Twigg, I have a visitor for you. You remember that....' before Mr Potts entered, his surgical retinue hot on his heels. Three strides took him to the patient's bedside. His team crowded in after him, completely filling the small room. Mrs Twigg had been sitting in her bed, quietly reading, a tartan blanket around her shoulders, but was visibly frightened by this sudden intrusion. She slid further down the bed in an unmistakable act of self-protection.

If ever a person had an appropriate name, it was Mrs Twigg. She was a tiny bird like figure, barely five feet tall, who couldn't have weighed an ounce more than six stones. Her face was pale and pinched; cheek bones prominent against dark sunken eyes. Her arms, partly hidden by the blanket she wore round her shoulders were like matchsticks, every anatomical feature sharply defined. Her hands, no more than skin and bone, looked skeletal; her nails claw-like, were white and shiny like enamel.

'Good morning, Mrs.....' boomed Mr Potts as he towered over her.

'Mrs Twigg,' Victoria added helpfully.

'That's right, Mrs Twigg. Don't look so frightened woman; no one's going to bite you.'

If these words were intended to reassure, they missed their mark. Mrs Twigg cowered from him, fear on her face. Instinctively, she pulled the bedclothes protectively to her chin as if to shield herself from attack.

Sister was now at her patient's side, across the bed from the consultant, a protective arm around Mrs Twigg's shoulders. 'This is Mr Potts,' she said quietly, 'one of the consultant surgeons. You remember that Dr Longfleet said that he would be coming to see you.'

'That's right,' reiterated Mr Potts, his voice echoing around the small room. 'Dr Longfleet has asked me to sort you out. Now, what seems to be the problem?'

He proceeded to extract a brief history from a hesitant and very apprehensive patient. He learned that Mrs Twigg was 45 years old, a mother and part time secretary, who had enjoyed good health until two years previously. She had then been troubled by vague abdominal pains, and had started to lose weight. She had been to see her GP who had given her some simple medication but later, when this had no effect, she was referred to the hospital. At first, it was thought that she might have a stomach ulcer. However, she did not respond to therapy, and then she developed bowel symptoms which also failed to improve with medication. All the while she had lost weight; in total, over three stones.

In the course of her illness, a wide variety of blood tests had been performed, an array of x-rays had been arranged, and various treatments had been tried, but all to no avail. Mrs Twigg's abdominal symptoms had continued, and despite Dr Longfleet's best endeavours, no firm diagnosis had been reached. Further, she was now anaemic and undernourished despite having received blood transfusions and a nutritious diet. She was in danger of a sad demise if the cause of her troubles could not be discovered and treated within the next few weeks.

'We'd better have a look at your abdomen,' Mr Potts said, pulling down the bed clothes, and lifting the patient's nightdress without asking or waiting for her permission.

Paul was startled by what he saw. Mrs Twigg's ribs stood out dramatically, like the timbers of an old wooden sailing boat. The bones of her pelvis, lacking any fatty layer, were prominent ridges in contrast to the hollow of her abdomen. The flesh on her buttocks and thighs had been lost, her skin hanging loosely in folds from her body. The victims of Belsen could scarcely have looked more emaciated.

Mrs Twigg winced as Mr Potts gave her abdomen a cursory examination. He then stood back.

'Right,' he said, addressing the patient. 'There's absolutely nothing for you to worry about. We'll get you across to the surgical ward, and we'll soon have you sorted out.' He looked across the bed. 'You can arrange that for me, can't you, Sister dear.'

Without further explanation, and denying Mrs Twigg the opportunity to ask questions, the consultant turned abruptly, and left the room. It had been a typical Leslie Potts performance. The consultant had a self-confidence which at times bordered on arrogance. He clearly was in little doubt that he would succeed where his medical colleagues had failed. Worse, he had little thought, or consideration for his patient or her feelings. He simply didn't recognise that his engagement with Mrs Twigg had been so unequal. The number of people crowding round her bed was intimidating. Mr Potts was standing, confident and healthy, fully dressed, surrounded by his team, armed with his medical knowledge, and the authority to decide on his patient's treatment. She was lying, in a strange, frightening environment, ill and anxious, half naked, her night dress barely covering her modesty, fearful of what the future might hold. Paul was appalled, but he was also aware that his boss was capable of performing surgery that was technically brilliant; he was able to perform life-saving operations that were beyond his consultant colleagues, and that his knowledge of surgical matters was second to none. What a shame, he thought, that these attributes were not matched by an equally good bedside manner.

Paul's every instinct was to stay behind to comfort Mrs Twigg, but he knew he was expected to follow Mr Potts as he led the way back to the ward office. No doubt Sister would soon be back at Mrs Twigg's bedside, comforting her patient, and apologising for Mr Potts' abrupt manner, whilst privately cursing him for causing her unnecessary distress. She would probably explain that the consultant surgeon was an extremely busy man, but assure her that he was also very clever, and would do his best to resolve her problems, whilst inwardly wishing she could give him a few lessons on how to improve his intolerable behaviour.

As they left the ward and walked back along the corridor towards the surgical wards, they chanced to meet Dr Longfleet coming in the opposite direction. With his entire surgical team and half a dozen medical students as an audience, Mr Potts was in his element. He addressed his colleague in a jovial tone, a beaming smile on his face.

'Ah, Bill. I'm so glad to see you. We've just been to see that emaciated lady of yours, Mrs.....'

'Mrs Twigg, Sir,' Victoria prompted once again.

'Yes, that's right, Mrs Twigg. She looks half dead to me. Have you been starving her? She's obviously got you foxed. You should have called for our assistance months ago when she had a little more flesh on her bones. I guess we'll have to take a quick look inside that abdomen of hers, and solve the mystery for you.'

Dr Longfleet was a quiet, intelligent and highly experienced physician who said nothing, nor did anything, without a great deal of thought. Although an inch or so taller than Mr Potts, and probably a dozen years older, he was slim and had a slight stoop suggesting that his responsibilities lay heavily on his shoulders. His small pinched face with its beak-like nose always wore a worried frown, and he peered at the world like a timid owl through small, round-rimmed NHS glasses. In the exchange that was to follow, he was no match for the ebullient, confident surgeon. He spoke hesitantly in a voice that was scarcely more than a whisper.

'Oh, er, hello Leslie. Thank you for coming to see Mrs Twigg. I'm very grateful to you. I can't deny she's been causing us a lot of concern. But when we asked you to see her, we weren't actually thinking about surgery. We thought you might care to go through the various tests we've performed on her, and give us the benefit of your opinion. I don't feel that an exploratory operation is the answer.'

'Nonsense, dear fellow,' Mr Potts said in a voice loud enough to startle two student nurses who happened to be passing, 'You've obviously done every test under the sun. I'm sure a quick look inside her belly will solve the problem. Obviously, I'll let you know what we find. Then we'll feed her well, fatten her up, and let you have her back to recuperate.'

'But that's the point, Leslie. She is eating well; the trouble is that the food she takes doesn't seem to do her any good. She doesn't absorb it. There's clearly something amiss with her intestines, but I doubt it's anything that can be removed surgically. We really wanted you to consider the entire file and advise us if we're missing something.'

Mr Potts laid a condescending hand on his colleague's shoulder. 'You worry too much, Bill. Just leave the matter with me, dear chap. We'll have her fit and well before you can say Jack Robinson.'

Dr Longfleet looked unconvinced. 'But Leslie, I, er, think that perhaps....' but his colleague had already turned to leave, and the physician lacked the confidence to press the matter. However, the expression on his face suggested that he was far from happy at the prospect of his patient having an exploratory operation.

****

The day after Mr Potts visit to the medical ward and his encounter with Dr Longfleet, Mrs Twigg was transferred to the surgical ward. Patients such as this were medical mysteries representing an academic challenge. Paul knew that occasionally the answer could be found by a careful review of the patient's story, a thorough clinical examination, and some work in the medical library, refreshing one's memory of those rare conditions only mentioned in the smallest print of the thickest text books. It would be wonderful if the surgeons could resolve the problem that had so baffled the physicians, and thereby restore Mrs Twigg to health; better still if he could be the one to do it, particularly if this could be achieved without resorting to surgery. In Mrs Twigg's emaciated state, an operation would be a risky undertaking.

Dr Longfleet had invited his surgical colleague to see Mrs Twigg with a view to casting a fresh eye over the case, seeking reassurance that nothing had been overlooked. His particular expertise was not in diseases of the gut, but in endocrinology, the study of glands and hormones. Paul recalled how the house officers had enjoyed a laugh at his expense at the last hospital Christmas revue. To the tune of '*June is bursting out all over*' they had sung a witty lyric about him:

June is bursting out all over, where once she was skinny and so thin,
'til she went to see Bill Longfleet, at his rooms down in St John Street
and he fed her on synthetic oestro Gin.
Endocrinology is charming, testosterone for men is quite the thing, so if you're short of male emotion, just take Billy's little potion, and your love affairs will really start to swing.
So, if your libido is low, take Bill Longfleet's pills and go!

Paul also recognised that, despite Dr Longfleet's reservations, Mr Potts had already decided to explore Mrs Twigg's abdomen at the earliest opportunity. The consultant had apparently assumed that further investigations would not prove fruitful, and that time would be wasted during which the patient would continue to deteriorate. Paul was concerned that so little consideration had gone into the decision, and resolved to take a particular interest in Mrs Twigg himself. His conscience would simply not allow him to stand by until the surgery was undertaken.

That evening, he started by going through her extensive medical records. There was no doubt she had been exhaustively investigated. When her abdominal pains had started, she had weighed ten and a half stones. There was a suggestion she might have had a stomach ulcer, and also evidence of some mild inflammation of the bowel, but nothing conclusive. Unfortunately, when treatment for these conditions had been introduced, there had been no improvement whatsoever, and all the while, her weight loss had continued. Whilst on the medical ward, she had been weighed twice a week; the chart showing a continuing downward trend. She now weighed precisely six stones and two pounds.

At one stage a psychiatrist had been asked to see her. He had noted that Mrs Twigg seemed a little depressed, but concluded that this was the result of her having a debilitating illness, rather than the cause of it. Specifically, he did not think she had anorexia nervosa, not least because the nursing staff confirmed she had a good appetite, ate all her meals and seemed to enjoy them. Paul noted however, that the central part of the bowel, the small intestine, had not been investigated. Since this was the part of the gut where many of the nutrients in food are absorbed, it struck him that this was a notable omission. He felt excited. If this discovery led to the correct diagnosis, not only might Mrs Twigg be spared an unpleasant operation, but it would also be good for his reputation! Undoubtedly, it would be a feather in his cap if he could solve a mystery that had defied a consultant physician. All trainee surgeons needed a good reference if they were to progress in the highly competitive specialty of surgery.

Paul went to the ward and listened carefully as Mrs Twigg retold the story of her illness; a story she had repeated innumerable times to the many doctors she had already met. Concentrating on symptoms that arose in the small bowel, he probed for any clues that might suggest some rare cause of disease; strange habits, unusual pets, exposure to noxious substances or travel to exotic locations. And he struck gold! Two years previously, Mrs Twigg had travelled to Nigeria. Her sister worked for Oxfam, and she had gone out to visit her. She had stayed for a month.

'Were you ill when you were out there?' Paul asked.

'Well yes, I had diarrhoea there,' she replied, 'but many people did, you rather expected it.'

'Did you tell the doctors on the medical ward about it?'

'No, I don't think so. They didn't ask, and it didn't seem important. And anyway, it was a long time ago.'

Paul examined her thoroughly, but the only abnormalities he could find were the result of her profound weight loss, not the cause of it. He could find no sign of any underlying disease.

He reviewed the notes again. The trip to Nigeria had not been picked up by Dr Longfleet, nor had any tests for tropical diseases been performed. He felt exalted; surely this was the breakthrough for which everyone had been searching. His knowledge of diseases that could befall travellers to African countries was limited, but he did recall from his student days there were many infections that could affect the small bowel. Surely one of them must be the cause of Mrs Twigg's profound weight loss. A diagnosis would be found without an operation after all.

Excited, he went to the hospital library. On a top shelf, there were three books on tropical diseases. They were covered in dust; only rarely was there a need to refer to them at an inner-city hospital in the UK. He picked up the slimmest volume, but even this ran to 600 pages. He flicked through it in dismay. Although medically qualified, he recognised only a tiny fraction of the diseases listed. Most had long unpronounceable Latin or Greek names, and were caused by all manner of noxious bacteria and viruses. There were diseases caused by fleas and lice most of which he had never heard. Others were due to infestations of the gut, such as amoebiasis and giardiasis. Then there were a variety of different worms such as the tapeworm, as well as round worms, thread worms, whip worms, hook worms and Guinea worms that could be over a metre long. Paul shuddered at the thought of that! Most of them were endemic in Africa. He noted that many of these diseases were associated with a fever, but importantly most caused vague abdominal pain, loose stools and weight loss, symptoms that Mrs Twigg had!

He discussed the situation with Victoria.

'Did Mrs Twigg have a fever when she was on Dr Longfleet's ward?' she asked.

'Occasionally her temperature was slightly raised, but it was never very marked.' Paul replied.

'And I take it there haven't been any tests to look for weird and wonderful parasites in the stool?'

'No.'

'Then we need to monitor her temperature carefully, and to ask the laboratory to examine the stools,' Victoria commented. 'An x-ray of the small bowel is the next logical step, but we'll need to contact Mr Potts to obtain his permission. It involves the patient receiving quite a lot of radiation, and takes a consultant radiologist the best part of an hour to perform.'

'We could request it now,' Paul suggested. 'It always takes a day or two to arrange, and we could cancel it if the boss doesn't agree.'

'Well, let's hope he does agree. We certainly need to dissuade Mr Potts from charging in with an operation!'

****

'What are the latest blood tests on this patient, my dear?'

Mr Potts had arrived at Mrs Twigg's bed during his next ward round. The question was directed at Janet, his house officer.

'Please do not patronize me, Mr Potts. I am not *your dear.*' Janet replied primly.

'Please do accept my apologies Miss.....' he paused. 'Look, you'd better tell me if it's Miss or Mrs or perhaps M/s so that I don't get into a further trouble.'

Mr Potts smiled; he was enjoying the exchange. To him toying with his tall, elegant blond house officer was a game, no more than a little light amusement on a routine ward round.

'I have already told you Mr Potts, that it's Miss Smith, but since my marital status is of no relevance on this ward round, I should appreciate it if you would call me Dr Smith.'

'That's fine. Then that's what I shall try to do, but I've no doubt you will correct me should I forget!'

'Now, let's get down to business.'

He turned to Mrs Twigg, seemingly having forgotten he had just asked to be told her latest blood tests. 'I'm pleased you've moved to my ward. This is where we get things done. As you know, Dr Longfleet has run dozens of tests, but he hasn't managed to sort you out. He and I have had a little chat about you, and we both agree that we need to have a look inside that tummy of yours to find the cause of your troubles. I'm sure that's the best way to put you on the road to recovery.'

They hadn't agreed, but Mrs Twigg wasn't to know that!

Mrs Twigg, overawed by the consultant's domineering tone, was too frightened to reply. The consultant towered over the timid little woman who shrank from him like a field mouse from a hungry tom cat.

Mr Potts took her silence as consent.

He turned to Janet. 'Now my dear, is there.... I do apologize, I mean *Dr Smith,*' Mr Potts added with a grin on his face, and a sideways glance at the other doctors and nurses, 'is there a slot on tomorrow's theatre list?'

'I'm afraid not, Mr Potts.'

'Well never mind. Arrange the operation just as soon as there's time in theatre.'

He had spent less than two minutes at the foot of her bed, and was ready to move on.

'Sir,' Paul said, somewhat hesitantly, aware of the consultant's unpredictable mood swings, 'Victoria and I have been reviewing the history, and have learned that Mrs Twigg spent some time in Africa a couple of years ago. It raises the possibility of tropical diseases that haven't been investigated. Also, no tests of the small bowel have been undertaken. We thought it would be useful to get that part of the gut x-rayed. We might get some further information without resorting to surgery.' As he spoke, he glanced at Mrs Twigg, who nodded weakly.

'I'm sure that Mrs Twigg feels that she's had more than enough tests already, and just wants to get on with an operation to sort things out,' replied Mr Potts.

It was difficult for Paul to pursue the conversation in front of the patient, so he didn't persist. He decided to wait until the ward round was over, and then argue his case in the privacy of the office.

The moment that the round was over however, Mr Potts stated that he had urgent matters to attend to, and was not able to linger for a drink and a biscuit.

'Before you go Sir, may I have a word about Mrs Twigg?' Mr Potts looked impatient, but said nothing so Paul ploughed on.

'Mrs Twigg hasn't had any tests to look for tropical diseases. I know it's some time since she was in Nigeria, but an infection in the small bowel might explain her symptoms. It could also cause her to be malnourished and lead to her weight loss.'

But Mr Potts was unimpressed. 'Lambert,' he said, 'an African infection of the gut would be associated with an obvious fever and profuse diarrhoea. I'm sure that a cancer hidden in the pancreas or liver is the cause of her problems. The quickest way to solve the problem is to explore her belly. I'm sure that's what Mrs Twigg wants.'

Paul knew that he ought to 'stick to his guns', but lacked the confidence to do so. He wanted to say, '*I honestly don't think that is what Mrs Twigg wants*', but hadn't the courage to say so.

Victoria though was not so reticent. 'Some stool cultures and an x-ray of the small bowel shouldn't prove to be too much for Mrs Twigg, Sir, and it would only take a couple of days to arrange. It might avoid surgery.'

'Alright,' Mr Potts replied. 'Since my next theatre list is already fully booked, you have until Friday to run your tests. But we can't wait any longer than that. If we do, poor Mrs Twigg will have faded away altogether. But I bet you a pound to a penny, we'll end up exploring the abdomen.'

Paul heaved a sigh of relief. He was certain it was the right thing to do, and was grateful to Victoria for her support. He was also glad he wouldn't have to admit that the small bowel x-ray had already been arranged; it was in fact scheduled for the next day.

****

As it happened, had either Paul or Victoria taken the bet they had been offered by Mr Potts on the chances of further tests solving the mystery of Mrs Twigg's illness, they would have lost their money. None of the tests they arranged added anything to their understanding of her problem. Her temperature chart remained as flat as a pancake, no African parasites were found in the stools, and the x-ray of the small bowel was normal. And so it was that on Friday morning, with an anticipation normally associated with reading the last chapter of a good detective novel when the identity of the murderer is to be revealed, Paul joined Mr Potts and Victoria in theatre as they prepared to explore Mrs Twigg's abdomen. The skin was painted with an antiseptic iodine solution, sterile drapes were laid around the operation area, and when the anaesthetist gave the nod, Mr Potts set to work.

As a surgical trainee, Paul found it educational to observe different surgeons at work. On the ward, Mr Potts was dour and taciturn, a man of few words. He conducted his rounds quickly, rarely spending more than a couple of minutes with any of his patients, making it necessary for his junior staff to return later to explain the decisions that had been made about them. But his personality changed when he walked through the doors of the surgical theatre. He came to life, and had this been a production in a West End or Broadway theatre, he would have been the director, the producer and the leading player all in one. He selected the work to be performed, he chose the supporting cast, and his was the name at the top of the bill. He was indeed the star of the show. Whilst operating he became expansive, verbose and indeed 'theatrical'. Not for him the thin, baggy, cotton trousers, tied with a pyjama cord round the waist, or the shapeless, green 'scrubs' worn by the rest of the staff. He wore a specially designed, tailored, blue cotton suit, with his name prominently embroidered on the pocket. He tied a white, crepe bandage around his forehead to act as a sweatband, and wore one of the newly designed surgeon's lamps, a modification of the original minor's lamp, on his forehead.

Mr Potts had a supreme confidence in his own surgical ability. He delighted in demonstrating his considerable technical skills to his staff, particularly to the nurses, whilst relating tales of disasters that had befallen other surgeons. Paul knew though from previous experience, that just occasionally this self-assurance was misplaced. Different surgeons operate at different speeds. Some are slow, methodical and excessively cautious, checking and double-checking every stage of the procedure as they work. By contrast, Mr Potts worked quickly, completing operations in a fraction of the time it would have taken some of his colleagues. At times, his work was quite brilliant. He was capable of performing extremely intricate and delicate procedures with a skill that was the envy of others. However, once or twice, Paul had seen him get into trouble, causing unnecessary bleeding when overconfidence had caused him to be a little too casual when dealing with a large artery or vein. Thanks to his ability and experience, he had always been able to retrieve the situation, but for a moment the reason for his sweatband had become apparent.

'Now,' Mr Potts declared as he took the scalpel that Sister handed to him, 'we'll soon find out what's confounded the physicians for the last two months. There comes a time when one peek inside the belly is better than a hundred blood tests and x-rays. My guess is that we'll find a tumour somewhere, possibly hidden in the pancreas or liver. Those are both areas which are difficult to demonstrate on x-ray. Then we'll be able to chide Dr Longfleet for taking so long to seek our advice,' he added, winking at the nurses.

Paul had never seen such a thin abdominal wall, even in a child. Mrs Twigg's skin was as thin as gossamer, as fragile as tissue paper, and there was no fatty layer beneath it at all. The muscles too were incredibly wasted, as thin as a slice of bacon, instead of being as thick and healthy as a decent steak. Within a couple of minutes, Mr Potts had made an incision four inches long. He started by examining the stomach, duodenum and pancreas, inspecting and feeling each in turn, but he could find no abnormality. He then turned his attention to the intestine and examined its entire length. Again, he drew a blank, so he extended the incision upwards to look at the liver, spleen and gall bladder. But everything was completely normal.

'This is very strange,' he said, 'there must be a tumour in here somewhere.'

He extended the incision downwards, such that it now stretched virtually from ribs to pelvis. This allowed an examination of the uterus, fallopian tubes and ovaries. Thanks to the lack of fat inside the abdomen, all these organs were very easily seen but, once again, they were all entirely normal.

For the first time, Mr Potts seemed to have doubts.

'Miss Kent,' he said, 'have a good look round. See if you can find anything, perhaps something I've missed.'

Five minutes later, however everyone was forced to the conclusion that there was no abnormality in the abdomen.

'Damn,' exploded Mr Potts, 'that fool of a psychiatrist was obviously wrong. She must be a bloody anorexic after all.'

He turned to Victoria. 'Keep her in hospital for a couple of weeks. Put her in a side ward, and get Sister to monitor every single scrap of food that goes in and comes out. We'll soon find out what she's up to.'

With that, he looked at the clock on the theatre wall. 'I must be off now. I've some more profitable work to do in my rooms. Close the belly for me Miss Kent. And do it carefully; she's so wasted; it will be a miracle if it heals.'

He stormed out of the theatre without a further word, tossing his cap and mask onto the floor as he left.

****

For the next ten days, Mrs Twigg remained imprisoned in her side ward. At first, she was confined to bed, but even when she became able to sit out, she wasn't allowed through the door. Since the side room had a wash basin but no toilet facilities, a commode was provided for her. All the food and drink that she was given was monitored, as were any remnants of food that she left on her plate; not that there were many, for she had a reasonable appetite. Her weight was recorded daily. She dropped a pound or two in the first few days after her operation which was to be expected, but to everyone's dismay and consternation, her weight lost continued. Two weeks later, Mrs Twigg was five pounds lighter than she had been when she left the medical ward! Dr Longfleet came to the surgical ward, and enquired after her progress. There was an awkward silence when he heard that an exploration of her abdomen had been performed, but that no disease had been discovered. He frowned but made no comment. As her weight fell, the anxiety of the surgical team increased, for it was inevitable that within the next few weeks, like frail grannies twice her age, she would develop a chest infection and die; she was far too weak to cough to clear phlegm from her chest. Amazingly, despite her emaciated condition, her abdominal wound healed, but she remained as much a mystery to the surgeon team as she had been to the physicians.

Paul and Victoria agonised over the situation. They spent hours in the medical library scouring specialist medical text books looking for ever rarer causes of weight loss. They studied the latest research articles and academic journals. They reviewed reports of malabsorption, allergies, infections, hypersensitivities and neurologic abnormalities of the gut. They spoke with consultants at the London School of Tropical Medicine hoping for enlightenment. They arranged ever more complex laboratory tests for ever more exotic medical conditions, but all to no avail. As the days passed, Mrs Twigg got weaker and weaker until she was scarcely able to get out of bed unaided. Eventually, even Paul and Victoria were forced to accept that it was only a matter of time before the pathologist would be invited to undertake a post mortem examination to identify whatever it was that had defied diagnosis during life.

A couple of days later though, Victoria and Sister Rutherford were working in the ward office discussing the situation, when Billy Atkins, one of the hospital porters, came in with the morning post, mainly laboratory reports and other interdepartmental mail.

'What is it that's so attractive to the pigeons on the roof of the Surgical Three theatre?' he asked.

'What do you mean?' Sister Rutherford asked.

'Well Surgical Three is on the ground floor. You look down on its roof as you approach this ward along the top corridor. There are always a few birds flying about the hospital grounds, picking up scraps of kitchen waste, but there must be a dozen or more pigeons on that roof at the moment. They've been there for a couple of weeks now. There must be a reason for it.'

'If you've got a moment, will you show me what you mean,' Sister said.

'Of course, no trouble,' replied Billy, and all three walked down the corridor. Sure enough, ten or more pigeons were busy pecking at the roof of the theatre.

Victoria looked at Sister, and she looked at Victoria. Simultaneously the same thought had occurred to them both. Sister looked thoughtful. 'Are you thinking what I'm thinking?' she asked.

'We need to be certain before we challenge her,' Victoria replied.

'Fair enough,' Sister replied. 'I suggest we let her have her lunch, then watch from this window.'

Their suspicions were quickly confirmed. Mrs Twigg was supervised while she ate the cottage pie and beans that she had been given. Her empty plate was then removed by the nurses, and she was left to her own devices. Five minutes later, from their vantage point on the corridor, they saw her throwing something out of the window.

'She ate all her food,' Victoria said, 'so she must be making herself vomit by putting a finger down the back of her throat. Then, when nobody's looking, she's been feeding her vomit to the birds. No wonder all the investigations have been normal! Would you believe that the casual observation of a porter can solve a problem that has confounded the best medical brains within the hospital?'

Victoria rang Paul to tell him that the mystery surrounding Mrs Twigg's illness had finally been solved, or as she actually said, 'Sister and I have finally *'twigged'* the cause of the problem!'

Paul received the news with mixed emotions; surprise and delight that a diagnosis had finally been made, and a sense of anger that for many months Mrs Twigg had put her life at risk, and caused so many people such anxiety and distress.

'She's made complete fools of all of us. The boss isn't going to be best pleased,' Victoria commented.

Inevitably there was concern as to how Mr Potts would react when he was told the cause of Mrs Twigg's troubles. Victoria argued it would be best to inform him of the latest developments in the office, rather than in Mrs Twigg's presence at her bed side. Rather cautiously, she raised the subject, and told him what they had discovered.

When she had finished there was a long pause, finally broken by Mr Potts.

'Damn her. She's quite deliberately deceived the lot of us, and I confess that includes me. I presume she's still in the side room. Bring her out on to the main ward. It will be easier to keep an eye on her there; Sister, make sure someone sits with her for a couple of hours after every meal; and Lambert, get that psychiatrist to see her again.'

And so the saga of Mrs Twigg came to an end, and she actually started to gain some weight before she was transferred to the care the psychiatrist. All in all, it had been a fascinating case, and a lesson for Paul that you can't always believe what a patient tells you!

Author's notes

The condition ascribed here to Mrs Twigg is now known as 'Bulimia Nervosa'. It is a clinical variation of anorexia nervosa, and was first recognised as a clinical entity by Professor Gerald Russell in London in 1979.

Since the advent of three-dimensional imaging and keyhole surgery, exploratory abdominal operations are now rarely performed.

Thought for the day

The kind of doctor I want is one who, when he is not examining me, is at home studying medicine.

George S. Kaufman 1889 – 1961

Chapter 22   Mr Walton's Party Trick

4th December 1970

It was another Tuesday afternoon and another thirty minutes wasted waiting for Mr Potts to arrive. When he did, to Paul's surprise, on exiting the office he turned right towards the side wards, instead of turning left to pass through the double doors onto the main ward.

'All your patients are on the main ward today, Sir,' Paul commented.

'Not today, they're not Lambert.'

The consultant raised an eyebrow to Sister Ashbrook. 'Which side ward Sister?' he asked.

'Room three, Mr Potts.'

Paul's heart gave a lurch; surely there couldn't be a patient of whom he was completely unaware. What the hell could he say if Mr Potts asked about his clinical condition? Junior hospital doctors were expected to know everything about their consultant's patients at all times.

Paul looked at the occupant of the side room in some surprise. He was a man in his fifties who, unlike every other patient on the ward, was wearing his outdoor clothes, a man whom he had never seen before. Paul prided himself on always being well informed of all the patients, particularly those of Mr Potts. Where was Sir William's patient, a man with stomach cancer whom Paul had seen in this very side ward not two hours before? How on earth had this man gained access to the ward without his knowledge? No new patients were scheduled for admission, nor had it been their day to accept emergencies. Presumably this patient had been slipped in from the consultant's private rooms.

'Hello, Mr Walton,' Mr Potts began, 'I'm grateful to you for agreeing to come in like this at short notice. It will help me to judge just how bright these 'would-be doctors' are.'

He turned to the students who were crowding round the bed, each hoping that they would not be the one he picked on to be interrogated. His eye fell on Miss Croft, a tall, slim blond who was the only girl in the group.

'Miss Croft, you look to be a bright attractive young thing. Come and examine Mr Walton's legs.'

The prejudice in the words was lost, or possibly ignored, by the student, but not by Janet who bridled at the sexual implication. She was bursting to express her indignation, but managed to hold her tongue at the last minute.

Mr Walton took off his trousers and lay on the bed. The sight that met Paul's eyes was quite extraordinary. Not only did the patient have the worst varicose veins he had ever seen, but both legs were discoloured by severe varicose eczema that extended from his ankles to his knees. A small ulcer was developing on the inner aspect of one ankle.

'Now Miss Croft, describe carefully what you can see,' Mr Potts instructed.

Belying the old adage that all blonds are dumb, Miss Croft accurately and succinctly described the appearance and correctly made a diagnosis of varicose veins with associated complications.

'Well done, well done indeed. Not only good looking but smart as well,' Mr Potts remarked, beaming.

This second remark was too much for Janet.

'What on earth is the relevance of Miss Croft's appearance? Surely what matters is the accuracy of her diagnosis.'

Mr Potts face creased into a huge smile. A further opportunity for him to cross swords with his prickly house officer would add a little spice to his day.

'Well, my dear, diagnostic accuracy is important of course, but coming from pretty lips makes it easier on the ear, don't you think?'

'Would you have made such a comment on the appearance of one of the male students?'

'I doubt it, Janet, my dear, I doubt it very much.'

'My name is Miss Smith, or Doctor Smith if you prefer, as you well know; and I am not *your dear*.' Janet's voice was clear, cold and precise.

Paul was astonished at Janet's bravery in challenging Mr Potts in such a bold and direct manner, and amazed that she always got away with it.

Mr Potts stifled his laughter. 'Touché,' he remarked, holding up a hand to show that the exchange was at an end. He then turned to the rest of the group.

'Now I want you all to watch very closely whilst Mr Walton performs his party trick. Afterwards I shall ask you to explain what you see. Miss Croft, will you help Mr Walton off the bed please.'

As he spoke, he nodded to Jimmy the ward orderly who had slipped into the room unnoticed. With a big smile on his face Mr Walton sat up, Miss Croft supporting him by one arm as he did so. As the patient swung his legs over the side of the bed, Jimmy positioned himself to support the other arm. For a few seconds Mr Walton stood facing the students who were wondering what they were supposed to observe. Then quite suddenly, the colour drained from his face, he swayed slightly and with glazed eyes, his knees buckled and he collapsed. Fortunately, Jimmy, who clearly knew what to expect, caught Mr Walton before he hit the floor, and shovelled the unconscious patient back onto the bed. Miss Croft, taken completely unawares, gave a high-pitched yelp partly in surprise but mainly because one of Mr Walton's flailing arms had struck her a forcible blow across the chest as he fell.

Jimmy made the now-comatose patient comfortable and then, with a quick 'thumbs up' to Mr Potts, he left the room as silently as he had entered.

'Now,' Mr Potts asked, 'Who knows what the patient's pulse will be right now?'

The students were too stunned to respond.

'Well, who can tell me how we should treat the patient?' Again, there was silence.

But Paul knew and so did Victoria. Appalled that Mr Potts was prepared to leave the patient to recover spontaneously, they both dashed to the foot of the bed, grabbed one leg each and elevated them as high as they could. Thirty seconds later, Mr Walton slowly came round. He still looked a ghastly colour and his brow glistened with sweat. Suddenly, he retched. Sister Ashbrook grabbed a vomit bowl just in time to prevent Mr Wilson's partly digested lunch spraying over the bedclothes.

Mr Potts ignored the patient as he quizzed the students on the events they had witnessed. Why had Mr Walton lost consciousness, had they noticed what had happened to his veins when he adopted an upright posture, what had happened to his pulse before and after his collapse, why had his face been so pale? Despite being prompted by the consultant, it took the students several minutes to regain their composure and explain what they had seen. Eventually though, Mr

Potts helped them to understand that when Mr Walton stood up, such a vast quantity of blood had dropped into his huge varicose veins that there simply hadn't been enough blood available to be pumped to his head. His blood pressure had dropped dramatically and his brain had been starved of oxygen causing him to faint. Paul was appalled. How many brain cells had suffered as a result? And the manner in which the patient had willingly demonstrated the effects of a sudden loss of circulating blood, suggested that this wasn't the first time Mr Potts had asked him to perform for the benefit of the students.

'Thanks Mr Walton, that was very helpful,' Mr Potts said. 'We'll get you a cup of tea and some toast, and give you a couple of minutes to recover before you go. If you pop in to see my secretary on your way out, she'll see you alright for your trouble.'

He turned for the door. 'Let's get on with this ward round.'

Later, back in the ward office, after Mr Potts and the students had departed, Paul turned and addressed Victoria.

'What are we going to do about Mr Walton. Every time he performs that 'party trick' of his, he's knocking off dozens of brain cells; I don't suppose the boss has explained that to him.'

Victoria, whose views on the matter coincided with Paul's, suggested that they ought to express their concerns, so together they went back to the side room. Mr Walton was just gathering his things together before going home.

'Did you come here today purely to help to teach the students?' Victoria asked.

Mr Walton, now fully recovered, grinned hugely. 'Yes, it's something Mr Potts asks me to do a couple of times a year. It allows me to have a day off work, and he gives me a bob or two for my trouble.'

'Has he ever suggested operating on your veins?' Paul asked, fearful that Mr Potts might deliberately be deferring Mr Wilson's treatment to enable this demonstration to be repeated for the benefit of each new batch of students.

'Yes, he has. I'm on the waiting list, though first I have to get rid of this nasty ulcer and angry skin rash. That's why I wear these compression stockings.'

'Fair enough,' Victoria replied, 'but if I was you, I should call it a day. You see, every time you faint, your brain gets starved of oxygen. It won't be doing you any good in the long-term.'

'But I quite enjoy it. I get a day off work, I'm not out of pocket and if it helps the students to become good doctors, surely that's a good thing?'

'Well, the decision must be yours, but if it were me, I should definitely put my own health first!'

'And so would I,' Paul added emphatically.

Thought for the day

It may seem a strange principle to enunciate as the first requirement in a hospital that it should do the sick no harm.

Florence Nightingale 1820 - 1910

Chapter 23   Mr Cullen's Vasectomy Operation

12th December 1970

Sir William was in his outpatient clinic, reading a letter he received from one of the local General Practitioners. It had been a long and tiring session, and he wondered if his age was finally catching up with him. Dealing with 20 patients in an afternoon was exhausting. He saw most of the patients himself, training Paul as he went, but occasionally he passed one to his registrar to see on his behalf. He tossed the single sheet onto the desk.

'Here you are, Lambert,' he said with a sigh. 'Making the diagnosis in this case shouldn't be too difficult.' Then he laughed. 'Mind you, you'll probably need all your diplomatic skills if you're to handle things successfully!'

Paul picked up the letter. It was quite brief.

'Dear Sir William,
Re James Cullen, Aged 34
Thank you for seeing Mr Cullen. I am afraid that the vasectomy operation he had a few years ago on your unit seems to have failed. I would be grateful if you would see him and advise. With thanks and good wishes,
James Hattersley, MB Ch B'

In the 60s, vasectomies were becoming increasingly popular, and by and large, were proving to be a reliable form of contraception. However, in a tiny number of cases, despite having had the procedure, some men had fathered children, and had demanded and received financial compensation. The payments were made, not because the operation had failed, since that could happen even to the best surgeons in the land, but because the patients had not been warned in advance that there was a possibility of failure.

Concerned that this might have happened in Mr Cullen's case, Paul checked the notes, and was pleased to find that the *'consent for operation'* form, signed by Mr Cullen before the operation was performed, specifically mentioned this possibility.

Paul went to see the patient, and found him sitting hand in hand with his wife. They seemed a pleasant couple. He was a quietly-spoken accountant, but a cautionary bell rang in Paul's ear when he learned that Mrs Cullen was the secretary for a firm of local solicitors; she probably had ready access to expert legal advice. Knowing he would need to ask Mr Cullen some awkward, personal, and potentially embarrassing questions, he asked if he would prefer his wife to wait outside during the consultation.

'No, I'm perfectly happy for Anne to be present. She's as keen as I am to get this matter sorted out.'

Without prompting, Mr Cullen opened the conversation. 'I'm afraid my vasectomy operation has failed, Doctor. I'm not blaming anyone; I was warned that this was possible. But I'd like to have the operation completed.'

At his side, his wife nodded in agreement. Mr Cullen went on to say he and his wife had been married for eight years and had two healthy children. Three years previously, having decided their family was complete, he had undergone the sterilisation procedure.

'And you say the vasectomy has failed?'

'Yes, my wife became pregnant and had a miscarriage.'

'A miscarriage or an abortion?' Paul asked.

'A miscarriage. It happened a couple of months ago. We were on holiday near Inverness in Scotland at the time. Anne was rushed to the hospital. She was bleeding, and had to have an emergency operation.'

There was a pause as Paul considered how to phrase his next question. 'Are you absolutely certain that it's the vasectomy that has failed?'

Mr Cullen looked puzzled, as if no other possibility had entered his mind. 'Yes, of course. What else could have happened?'

Paul wondered if his patient was really as naïve as his question suggested.

'Well,' he said, speaking as gently as he could, 'vasectomy operations can fail, although such an event is rather unusual. It probably doesn't happen more than once in every couple of thousand operations. However, you must realise that if a woman becomes pregnant, it doesn't automatically follow that her husband is responsible.'

'Oh, there's absolutely no question of anyone else being involved.'

Paul glanced at Mrs Cullen. He judged that she was probably little more than twenty-six or twenty-seven, significantly younger than her husband. She wore a smart suit, tailored to her slim figure, over a starched white blouse. With her skirt cut just above the knee and black, high-heeled shoes, she certainly wasn't 'mumsy', despite having two children. She was a good-looking woman who clearly took trouble over her appearance. No doubt, some of the young solicitors with whom she worked would find her attractive. But was she flighty? Would she be the sort to play away from home? It was impossible to tell, of course, but Paul thought it unlikely. She was not afraid to meet his gaze, and appeared to be as shocked as her husband at the suggestion that she might have been unfaithful.

'There's absolutely no question about it,' she said emphatically. 'We're a happily married couple. We're devoted to each other; we love each other to bits.'

One of Sir William's favourite expressions came into Paul's head. *'Common things occur commonly'*. If he had heard his boss say that once, he'd heard him say it a dozen times; and a wife cheating on her husband was undoubtedly a more frequent event than a vasectomy operation failing!

'Look,' he said, 'before we jump to any conclusions, we need to confirm that the operation has definitely failed. The way to do that is to run a sperm check.'

'That truly won't be necessary,' Mr Cullen replied, placing his arm around his wife's shoulders. 'I trust my wife, implicitly.'

It was an interesting reply. Was Mr Cullen prepared to have further surgery, rather than risk having to face what might prove to be an unpalatable truth?

'Nonetheless, we do need to arrange the test,' Paul said firmly. 'From a medical point of view, it would be wrong to arrange another operation without making certain that the first one has failed. It needn't take more than a few days.

'Alright, Doctor, if it has to be, it has to be. But I can assure you that it will confirm that the operation has failed.'

Paul glanced again at Mrs Cullen, trying to judge if she was as confident of the result as her husband. Since qualifying as a doctor, he had heard of this situation twice before, and in both cases the sperm count had been zero, proving that the vasectomy operation had been successful. It meant that the two men were incapable of fathering a child, and had to look elsewhere for the cause of their wives' pregnancies. On each occasion, even though the wife had not been present, it had been difficult for the doctors to explain the situation to their patients, and heart-breaking for the men receiving the news. But Mrs Cullen didn't look in the least concerned that a test was to be performed that might prove she had been unfaithful. Paul was therefore left in no doubt that when the couple attended again, it would be clear that the operation had indeed failed, and arrangements would be made for the vasectomy to be repeated.

Paul completed the request form, told Mr Cullen to go to the laboratory to pick up a specimen jar, and to produce a sample at his leisure. This induced a fit of giggling in Mrs Cullen that confirmed Paul's belief that there was no question of her being unfaithful.

****

A month later, again working in the clinic, Paul recognised the name on the notes of his next patient, those of Mr Cullen. He opened the record, flicked through the pages, and found the report of the semen analysis that he had arranged.

'Sample of semen,' he read, '*four millilitres of cloudy viscous fluid. Number of motile spermatozoa: nil. Number of non-motile spermatozoa: nil.*'

His heart sank. The message from the laboratory report was unmistakable. Mr Cullen's vasectomy operation had not failed. The sperm test confirmed that he was sterile. He was not capable of fathering a child.

Paul, through the nature of his work, had been exposed to a wide range of human emotions. He had experienced the delight and exhilaration when a critically ill patient had survived against the odds. It gave him a 'high' every bit as powerful as any drug. At times, he had enjoyed the gratitude of his patients, and their relatives for the care he had given in difficult circumstances. But he had experienced less pleasant emotions just as keenly; the appalling sense of failure when a life had been lost, or the profound feeling of inadequacy when a desperately ill patient defied diagnosis. Not the least distressing of the situations he had faced was the task of relaying bad news. In the four years since he qualified, it had been Paul's misfortune to inform several patients that they had an incurable disease. He had experienced the anguish of telling a man that his young wife had died unexpectedly after routine surgery, he'd even had the unenviable task of informing a mother that her four- year-old daughter had lost her life in a road accident. This present situation was less dramatic, but the information he had to impart would nonetheless cause significant distress. He had to tell Mr Cullen that his wife had been unfaithful. He held the evidence in his hand.

Entering the cubicle, he hoped that Mr Cullen would be on his own; it would be easier to break the news to him man to man if his wife had remained at home. However, it was not to be. They were both waiting to see him, eager to hear the result of the test. As before, they were sitting hand in hand, looking at him expectantly. There seemed little point in spending time on pleasantries.

'Good morning,' he said before turning to Mr Cullen. 'I have the result of your sperm count here. The sample that you produced did not contain any sperm.'

'What does that mean, Doctor?' It was Mrs Cullen who asked the question. Paul examined her face carefully; she looked puzzled rather than guilty or ashamed. He thought the implications were perfectly clear, but knew he had to be polite and professional.

'It means that your husband is not able to father a child,' he said.

'But that must be wrong,' she insisted. 'He has fathered a child. I became pregnant.'

'Couldn't there be another explanation?' Paul asked.

It was Mr Cullen who answered, his tone forceful. 'If you're suggesting that my wife has had an affair, Doctor, you can dismiss the idea. She and I love each other dearly. I would never cheat on her, and I know with absolute certainty that she would never cheat on me. I trust her implicitly.'

It was on the tip of Paul's tongue to make a sarcastic comment about an immaculate conception, but he thought better of it! For a moment, there was an uneasy silence.

'I know exactly what you're thinking, Doctor,' Mr Cullen persisted, 'but there just has to be another explanation. Could the vasectomy operation be failing intermittently, sometimes sperm getting though, and sometimes not getting through, perhaps depending upon the strength of the gush?'

'No,' Paul explained, 'it doesn't work like that. The vasectomy operation blocks the sperm as they leave the testicles, so they never reach the storage reservoir. The ejaculation, or 'gush' as you call it, is the fluid leaving the reservoir and coming to the surface. I've never heard of a case of an intermittent failure.'

'Well,' Mr Cullen said emphatically, 'I still want to have the vasectomy repeated. I really can't risk my wife having another miscarriage. She had a painful and distressing time. Even after she'd miscarried, she had to have an anaesthetic and an operation to ensure her womb was completely empty.'

'Look,' Paul said, 'if we knew that the operation had failed, as happens from time to time, we would willingly do a further operation for you. But with this sperm test, we wouldn't be justified in performing more surgery.'

'We would be quite willing to pay to have it done.'

'It's not a question of paying; it's a question of whether it's the right treatment for you.'

It was Mrs Cullen who spoke next. 'I'm afraid we're not satisfied, Doctor Lambert. If you're not prepared to repeat the operation here, then we'll go elsewhere.'

'I'm afraid you can expect the same answer if you do look elsewhere,' Paul said.

'Well, that's what we're going to do,' she said doggedly.

Yes, and try to persuade another surgeon to perform a completely unnecessary operation on your husband, Paul thought, when you know perfectly well that you've been unfaithful.

They had reached an impasse, and a long silence ensued. Paul needed guidance on how to proceed, and decided that this was an appropriate moment to speak to Sir William. He was in no doubt the information he had given was correct, but throughout both consultations, he had been impressed by Mr Cullen's belief in his wife. But there were other possibilities. Maybe he was so desperate to believe that his wife had remained faithful, that he was prepared to have an unnecessary operation to save his marriage. Or, perhaps he thought that Paul was young and inexperienced, and there was another explanation of which Paul was ignorant. Paul found it unsettling.

'Look,' he said after a long pause. 'If you'll excuse me for a moment, I'll have a word with my consultant, and see what he has to say.'

Never one to be hurried when considering the most appropriate management in any particular situation, Sir William listened carefully to the story, as he always did.

'I've never heard of an intermittent blockage after a vasectomy operation,' he said, 'but I suppose it's theoretically possible. In any case, it won't do any harm to get the sperm test repeated. It will be a month or so before we see them again, which will give them a chance to consider the more obvious explanation. Also, since you say she had a miscarriage, you'd better get the notes from the hospital in Scotland, to check that it was well-documented.'

For a moment, he paused, then smiled and added, 'But you know what I always say, Lambert; *'common things occur commonly.'* The odds must be overwhelmingly in favour of the child being fathered by a third party.'

Mr and Mrs Cullen agreed to Sir William's plan without hesitation, and were still hand in hand as they left the clinic. Although Paul was impressed by Mr Cullen's belief in his wife, he suspected that eventually, he would be forced to accept she had been unfaithful. He would await the further sperm test result with interest.

****

A week or so later, the notes documenting Mrs Cullen's treatment in Inverness arrived through the post. They included a copy of the letter written to her GP summarising her management whilst in hospital. It described how Mrs Cullen had been admitted as an emergency with bleeding. She had told the staff that her periods *'were always erratic'* but admitted that *'she might have missed a period or two.'* Her urine test was strongly positive, indicating she was pregnant. She was admitted to the ward for bed rest in the hope that this might avert the miscarriage, but regrettably, this policy had proved unsuccessful. She had continued to bleed, and then started to pass clots and tissue. Subsequently, she had been taken to theatre, and her uterus had been emptied. The operation note, written by the consultant who performed the surgery, stated that *'products of conception'* had been removed. There seemed to be no doubt that Mrs Cullen had indeed been pregnant, but for final confirmation, Paul looked for the laboratory report of the tissue removed from the womb. But there wasn't one.

He discussed the situation with Sir William.

'Has the second semen analysis been reported?' he asked.

'Yes, it has, and the result is the same as before; no sperms were seen.'

Sir William thought for a moment. 'Alright,' he said, 'I haven't met the couple yet, but when they next come to the clinic, we'll see them together. In the meantime, Lambert, you telephone the laboratory in Inverness. Find out if the tissue removed from the womb was actually sent to the lab. It's possible it was sent and analysed, but for some reason, the report never found its way into the notes. My job will be to speak with one of the gynaecologists at St Margaret's. Gynaecology is not my specialty; it will be useful to get the view of an expert.'

In the clinic the following week, Paul introduced Sir William to Mr and Mrs Cullen.

'Have you had the result of the test, and the report from the hospital in Scotland?' Mr Cullen asked eagerly. His arm was around his wife's waist, but for the first time, Paul detected some anxiety in his voice, and a hint of concern on his face.

Sir William deflected the question by commenting that he would come to the information from Inverness in due course.

'Mr Lambert has told me about this problem,' he began, addressing Mrs Cullen, 'but first, I would like you to tell me the story yourself.'

Paul wondered if Sir William was simply being thorough, taking a history himself to check he had all the facts, or whether perhaps, he was quietly making his own judgement of the couple, particularly about Mrs Cullen. Without challenging her directly, he had put her in the position of having to restate her loyalty to her husband, which she did without hesitation. In the background, Paul listened to the tale with which he was already familiar, all the while carefully observing Mr Cullen. Again, he felt that doubt was beginning to develop in his mind. Perhaps he was now beginning the think the unthinkable about his attractive young wife.

'I see,' said Sir William, when Mrs Cullen had finished her story. 'Now let me tell you the result of our detective work. The repeat semen analysis confirms the previous one, no sperms were seen.'

As he spoke, Paul now watched Mrs Cullen. No concern showed in her face, there was no trace of guilt; she just looked puzzled. If she had indeed been unfaithful, she was a remarkably good actress.

Sir William paused. 'We also have the notes from the Inverness hospital where you were treated. The consultant there was in no doubt about it. He was certain you were pregnant, and he was confident that you had a miscarriage.' Sir William paused again, all the while watching his patient. For the first time, there was undoubtedly a trace of alarm on Mrs Cullen's face.

'However,' Sir William continued, 'they did not confirm the diagnosis by sending tissue to the laboratory. There was no analysis of the contents of the womb.'

'So, what does that mean?' Mrs Cullen asked cautiously.

'It means that they never actually proved you had a miscarriage. It's just possible they made a mistake.'

'Well, that's it,' Mr Cullen remarked immediately, turning to his wife, relief written large on his face. 'That's the explanation. You mustn't have had a miscarriage after all. It must have been something else. Oh, thank you, Doctor, for sorting it out. We have been so worried; this is such a relief. And I suppose that means I don't have to have the vasectomy operation repeated after all.'

They flew into each other's arms, and hugged long and hard. Mr Cullen had his back to Paul, but over his shoulder, he could plainly see his wife's face. She looked enormously relieved. Smiling, she caught Paul's eye, then winked as she mouthed *'thank you'* silently to him.

After they left, Paul spoke with Sir William. 'I know there was no pathology report Sir, but surely a consultant gynaecologist can recognise the products of conception!'

'Yes,' he replied, 'I rang and spoke with him, and he was in no doubt. In fact, the reason he didn't send the specimen to the laboratory was that he was certain of the diagnosis.'

'And the pregnancy test on the urine was positive as well,' Paul said.

'Yes, it was.'

'And neither of the sperm tests showed any sperms.'

'No, indeed they didn't.'

'Sir, surely you don't believe that there's been a mistake. You do accept that she was pregnant.'

'Lambert,' Sir William said quietly. 'It doesn't matter what I believe, or what you believe; it's what Mr Cullen believes that matters. I don't know whether he suspects his wife has been unfaithful or not. It's possible that in his heart, he knows that she has. But he obviously wants the marriage to continue. Besides, there are two young children to consider. What would be gained by forcing an unpalatable truth on him, and risking a break up of their marriage? Better to leave things as they are. But I do hope Mrs Cullen has learned her lesson.'

Afterward, Paul reflected on the whole episode. He was in no doubt that had the situation been left in his hands, had he not sought Sir William's advice, he would have insisted that the vasectomy had not failed, and left Mr Cullen to draw the inevitable conclusion. But Sir William had seen the wider implications, and shown great wisdom. In doing so, he had demonstrated there was more to medicine than simply making the correct diagnosis.

Thoughts for the day

It is always the best policy to speak the truth – unless, of course, you are an exceptionally good liar.

Jerome K Jerome 1859 – 1927

When my love swears that she is made of truth

I believe her, though I know she lies.

William Shakespeare 1564 - 1616

Chapter 24   Lodgers

6th January 1971

Paul was fresh out of bed, his face covered in shaving foam, when the telephone rang. It was Sister Ashbrook on the male ward and it was obvious from the tone of her voice that she was worried.

'Paul, I've just come on duty and found that an orthopaedic patient has been admitted to the ward during the night. What's worse, he's in one of Mr Potts' beds. You'd better get rid of him fast, or there's going to be a dreadful scene when he arrives for his ward round later this morning.'

Paul recalled a warning he had received from Victoria a couple of weeks before. Apparently, during the previous winter, many patients had been admitted having slipped on the snow and ice and suffered broken wrists, ankles and hips. At times, when all the orthopaedic beds were full, patients had overflowed and 'lodged' in Mr Potts' beds. This had upset him and he had decreed that 'lodging' in his beds would not be permitted in the future.

'What's his objection to them?' Paul had asked.

'I honestly don't know,' Victoria had replied. 'Possibly one of his patients couldn't be admitted because there was an orthopaedic patient occupying a bed on our ward. But his edict creates great difficulties for the orthopaedic staff. If their beds are already full when someone requires admission, there's really not much they can do about it. If there's a major road accident with multiple victims, they have no option but to place their patients wherever a bed is available. And frankly, Mr Potts is being a bit hypocritical because from time to time, we lodge patients on the orthopaedic wards! But, be warned, if he spots a 'lodger' here, he gets extremely angry and we all suffer. So for the sake of a quiet life, please try to keep orthopaedic patients out of his beds if at all possible.'

'Not to worry,' Paul reassured Sister Ashbrook on the phone. 'I'll have a word with their houseman and get him shifted.'

Paul chanced to meet Jane Holme, the orthopaedic house officer, at the breakfast table. She looked weary, having been up for a couple of hours in the night. He spoke to her about the orthopaedic lodger.

'Oh, he's an old boy of about 85,' Jane replied, spreading marmalade thickly onto her toast; she believed that a generous helping of sugar helped to sustain her through the day. 'He fell yesterday whilst he was out shopping. He's broken his wrist and sprained an ankle. His wrist was straightened under an anaesthetic last night. Normally he wouldn't have been admitted, but he lives alone; he's got no close family and no carers. We'll have to fix him up with some support before he goes home. But don't worry; he'll only be with you for a day or two.'

'Have you no beds in the orthopaedic ward?'

'Sorry, but we haven't. Yesterday was a busy day for us. We've overflowed onto Surgical Two as well.'

It was clear that the lodger would need to stay where he was and that Mr Potts would have to accept the situation. Paul wasn't particularly concerned, after all, only the week before, when all their beds were full, a patient of Mr Potts with appendicitis had been placed on the orthopaedic ward.

As usual, at 8.30 am, Paul met Victoria on the male ward to undertake a quick review of the patients before Mr Potts arrived. By this time, however, Sister Ashbrook had become quite agitated.

'You simply must get rid of the orthopaedic patient. All hell will be let loose if you don't.'

Paul explained that the patient couldn't be discharged home for social reasons, nor was there any prospect of moving him back to the orthopaedic ward.

'Don't worry, Sister,' he added. 'I'm sure Mr Potts will understand.'

'No, he damn well won't,' Sister snapped. She looked pleadingly at Victoria, who turned to Paul.

'Paul,' she said, 'you do a quick ward round and make sure everything is shipshape before Mr Potts arrives. I'll see what I can do about this orthopaedic patient.'

As Paul worked his way, patient by patient, down the ward, it was impossible not to notice the orthopaedic lodger. He was in a bed halfway down on the left-hand side, his freshly applied 'Plaster of Paris' cast and brilliant white triangular sling stood out like a beacon of light amidst the general surgical patients. A pair of crutches and a walking frame stood at his bedside. Paul thought Victoria was on a fool's errand; it would be impossible to hide his presence from Potts.

An hour later, when Mr Potts came to do his ward round, Paul was anxious to see if his reaction to the orthopaedic lodger would be as ferocious as Victoria and Sister Ashbrook had feared, but to his great astonishment, the patient, together with his crutches, plaster cast and walking frame, had vanished into thin air. The bed was empty; indeed, it had been remade with fresh linen. Even the bedside locker was bare. All that remained was an empty bed awaiting its next occupant. Paul looked at Victoria in amazement as they walked past the spot where the lodger had been. She caught his eye, but said nothing. She just winked and her face eased into a slightly smug smile. The round was completed without undue incident, and without any temper tantrums from the consultant, but the minute Mr Potts departed, Paul demanded to know how Victoria had managed to weave such magic.

'Easy,' she said. 'The patient had his wrist fracture reduced last night. That means he needs a check x-ray today to see that the bones have been set in a satisfactory position. The patient is now in the radiology department having his x-ray. The rest of the transformation is down to Sister. She goes along with the subterfuge for the sake of peace and quiet. We've both seen Mr Potts' reaction to orthopaedic lodgers and believe me, when you've witnessed it once; you don't want to see it again.'

'Well done, well done indeed,' Paul commented, admiration evident in his voice.

****

Not too long afterward, he needed to have a further chat with the orthopaedic houseman.

'Hi, Jane,' he began, trying to sound cheerful but knowing he had a favour to ask. 'I'm told by our ward Sister that you've placed a lodger on our ward. I'm afraid we need the bed for today's admission,' he lied. 'I'd be grateful if you could take him back to your ward as soon as possible.'

'Don't tell fibs,' Jane chided him. 'He's on your ward because you *haven't* any admissions today! I know because I checked. You've got a Leslie Potts ward round this morning, haven't you; and you're afraid he'll cause a scene? I've heard all about his allergy to our orthopaedic patients. What happens if he comes into contact with one? Does he swell up and come out in blotches?'

Paul smiled. 'So far, I haven't actually seen what happens, but I'm told he loses all self-control, and breathes fire and brimstone like a dragon. Apparently, he roasts any junior doctors who happen to be around, folk like Victoria and me. But OK, you're quite right, I confess we haven't got an admission today – but it still means that you've got to take him back, pronto!'

'I'm sorry, Paul, but that won't be possible. There was a major road accident on the by-pass last night. We've got lodgers all over the place. I'm afraid one of you will have to act as St George!'

'Is there no chance of moving him at all?' Paul pleaded. Much as he would like to slay Mr Potts, he didn't think he was up to it.

'No, and frankly, I really don't see why your team is always pushing for special treatment. None of the other units harass us the way you do. You lodge patients on our ward from time to time. You should be prepared to give and take.'

'I know that Jane, and truly I don't mean to hassle you, but unfortunately Mr Potts isn't as reasonable as the other consultants.'

'Well, as I say, I'm sorry,' Jane said firmly, 'but the fact remains. We've no slack on our ward, and if we had a spare bed, we would bring a lodger down from Surgical Four. We've three patients up there, and you've only got one. Anyway, it would be difficult to move him. He's trussed up on a Balkan beam.'

Paul groaned. This was a real problem. A 'Balkan beam' was a bed adapted by the addition of four vertical posts, one at each corner. It looked like a four-poster bed with cross beams at the top. The frame was used to support a fractured femur in a sling and, in all likelihood, there would be a giant weight or a large bag of water swinging at the foot of the bed, applying traction to the leg. Although the bed could be wheeled gently on the flat, to move the patient down to the orthopaedic ward in the lift would mean taking it apart, causing the patient pain, risking disturbing the alignment of the broken thigh bone, then reassembling it. The whole process would take at least an hour. Paul sighed. It seemed he was destined to witness Mr Potts' reaction to a lodger, though he doubted it would be quite as dramatic as Sister and Victoria suggested.

Then he had a moment of true inspiration. He rang the ward and had another word with Sister Ashbrook. He would need her assistance if his plan was to succeed, but recalling how she had been complicit in hiding the elderly man with the broken wrist, he was certain she would agree to help. He had seen Victoria pull the wool over Mr Potts' eyes when she'd managed to made a lodger melt into thin air. Would he be as successful, or would the slightly devious use of language he would need to employ land him in trouble? His plan was not without risk, and if it didn't work, what would Mr Potts' reaction be? Presumably Paul, rather than the lodger, would become the focus of the consultant's fury and, if so, Heaven help him.

When Mr Potts came to undertake his ward round, he was in an effervescent mood. The team left the office and approached the patient in the first bed, Janet pushing the trolley containing the patients' notes in front of her.

'Good practice for your future pram pushing days,' Mr Potts remarked with a grin on his face.

He had obviously decided to enjoy himself by teasing Janet, his feminist house officer; he was always pleased if he could get her to react. Paul hoped that on this occasion, she wouldn't. There would be fireworks if he realised there was a lodger on the ward, and it would be ten times worse if he was already riled. Janet glared at the consultant, met him eye to eye, but kept her lip buttoned; she had decided that on this occasion her response would not be with words but with actions. As the group moved to the next patient, she deliberately left the trolley behind. They were three beds further down the ward before Mr Potts asked for some information that was held in the patient's clinical record.

'Where are the patient's notes?' the consultant wanted to know, his eye searching in vain for the missing trolley. As one, the group turned, and saw the trolley isolated and abandoned like a wartime casualty after the cavalry have charged on.

'I parked the *pram* five minutes ago,' Janet replied coldly, standing tall, glaring at the consultant and making no movement to go and retrieve it. She added the word, 'Sir,' somewhat belatedly.

A shocked silence enveloped the group in anticipation of an imminent storm. A flash of anger crossed Mr Potts' face. Then his features softened and broke into a smile. Finally, he laughed out loud.

'So you have, my dear, so you have. I do so like a pretty girl with a bit of spirit. Well done.' Then he stopped and with a twinkle in his eye added, 'I suppose you wouldn't care to carry the notes in your arms, rather than push the pram? Carrying notes is a bit like carrying a baby, you know – good practise for later life.'

Seeing the expression of disgust on Janet's face, he added, 'No, I don't suppose you would.'

He turned to Paul. 'Let me give you a bit of advice, Lambert,' he said, with mock seriousness. 'In a few years' time, when you're a consultant, be very careful when appointing female staff. By all means, employ a woman to be your house officer. They won't be with you long enough to get pregnant, and in any case, you'll work them so hard that they won't have the energy to take the preliminary steps. But never appoint a woman to a long-term post. Invariably they get pregnant, and it plays havoc with the duty roster.

Now, Sister Ashbrook, do you think one of your lovely nurses would be kind enough to act as mother and fetch the trolley? It's time we got on with our work.'

The consultant turned again to his house officer. 'Now tell me about this next patient, my dea..... oh, I'm so sorry, Miss Smith, or is it Doctor Smith? For the life of me, I can never remember which you prefer and I'm not allowed to say 'my dear', am I? I'm afraid I just can't get used to all this political correctness; you really must forgive me.'

Janet simply ignored him. She had decided not to rise to the bait, and not to push the notes trolley for Mr Potts ever again!

During these exchanges, Paul was becoming increasingly anxious. They were coming to the last few patients and so far, nothing had raised any suspicion in Mr Potts' mind that there might be an orthopaedic lodger on the ward. But the most critical, most dangerous part of the deception was yet to come. All that remained was to see the patients in the side wards, which were shared by the two consultants. As Mr Potts saw the patient in the first room, Paul lingered at the back of the group, thereby able to make a quick exit when the consultation was over.

The door to the second side ward was closed, the blind covering the window pulled down. Paul made sure he reached the door first. Mr Potts normally barged straight in without knocking, but found Paul barring his way.

'I'm afraid we had a death on the ward earlier today, Sir,' he said. Strictly speaking, it wasn't a lie, though it was deliberately misleading.

For a moment, Mr Potts looked concerned.

'Not one of mine, I hope,' he said.

'No, sir. He wasn't a patient of yours,' Paul replied honestly.

The consultant's cheery disposition seemed to be enhanced by this information.

'So! Old Sir William has been killing them off, has he?' he joked. 'What was it, a simple toenail operation that went wrong?'

Remarks like this were commonplace between medical staff at all levels in the hospital; it wasn't unusual for one consultant to have a dig at the expense of another, or for surgeons to rib the physicians. Victoria and Paul smiled dutifully at the remark, but Sister Ashbrook took exception.

'Sir William may be nearing retirement,' she protested, 'but he remains a very safe surgeon and a very fine gentleman.'

'I was only joking, Sister dear,' Mr Potts replied, smiling and pleased to have prompted a reaction from his Ward Sister, 'there's no need to spring to his defence. But you must admit; he is getting a bit close to his sell-by date.'

Paul knew he was only teasing, but wasn't sure that his Ward Sister did. She looked furious, but without Janet's self-assurance, she didn't have the confidence to bandy words with the consultant.

Thankfully, the rest of the round passed off without further incident, and when Mr Potts had departed and the tea and biscuits had appeared, Paul turned to Victoria.

'Did you happen to notice the orthopaedic lodger on the ward today?' he said, helping himself to a chocolate biscuit, a satisfied expression on his face.

Victoria looked surprised. 'No, I didn't.'

'Actually, he has a broken leg and he's strung up on a Balkan beam. I'm amazed you didn't spot him.'

Victoria thought for a moment. 'Ah,' she said, 'that must be the 'deceased' patient in the side room! I can see you're learning, Paul; you're obviously a candidate for promotion. But when you make consultant grade, I do hope that you'll ignore his intolerable sexist advice about appointing female members of staff.'

Thanks to the cooperation of the nursing sisters, a degree of subterfuge and a run of good luck, Victoria and Paul managed to conceal the presence of the occasional orthopaedic patient from the consultant's eagle eye for many weeks. Good fortune, however, does not last forever, and the day duly arrived when Leslie Potts was destined to find a lodger in one of his beds. To make matters worse, there were actually two lodgers, and both were highly conspicuous in the middle of the Nightingale ward. It was inevitable that the consultant would spot them! One lodger had a surgical collar around his neck, and an arm encased in Plaster of Paris, as brilliantly white as virgin snow. The other was imprisoned in a Balkan beam, his leg in a heavy metal splint exposed above the bedclothes, with numerous weights and pulleys hanging over the foot of the bed.

Desperately, Victoria and Sister Ashbrook had tried to conceal them, but without success. Neither needed to leave the ward for further x-rays, and there wasn't a side ward available into which they could be hidden. Consideration had been given to placing them on the veranda for the duration of the ward round, but in winter, as the temperature was barely above freezing and snow was falling, this wasn't a practical proposition. It seemed that finally, Paul would witness the consultant's displeasure, and discover why Victoria and Sister Ashbrook were so apprehensive. The two junior doctors were painfully aware that when Mr Potts was in a bad mood, they were the ones most likely to suffer.

The medical students were also apprehensive. They too, were familiar with Mr Potts' unpredictable moods. Only the week before, he had objected to the beard grown by one of them.

'Beards have no place on a surgical unit,' he had said. 'They harbour germs. You will not be allowed on the ward until you have shaved it off.'

Another of the group, Simon Morris, had been despatched from the outpatient clinic for his untidy appearance.

'Jeans and sweaters are inappropriate attire for anyone aspiring to be a doctor,' he had insisted. 'Go and change this instant.'

The nerves of the patients awaiting the consultant's visit were also on edge. Most had heard that Mr Potts was not a man who suffered fools gladly. Their concerns had been heightened by witnessing the frantic preparations made by the nurses for the round; anxiously tidying lockers, straightening blankets and fluffing pillows. They had seen the porters, orderlies, and cleaners being shooed from the ward, and they had been given strict instructions to stay in their beds and to avoid unnecessary noise.

On this occasion, Mr Potts was a mere ten minutes late, and as he breezed into the room, he appeared to be in a good mood. He had a smile on his face as he ran his eye along the line of students.

'I'm pleased to see that you're all turned out smartly today. Even Mr Morris seems to have made a special effort.'

Then he put a hand loosely on Janet's shoulder, still addressing the students. 'And our lovely House Lady also looks well this morning, doesn't she? Although I'm not supposed to say that either, am I, my dear?'

With time Janet had come to regard her boss with contempt. She recognised that reacting to his provocation simply encouraged him, so she simply took a small step sideways which left his hand hanging awkwardly in mid-air. However, this further example of her consultant's sexist behaviour caused something inside her to snap. She decided enough was enough; the time had come to put a stop to it. But what, as a lowly house officer, could she do?

'Right, let's go and see our patients,' Mr Potts said, as he strode purposefully through the double doors and onto the ward. Sister was at his side, Victoria and Paul followed behind. Next in line was Janet. Holding to her resolution, she strolled alongside the notes trolley, which was being pushed by a student nurse. The medical students brought up the rear.

Mr Potts stopped abruptly the moment his eye fell on the two orthopaedic patients. The entourage following behind also came to a sudden halt, each bumping into the one in front, like railway trucks in a shunting yard. The consultant jabbed a finger at the two lodgers, then glared at Sister Ashbrook, eyebrows raised, brow furrowed and face flushed, his blood pressure rising.

'What are those patients doing on my ward, Sister?' he demanded. 'They're orthopaedic patients. They should be on the orthopaedic ward.' His voice was loud, his tone angry.

Sister hesitated, flustered. Victoria interceded on her behalf.

'I'm sorry, Mr Potts, but there was a nasty accident at the steelworks late last night. All the beds on the orthopaedic unit were taken, so, unfortunately, these two patients had to be placed on our ward.'

'Well, get rid of them at once!' he bellowed.

'We've already tried to do that, Sir. We've spoken to the staff downstairs to see if they have any spare capacity, but regrettably, they haven't. They admitted some patients this morning from their waiting list for surgery tomorrow. All their beds are full.'

'They've no damn right to admit more patients to their ward when we have their blasted lodgers here. Go downstairs immediately Miss Kent, and send their new admissions home. I will not tolerate orthopaedic patients on my ward. They're a bloody nuisance; they upset the staff and interfere with the smooth running of the ward.'

'I'm afraid I have no authority to do that, Sir, any more than the orthopaedic registrar has the right to come here and discharge our patients.' Victoria spoke quietly and respectfully. What she said was completely true, but her words cut no ice with her angry boss.

'Then go downstairs and tell their registrar to discharge their new admissions. It's quite intolerable that they should carry on admitting when their patients are clogging up my beds.'

To Paul, a couple of patients on the wrong ward seemed no more than a minor inconvenience, particularly as the beds on their ward would otherwise have been empty, and had he been wise, he would have kept quiet. Unfortunately, he didn't.

'I know its awkward, Sir,' he volunteered, 'but they did have some of our patients on their ward only last week. Surely, it's simply a matter of give and take.'

For a moment, there was silence, and then Mr Potts roared, 'When I want your advice, Lambert, I'll ask for it. Until then, shut up.'

In the silence that followed, all eyes turned on Paul, no-one daring to say a word for fear of aggravating the situation. Then Mr Potts started giving orders.

'Dr Smith, you stay here. Sister, prepare those two orthopaedic patients for transfer. You students, go and find something useful to do 'til I get back. Miss Kent and Lambert, come with me. We'll go to the bloody orthopaedic unit, and we'll find some empty beds, even if we have to discharge their patients ourselves. I'll show them they can't scatter patients around the hospital like confetti whenever and wherever they please.'

As Victoria and Paul followed Mr Potts off the ward, there was alarm on the faces of the patients in the vicinity. They were stunned by the behaviour of their consultant; if he threw temper tantrums like this when operating, were they wise to entrust themselves to his care?

Leslie Potts flew down the stairs two at a time and flung open the doors of the orthopaedic ward. A ward round was in progress. The junior orthopaedic doctors were present, together with the ward sister and a couple of her nurses. At their head was Mr Keenan, the orthopaedic consultant, a man built like an ox, who would not have been out of place in the front row of a rugby scrum. With his thick neck, broad shoulders and with pectoral muscles scarcely contained within his tight-fitting shirt, he towered over his fellow consultant. Mr

Potts though, blinded by rage, was not intimidated and marched straight up to him, David face to face with Goliath. Victoria and Paul followed apprehensively, a dozen paces behind.

'Sam, I need words with you!'

Sam Keenan looked up and saw Mr Potts, his face flushed and bristling with anger. Knowing his colleague of old, he summed up the situation in an instant.

'Ah, Leslie,' he said in a quiet appeasing voice. 'I've no doubt you've come to have a little chat about the two patients we've had to lodge with you. I'm genuinely sorry about that. Come into the office with me, and we'll see what can be done about it.'

Before Mr Potts had time to respond, Mr Keenan draped his arm around his consultant colleague's shoulder, and gently guided him to the privacy of the office. Victoria and Paul stood a little way apart from the orthopaedic team, and awaited events.

'Well,' Paul said, 'you did warn me, but I never expected anything like that. Why on earth does he get so angry? It's obvious that when one ward is full, urgent admissions have to be placed on another ward. It's give-and-take. Sometimes, we lodge on their ward, sometimes, they lodge patients on ours. It all balances out in the end.'

'Yes, obviously it does, but Mr Potts doesn't see it like that. He believes that the beds on his ward are sacrosanct. And to be fair, the orthopods ought to have taken their lodgers back this morning before they arranged further admissions to their own ward.'

'That's true, but why does he get so upset?'

'I honestly don't know. There's obviously some bad blood between them, though I can't see Mr Keenan ever upsetting anyone. He really is a gentle giant, and the most obliging man you could hope to meet. Maybe Mr Potts fell out with the orthopaedic consultant who retired recently. Perhaps he had a bad experience with a broken limb as a child. I really don't know, but I could do without it. There are more than enough problems for us to worry about without having to deal with explosions of rage by the consultants.'

The door of the ward office remained firmly closed for the next five minutes. Then the two consultants emerged, and rather formally shook hands. Mr Keenan, a twinkle in his eye and the hint of a smile on his face looked perfectly calm. Leslie Potts still looked tense, though he now appeared to be more in control than before, his rage having abated somewhat.

'Right,' he said to his registrars, 'now that's sorted, let's get back to our own patients.'

Victoria and Paul would have loved to have overheard the exchange between the two consultants, and to learn what agreement had been reached, but that remained a secret between them. However, they were fascinated to observe that both the orthopaedic patients had disappeared by the time they visited the ward later that day, and it was to be many months before any more orthopaedic lodgers found their way into Mr Potts' beds.

Thought for the day

Anger always thinks it has power beyond its power

Publilius Syrus 1st Cent BC

Chapter 25   Dr Janet Smith

10th January 1971

One wet January evening, Janet sat seething in her room as she considered what she could do about Mr Potts' appalling attitude towards women. She considered herself to be a fair-minded and reasonable woman, not one to be upset at some slight teasing, but on many occasions his conduct had been totally unacceptable. She recalled the Mickey McGovern affair. Certainly, he had defended her, and protected her from adverse publicity for which she was grateful, but in patting her bottom, and suggesting that she ought to find sexual innuendo acceptable, he had revealed that he was just as guilty of sexist behaviour as the young footballer had been. Maybe he wasn't quite as blatant as Mickey had been, but his prejudice against women was just as deeply ingrained. She also felt that although she was strong enough to stand up to him, to let him know that his sexism was not acceptable, others were not. Karen Croft clearly had not enjoyed being the subject of Mr Potts' personal comments when asked to examine Mr Walton's varicose veins, but as a young medical student, she was dependent on her consultant, and wasn't in a position to do anything about it.

Janet therefore decided that action was required; it was time for Mr Potts to be shown that his attitude towards women, his intolerable sexist behaviour, was simply not acceptable. Maybe a hundred years ago women had been subjugated, and a man could get away with such behaviour, but those days were surely gone. It was time for her to do her duty, and to speak up for her sex. But would he listen, and even if he listened, would he take any notice?

For several days, Janet considered the problem, and came to the conclusion that whilst she couldn't force him to change his beliefs, or his behaviour, there were opportunities for her to speak her mind, occasions when he would have no option but to listen to her views.

Later that week, Janet and Victoria were assisting Mr Potts in the operating theatre, as he excised a colonic tumour. Janet waited until the cancerous growth had been removed, and the continuity of the bowel had been restored. The difficult technical part of the operation now completed, all that remained was the closure of the abdominal incision, a routine procedure during which the surgical team were able to relax.

'OK, Sister dear,' Mr Potts said, 'we're nearly through, let's get this wound closed, and then you can get off home and organise the tea for your family. I'll have the Number One Dexon suture for the muscle layer now, please.'

This remark gave Janet the opening for which she was waiting.

'You know, Mr Potts,' she said, 'I really don't understand why you assume that preparing a meal is woman's work; perhaps Sister's husband will do it.'

And without giving the consultant a chance to respond, she continued. 'Recently, I was told a story by a friend of mine. She's a medical student, and all being well, she'll qualify as a doctor next year. She was observing a GP at work when an elderly lady attended, accompanied by her husband. They were asked if they minded the student being present during the wife's consultation.

Apparently, the old gent turned to my friend, and said, 'No, we don't mind at all. Everyone has to learn, don't they? So you're studying to be a nurse, are you?'

It was his wife who immediately corrected him. 'Don't be such an idiot, dear,' she said. 'Her badge says 'Medical Student'.

Do you see, Mr Potts, the old man had assumed that because she was female, she was training to be a nurse, not a doctor. Do you realise that 25% of medical students these days are female?'

'Yes, I did know that,' her boss replied, 'and I really don't know what the world is coming to! They'll qualify as doctors then go off, get married and then have babies. They'll hang up their stethoscopes and they won't practise medicine after the age of thirty. Such a waste.'

'You know, Sir', Janet retorted, 'I think it's rather sad that in some ways things really haven't moved on since 1862.'

'I've a feeling we're going to hear what happened in 1862,' Mr Potts commented to the other doctors and nurses who were listening to the conversation, admiring Janet for her bravery, but wondering if she were wise to challenge her consultant quite so forcibly.

'Well, it was in 1862, Mr Potts, that Elizabeth Garrett Anderson was the first woman to be granted a licence to practice medicine by the Society of Apothecaries. It really is an interesting story. You see, she'd been a nurse, but then educated herself privately, to become the first female doctor in this country. And guess what the Society immediately did?'

'I'm ready for the skin suture now, Sister dear,' Mr Potts said, avoiding the question, and perhaps hoping this would deflect the conversation onto a new topic. But it didn't; Janet was determined to make her point.

'The Apothecaries immediately changed the rules to bar any other women from being granted a licence. It was to be another fourteen years before the law was changed by virtue of an Act of Parliament.'

Victoria feared that if Janet persisted in expressing her views so strongly, Potts' short-fuse might be revealed.

'Actually, Janet,' she said, 'Elizabeth Anderson wasn't the first woman to become a doctor. A few years earlier, James Barry had that honour. James was actually a woman though she lived her life as a man; she took the Apothecaries exam and practised medicine throughout her life as a man.'

Mr Potts decided that he had heard enough.

'Right,' he announced, 'time for me to go. I'll leave you two girls to pop in the last few skin stitches whilst you continue your chat.'

He dragged off his hat and mask, threw them in the bin, and marched out of the theatre.

Victoria immediately turned to the house officer. 'Do have a care, Janet, I know you feel strongly about these matters, but at the end of the day, Mr Potts is the boss around here. When you leave, you'll need a reference, and he has a lot of influence, you know.'

'I've already got my next job,' Janet replied, 'in Australia. I don't need any favours from him, so I'm planning to continue my campaign to educate him until I leave.'

Victoria presumed that Janet would find just as many male dinosaurs in Australia; indeed, she might find even more than in the UK, but she kept these thoughts to herself.

Although Mr Potts walked away from Janet's fiercely-held opinions on that occasion, it was not too long before Janet was again voicing her opinions. The next time she was in theatre, it happened that Paul was assisting Mr Potts. Again, she waited until the difficult aspect of the operation was completed before opening the subject that was so dear to her heart.

'Do you happen to know Miss Kathleen Woods?' she asked Mr Potts.

'No, I don't think so,' he replied, 'who is she?'

'She's a consultant surgeon in London.'

Mr Potts looked up from his work. 'Then I'm surprised I haven't heard of her. What's her specialty?'

'Ear Nose and Throat, Sir.'

'Yes, now you mention it, I have heard of her; she wrote some nonsense in a surgical journal recently about sexism in medicine, didn't she? And if I remember correctly, she's not an ENT surgeon; she's just an N surgeon. Doesn't she only operate on noses? I ask you, how specialised can you get? Mind you,' he added, winking at Paul, and then at Janet across the top of his mask, 'as a female, maybe that's all she can cope with.'

These exchanges usually worried Paul, but on this occasion, Mr Potts was taking the fray to Janet, clearly relishing the challenge.

'Did you read the piece she wrote, Mr Potts?'

'No, I didn't, my dear', he said, his voice light-hearted, 'it wasn't a subject that interested me, so I skipped it.'

'Well, Mr Potts, in the article, she recalled how after explaining an operation at length to a patient, she was asked; *'Will I ever get to meet the consultant?'* You see, the unspoken assumption was that the head of the department must inevitably be a man. She also told how, when she was at the College of Surgeons receiving her Fellowship, she was standing with her husband when the chief examiner came up to her and said, *'You must be very proud of him.'* It shows, Mr Potts, that sexism is still alive and kicking in this country, and not just in this hospital,' she added pointedly.

Paul, conscious as ever that Mr Potts would only tolerate so much from his juniors, decided to intervene.

'I remember,' he began, 'when I was newly-qualified, being called to see a patient on the gynaecology ward. I was wearing my white doctor's coat, and I was 'wolf-whistled' by one of the gynaecology patients as I walked down the ward. This caused quite a lot of laughter, and there were comments and catcalls as well; *'he can give me the once-over anytime he wants.'* At the time, I simply felt embarrassed, but I can well imagine that such remarks addressed to a woman, perhaps who is on her own, or maybe in a quiet location, would be upsetting, if not frightening.'

'You should have been flattered, Lambert. They obviously thought you were a good-looking chap.'

'But that's exactly the point, Mr Potts!' Janet said. 'Women don't want to be judged on their appearance, they want to be recognised for who they are.'

'If that's the case, why do they spend so much money on their clothes, and so much time on their make-up?' was Mr Potts response, as once again he threw off his gown and departed, leaving Paul to complete the procedure.

To Paul's relief, that ended the conversation. He placed the last sutures in the patient's wound before he and Janet scrubbed again for the next operation.

Unsurprisingly, Janet's one-woman campaign against Mr Potts was the subject of much discussion in the doctor's residency, and as a result several of her female colleagues shared their own experiences with her. Janet was told of an occasion when a consultant asked a female trainee to perform some minor procedures in a side theatre whilst he worked in the main theatre. This included circumcision and vasectomy operations. When gowned up, she had approached one particular patient, scalpel in hand, to perform a vasectomy where upon he had leapt off the operating table, grabbed his trousers with one hand, his wallet and shirt in the other, and run off down the corridor shouting 'I'm not having any bloody women operate on my genitals!'

Janet stored such stories in her memory to be used as ammunition as and when the opportunity presented itself.

Her best chance to promote her views was always when she and Mr Potts were together in theatre, when he was unable to escape.

An opportunity presented itself the following morning, and she knew exactly which tale of sexist behaviour she was going to relate. But it transpired that she was not the only one to have made preparations for this third round of their battle of wits. On this occasion, Mr Potts called at a sweet shop on his way to the hospital, phoning to say he would be a few minutes late, and asking Paul to make the preliminary incision for him. Paul and Janet were therefore scrubbed, gowned, and wearing caps and masks at the table when he arrived. Before going to scrub himself, he went up to Janet, lifted her mask, put an enormous gobstopper in her mouth, and then slipped her mask back into place.

'Now, Sister dear,' he said, 'we'll be able to enjoy some peace and quiet whilst I whip this gall bladder out, and then perhaps one of your young angels will be able to rustle up some coffee and toast for us hard-working men!'

With blood-stained, sterile gloves on her hands, Janet was unable to respond, and was forced to fume in silence while Mr Potts chatted to Paul about the prospects for the English Rugby team in the forthcoming Calcutta Cup match against Scotland.

Thoughts for the day

Yes, injured woman! Rise, assert thy rights.

Anna Laetitia Barbauld 1743 – 1825

Do you not know I am a woman? When I think, I must speak.

William Shakespeare 1564 - 1616

Chapter 26   Cedric Brown: (A Drama in Three Acts)

20th January 1971   Act One   To the Pearly Gates and Back

It was 9 pm on a Saturday evening. Paul was in the Casualty Department, taking a short break, when he heard the familiar siren of an ambulance drawing up outside.

'Sounds like more work for us,' he commented. There was no anxiety in his voice, but his heart skipped a beat. He had now been qualified for four years, but there were still medical conditions beyond his competence.

Two minutes later, Sally, one of the Staff Nurses, popped her head around the door.

'I think you ought to see this patient straight away, Paul,' she said. 'She's got a nasty laceration on her hand.'

Paul didn't need to ask into which cubicle the patient had been placed. He merely had to follow the drips of fresh red blood on the polished linoleum floor.

The woman looked to be about 35-years-old. A quick glance at the Casualty card told him she was called Annie Nolan. She had a bloodied headscarf wrapped tightly around her right hand, which she clutched to her chest in pain. Paul thought the woman's face was vaguely familiar, although he couldn't place her.

'Hi, I'm Dr Lambert,' he said. 'Haven't I seen you somewhere before?'

Sally shot him an amused look, but made no comment.

'You may have, Doctor. I live just around the corner.'

She looked frightened and unkempt, but it was her clothes that reminded Paul why her face was familiar. She was wearing a cheap, leather mini-skirt, fish-net stockings, and a low-cut blouse that revealed a vast cleavage. The blouse had once been white, but was now covered with blood. The hospital stood on one of the main city thoroughfares, but opposite the main entrance, a tangle of narrow side streets led to a less salubrious area. Occasionally, Paul had passed Annie on one of these street corners when walking home from work. She had once approached him, and asked *'would you be looking for a little warmth and comfort this evening, Sir.'* No wonder Sally had been amused when he had suggested that he recognised Annie.

Slowly and painfully, Sally removed the scarf from Annie's hand, and wiped away the blood and clots, so they were able to inspect the damage. Paul had never seen such an injury before. There was a deep cut across the base of all four fingers. The lacerations must have been inflicted by an extremely sharp blade for the wound edges were clean and sharply defined. He asked Annie to make a fist, showing her with his own hand what he wanted her to do. She attempted this, grimacing with pain. Her thumb flexed but her fingers remained straight. The cut had gone straight down to the bone, dividing all the tendons that enabled the fingers to move. Unless these guy ropes could be reconnected, her right hand would be useless.

'How on earth did this happen?' he asked.

There was silence. 'Come on, Annie, we need to know.' But Annie had clammed up.

'Are you right-handed?' Paul asked.

Annie nodded weakly. That made the injury significantly more serious.

Paul turned to Sally. 'Can you put a pressure bandage on these wounds for me, please? I'll ask the Orthopods to come and see her. They're the experts. They get more practice repairing tendons than we do.'

'Annie,' Paul said, 'you're going to need this hand patching up under an anaesthetic, but we'll get the experts to sort that out for you. Are you injured anywhere else?'

She pointed to a two-inch cut on the back of her left forearm, and then took off her blouse. There was a shorter laceration on her left shoulder. Again, both injuries appeared to have been inflicted by an extremely sharp blade. Fortunately, however, in neither case was there any damage to underlying structures. Paul felt sure he could persuade the orthopaedic surgeons to suture these two cuts whilst they were repairing her hand, so he simply asked Sally to apply temporary dressings.

He had just returned to the office to record Annie's injuries in her notes when Sister Atkins, one of the Departments most senior Sisters, dashed in.

'Paul, there's a major stabbing in the 'resus' cubicle; we need you right now.'

Again, Paul experienced that twinge of doubt, and muttered a quiet prayer that he would be able to cope.

Assessing blood loss in an Afro-Caribbean is not as easy as may be imagined. In a Caucasian, the profound pallor and cold, moist skin are recognisable from the foot of the bed; but not so for black skin. There was, however, no difficulty in knowing that this particular West Indian, who Paul later learned was called Cedric King, was 'in extremis.' He was barely conscious, and had a large and expanding bloodstain on his shirt.

'He's been stabbed,' Sister said, rather stating the obvious. She was already at work, setting up a drip, and taking blood for a cross-match. 'Pulse is 115 per minute; blood pressure barely 90/60.'

Paul's rapid assessment revealed a single stab wound in the left upper abdomen, about an inch long. Inspection of the external wound offered no clue as to the extent of the internal injuries, but the whole abdomen was tender and rigid, a sure sign of serious internal damage. The knife, or whatever it was, that had inflicted this injury, had clearly caused either massive internal bleeding, or perforation of his gut, or possibly both.

'Blood pressure falling!' Sister shouted. 'Now 75 over 50.'

'Right. He goes straight to theatre. Tell them to expect a patient for an emergency exploration of the abdomen within five minutes. Get them to 'crash call' the anaesthetist, and tell him to meet us in the theatre.'

'Will do, Paul,' Sister said, already on her way to the phone.

'And, Sister, can you call the laboratory urgently as well. We'll need four pints of blood, maybe more. If possible, we'll have the same blood group, but there won't be time for a full cross-match. Your nurses can run the sample to the laboratory; we haven't time to wait for a porter. In the meantime, keep the plasma running.'

There was no need to check that Sister understood these instructions; with years of experience, she would have organised everything just as efficiently, even if Paul had not been there. 'And when you have a minute, you'd better inform the police,' Paul added.

Paul and Jimmy, the Casualty orderly, rushed the patient down the hospital corridor, pushing the trolley as fast as they could, scattering visitors and staff as they went. A nurse ran alongside holding the drip. Paul cursed the speed of the lift as they went up to the Surgical Five theatre on the first floor. Two minutes later, they reached the theatre to find the staff hard at work, preparing for the emergency.

The duty anaesthetist, Bill Jones, a contemporary of Paul's and a steady head in an emergency, was already present. 'What do you expect to find here?'

'Truly, I don't know,' Paul replied. 'He's clearly lost a lot of blood, so presumably, some major blood vessel must be severed, but the bowel may be damaged as well. We won't know until we get inside.'

The truth was that the wound could be two inches deep, or twelve inches deep. The spleen, liver, pancreas, or any major blood vessel could be bleeding. It might be something Paul was able to deal with, but equally, if it was the aorta or inferior vena cava, the huge pipes that carry blood to and from the lower trunk and legs, the injuries would be beyond his capabilities. He had no experience of operating on these vessels. He rang Sir William, who was the consultant on call. It was his resident housekeeper, Mrs Burton, who answered.

'I need an urgent word with Sir William.'

'He's reading in his study. I'll ask him to come to the phone.'

'No, wait,' Paul said, 'give him a message. Ask him....' but it was too late, Mrs Burton had put the receiver down, and was already on her way to fetch the consultant.

Paul grabbed one of the junior nurses. 'Hang onto this phone for me, will you? When Sir William comes on the line, tell him we have an emergency stabbing in theatre. Ask him to come as soon as possible.'

In the anaesthetic room, one of the nurses was pumping fluid into Cedric's left arm with a mechanical roller. Bill was passing the endotracheal tube through which the anaesthetic would be given, into the patient's throat. As soon as the tube was in place, he called to Paul.

'Paul, I'm going to bring him straight into theatre, we're in danger of losing him.'

Paul glanced at the heart monitor. The blood pressure was barely recordable, and the bleep from the cardiac machine raced along. They dragged the patient from the trolley onto the operating table. Then suddenly, the monitor's bleep changed to a continuous shrill alarm tone. The heart had stopped. Bill began cardiac massage, while one of the nurses squeezed the bag to blow oxygen and anaesthetic gases into the patient's lungs. Paul threw off his white coat, rolled up his shirt sleeves, dragged a plastic apron over his head, then pulled on a pair of surgical gloves. Sister passed him a knife. There was no time to cleanse the skin, or to put drapes around the abdomen. Paul plunged the knife into the skin, but there was no response from the patient;

whether he was unconscious, anaesthetised, or even dead, he had no idea.

Making no attempt to identify the separate layers of the abdominal wall, he made a large incision. The bleeding was minimal, thanks to the absence of any blood pressure. The belly was full of blood, some liquid, some clotted. Sister produced the strong surgical suction tube, and the liquid blood rapidly disappeared into the suction bottle at the side of the table. Within a minute, the two-litre bottle was full and needed replacing. Paul scooped out the clots, two-handed and placed them into a kidney dish. To his enormous relief, when the blood and clots were removed, the source of the bleeding was apparent. A large artery and two even larger veins feeding blood to the spleen had been divided. The application of several large pairs of forceps arrested the bleeding.

When a breathless Sir William entered the theatre moments later, he might have imagined he was in a military hospital in a war zone. The patient, his underpants about his ankles and his shirt around his neck, had a huge wound in his belly, without a surgical drape in sight. Blood was dripping down the side of the operating table, and forming a dark pool on the theatre floor. Paul was ungowned, still wearing his shirt and tie, his plastic apron heavily blood-stained with just a pair of gloves on his hands as a gesture to sterility. Bill, the anaesthetist, was pumping on the patient's chest, leaving Sir William in no doubt of the urgency of the situation.

'Have I time to scrub, Lambert?' Sir William asked, his voice calm and quiet.

'Yes, I think I've managed to stop the bleeding,' Paul replied.

'Good. In that case, I'll join you at the table in a couple of minutes. Since this is a cardiac arrest situation, I suggest you pack the area with some large swabs. That will apply a bit of pressure, and allow Jones some time to get on with the resuscitation.'

'I would appreciate that,' Bill gasped, now out of breath from his physical exertion. 'It will give me a chance to try to catch up with the blood loss.'

The next five minutes were spent with furious activity. Blood and plasma were pumped into Cedric's veins, and Bill passed a long needle between his ribs and injected adrenaline directly into the heart.

'Everyone stand back from the patient,' Bill instructed as he placed the two pads of the cardiac defibrillator onto Cedric's chest. He applied a massive electric shock to the heart resulting in a violent spasm which, for an instant, lifted the patient bodily off the table. But to no avail, the cardiac trace remained flat, and the alarm tone from the monitor continued.

'Everyone stand away again,' Bill instructed. He shocked the patient a second time, and miraculously the heart started to pump again. Initially, the beat was hesitant and weak, but gradually its strength and rhythm improved until it was able to restore the circulation. To everyone's relief, the cardiac monitor once more gave out its reassuring regular, if rapid, bleep.

With Sir William now at the table, Paul had a chance to relax. Appropriately scrubbed, gowned and gloved, Sir William looked across the table at Paul's blood-stained clothes.

'Lambert,' he said, 'I'll take over for a minute and ensure there's no further bleeding. You go and gown properly.'

Then he addressed the anaesthetist. 'Will it be alright if I tidy up in here?'

'I would rather you didn't, Sir,' Bill replied. 'I'd prefer you to take a breather while I get some more fluid inside him.'

In the changing room, Paul took off the bloodied plastic apron and placed it into the skip for disposal. He discovered that blood had dripped down from it onto his shoes and socks, so he shed them and put them to one side. He would deal with them later. He put on a theatre top and pants, and then with bare feet inside surgical wellington boots, he scrubbed properly and re-joined Sir William.

'Have you had a chance to look round the rest of the belly yet?' Sir William asked.

'No, I haven't, Sir. There just wasn't time.'

'Right, well, that's the next job. Is it alright, Jones, if we do that now?'

'Yes, that's fine,' Bill replied. 'He's been to the Pearly Gates and back, but he seems to be perking up a bit now. I've got his BP up to 100. It's quite amazing!'

Sir William undertook a thorough examination of the abdomen. Fortunately, apart from the damage to the blood vessels to the spleen, he found no other injury.

'What do you think we should do next, Lambert?' he asked.

'I suppose the spleen ought to come out, Sir,' Paul said.

'I'm sure that's right. It's lost its blood supply so it will die and get infected if left in place. This really is your operation, Lambert, but if you don't mind, I think I'd better do it to save time. The sooner we get this patient off the table the better, don't you agree, Jones?'

It was impossible not to respect Sir William; he was always such a gentleman. He didn't need to ask Paul's permission to take over the operation. Cedric was his patient. At the end of the day, he was the consultant responsible for his care, but even in this fraught situation, he had been at pains not to be seen to be pulling rank on Paul.

Expertly, Sir William swept his hand round the back of the spleen, and freed it from its bed. Then he applied ligatures to the blood vessels that had been damaged, using the clamps that Paul had applied twenty minutes or so earlier.

'Right,' he said, 'it's nearly time to close up, but before we do, we ought to investigate this stab wound a bit further. In due course the police will be asking for a report, and this is an ideal opportunity to do a bit of detective work.'

Together they looked at the entrance wound in the skin. It was about an inch in length, and the edges could not have been better defined had they been incised with a surgical blade. The knife that inflicted the injury must have been razor-sharp.

'And look,' Sir William commented, 'it must have been inflicted by a double-edged knife; the skin has been cut equally cleanly at both ends of the wound. Can you let me have something to use as a probe, Sister? Anything will do.'

Sister passed him a pair of forceps, and Sir William carefully inserted these into the stab wound. From the entrance of the wound below the ribs on the left side, the instrument passed slightly upwards for a full five inches. In doing so, it had passed, very fortuitously, in front of the patient's left kidney, then behind his stomach, before its tip had caused the catastrophic bleeding from the vessels going to the spleen. Had it penetrated another inch or so, it would have struck the aorta, the enormous blood vessel running down the back of the trunk supplying blood to the lower half of the body. This would surely have been fatal.

'So,' Sir William concluded, 'the blade that inflicted this wound was sharp, double-edged, not less than five inches long, and the direction of the blow was almost horizontal. You'll need to include all that in your police report, Lambert. Right, it's time to close up. You do it. I'll assist.'

'I'm afraid it's not a very tidy incision, Sir,' Paul confessed, 'it was done in a bit of a hurry.'

'As was entirely appropriate, I should imagine,' Sir William replied, glancing at the blood in the suction bottles. 'It looks as if you applied those clamps just in the nick of time.'

Slowly, carefully, under Sir William's watchful eye, Paul closed the wound as best he could, but it was a large incision, and impossible to make a neat job of it, thanks to the haste with which it had been created. Looking at it when he had finished, it reminded him of the bossed edges of a Cornish pasty. He hoped it would heal satisfactorily, but given the patient's perilous condition, that was something they would worry about later.

Amazingly, with further fluid replacement, and with his heartbeat stabilized, Cedric's blood pressure continued to rise, and to everyone's astonishment, he even woke up when his anaesthetic was reversed. Fears that he might have suffered brain damage during his cardiac arrest appeared to be unfounded.

Sir William and Paul went together to the surgeon's room to change. Paul was surprised to discover what Sir William had been wearing before being called into the hospital. Paul was accustomed to seeing him looking immaculate in his city suit, often with a rose in the buttonhole of his lapel. It was incongruous to see him wearing dirty, brown corduroy trousers, and an old woollen jumper sporting several holes.

Sir William saw Paul washing out his blood-stained socks in the sink, and placing them on the radiator to dry.

'I'll leave you now,' he said, 'but if you wait here for five minutes, I'll ask my housekeeper to come across with a pair of my socks.'

'That's very kind, Sir,' Paul said. 'I was wondering what I should be able to wear for the rest of the day.'

Sir William started towards the door, then stopped and placed a hand on Paul's shoulder.

'You did a good job there, Lambert. Well done. It's important to know how to do things by the book, but equally important to know when to break the rules. The patient should be very grateful to you.'

The next day, Cedric King was as well as could be expected after the drama of the night before. Inevitably, the local press got hold of the story, and described his condition as *'comfortable'*, which was certainly a misnomer since he was in a considerable amount of pain from his large abdominal incision.

For the first time since his arrival in Casualty, he was conscious, and the nurses and doctors were able to communicate with him. Far from being grateful that his life had been saved, they found him to be foul-mouthed, rude and aggressive. Fears that this was due to oxygen starvation of the brain during his cardiac arrest were dispelled when it was subsequently learned this was his normal personality. He wasn't asked about the events leading up to the stabbing, nor did he volunteer any information.

Paul chatted to one of the police constables who had been posted in the corridor outside his side room waiting to interview him. He looked thoroughly bored.

'I don't think you need to wait,' Paul suggested, 'we'll let you know when he's fit for an interview.'

'My sergeant says I've got to wait; we don't want him to do a runner. By the way, Doctor, we'll need a full written report of his injuries in due course, but it would be helpful if you could give me a brief account now.'

The constable listened with interest, and made notes as Paul described Cedric's life-threatening injuries and cardiac arrest. 'I suppose that the woman with the cuts on her hands must have been involved in the same incident,' Paul suggested.

'We weren't aware there was a second victim,' the constable said. 'Was she admitted as well?'

'Yes, she's downstairs on the orthopaedic ward.'

'In that case, I need to speak with my sergeant. We'll need to interview her as well.' To Paul's surprise, he then commented, 'You might have done us all a favour, Doctor, and not tried quite so hard to save him! There are far too many villains in this city.'

'So he's known to the police, is he?'

'He most certainly is. He heads one of the most vicious gangs in the city. He's in the protection business; *'pay us a weekly sum, and we'll make sure that your business doesn't catch fire'*, that sort of thing. We've been after him for years, but never managed to pin anything definite on him.'

Two days later, the police interviewed Cedric King in his hospital side ward. They also asked Annie for a statement, but she refused to speak with them; neither would she give any account of how her injuries had been sustained to the medical staff. Later, a more senior officer tried to extract some information from her, but again she refused to cooperate. She even declined to make any comment when informed that Mr King had signed a statement alleging she had stabbed him in an unprovoked attack, and that she faced a charge of attempted murder. It seemed that Annie was more afraid of Cedric and his gang than she was of the police and prison.

Inevitably, there was much discussion on the case in the hospital. It was confirmed that both Annie and Cedric had been brought by ambulance to the hospital from the same address: Annie's flat. It was therefore assumed that Cedric had been Annie's client. But who started the fight, and why? And how was it that they had both suffered such severe injuries? Cedric was twice the size and weight of Annie. If there had been some dispute between them, he wouldn't have needed to use a knife. He could simply have knocked her out of the way with his fist. Did that mean that Annie had stabbed Cedric first, and that he had then retaliated before collapsing with his own injuries?

Paul wondered whether Sir William might have an opinion on the matter, but later, when he spoke with him, Sir William declined to speculate.

'Lambert, your role is simply to present the facts when asked to do so, not to pass an opinion or to speculate. You saved the man's life. That was your job, and you did it well. Leave others to work out what happened and why. It's the police's job to investigate the crime, and then it's up to the legal profession to decide whether the evidence stands up in court, and to pass judgement.'

'But aren't you curious to know what happened? Paul queried.

'Of course, I am. But I'm patient enough to wait until the judge delivers the jury's verdict,' Sir William replied, with a twinkle in his eye.

****

Three days later, in the middle of Sir William's round, the calm of the ward was shattered by a terrible scream, then loud shouts. They came from the corridor where the side rooms were situated. It was a deep male voice.

'HELP ME. SOMEBODY HELP ME. OH, MY GOD, I'M GOING TO DIE!'

A moment later, a junior nurse dashed towards them, eyes wide in alarm, bloodstains down the front of her apron. By the time she reached Sister, she was sobbing, her words poured out in a torrent.

'It's Mr King, Sister. I was just dressing his wound when something awful happened. One minute he was fine, the next, his wound exploded. Oh, Sister, he had a coughing fit, and then....' Her sobbing got worse, and she was unable to continue.

Sister turned to Sir William, 'Please excuse me, I think I'd better go and see what's going on.'

'Of course, Sister,' the consultant replied. 'I'm sure that Staff Nurse will prove to be an able deputy. I suggest that Lambert goes with you as well,' he added, already having a shrewd idea of the diagnosis. 'It sounds as if Mr King will need to go back to the theatre.'

When they entered the side ward, they found that Victoria Kent was already there. She had heard the commotion as she happened to be passing. The scene that met their eyes was certainly dramatic, though not one that particularly alarmed them. It was a situation they had both met before. Cedric was lying on his back, pale and shocked, not merely due to the problem with his wound, but fearful that his days were at an end. The bedclothes were thrown back, revealing that his long abdominal wound had parted from top to bottom. The entire length of his intestines had mushroomed out. His guts were lying in a pool of watery, infected, pink fluid in the bed beside him.

'My God, I'm dying. Help. Help me, please!' Cedric moaned.

'No, you're not dying, Mr King,' Victoria said, her voice quiet and calm. 'You've got what we call a burst abdomen. Your wound hasn't healed. I'm afraid it will mean going back to theatre to stitch it up again.'

'But it's awful, Doctor. What is all that?' Cedric asked, pointing at the wriggling glistening mass.

'It's your intestines, but don't worry. We'll give you an anaesthetic, pop them all back inside, and then stitch you up again.'

Cedric, reassured by Victoria's words, gained a degree of self-control. 'But why has it happened?'

'We can go into that when we've sorted you out,' Victoria replied, unwilling to enter into a detailed debate when a further operation needed to be arranged.

Within the hour, Paul was assisting Victoria, as she closed the wound, using strong thick sutures reserved especially for this purpose. At the end of the operation, the entire abdomen was encased in a strong corset to offer the wound extra support as it healed.

Unfortunately, following his second operation, Cedric developed further complications. He suffered a severe chest infection, blood clots in his legs, and a mild heart attack. All in all, he was in the ward for seven long weeks, during which time he proved to be unpleasant, demanding and abusive.

Just as bad were his visitors; a string of undesirable-looking men of various nationalities, though mainly Afro-Caribbean. All looked rough and tough, were unshaven, and judging from their scars and broken noses, mainly gained a living with their fists. At times it seemed that Cedric was running his criminal organisation from his side room, but whether this was related to drug distribution or a protection racket was never discovered. Everyone in the ward was relieved when he was finally strong enough to go home.

Thought for the day

One murder made a villain – Millions a hero.

Beilby Porteous 1731- 1808

Chapter 27   Cedric King   Act Two: Trial by Jury

Some six or so months later, Paul learned that he was to be called as a witness for the prosecution in the case of *The Crown versus Miss Annie Nolan.* The charge was one of *'attempted murder'*. Although he had previously appeared in a coroner's court, he had never been a witness in a criminal court, and ignorant of court procedures, he again sought advice from Sir William.

'Lambert, you are quite right, appearing in court can be quite an ordeal, and it's sensible to prepare yourself in advance. Here in the hospital, you are in a familiar environment, but for your patients this is a strange, unfamiliar, and often frightening place. The same is true in court, except that now it is you who are out of your comfort zone, and the lawyers who are at ease. But there are a number of things you can do to prepare yourself.

You will be interrogated on your statement, so go over it carefully before the trial. Before answering any question, always pause and think. Don't be rushed into saying something you can't substantiate, and always confine yourself to facts. Remember that barristers are slippery customers; they may try to lead you astray. They will often present a scenario to you, and ask you to agree with it. If they do, it is tempting simply to say *'Yes'*, but much safer to say *'I agree that what you are suggesting is possible.'*

Remember also that you will be cross-examined by the defence team. They will attempt to pick holes in your evidence, or try to trick you into saying something you don't mean. Their questioning can be quite aggressive. At times, you may think that you are the one on trial, not the defendant, but just stay cool. Remember, you are only there as a witness to what you saw and did. As I say, just stick to the facts.'

Paul had been anxious before he went to see Sir William, but came away feeling even more apprehensive about the forthcoming trial. Nonetheless, he went over his witness statement several times, and determined that when he was in court, he would to try to stay calm and follow his consultant's advice.

The summons that Paul received had been accompanied by a letter from the prosecuting counsel, requesting a meeting an hour before proceedings were due to commence. The court clerk showed him into an office where the barrister was waiting.

'This is Dr Lambert, one of the witnesses,' the clerk said.

The barrister, Vincent Egerton, QC, was far younger than Paul had expected, perhaps no more than late 30s. Tall and slim, he had a stern, bony, angular face, a sharply-pointed nose and strikingly blue eyes that contrasted with his jet-black hair. He spoke with a clipped, slightly high-pitched voice, with an accent suggesting he had come from a privileged home, and had the benefit of an expensive education. He was sitting behind a mahogany desk, the inlaid top covered with legal papers, some loose, others rolled and tied with red ribbon, surmounted by his barrister's wig. He did not rise when Paul entered, but waved loftily at a chair across the desk. For three or four seconds, he simply looked at Paul, his eyes focusing on Paul's face. His gaze was penetrating, suggesting he could infiltrate your skull, and discern your innermost thoughts. Paul reminded himself that Sir William had said he had nothing to fear; he was there simply as a witness to the facts, but this man's gaze made him feel distinctly uneasy. Already, he felt that it was he who was on trial, and not Annie Nolan.

'Right, Lambert,' he said sharply, his inspection of Paul complete, 'have you appeared in court before?'

In the hospital, Paul was accustomed to being referred to simply as 'Lambert'. The consultants rarely used a prefix. It was hospital custom and practice, and Paul took no offence at it. Outside the hospital however, to address someone simply by their surname might be regarded as being impolite, bordering on rude. Paul presumed the barrister was establishing the relationship he considered would be appropriate between them. When Paul had confirmed that this was indeed his first court appearance, Mr Egerton proceeded to give advice on how Paul should present his evidence.

'I shall lead you step by step through the statement that you've provided. I take it you have familiarised yourself with it?' Paul nodded. 'It will all be entirely straightforward. I want you simply to answer my questions. Do not be tempted to add any additional thoughts you may have, no matter how relevant you think they may be. Is that absolutely clear?'

Again, Paul nodded. 'You will be the second witness I shall call. The first will be Mr King, the victim of this appalling attack. I want you to listen carefully to his evidence. It's possible that when I have led you through your own statement, I shall ask you a question or two that may arise from he has said. Are you happy with that?'

For a third time, Paul nodded. 'Then that will be all, thank you.'

The entire meeting had lasted precisely three minutes, and Paul hadn't spoken more than half a dozen words. He was shown to a waiting room. The proceedings were not due to start for a further hour. Then he was told that there had been a delay. No explanation of the delay was offered. For two hours, Paul sat twiddling his thumbs, thinking of all the useful things he could have been doing at the hospital, if the court officials were more considerate of the time of others. He vowed that if ever he was called to court again, he would bring a book with him.

Finally, a clerk came to collect him, and led him through into the courtroom. There he saw Cedric King for the first time in six months. He had been accustomed to seeing Cedric as a patient, lying in a bed, and had not appreciated what a huge man he was. Broad across the shoulders, he was not less than 6 ft 2 inches tall. At first, Paul scarcely recognised him, his Rastafarian dreadlocks had become a neatly parted 'short back and sides', and he was wearing a smart grey suit, which struggled to contain his enormous belly.

Then Annie was led into the dock. By comparison, she was a tiny mouse-like figure, dwarfed by the stout prison guard at her side. She looked petrified, and cowered from the gaze of the jury, the lawyers, their clerks, and the visitors in the public gallery.

Everyone was instructed to stand as the judge entered. Judge Phillips was almost as wide as he was tall; he waddled slowly to his seat. He looked to be at least seventy years of age. Paul was later to discover as the trial progressed, that having taken his place in his high chair, he scarcely moved. He sat with eyes half-closed, and with his head bent forward as if he were hard of hearing. There were times when it seemed to Paul that he might have nodded off, though perhaps he was simply concentrating on the proceedings.

As Paul surveyed the court, the polished oak benches, the dark panelling on the walls, the jury segregated to one side watching intently from their box, the public gazing down from the gallery, and the barristers and the judge with their robes and wigs, he found it hard to decide whether the scene was one of dignity and solemnity, or of farce and pantomime. Paul recognised a number of faces in the public gallery. He had seen them visiting Cedric in his hospital bed. Although Cedric's appearance had changed markedly, theirs had not. They still looked a rough, tough group of men that Paul would not have wished to meet in a back alley on a dark night.

After the judge had addressed the jury, gravely reminding them of their responsibilities, Cedric was invited to take the stand. He was sworn in, and began to give his evidence. If Vincent Egerton had spent little time with Paul, he had clearly rehearsed Cedric at great length. The answers he gave to the prosecuting barrister's questions were delivered confidently in a slow, deep, monotone as if they were being read, or had been memorised. From time to time, his counsel needed to prompt him. At one stage, he caused a laugh when he gave an inappropriate answer to one of the questions. He then apologised, *'Oh, sorry, Sir, that's the answer to the next question, isn't it?'*

Essentially, Cedric's story was that he had gone to one of the local pubs with a group of his friends to celebrate a win on a horse he had backed. During the evening, he had drunk several beers, though not to the point of being drunk. He stated that he fell into conversation with a woman that he now knows to be Annie Nolan, the defendant. They struck up a friendship, and in due course walked to Annie's flat, where after further drinks, sexual intercourse took place. Cedric insisted that this was consensual. He alleged that before he was fully dressed, Annie had demanded money from him. He was adamant that he did not know she was a prostitute. He stated he had never found it necessary to pay for sex. He thought he had been *'doing her a favour'*, and he was dammed if he was going to give her any money.

He said Annie then flew into a rage, and attacked him with her fists. He simply laughed at her, and pushed her aside. However, she found the knife he carried in his belt, and attacked him with it. He strenuously denied he had done anything to provoke the attack. He was asked why he found it necessary to carry a weapon, a six-inch, double-edged knife. Did he not know it was illegal to carry an offensive weapon? He acknowledged that he did know it was illegal, but stated that in the environment in which he lived, he felt more secure carrying it, although he would never have dreamed of using it.

Vincent Egerton then led him through the period that he had spent in the hospital. Cedric told the jury he had actually died whilst on the operating table. He made great play of the fact that his wound had burst open, and that all his intestines had ruptured into the bed. This was stated to be a further life-threatening episode. Clearly, the barrister wished the jury to agree with him that the crime was indeed *'attempted murder'*, not merely *'grievous bodily harm'*.

Cedric was not asked, nor did he offer any explanation of Annie's injuries. This surprised Paul, and it was only later he came to understand the reason why. Otherwise, the account that Cedric gave sounded entirely credible.

Cedric was dismissed, and a few moments later, Paul was called to give evidence. As he took the stand, he again told himself not to be nervous. There seemed to be no need. Mr Egerton had been extremely gentle with Cedric. Questions had been posed quietly and politely, and nothing unexpected had been asked. The barrister had simply led Cedric through his prepared statement. Paul reminded himself he was only there to testify to the facts, and vowed not offer any opinions. But he couldn't help feeling nervous in this strange environment. He clearly understood Sir William's remarks about the apprehension of patients when they were in an alien hospital setting.

With his right hand on the Bible, he was sworn in. *'I swear by Almighty God that the evidence that I shall give, shall be the truth, the whole truth, and nothing but the truth'*. He was about to add *'so help me God'*, and was then surprised to discover that those words were not actually written on the card! He stopped himself just in time.

Mr Egerton asked Paul's name, his job, and established that he was on duty at the City General Hospital on the night in question.

'Tell me, Dr Lambert, did you see my client, Mr Cedric King, in the Casualty Department of the City General Hospital, and did you treat him for the wounds he had received?'

Paul noticed that in the arena of the courtroom, he was addressed with a title, albeit an incorrect one. For a moment, he thought of pointing out that as a surgeon, he was 'Mr Lambert', not 'Dr Lambert', but then thought better of it.

'Yes, I did,' he confirmed.

'Can you describe for the jury the physical state Mr King was in when you first saw him?'

'He was bleeding profusely, and was in a state of shock.'

'Would you say that his injuries were serious?'

'Yes, I would.'

'Would you say they were life-threatening?'

'Yes, they were.'

And so it went on, Mr Egerton leading Paul through a series of questions to establish what had happened during Cedric's seven-week stay in hospital. The questions were all entirely straightforward, and Paul began to feel more relaxed and confident.

He then asked Paul if Cedric's wound gave any indication as to the type of knife that caused it.

Paul explained that the wound indicated that the knife was double-edged, was at least five inches long, and not less than an inch wide at a point at this distance from its tip.

'Dr Lambert, I am going to show you a knife. I would like you to look at it carefully.'

He passed Paul a horrendous looking dagger. It was heavy, and at least eight inches in length. It had a wooden handle, and was double-edged.

'Dr Lambert, would you agree that the injury you treated was entirely consistent with an assault with such a knife?'

'Yes,' Paul said cautiously, 'the injury may well have been caused by such a blade.'

'And would you not agree, that in all probability, it was in fact, this particular blade, that caused Mr King's life-threatening injury?' the barrister asked quickly and confidently.

It suddenly struck Paul that he was now being asked for his opinion, rather than merely for verification of facts. He recalled Sir William's cautionary words, and vowed to be careful. He suspected he had very nearly fallen into a carefully contrived trap.

'Not necessarily,' Paul responded, 'but it is possible that a blade such as this could have caused the injury that I treated.'

For a second, Paul wondered whether he saw the slightest look of irritation on the barrister's face, but if he did it was gone in a flash.

'You said in your evidence, Dr Lambert that the horrendous, life-threatening bleeding suffered by my client was caused by an injury to the blood vessels leading to the spleen. Will you please tell the jury the tissues through which the blade must have passed to reach this point?'

'The blade would have passed through the skin, the fat beneath the skin, then the abdominal muscles, and then a layer of fat inside the abdomen, before it hit these vessels.'

'Do you agree that the tissues you have described are generally known in medical parlance as soft tissues?'

'Yes, that is correct.'

'And therefore, as such, they would not offer a great deal of resistance to a blade as sharp as this one?'

'No.'

'And so a stab wound five inches deep, caused by a very sharp blade, such as the one I have just shown you, would not require a great deal of force to inflict it.'

Paul thought carefully. Strictly speaking, the words, as spoken, were a statement, and as such, they didn't require an answer. The inflection of the voice though, posed them as a question. Again, Paul realised he was being asked for an opinion.

He paused before answering. 'No, in my opinion, it would not have required a great deal of force.'

'And therefore, it could well have been inflicted by someone of a very slight build, such as Miss Nolan, for example.'

This was another statement, despite the enquiry in the voice. Paul decided not to reply.

'Well, Dr Lambert?'

'It *could* have been inflicted by such a person,' Paul said, emphasising the word *could*. 'But it could also have been inflicted by someone of average or heavy build.'

'Dr Lambert, I would now like you to consider how such a wound might be caused. Since the wound was to Mr King's left-side, presumably, the attack was from an assailant who is right-handed.'

'I am not sure that I understand,' Paul responded.

Mr Egerton came and stood in front of Paul. He raised his right arm, holding a pen in his fist to mimic a knife. 'To stab you in your left side, I would have to be using my right hand, wouldn't I?'

'Not necessarily. You are assuming both parties were standing face to face. I understood from Mr King's evidence that this confrontation took place in a bedroom. Mr King might have been lying on a bed at the time. You are also assuming that the assailant had the use of their right hand at the time of the attack.'

Mr Egerton looked puzzled. 'What do you mean by that?'

Sir William later explained to Paul that a good barrister would never ask a question to which he does not already know the answer.

'Well, if the question refers to Miss Nolan, at some stage, she sustained a nasty injury to her right hand.' Paul was sure he detected a flicker on Mr Egerton's face, this time of surprise before the mask clamped down again.

'How do you know that?' he asked.

Another mistake; this was a question to which he obviously did not know the answer.

'I know because I treated her in the Accident and Emergency department on the same night that I treated Mr King. In my opinion, after she sustained the injury, it would have been very difficult, if not impossible, for her to grip a knife in her right hand.'

There was a prolonged pause. Paul glanced at the judge. He had been listening to Paul's evidence with much the same bored expression that he had listened to Cedric's, but now he looked alert and interested.

'Mr Egerton,' he said, his voice a deep growl. 'It is now nearly 12.30, and in view of this development, I expect that Dr Lambert is going to be on the stand for some time. Would this be a good opportunity for us to break for lunch?'

'Yes, Sir, I think it would,' the barrister said.

'Right,' said the judge. 'The court will reconvene at 2.30.'

'All stand,' shouted the court clerk, and everyone stood while Judge Phillips descended from his seat, and left the court. Left standing in the witness box, Paul was stunned. Mr Egerton's response to his last two answers suggested he hadn't been aware that Annie had also been injured in the fracas that had taken place. It seemed inconceivable, yet he had appeared genuinely surprised at the news.

In an instant, Mr Egerton was at Paul's side. 'Lambert, come with me,' he ordered.

He marched Paul back to his office, tight-lipped and angry. As soon as they were on their own, he slammed the door.

'When did you treat Annie Nolan?' he demanded to know, his voice was sharp and cold, his eyes piercing.

'It was the same night that Cedric King was admitted. She arrived about five minutes before he did. I'd already examined her when I was called away because Cedric was seriously ill.'

'Did they come from the same location?'

'I don't know for certain, but I always supposed they did.'

'What were her injuries?'

Paul described the lacerations on her right-hand, and explained that the division of all the tendons to her four fingers meant she would not have been able to grip a knife. He also mentioned the minor injuries to her shoulder and arm. There was a long pause.

'I see,' he said slowly. His face had lost the superior confident expression to which Paul had become accustomed. He looked distinctly worried.

'Okay, Lambert, that will be all. I shall have no further questions for you this afternoon.'

Paul was being dismissed, but the events in court puzzled him. 'Didn't you know that Annie had also been injured?' he asked the QC.

'No, I didn't.'

'Surely you get copies of the defence statements?'

'Yes, normally, we do. But Miss Nolan decided not to make a statement.'

'Not even to her defence team?'

'No, not even to them. I understand she simply clammed up. She hasn't given an account of events to anyone, not even to the police.'

'Why on earth would she do that?' Paul asked.

'I really couldn't say,' Mr Egerton replied flatly. But Paul knew the answer, and he suspected that Mr Egerton did as well. He remembered what the police had said about Cedric's occupation. He was in the protection racket. His weapon was fear. Annie was afraid to describe what had occurred in her flat; so afraid, in fact, that she was prepared to risk being found guilty of attempted murder, rather than to try to defend herself.

'Does that mean that I'm now free to go?'

'No, it doesn't. Technically, you are still on the witness stand. The judge will be the one who will tell you when you are able to go.'

Paul had expected to be called back at two-thirty, but it was after three-thirty when the trial recommenced. When he was eventually called, he again took his place in the witness box. The judge turned to Mr Egerton.

'Do you have any more questions for Dr Lambert?'

Having been assured that the barrister had no further questions for him, Paul was surprised to hear him say, 'Yes, just one or two, my lord.'

Had he been deliberately misleading Paul, or had he had second thoughts?

Mr Egerton began by reminding Paul that he was still on oath.

'I would like to ask you a few questions, Dr Lambert, about Mr King's convalescence after his operation. I understand he was in the hospital for seven weeks altogether. I presume therefore that there must have been one or two complications.'

'Yes,' Paul said, 'he developed an infection in his wound.'

'Would you describe this as a minor infection, or a major one?'

'Oh, certainly a major one,' Paul responded confidently, 'and healing is always impaired when an infection is present. Mr King's wound failed to heal.'

'What do you mean by that?'

'Well, he suffered what we call a burst abdomen. All the stitches in his operation wound parted, and his entire gut mushroomed out through the wound like a volcano erupting. It can be a life-threatening event.'

'You describe it in a very dramatic way, Dr Lambert.'

'Well, it was a very dramatic event.'

'I understand that as a result of this problem, Mr King had to go back to theatre to have his wound re-sutured, and it then took a further five weeks before he was sufficiently fit to be allowed to go home.'

There was a long pause while Mr Egerton perused his notes, allowing Paul a moment to reflect. The questions he had been asked had all been straightforward; he was confident that his answers had been factual, but he wondered in what way they were relevant to Annie Nolan's trial.

'I have been looking at the operation note you wrote, Dr Lambert, after you had performed surgery on my client. It states quite clearly that you did not wash or scrub your hands before this operation.'

For the first time, it dawned on Paul where this line of questioning was going. This devil of a lawyer was attempting to pin the blame for Cedric's torrid post-operative convalescence on him. He felt a surge of anger flow through him.

'Yes, that right,' he admitted.

'And the operation note also states quite clearly that you did not put any antiseptic on the skin before you started to operate. Is that also correct?'

'Yes.'

'Nor did you put any sterile drapes around the wound.'

'No, I did not.'

'Surely that's highly irregular, and presumably its why Mr King had such a difficult time, indeed as you said yourself, '*a life-threatening*' time, after his operation. So, I think we must conclude,' Mr Egerton said, a superior tone to his voice, 'that the infection was caused by your surgery.'

Angry though Paul was, he now began to think a little more clearly.

'There was an extremely good reason why I didn't wash my hands, or put any antiseptic on the skin, or place drapes around the wound in the usual way. Mr King was bleeding to death. It was infinitely more important to stop the bleeding than to worry about possible future infections.'

'And that is your opinion, Doctor?'

'Yes, that is my very definite opinion.'

'But that is the opinion of a very junior surgeon, is it not?'

Paul riled at that, his anger welling up once again. 'I am four-years-qualified, and I'm a Fellow of the Royal College of Surgeons.'

But Mr Egerton knew more about him than he imagined. He had obviously done some homework. Paul wondered whether this was the reason behind the delay before the afternoon session began.

'Tell me, Dr Lambert; what training do you still have to do before you are able to apply to be a junior consultant.'

'Well, I have to complete my job as a Registrar and then, all being well, hold a Senior Registrar job.'

'And would it be fair to say that you can expect to be a Junior Registrar for another two years, and then a Senior Registrar for a further four years making a total of six years in all?'

'Yes,' admitted Paul through gritted teeth.

'And, although you say you have been qualified for four years, as I understand it, the first of those four years was your probationary year, when you were not permitted to treat patients unless under supervision. And of the remaining three, one was spent in the university studying anatomy, when you didn't see any patients at all. Is that also correct?'

'Yes.' Paul felt like a cornered mouse. Wherever he ran, the cat was covering his retreat, blocking him in.

'So in practical terms, you have two years experience of surgery, and six years of training in front of you. You are, therefore, one-quarter of the way through your surgical training.'

He turned to the jury to deliver his final insult. 'I think therefore, it is reasonable to conclude that Dr Lambert is a junior and inexperienced surgeon.'

Without allowing Paul a chance to comment, he addressed the judge. 'Thank you, my lord; I have no further questions for this witness.'

The counsel for the defence was Lionel Baxter, QC. Twenty or so years older than Mr Egerton, he was small in stature, very stooped, and with his wig and black gown, looked like a grey-headed crow. He spoke with a soft, Scottish accent in a quiet voice, allowing long pauses between his questions.

'I believe that the court has been doing you a disservice,' he said, glancing towards Mr Egerton, 'Having proven your competence in an exacting assessment of your knowledge and competence, you are a Fellow of the Royal College of Surgeons, and therefore entitled to be addressed as Mister Lambert. Is that correct?'

'That is correct.'

'So Mr Lambert, you treated the defendant, Miss Nolan, I believe.' Again, this was a statement, dressed up as a question.

'Yes,' Paul replied.

'Mr Lambert, will you please describe for the benefit of the jury, the injuries sustained by Miss Nolan, particularly the injuries to her right hand.'

Paul explained that Miss Nolan had suffered a cut across the base of the fingers of her right hand.

'So that the jury can be completely clear, please will you demonstrate with this ruler the exact site of these cuts.'

Paul turned the palm of his hand to face the jury, and placed the ruler across the base of his four fingers.

'In every case, the cuts went down to the bone, and the tendons were divided,' he said.

'I am sure you understand that I am not a doctor, nor indeed are the members of the jury, so perhaps you would explain, in lay terms, what tendons do, and how they enable to fingers to move.'

Paul explained that the muscles that move the fingers are situated in the forearm, and are linked to the bones of the fingers by strong, string-like tendons.

'If I have understood you correctly, if all the tendons were cut, Miss Nolan would not be able to bend her fingers. She would not be able to make a fist and certainly not able to grip a knife.'

Mr Baxter picked up the knife that had already been exhibited, before continuing. 'So at the time, presumably the knife must have been held by somebody else?'

'Yes, or I suppose held by Miss Nolan in her left hand.'

'I suppose that is theoretically possible,' Mr Baxter said thoughtfully, 'though it must be unlikely because we know that Miss Nolan is, of course, right-handed.'

Mr Baxter paused, allowing the jury time to digest the implication of this statement before continuing. 'You say Mr Lambert, that Miss Nolan had other injuries.'

Paul described the injury on the back of her left shoulder, and the one on the middle of her left forearm on its outer aspect. He picked up the knife and handed it to Paul.

'It is possible,' he said, addressing the jury, 'that it may later be suggested by the prosecution that Miss Nolan's wounds were self-inflicted.'

He turned back to Paul. 'May I ask you please to take the knife, and show me how someone might inflict the injury to the shoulder upon themselves?'

Paul took the blade and demonstrated the impossibility of applying the knife to the point on the back of the shoulder where the injury had occurred. Mr Baxter then walked towards Paul, took the knife from him, and then stood at Paul's side, the blade now held in a firm grip in his right hand. He then turned as if to replace the knife on the table, but suddenly spun around, screamed, and lunged, his hand raised high as if to stab Paul's head. Alarmed, Paul shrank from him, but trapped in the witness box, could not take a step back. Instinctively, he raised his left arm to protect his face. Mr Baxter's hand came down, and Paul was struck a blow on his left forearm, on its outer aspect, halfway from wrist to elbow. But it wasn't the knife. During the moment his back had been turned, the knife had been exchanged for the ruler. Now Mr Baxter froze, the ruler still held in his hand remained in contact with Paul's arm.

'Is this where Miss Nolan was cut?' he asked.

'Yes, it was.'

'And was the line of the cut, in the line that this ruler is now positioned?'

'Yes, it was.'

Quietly satisfied he had demonstrated that this wound was almost certainly the result of self-protection, he turned to the jury.

'Interesting,' he said quietly before addressing the judge. 'I have no more questions for this witness, my lord.'

Paul left the courtroom burning at the injustice of the mauling he had received at the hands of Mr Egerton. He had belittled Paul, called him junior and inexperienced. He obviously held Paul responsible for Mr King's long and complicated convalesce, blaming him for the pain and suffering caused by his burst abdomen, and the gross infection that had occurred. It was grossly unfair. Damn it, he had saved the villain's life. There simply hadn't been time to take all the precautions that normally prevent wound infection.

But Paul was also confused. He couldn't understand why Mr Egerton had turned on him. The trial was supposed to reveal who had inflicted Cedric's stab wound, not to discuss his post-operative problems. So the next day, when Sir William asked him how the trial had gone, Paul explained what had happened and poured out his anger. Sir William too, was amazed that the prosecution team had not known of the injuries Annie had suffered, but suggested it probably explained Mr Egerton's attack on Paul.

'When the QC realised that both parties had been injured,' he said, 'and that Annie's wounds had almost certainly been suffered in self-defence, he would have recognised that the charge of attempted murder was unlikely to succeed. With it, the chances of obtaining damages from Annie would disappear, not that it was likely she had much money anyway. However, he would know that as a doctor, you carry medical insurance. If he can lay the blame for Cedric's problems on your shoulders, there could be a significant payout for his client.

Unfortunately, it's now being recognised,' Sir William continued, 'that if there's an accident in which no one can be held responsible, there may still be money to be made if the legal team can find fault with the medical treatment.'

'Does that mean that I'll face an allegation of negligence in the civil court' Paul asked.

'I'm afraid it probably does, but I shall take great pleasure in ensuring that it is unsuccessful,' Sir William answered.

Thoughts for the day

I know you lawyers can, with ease,

Twist words and meanings as you please,

By language, by your skill made pliant,

Will bend to favour every client

                                                John Gay 1685 – 1732

A man without money need no more fear a crowd of lawyers, than a crowd of pickpockets.

                                      William Wycherley 1640 - 1716

Chapter 28   Cedric King   Act Three: Litigation

It was at 10.30 on a Saturday morning two months later, that the postman delivered a first-class letter with a London postmark. It was a letter which was to cause Paul much heartache.

'Dear Mr Lambert,' he read,
'Re. Cedric King, aged 42.
We act on behalf of the above-named client who has suffered both physically and mentally as a direct result of your negligent medical attention. Please be informed that the extent of the injuries which result from your negligence has been assessed at £65,000. Within the next two weeks, we will write again, detailing an inventory of the damages claimed.
Yours sincerely,
James Curtis
(on behalf of Curtis, McKay, and Westwood.)'

It was the word 'negligent' that hurt Paul most. He didn't consider himself to be negligent at all. He believed himself to be a conscientious doctor, and a hard-working member of the team. It was his nature to complete a task on the ward himself, rather than delegate it to a colleague, even if that meant going off duty late. He worried about his patients if they weren't responding to treatment, checking their progress to ensure that everything possible was being done for them. How dare they suggest that he had been negligent?

And the patient making the accusation of negligence was Cedric King of all people. The mere mention of his name brought every detail of his treatment flooding to his mind. He recalled vividly Cedric's emergency operation, his cardiac arrest; even going home wearing Sir William's socks. Damn it, without the operation he had performed, Cedric would now be dead.

Paul thought for a minute, grim-faced. He needed to inform the Medical Defence Union (MDU) about this. They were the experts in defending doctors when they get into trouble, and he also needed to speak to Sir William.

It was Monday lunchtime before Paul was able to speak to the consultant in his office. Sir William listened to Paul's concerns, read the solicitor's letter then laid a hand on Paul's shoulder.

'Lambert,' he said quietly, 'this claim has absolutely no chance of succeeding. They're just fishing. They're hoping that the MDU will offer a small payment to settle the case out of court without them incurring too many legal costs. All you need to do is to acknowledge the solicitor's letter, inform them that you will be represented by the MDU, and let me know how things develop. And don't worry,' he added kindly.

But despite Sir William's reassurance, Paul did worry; unfortunately, it was his nature to worry!

One afternoon, several weeks later, the typed list of the admissions planned for the following week arrived on the ward. This advanced warning gave the ward sisters the opportunity to plan the nurses' off-duty, and make the best use of the available beds. Sister Ashbrook swept her eye over the details of the patients and their proposed surgical procedures. One name immediately caught her attention. She groaned. Cedric King was to be re-admitted for the repair of an incisional hernia. She turned to Victoria, who chanced to be working in the office at the time.

'Did you know that Cedric King needed further surgery?' she asked.

'Yes, I did. He was seen in the clinic recently. When his wound finally healed, it was so weak that it offered no support to the guts inside his belly. It now bulges forward and looks like a nine-month pregnancy. It's also causing him a lot of pain, so he's coming in to have it repaired.'

'Will he be in for long, do you think?' Sister asked, concern in her voice.

'I'm afraid so. The rupture is huge. He'll be in for at least a week, possibly longer.'

Sister swore under her breath. 'He caused no end of trouble when he was here last time, and he attracts the most undesirable visitors. Perhaps I'll put him in the end side ward and then he'll be as far from the other patients as possible!'

Paul too was dismayed when he heard the news. Cedric's burst abdomen, and the wound weakness from which he now suffered, all stemmed from the operation that he had performed, an operation that

Cedric alleged had been performed negligently. In the circumstances, he didn't see how he could possibly be involved in Cedric's management. He went to have a private word with Sir William, as he always did when he needed advice on a moral or ethical issue. He explained his dilemma, and asked to be excused involvement in the case. To his surprise, his request was denied.

'No, Lambert,' he said. 'I don't believe for a minute that Mr King blames you for his problems. In his heart, he probably appreciates that you saved his life. It's simply that by suing you, he hopes to win some compensation, not from you personally, but from the medical insurance company. When he comes onto the ward and you prepare the operation consent form for him to sign, specify that his operation will be performed by me, with you acting as my assistant. Also, make sure you perform small practical procedures on him, such as taking blood and putting up drips.'

Sir William smiled. 'You see, if he really believes you're a negligent doctor, he won't allow you to be involved in his treatment, but if he puts his signature to a form that states that you will be operating on him, he will undermine his own case.'

Fortunately, Cedric made a good recovery after his hernia operation, and as the days passed, Paul began to feel more confident that Cedric's claim of negligence could be rebuffed. Sir William's plan had worked well. Paul had been personally involved in his care, and Cedric had not objected to him assisting at his operation. One day, though, Cedric called Paul back to his bedside. He looked angry.

'Doc, I need a word,' he growled, his tone belligerent.

Paul wondered if he was about to mention the negligence claim, but when he spoke, it was on quite a different subject.

'Get that young male orderly to come to see me.'

'You mean Charlie?' Paul asked.

'That's the one. He and I have some unfinished business to discuss.' Cedric's voice was threatening.

'What sort of business?'

'That's nothing to do with you, but if he knows what's good for him, he'll make damn sure he comes to see me today.'

Everybody loved Charlie. He was the hospital's local 'character', and it was impossible to be glum when he was around. Officially, he was the hospital barber, but in practice he was the quick-witted hospital comic and prankster. Cheeky and cheerful, he radiated good humour wherever he went. He was good-looking, tall, and slim, his height exaggerated by the shiny, black drainpipe trousers he always wore.

He was a smoker and regularly slipped to various secret haunts to indulge this weakness. Frequently, he would 'just have left one ward', but failed to arrive at the next. To solve the problem of locating him, he was issued with a radio pager, but this did little to improve the situation. He rarely responded to calls, and when finally located and challenged, he would simply say, *'I think the batteries must be flat',* with a cheeky grin on his face.

A regular reader of the Racing Times, he was known to have a flutter on the horses, and he often discussed runners, riders and likely winners with the patients. It was widely known that his periodic absences from duty, other than when he slipped off to 'have a fag', were due to him acting as a courier between the patients on the ward and the local High Street bookmaker.

Feeling apprehensive, and sensing that Charlie was in some sort of trouble, Paul bleeped the young orderly, but as so often happened, Charlie didn't respond. A few casual enquiries however, led Paul to the yard outside the laundry at the back of the hospital. He found Charlie sitting on one of the large, wicker laundry baskets, having a quiet cigarette. Paul made a casual remark about *'cancer sticks being bad for his health',* a comment which Charlie would normally have rebuffed with a smile and a joke, but Charlie looked drawn and anxious, and when he got up, he was limping. There was also a bruise on the side of his face.

'You've been in the wars,' Paul said cheerfully, 'fighting over one of the nurses, I suppose.'

'No, Paul, I simply slipped and fell over. I rather overdid the booze last night.'

When Paul explained that Cedric wished to see him, Charlie swore.

'Paul. I can't go and see him,' he said anxiously. 'You'll have to make some excuse for me. Tell him I'm not on duty, or that I've gone off sick.'

'Is there a problem? Are you in some sort of trouble with Cedric?'

Charlie sat down again on the laundry skip. 'Yes,' he confessed, 'I am. I owe him some money.'

'Much?' Paul asked.

'Yes, quite a lot.'

'And you can't pay him back?'

'I'm afraid not.'

'Do you want to tell me about it?'

Charlie explained that some of the men on the ward liked to have a flutter on the horses. For many years, he'd taken their stake money to the bookies, and placed the bets for them. Few patients though knew much about horse racing, many had never placed a bet before, and their wagers usually lost. Charlie therefore had stopped placing the bets; instead, he'd simply pocketed the money, then paid out if anybody won.

For many months, his system had proved to be profitable. Then Cedric asked him to put a big bet on an outsider. Charlie recognised that there was a risk if he didn't place the money at the bookies, but he got greedy. He explained that the wretched horse won at twelve to one, and as a result he owed Cedric a couple of hundred pounds which he simply didn't have.

'So Cedric set his henchmen onto you?'

'Yes, I was followed when I went home from work last night. There'll be worse to come if I can't pay.' He looked appealingly at Paul.

'Look, I'm afraid I don't have that sort of ready cash, Charlie. I could ask if he was prepared to accept a smaller amount.'

Charlie looked desperate. 'No, Paul, he wants the whole lot. Would you ask him if I can pay him back over a few months?'

'I'll see what I can do,' Paul said, but knowing that Cedric was in the protection business, he didn't feel hopeful. Extracting money by extortion was right up Cedric's street, and so it proved. When Paul went back to Cedric's room, he found the villain in an uncompromising mood. Paul decided to be honest, and admitted that Charlie hadn't actually placed the bet. He suggested that Cedric might be prepared to take his stake money back and forget the matter. Cedric though simply laughed scornfully.

'He told me he'd placed the bet. If the fool didn't, that's his fault. He owes me the money. You can tell him from me that if he doesn't pay by this time tomorrow, he'll get worse treatment than he's had so far.'

'You arranged for him to be beaten up?'

'Maybe I did, maybe I didn't. Now you go and tell the idiot to bring me my money.'

For the next couple of hours, Paul went about his duties much distracted. Cedric was obviously vicious, and was prepared to use violence to force Charlie to pay. Even though he was stuck in a hospital bed, he clearly had friends outside who did his dirty work for him, and unfortunately, Charlie, through his own stupidity, had fallen foul of him.

Later, Paul discussed the problem with Victoria. They both felt that the matter should be handed over to the police, but equally realised it would be inappropriate to involve the police without their consultant's permission. So Paul rang Sir William who suggested Paul join him at his home for a drink.

Sir William's house was only a hundred yards away. It had originally been the lodge to an old hall, which had long since been demolished to make room for the hospital, so in less than five minutes, Paul was ringing the front door bell. Paul imagined that Sir William might resent being disturbed in the evening, but in fact, he seemed pleased to have a visitor.

'I don't get many folk calling during the evening, Lambert, so it's good to see you. May I offer you a drink, perhaps a sherry or a whisky?'

'No, Sir, I'd better not, I'm on duty.'

'Well, if you don't mind, I'll have a whisky, and you can tell me what's on your mind.' He poured himself a generous drink, settled comfortably into his armchair, and then listened without interruption.

'I'm sorry to trouble you in the evening, Sir, but something has cropped up upon which I need some advice,' Paul began, before telling the story of Charlie's scam, and how it had backfired on him. He expressed concern about what might happen to Charlie if he were unable to pay the money he owed.

'And you say Charlie has been assaulted already?'

'Yes, he has.'

Sir William sat pensively for a moment. 'Okay, Lambert, I don't think we'll involve the police just yet. I'll sleep on the problem overnight, but perhaps you would ask Charlie to come and see me first thing in the morning.'

Charlie must have shared his problem with others for, by the next morning, the hospital grapevine was hard at work, and his dilemma was being widely discussed. Charlie was a popular character, and a collection was started in the hope that enough money could be raised to get him out of his difficulties. However, Charlie didn't turn up for work the next day, giving rise to grave concern. Rumours abounded.

Some suggested he must have been assaulted again, whilst others thought that he was probably lying low. All the while, Cedric remained a patient on the ward. The staff found difficulty in continuing to treat him, but managed to maintain a professional, if cool attitude towards him.

Two days later, Charlie raced into the office, a huge smile on his bruised face. He was bursting to tell everyone the news.

'Sir William was amazing,' he said, 'an absolute star.'

Charlie explained that Sir William had made him go to see Cedric to suggest that he offer to pay off the money on a weekly basis. He had however, supplied him with a pocket Dictaphone to secrete in his coat, in anticipation that Charlie would be threatened with violence. And Cedric did just that! He boasted that his boys had been responsible for the first attack, and threatened to arrange a much more vicious assault if the debt were not paid.

'And I got it all recorded on tape,' said Charlie gleefully. The next day, armed with the tape recording, Sir William had visited Cedric's side ward, and a negotiation had taken place. The tape recording would be locked away in Sir William's safe, and Charlie's debt would be cancelled.

'I don't even have to pay the stake money back,' Charlie said a huge grin on his face.

'Mind you there is just one snag. Sir William says that if he catches me acting as a bookie's runner in the future, he'll post the tape to Cedric!

By the way, Paul, Sir William says he got some news for you too. He didn't tell me what it was, but said you would find out about it soon enough.'

Sir William said nothing to Paul, but a week later, he received another first-class letter, once more with a London postmark. It read:

'Dear Mr Lambert,
Re Cedric King, aged 42.
We write to inform you we have received further instructions from our client to the effect that he no longer wishes to pursue his claim for negligence against you.
Yours sincerely,

James Purvis
(on behalf of Quinell, Purvis, and Weekes.)'

Thought for the day

My life was simply hellish, I didn't stand a chance,

I thought that I should relish, a tomb like General Grant's

But now I feel so swellfish, so Elsa Maxwellish,

That I'm gong to give a dance.

Cole Porter 1891 - 1964

Chapter 29 Malcolm's Toolbox

1st February 1971

After the incident with the gobstopper, Janet abandoned her campaign against Mr Potts. Reluctantly, she was forced to the conclusion that he actually enjoyed sparring verbally with her, was never going to change his views, or to value the role of women in society. She therefore resolved to deprive him of that pleasure. Thereafter, whenever he made an inappropriate comment, or addressed her as 'my dear', which he often did as bait tempting her to rise to the challenge, she simply ignored him. Finally, the first day of February dawned, and a new house man arrived. He would overlap with Janet for one week. Janet's plans were then to wait until her fiancé's contract came to an end before she returned to Australia to take up a medical post there.

Appointed not by Mr Potts, but by Sir William, the new house officer could not have been more different than Janet. Paul recognised him as one of the students who had studied on the unit a couple of years previously.

'I think you've worked with us before,' Paul said, as he greeted the newcomer on the ward

'Err, yes,' he said. 'I'm Malcolm Chapman.'

Hearing the name refreshed Paul's memory. Malcolm had been the brightest student they had taught on the unit for many years. Academically, he was brilliant. His knowledge of surgical diseases had almost been as comprehensive as his own. When Paul had been teaching the students, there had been times when he had struggled to answer some of Malcolm's searching questions. Paul had little doubt that Malcolm had been appointed because he had scored the highest mark in the surgical exam as a medical student.

In appearance, he was unremarkable, certainly not one to stand out in a crowd. He was at least six inches shorter than Janet, and had a waistline that hinted at a sedentary lifestyle. His face was round, pale and pasty, and with his stumpy nose, his NHS glasses and untidy, short, brown hair, he had an owlish appearance.

When he appeared on the ward however, the most remarkable thing about him was his white coat, which would have suited someone of a rather grander stature. It drowned him, almost reaching his ankles. The effect was to make him appear shorter and fatter than he really was. Further, the coat had been adapted by having several large, additional pockets sewn into it. Each pocket bulged with assorted items of equipment. In one was a selection of pens and pencils, in another a ruler and stethoscope, and from a third overflowed an assortment of request cards for various blood, urine and x-ray investigations. Further pockets contained syringes, needles, swabs and plasters, as well as a tendon hammer and a tuning fork to enable examination of the nervous system. The final pocket held tools to take temperatures, blood pressures and even gloves and lubricating jelly with which to perform a rectal examination. Paul suppressed a laugh. He couldn't decide whether their new houseman looked more like a Michelin Man in a white coat, a wartime spiv selling rationed goods, or a mad professor from a horror movie.

'You've come well prepared,' Paul commented cheerfully, though privately he wondered what Leslie Potts would make of Malcolm's appearance. 'And of course,' he added, 'you're very welcome. I trust you'll enjoy working on the Surgical Five unit.'

When Mr Potts arrived, his eyes alighted on the new member of staff. 'You must be our new house officer,' he said.

'Yes, Sir, I'm M-Malcolm Chapman, S-Sir,' Malcolm replied, his face reddening.

'What are you wearing, boy?' the consultant queried.

'M-my white coat, Sir.'

'I can see that, I'm not a complete fool! But what on earth have you done to it?'

'I've arranged for some extra pockets to be added, Sir.'

'For heaven's sake, why?'

'It will enable me to be more efficient, S-Sir. I shan't have to return to the office every time I need a piece of equipment.'

'Well, you look like a bloody stuffed rabbit. Go and take it off at once, and don't come back onto the ward looking so ridiculous ever again.'

'You mean, go now, Sir?' Malcolm asked.

'Yes, now. Go, go!'

Paul felt sorry for the young man, seeing him treated so unfairly, particularly as it was his first day in his new job, but he knew better than to interfere. He would take Malcolm to one side later, sympathise and explain that he was not the first to be treated in that fashion by Mr Potts, nor indeed would he be the last.

Malcolm left the ward with his tail between his legs, to reappear twenty minutes later, burning with indignation, but wearing a more conventional white coat. He resented that his enterprise had not been appreciated, and was angry that he had been criticised by his consultant, particularly as his chastisement had been delivered in front of the whole team. He had studied long and hard for the final medical school examination, and had obtained high marks. Then, when most of his colleagues were enjoying a well-earned holiday, he had shadowed Janet to prepare himself for his first job as a house officer. He had noticed how frequently the doctors interrupted a patient's treatment at the bedside to return to the office for an item of equipment. How much better, he had thought, if all these items were on hand; hence his initiative with the extra pockets on his white coat. Although bewildered by the manner in which he had been treated, he refused to be down-hearted. In fact, the episode made him more determined than ever to prove his worth to his consultant. He vowed that in the months to come, he would prove himself to be hardworking, knowledgeable, and resourceful.

When Paul next visited the ward, he noticed that a modification had been made to the notes trolley. The trolley was a large wooden box on wheels, the open-top being divided by partitions to create a space for each of the patient's notes and x-rays. At each end, there was a horizontal bar or handle, akin to that on a pram, to allow the trolley to be pushed around the ward. Over each of the horizontal bars, a white flannel sheet had been draped, attached by a pair of jubilee clips. On each sheet were three large pockets. It appeared that Malcolm's white coat had been cut up and draped over the ends of the trolley. Moreover, the pockets were stuffed full of the various items that Malcolm had previously had in his white coat; the investigation cards, instruments, blood bottles, needles and syringes.

Paul immediately saw the value of the trolley, but wondered what Mr Potts' reaction to it would be. It wasn't too long before he found out.

When the consultant arrived for his next ward round, his juniors as usual were waiting for him in the office, but Mr Potts merely put his nose around the door.

'Come on, let's get on with this ward round,' he said.

As was his normal practice, he marched swiftly to the far end of the ward, and stopped by the end bed, waiting for his staff to catch up with him. Most consultants started their rounds at the ward entrance, but Mr Potts preferred to see his patients by working in reverse order. This saved him from being hijacked with supplementary questions from patients on the return journey. Malcolm arrived last, pushing the now rather heavy and cumbersome trolley. Leslie Potts' eye immediately fell upon it.

'What the hell is that?' he demanded.

All eyes turned upon Malcolm, who blinked behind his round, metal-rimmed glasses. He looked like a timid owl, but had come prepared to stand his ground.

'I know you didn't approve of my m-modified white coat, Mr Potts, Sir' he said quietly, 'so I've made a modification to the notes trolley instead. I hope you approve of it.'

'Well, I don't,' snapped Mr Potts. 'What on earth is the purpose of it?' he demanded to know, though the answer to his question was perfectly obvious.

'It's to save t-time on the ward round, Sir,' Malcolm replied entirely reasonably, 'so when you require a piece of equipment, we shall already have it to hand, and we shan't keep you waiting.'

'But those drapes will attract germs; all our patients will end up with infections,' Leslie Potts said, casting around for a reason to justify his disapproval. 'We can't have a mobile bacteria carrier on our wards rounds, get rid of it.'

'But I've thought about that, Sir,' countered Malcolm, 'the staff in the linen room have made a duplicate set for me. We can get these laundered whenever necessary.'

Paul and the Sister Ashbrook shuffled uncomfortably. They thought Malcolm had shown commendable initiative. Had they been braver, they might have given him some verbal support, but they didn't. They actually felt that Malcolm's best plan would be to shut up, and let the matter drop. They recognised that Mr Potts had made up his mind, and that this exchange would inevitably end with Malcolm being shouted down.

Mr Potts was not accustomed to having his decisions dissipated by logic, or challenged by junior members of staff. 'But it looks like a baby's pram,' he blustered. 'If we're going to have some damn thing looking like a pram on the ward, for God's sake, give it to Janet, then at least it will be pushed by a woman.'

Janet, who already stood an inch or two taller than Mr Potts, raised herself to her full height, and glared at him, fixing him with her cold, penetrating gaze. Would she break her new resolution and answer him back? In the silence that followed, Paul prayed that she wouldn't.

But Janet's glare melted into a half-smile. 'Do you have a family, Mr Potts?' she asked sweetly.

'Yes, I do. Why do you ask?'

'Then I do hope, Mr Potts, that when your children were babies, you took your fair share of domestic duties, not only feeding and washing them, but changing their dirty nappies as well, as every good husband should.'

Never before had a junior doctor dared to speak to the consultant in such a way, and his face contorted with anger. There was a prolonged silence as everyone waited for him to explode. But he didn't. Controlling his temper, he turned to Malcolm.

'Alright,' he said quietly, 'this time you win. I will tolerate the trolley on the ward today, but when I return for my ward round next week, I'd prefer to see the trolley back in its normal state.'

The words were spoken as a request, but everyone realised that in reality, it was a strict instruction.

****

A few weeks later, Malcolm collared Paul after lunch in the hospital canteen.

'Paul,' he said, 'do you have a minute? There's something in my room that I'd like to show you. I thought I'd better let you see it before I unveil it on the ward.'

Malcolm led the way to his room, and when the door was closed behind them, he showed off his latest creation. Paul looked, and groaned. Malcolm had designed and constructed a wooden box some two feet long and nine inches wide. The top was hinged, and when the lid was opened, a number of compartments of different shapes and sizes were revealed. The design was good; the wood was sturdy, and the handiwork beautiful. The box had dove-tailed joints, a brass handle and hinges, and a lock inset into the front.

'It's a wonderful piece of work,' Paul said, knowing how little time housemen had for rest and relaxation, 'did you make it yourself?'

'Yes, I did,' Malcolm said. 'I was off duty last weekend, and spent most of my time on it.'

'It's for carrying cards and equipment on the ward, isn't it?'

'Yes, and I want to know if you think Mr Potts will take exception to it. He doesn't seem to approve of my various initiatives. I don't want to be embarrassed on the ward yet again.'

Paul knew exactly what Mr Potts would say if he saw it. With sarcasm flowing from his lips, it would be something along the lines of *'I'm not having anyone looking like a plumber or joiner traipsing after me while I do a ward round. Get rid of it at once.'*

'Look, I'm sorry, Malcolm, but I honestly don't think the boss will approve. In fact, I don't think it would be wise to let him see it. I do understand that it saves time to have everything to hand when seeing a patient, but I'm afraid the boss won't see it that way.

Malcolm looked crestfallen, 'But why should he object?' he asked.

It was a perfectly reasonable question, but Paul knew that they were not dealing with a reasonable man.

'Take my advice, Malcolm, use it if you like when you're working on your own, but please don't take it on his ward rounds. He's God around here, and if he's decided he doesn't like your bright ideas, then I'm afraid he's not going to change his mind.'

Advising Malcolm in this way brought to his mind some advice that he'd received when he had been a houseman. *'Don't try to buck the system,'* Mo Khan had said to him. *'You won't change it. It was here long before you came, and it will still be there long after you are gone.'*

Malcolm did use his joiner's wooden box when working on the ward, and it wasn't long before he became quite a celebrity in the hospital as he carried the box around with him wherever he went. Following Paul's advice, though, he was always careful to leave it in a quiet corner of the office whenever Mr Potts was around. One day, someone referred to him as 'Chippy' Chapman, and the name stuck. He became known simply as 'Chippy' for the rest of his time on the unit.

****

'Sister, for God's sake, get one of your nurses to investigate that noise. How can I concentrate on what Mrs Andrews is saying with that din going on?'

Mr Potts was at a patient's bedside with his team of doctors and nurses. A loud hammering noise was coming from the corridor leading to the ward.

Sister turned to the nurses, 'Staff Nurse, would you mind?'

Staff Nurse went to investigate, but before she reached the end of the ward, the banging had stopped. She looked down the corridor, visited the office, and investigated each of the adjacent rooms, but could find nothing amiss. She returned a minute later, and Mr Potts shot her an enquiring glance. Staff Nurse shrugged her shoulders.

'I'm afraid I've no idea what it was, Sir. The noise stopped before I reached the office, and there were no workmen there.'

'Well, at least it's quiet now.' Mr Potts responded. The ward round continued, and the incident was quickly forgotten.

At the end of the round, Mr Potts left to have his lunch, Paul slipped away to Casualty to treat a patient with bellyache, and 'Chippy' Chapman went back to the office to pick up his carpenter's box. He had hidden it on the floor behind Sister's desk, out of Mr Potts way. To his surprise, he found he couldn't lift it. He tried again, but to no avail. The box appeared to be stuck to the floor. He put two hands to the handle and tugged with all his might, he tried to rock it from side to side, but it wouldn't budge. Mystified, he opened the lid, but the contents were as he had left them. He emptied the box and solved the mystery. He discovered that two huge nails had been hammered through the wooden base, firmly attaching it to the floorboards.

'What the hell....' he began, then remembered the hammering that had disrupted Mr Potts' ward round.

Grimly, he turned to Staff Nurse. 'Did you happen to see who did this?' he asked.

'No, I didn't,' she replied, 'but Bill Taylor was in the office when I looked in, and now I think about it, he did have a guilty look on his face.'

'Was there anyone else in the office with him?'

'No there wasn't. I'm sure he must be responsible.'

Bill was the House Officer from Surgical Three, the rival surgical unit situated on the ground floor. Malcolm vowed that he would find an opportunity to gain his revenge. But that would have to wait. The immediate problem was to release the box from the floor. He wondered if he could free it with brute force, but quickly realised that to do so would irreparably damage the box, which he had spent so much time on crafting.

Staff nurse came to his rescue. 'Chippy, you get on with your jobs; I'll ask the hospital maintenance team to free it.'

That evening, Malcolm discussed with Paul how he might get even with Bill. Various schemes were suggested: cotton wool in the bell of his stethoscope, itching powder on the collar of his white coat, glue in his theatre boots and so on, but all these ideas seemed a little childish and unsuitable. The matter was left unresolved, but later, Malcolm said he had the germ of an idea which he would like time to develop. He suggested there should be no further talk about the episode with the toolbox, while he considered the possibilities, so that Bill would have no suspicions that revenge was planned.

One late afternoon, a week later, Malcolm was furious to discover that his precious workbox had once again been nailed to the floor. On this occasion, no one heard the deed being done, nor was any suspicious activity noticed. Nonetheless, Malcolm was in no doubt of the culprit, and was even more determined that he would be avenged. On this occasion, though, there were more immediate consequences.

At 8:15 that evening, Sister Morrison was sitting at her desk in the Surgical Three office supervising the 'nurse handover', the twice-daily routine that took place when the day staff and night staff changed shifts. Around her, in a wide semicircle, her nurses were listening intently to her, a mother hen fussing over her brood of chicks. Sister was detailing the care that each of the patients had received during the day, and giving the night staff their instructions. It had been a long and tiring day, and she was looking forward to getting home and putting her feet up. She was speaking of the final patient when a drop of water fell onto the nursing record that she was holding. Surprised, she looked round to see where it had come from. Then a second drop fell, larger than the first. She looked up at the ceiling. Immediately above her head, the white plaster had turned a dirty grey colour, and was bulging ominously over an area three feet across.

'Oh, my God,' she exclaimed. More drops fell, their size and frequency increasing, and as she watched, a crack appeared at the apex of the swelling. The drops became a steady trickle.

'The whole ceiling's going to come down!' she shouted, as she took evasive action. 'Help me move this desk and these patient records.'

Even as she spoke, a huge chunk of plaster crashed down onto the desk where she had been sitting just a few moments before. It was followed by a cascade of dirty brown water. The patient records that had been on the desk were soaked. Watery debris splashed onto the nurses' shoes and stockings. It covered the floor and splattered the surrounding walls. In a matter of seconds, the office looked as if a tornado had ripped through it.

The nurses had scattered in all directions, some in a state of shock. It was Sister Morrison who recovered first.

'Nurse Webster,' she said, 'Surgical Five is above us. Run up and see what the problem is. Some fool must have left a tap running.'

Five minutes later, the nurse was back. 'There's no problem upstairs,' she reported, 'everything's fine.'

Sister looked up at the ceiling from which a steady trickle of water still emerged, adding to the lake on the floor. 'Then there must be a leak in one of the pipes,' she concluded.

Quickly, she organised her staff. She instructed the night staff to start their nursing duties, and then asked for volunteers from the day staff to stay behind to clear up. She arranged for buckets to be placed under the continuing leak, called the maintenance team, and then got busy with mops and towels to tidy up the mess.

Unfortunately, the hospital plumber had gone home for the night, and it was thirty minutes before he could be called back. All the while, water cascaded into the office. Noting that the Surgical Five office lay immediately above the Surgical Three office, he went up to investigate. He inspected the floor for any signs of moisture, but could find none. He failed to spot a tiny hole in the lino where Malcolm's box had been anchored just a couple of hours earlier. With water still streaming into the ward below, he shifted the office furniture, rolled back the lino, and then started to raise the floorboards. Twenty minutes later, he identified the problem: a neatly punched hole in a water pipe. He scratched his head wondering what could have caused it. Had he been aware that a few days earlier, his colleague had come to Malcolm's assistance, he would probably have put two and two together. As it was, having identified the appropriate stopcock, he repaired the leak, before replacing the floorboards and lino.

It wasn't until the next morning that Bill Taylor learned what had happened. He arrived on the ward, and turned into the office only to find that the room was empty. All the furniture had been moved into a side ward which now served as a temporary office. He saw the floor, still wet from the drenching it had received the night before, noted the dirty stains on the walls, and the buckets catching the last few drops of water that still seeped through the ceiling.

'What on earth has happened here?' he exclaimed before, with sudden horror, he realised that he had caused the problem. He experienced a terrible spasm of guilt, but decided at the same moment, to play the role of an innocent bystander. So long as no-one pointed the finger of blame at him, he would keep quiet, and hope people would assume the burst pipe was an act of God.

****

Late one Saturday evening, some weeks later, Bill was working in the Casualty Department. Midnight approached, the time when, having been encouraged by landlords to sup a hurried final pint at 'last orders', the pubs disgorged their intoxicated customers onto the street. Some made their way home without incident, but others embarked on escapades they would regret before morning. Many were drunk and likely to fall down steps or walk into lampposts; others were belligerent, and taking offence at some minor comment, got involved in fights.

It all made work for the Casualty staff, not least because the local Bobbies felt obliged to bring the miscreants to hospital to be medically assessed before locking them up in the cells for the night, and transporting them to the magistrate's court the following morning.

Bill was weary and ready for bed. He felt abused. These patients' problems were self-inflicted, and he had little sympathy for them. Some were aggressive, others were 'lippy', making comments to the nurses they thought were funny, but were in fact, frequently crude. However, he was conscientious, and although tired, he continued to work until the waiting room was empty. He was just relaxing with a well-earned snack of tea and toast when one of the staff nurses came into office.

'I'm afraid another case has just arrived, Bill,' she said. 'I've put her in cubicle two.'

With a look of resignation on his face, Bill went to see the patient, desperately hoping it would be the last, and that when he finally got to bed, he would not be disturbed before morning. The woman on the couch in the cubicle was young and attractive. She wore a university college scarf around her neck, and Bill was pleased to observe that she appeared to be sober. Accompanying her was a man perhaps ten years her senior. He looked an unlikely companion. He was big, burly, and looked unkempt with two days' growth on his chin. He had a bruise on one cheek and a cut above his eye, which Bill judged to have been recently inflicted. Unlike the girl, who was nicely dressed with a pencil skirt, black leather shoes, and a tight-fitting jumper that emphasised her shapely figure, he wore dirty jeans, an old, food-stained sweater, and steel-capped boots.

Bill picked up the Casualty card and introduced himself. The girl was called Penny. She was a 19-year-old student living in one of the University halls of residence.

'Tell me what happened, and where you're hurt,' Bill said, noting the receptionist had written *'road traffic accident'* on the Casualty card.

'I fell off my bike earlier this evening,' Penny explained. 'I landed heavily on top of the bike, and the end of the handlebars stuck in my chest. I didn't think too much of it at first, but it really hurts now.'

'Have you hurt yourself anywhere else, or is it just your chest?' Bill asked.

'I've a pain in my knee, and my elbow aches a bit, but nothing serious.'

'Is the chest pain there all the time?'

'No, if I keep absolutely still, it doesn't hurt at all, but as soon as I move, it hurts a lot; and if I cough, it's absolute agony. It's like a dagger stabbing into me.'

'It sounds as if you've injured a rib, you might even have cracked it. Have you noticed any change in your breathing?' Bill asked, knowing a fractured rib might easily have punctured a lung.

'Yes, I do feel a bit tight-chested, you know, slightly short of breath.'

'Okay, well, I'd better have a look at it. Can you slip your top off, please?'

Penny looked at her companion. 'Would you mind Pete,' she said.

'I don't mind staying to look after you,' Pete replied in a gruff voice, looking at the pretty young woman who was about to disrobe.

I'm sure you wouldn't, thought Bill.

'Quite sure, thank you,' Penny replied in a firm voice.

'OK, I'll just wait outside in case you need me,' Pete said as he left, somewhat reluctantly.

After Pete left the cubicle, Bill asked whether Pete was a friend of hers, curious to know the relationship between this rather rough-looking character and the well-spoken girl who clearly came from an upper-class background.

'Good gracious me, no!' she exclaimed as she slipped off her sweater. 'He's the janitor at the hall of residence. The college tutor asked if he would mind driving me here to be seen.'

Bill was a rather shy bachelor who had only recently qualified as a doctor. As he gazed at the slim figure lying on the couch before him, her skimpy red bra struggling to contain her full figure, he wondered how long it would be before medical professionalism obliterated his natural male emotions. His face flushed slightly, aware of the conflict in his mind.

'Would you like me to get a chaperone,' he asked?

'No. You're a doctor, aren't you? You must have examined dozens of women of all shapes and sizes.'

He had examined many female patients in the short time he had been qualified, but most had been elderly women with folds of loose flesh hanging from their dumpy bodies. None had been as attractive as the young woman lying in front of him.

'Inspection first, percussion second and auscultation third. Start with the back of the chest', he said to himself, repeating the instructions his mentors at medical school had instilled into him as he attempted to distract himself from Penny's beautiful body.

'Inspection first', he said out loud. 'Sit up straight and take a deep breath for me, please.'

The chest moved symmetrically, but Penny winced as she felt a stab of pain in her side. In textbook fashion, he diligently percussed the upper, middle, and lower regions of her back, carefully comparing one side with the other. No abnormality there. Finally, auscultation. Bill took his stethoscope out of his pocket.

'Breath in,' he instructed as he listened for any abnormal sounds, 'and out,' he said. He decided there was an equal volume of airflow on both sides, nothing to suggest a punctured lung.

Now he had to examine the front of her chest. He knew that to undertake a complete examination, he should ask Penny to remove her bra; that is what he had been taught to do at medical school, but he found himself too embarrassed to ask. Once more, he inspected, then percussed and then listened to the upper and lower parts of her chest, but this time omitting the middle region.

Bill placed his hands on either side of Penny's chest, and pressed firmly to apply compression to the rib cage. Penny squealed with pain. 'My God, that really hurt.'

'I am afraid that means you've broken a rib,' Bill said. 'Pop your top on, and I'll arrange an x-ray for you.'

'But, Doctor, it's my left breast that hurts most. That's where the handlebar of my bike really stuck in. I'm worried because I seem to have developed a lump there. You don't think it's done any damage do you? My Mum had breast cancer when she was only in her 40s. I'm petrified that I might get that too. You will check it for me, won't you, just to make sure?'

Uninvited, she slipped off her bra.

'*Observation, then palpation,*' Bill said to himself. Observation first. As he looked at the nubile figure before him, his emotions were once more in turmoil. A hint of perspiration appeared on his brow.

'Lie back on the couch, and put your left arm behind your head,' he said, knowing that this was the correct position for a breast examination.

'*No asymmetry between the two breasts*,' his medical training said. '*What a beautiful figure*,' his male brain responded.

'Where does it hurt?' he asked.

She pointed to an area behind her left nipple.

'*No obvious bruising,*' the doctor in him decided. '*How desirable,*' his baser emotions replied.

Tentatively he laid a hand on her breast. His fingers could detect no obvious lump. He probed more deeply.

Suddenly, the girl recoiled and screamed at the top of her voice. 'Get off! Get off, you fiend!'

Bill recoiled, hands raised in a posture of innocence.

'But I....'

But his protestations of innocence were drowned out as Penny continued to shout. She sat up, and started flailing at him with her fists, her breasts bouncing up and down like balloons on a restless sea, all the while screaming at the top of her voice, 'Rape, rape, help, someone please, please help me!'

Bill continued to protest, but by this time, Penny was wide-eyed, and hysterical.

In a flash, Sister appeared through the door. 'What's going on?' she cried.

Summing up the situation in an instant, she glared at Bill. 'How dare you?' she said, as she gathered the sheet from the couch, and threw it around Penny, who was now cowering in a corner, crying uncontrollably, hands across her chest, trying to protect her modesty.

'But I... I did nothing,' Bill wailed. 'I was simply examining her. She said she had a pain in the breast. I wouldn't dream of....'

Again, he was interrupted, this time by Pete who entered, his face bursting with rage.

'It's him, it's him!' Penny screamed, pointing directly at Bill. 'He's a sex maniac, a pervert. He's been groping me.'

Pete reached Bill in one giant stride across the small cubicle. He picked him up by the lapels of his white coat, and lifted him bodily off the floor. Bill's feet dangled in fresh air. Pete thrust his face within two inches of Bill's. 'You filthy little swine, you'll pay for this, you pervert.'

At that moment, two more figures entered the crowded cubicle unannounced; one was Malcolm, the other Paul. Malcolm held a video camera to his eye, and it purred quietly as he focussed on Bill's petrified face, and then panned to Penny. Now discreetly draped with the hospital sheet, she had a huge grin on her face. Malcolm continued filming for a couple of minutes taking time to photograph all the characters in the charade which he had so carefully choreographed. Initially, Bill had looked absolutely terrified then, when Malcolm had entered, he appeared bewildered. It took quite some time before it finally dawned on him that he had been duped. He growled at Malcolm.

'You bastard, you utterly despicable bastard.'

Satisfied that he had a complete photographic record of the scene, Malcolm stopped filming. The revenge he had planned had gone with a precision of which the military would have been justly proud.

'Let me introduce you to Penny,' he said to Bill. 'She's my sister. She's a drama student at the College of Performing Arts. She's a great actress, isn't she?'

Then he turned to Penny's companion. 'And this is Pete. He's not really the caretaker at the college. He's actually the captain of London Irish rugby team. He's Penny's boyfriend. He played in a match this afternoon, which explains why his face has been knocked about a bit.'

Malcolm turned to the Casualty Nursing Sister. 'I'm sorry, Sister, that we didn't let you in on our little secret, but I must say you played your part to perfection. We thought you might not be quite so convincing, if you knew in advance what was going to happen. Now, Paul,' he said, 'would you be kind enough to retrieve my little box of tricks so I can put this camera of mine back in a safe place?'

Paul slipped out of the cubicle and returned a few seconds later with Malcolm's 'toolbox'. With a glance at Bill, Malcolm opened the lid, put the camera safely in, then closed and locked it.

'I trust that will teach you not to mess with my belongings in the future.'

Thoughts for the day

Revenge is a dish that can be eaten cold.

Late 19C Proverb

If you prick us, do we not bleed?

If you tickle us, do we not laugh?

If you poison us, do we not die?

And if you wrong us, shall we not revenge?

William Shakespeare 1564 - 1616

Chapter 30 A Game of Cricket brings a Moral Dilemma

21st June 1971

In the fifties, sixties and early seventies a community spirit existed within UK hospitals. This spirit was particularly in evidence at Christmas, when everyone went out of their way to create a cheerful atmosphere for the patients who were unable to be at home with their loved ones. For many, the highlight came on Christmas Eve when the nurses' choir in their maroon capes and starched white caps sang carols around the tree in the middle of the ward, a heart-warming sight.

On Christmas Day, the catering staff came on duty early and worked hard in the kitchens roasting turkeys, one for each ward. These were carved by the consultants in the centre of the ward, and then served to the patients by his wife and family. Father Christmas flew in, you could hear his reindeers' bells jingling in the corridor, before he distributed presents, usually a bottle of beer for the men, and some toiletries for the women. The Salvation Army brass band also visited and played carols in the corridors. There were far too many players for them all to squeeze onto the ward, but the warmth of their music reached every bedside.

The staff also came together to perform the hospital pantomime, a very popular event, which was a wonderful opportunity for the junior doctors and nurses to poke fun at the consultants and the hospital matron. They took it all in good heart of course, indeed were affronted if they were not the butt of at least one good joke.

At the City General, other special social events were the fund-raising summer fair and the annual cricket match between the hospital consultants and the junior doctors. This was always eagerly anticipated, not only by the participants, but also by the rest of the hospital staff, many of whom came along to watch. There were usually some good-looking bachelors on the junior doctor's team, which guaranteed the attendance of a number of young nurses. Others came along privately hoping that some of the more pompous consultants might find a way of embarrassing themselves. Given that several of them were both unfit and overweight, there was a fair chance that they wouldn't be disappointed! The format was a limited-over match, with everyone except the wicket-keeper required to bowl two overs. An additional rule was that you couldn't be 'out' first ball. This generally worked well, except on the occasion when a consultant was 'out' on the second ball he received, as well as the first. Then, when given a further chance by the benevolent umpire, who chanced to be one of his consultant colleagues, he proceeded to be 'out' on the third ball as well! A unique and unforgettable hat trick!

The juniors, young, athletic and keen to have some fun at the expense of their consultant chiefs, never had any trouble fielding a team. The consultants on the other hand, some elderly, staid and possibly afraid of public embarrassment, often had to supplement their side with friends, relatives, or their colleagues in general practice. Since the object of the game was to relax, have fun and break down barriers, there was an unwritten rule that 'regular' cricketers, for example, members of local league cricket clubs, were not allowed to play.

The venue was the park adjacent to the hospital. Built originally on land that had formed part of a wealthy merchant's country estate, the City General Hospital had started life in Victorian times situated amongst pleasant green fields. Over the years though, it had become engulfed by urban development as the city expanded. Fortunately, the area immediately adjacent to the hospital had been preserved as a park for the recreation and enjoyment of the public.

In the absence of a cricket pavilion, the teams gathered in two informal groups on the edge of the field. Many student nurses were present, eager to support the junior doctors who in turn, were keen to impress with a display of their sporting prowess. Inevitably, there was quite a contrast between the teams. The junior doctors were aged between 23 and 35 and, with one exception, wore green theatre vests and trousers. The 'odd one out' was the only female member of the team, Victoria. The age of the consultant team ranged from 30 to 60 and again there was one exception, Mr Potts' nine-year-old son. They were of various shapes and sizes, sporting a motley selection of attire, some in regular cricketing whites, some in theatre greens, and others, since it was a warm summer's day, in beach shorts.

There was much curiosity to see which of the consultants had been brave enough to play. Normally respected by virtue of their seniority and experience, many were liked and admired, but one or two, such as Mr Leslie Potts, were domineering and autocratic. Would they be shaken from their lofty perch, and brought down a peg or two? And how would others fare, given their generous waistlines?

Paul looked across at the consultant group. He knew most of them, but there were three or four unfamiliar faces, presumably local general practitioners who had been drafted in to make up the numbers. Leslie Potts was there of course, immaculately attired, his white trousers starched and pressed, wearing cricket boots and a white sweater. There was a club motif on both his sweater and cap. In the days before the match, he had bragged of his athleticism, and spoken of previous success on the cricket pitch. Paul had taken this as arrogance, but perhaps he was a good cricketer after all. Maybe his self-praise had been justified and not merely the product of a big ego, a lively imagination, and a desire to impress the nurses! By contrast, Professor Butterworth, the head of the University's Faculty of Medicine, who was not the smartest of dressers at the best of times, had merely taken off his jacket and tie, tucked the bottom of his brown corduroy trousers into his black socks and donned a pair of white tennis pumps. The Professor was known to be a character with a lively sense of humour, but clearly, he was not a cricketer!

Mrs Potts, together with her son and daughter, were amongst the consultants group. Paul had met the Potts family four years before, when he had been the house officer on the unit. They had visited the ward on Christmas Day when as was traditional, Mr Potts had carved the turkey using the longest and sharpest knife that was available in the operating theatre; the one normally reserved for amputating limbs! Mrs Potts and her daughter had helped the nurses to serve lunch to the patients. Paul decided that propriety dictated that he should walk over to chat with her. She was a striking figure; tall and slim, with an exuberant and bubbly personality, quite a contrast to her dour and brusque husband. She shared her outgoing disposition with her son. His name was Andrew and he had been five years old when Paul had last seen him. With his mother's blonde hair, blue eyes and a cheeky grin, he had caused chaos on the ward within five minutes of arriving. He had brought two of his Christmas presents with him; a clockwork car and a football. The car, whose speed had disappointed on the lush lounge carpet at home, went like a formula one racer on the polished linoleum of the ward floor. It frequently disappeared under patients' beds or items of medical apparatus, and in a flash, Andrew went after it, knocking over anything that stood in his way. Much to Sister's annoyance, his father had done nothing to curb his enthusiasm! After a drip stand and two commodes had been sent flying, their malodorous contents having been spread far and wide, Paul had taken him to the far end of the ward, and set up two chairs to act as goal posts. Then he had acted as a goalkeeper, whilst Andrew had taken penalty kicks with his new football, screaming with delight with every goal that he scored. This was not a role included in Paul's job description, but it proved to be an effective way of preventing further damage to ward equipment!

On this occasion, like his father, Andrew was correctly and smartly attired. Although only nine years of age, he was wearing long white trousers, cricket boots and pads. He was playing flamboyant strokes with his junior cricket bat as Sir William, dressed in his umpire's white coat (no doubt borrowed from one of the housemen, then washed and starched in the hospital laundry), tossed a tennis ball to him underarm. As always, the senior consultant wore a fresh red rose on his lapel. Clearly Andrew was a *'chip off the old block'*, a showman in the making, like his father.

Also standing with the consultants was Frederick Swindles, the obsequious secretary to the consultant's management committee. Paul had met him when being interviewed for his job at the City General. He had been co-opted as an umpire. He was a slightly built, insignificant, greying, middle-aged man, who tried to raise his status by insisting on being called 'Frederick', but who was in fact, known simply as 'Fred'. In stark contrast to Sir William, he was wearing a crumpled, brown jacket over a hand-knitted woollen cardigan, a shirt and tie of discordant colours and scuffed shoes. Having started as an office junior, some twenty years before, he had been promoted over the years to his present post, but had never left the secluded security of the administrative department. Knowing how he loved to inveigle his way into the good books of the consultants, Paul doubted that the junior doctors would benefit from many of his umpiring decisions.

As Paul watched, and much to his surprise, Janet arrived; he had thought that she had left the country a couple of months previously to take up a post in Sydney. She amazed him by waving merrily to Mr Potts. Paul knew how much she detested the consultant and couldn't understand her action. Surely the two of them hadn't suddenly made up their differences. Unsurprisingly, with his wife close at hand, Mr Potts did not respond in kind. Instead, Paul saw him stiffen slightly, and then half turn his back as he continued to chat with his consultant colleagues. Janet however, waltzed straight up to Mr Potts, put her arms round him and gave him a hug. For one dreadful moment, Paul thought she was going to kiss him. She didn't, but the familiarity of the greeting was unmistakably. What on earth was she doing? Then suddenly, Paul understood the game she was playing. Presumably Mrs Potts knew, as everyone in the hospital knew, that her husband had an eye for a pretty girl with a curvaceous figure; Janet was aiming to embarrass Mr Potts in front of his wife by suggesting that the relationship between them was not merely that of consultant and junior doctor.

'Hello Leslie,' she breezed, beaming at him. 'I've been looking forward to this match for weeks. I must say you really do look the part. I'm sure that you'll play a starring role.'

Her words jarred. House officers never addressed consultants by their Christian names. It was unheard of.

Mr Potts had no option but to respond. 'Ah. Good afternoon, Dr Smith. I see you've come to watch the match.'

'Yes, I have,' Janet responded, taking his arm, 'and I'm looking forward to it immensely. I'm expecting you to score lots of runs, and take a few wickets.'

'Thank you, my dear,' Leslie Potts replied, the coolness in his voice unmistakable. 'That's very kind of you to say so, but I think you're in the enemy camp. The resident's team is over there.'

Paul had been chatting with Mrs Potts, and both had witnessed the exchange between Janet and her husband.

'Who is that young woman?' Mrs Potts asked her voice cold and prim.

'It's Dr Smith, one of the house officers,' Paul replied, thinking it unwise to volunteer that the '*young woman*' in question, had been selected by her husband to be his house surgeon, and had received a good deal of his personal attention whilst undertaking the job.

'I see. Perhaps you would just excuse me for a minute, Dr Lambert.'

But Sir William had also seen the exchange, and showing commendable diplomacy, moved in to defuse the situation.

'Leslie,' he said cheerfully. 'I think we're ready to begin the match.'

Then to Janet he added, 'Dr Smith, I believe Dr Hill is the captain of the resident's team. Could I trouble you to ask him to come across, and we'll get the game started?'

With Janet cleverly despatched, and Sir William engaging Mr Potts and his wife in conversation, the tension had eased by the time Richard Hill wandered across to join the group.

'Now,' said Sir William, 'before we have the toss, can we have an agreement about the rules.'

'What we suggest,' Richard said, 'is that, as is customary, the match be restricted to twenty overs, with everybody bowling two overs. This is a friendly game, we want everyone to feel involved, and to play an active part.'

'Are the consultants happy with that arrangement?' Sir William asked.

Mr Potts, the self-appointed captain of the consultant's team, nodded his agreement.

'Unfortunately,' Richard continued, 'we have a slight problem. Some members of our team are on duty, so they are carrying their 'pagers' in their pockets. It means that there may be some coming and going during the course of the match.'

'I'm sure that will be acceptable,' said Sir William, without referring the matter to his fellow consultant. 'And I'm delighted to see that Mr Khan has returned to join us this afternoon; he was one of the best trainees that it's been my pleasure to have on the unit. I also see that Miss Kent is playing for your team.'

'Yes,' responded Richard. 'We've struggled to get a full team, and Victoria has agreed to make up the numbers. I hope you have no objection, Mr Potts?'

'No objection at all. In fact, it should add to the merriment.'

'Right,' said Sir William. 'Are we ready to toss?'

Both captains agreed, a coin was flipped which Richard duly won. He decided that the juniors would bat first.

There was polite applause and a few catcalls from the spectators, as the consultants, led by Mr Potts, took to the field, his son at his side. Professor Butterworth, now wearing wicket-keepers' pads over his corduroy trousers, looked even more incongruous than before. The cheering grew louder when Richard, who had many female admirers, took to the field, bat in hand. He looking determined, and had a steely glint in his eye. Tony Myers, one of the medical house officers accompanied him to the crease. A trace of a smile crossed Richard's face when it became apparent that Mr Potts planned to open the bowling for the consultant's team. Richard had previously worked on Mr Potts' firm, had frequently been criticised and belittled by the consultant in front of the nurses, and saw the match as an opportunity to settle the score. It seemed that the spectators were to be treated to a fascinating contest.

Mr Potts claimed to have had significant success as a cricketer in his youth, both as a batsman and as a bowler. Paul waited with interest to see whether this self-confidence was justified. Stockily built, he delivered the ball with reasonable accuracy, at a good medium pace, off a shortish run. Richard though had a good 'eye', he was young and fit, and he swung his bat lustily, attempting to hit every ball out of the park. His cricket bat became a weapon with which to gain his revenge. Mr Potts first over yielded four boundaries, two of them sixes. It was entertaining stuff, with every blow being cheered by the crowd as the score rattled along. A look of grim satisfaction appeared on Richard's face.

Whilst Leslie Potts may well have been a reasonable cricketer in his youth, and still retained much of his cricketing skill, he had not retained his fitness. Before he had completed the second of his permitted overs, he was red faced and blowing like a steam locomotive. He did however have the satisfaction of taking the first wicket as Richard, attempting one blow too many, didn't quite middle the ball, and holed out on the square leg boundary. Mr Potts was ecstatic, appealing loudly to the umpire. When Fred's index finger was raised, he danced with delight as if he had just won the £75,000 jackpot on Littlewoods pools. After only three overs however, the resident's score had reached 36 for the loss of one wicket, 30 of them coming from Richard's bat.

The first bowling change introduced an athletic looking man of about 35, one of the local general practitioners. It was later learned that he had previously played cricket for one of the minor counties! Unfortunately for the junior doctors, it seems that no one had informed him that this was a friendly game, and he bowled fast and straight with devastating effect. The score of 36 for one, rapidly became 48 for four, and one of the wickets to fall was Paul's. At school, he had enjoyed playing cricket, but had only been an average performer, and was no match for this 'ringer'. He did manage to survive a couple of deliveries, even nicking one through the slips for a boundary, but then, more concerned with his own safety than protecting his wicket, he completely missed a fast, straight full toss, and was comprehensively bowled.

In the next few overs, the score crept up slowly, but came to a complete halt when Leslie Potts Junior came on to bowl. Clearly imbued with his father's huge self-esteem, he took a 20 yard run up, which he covered with impressive speed, only to come to a complete halt, when he reached the wicket for his delivery stride. Without the strength to propel the ball the full 22 yards to the other end of the pitch, the ball dribbled to a halt five yards short of the batsman. There was a suggestion, shouted from the ranks of the residents' supporters, that since the ball had not reached the batsman, it should be designated a wide, but Sir William, who was umpiring at the bowler's end, decreed otherwise. After three such deliveries, Sir William suggested to the batsman, that 'Potts Junior' should be permitted to bowl from a point a third of the way down the pitch. This was readily agreed, (not that anyone would have dreamed of disagreeing with the hospital's most senior consultant), but even so, the ball only reached the batsman grubbing along the ground. Scoring was impossible and as a result young Andrew was the only bowler to bowl two maiden overs.

After 12 overs, with five wickets down, the score had only reached 73, disappointing after Richard had given the team such a bright start. This quickly became 73 for six when Professor Butterworth surprised himself by holding a sharp catch behind the stumps, off the bowling of Mr Keenan, the orthopaedic consultant. This brought Victoria to the crease. Strangely, of all the members of the resident's team, she was the most appropriately attired. She wore smart white flannels, a white shirt and cricketing pads that actually fitted her. Mr Keenan was a giant of a man; not less than six feet two inches tall, weighing at least eighteen stones. It was easy to imagine him straightening broken bones without the slightest difficulty. Red-faced, bull necked, and as broad as an ox, he towered over Victoria, who looked positively petite in comparison.

'Would you prefer me to use a tennis ball?' Mr Keenan asked from the bowler's end. It was genuinely a courteous question, in no way intended to be derogative. Clearly, he had not seen the county badge on Victoria's sweater, nor had he noticed the rather professional way in which she asked the umpire for a middle and leg guard.

Victoria answered, firmly but politely, 'That won't be necessary, thank you, Sir.'

'OK,' the bowler responded. 'Then I'll bowl nice and gently.'

'Just as you wish,' came the reply.

The first ball was a slow long hop, well outside the off stump. It sat up invitingly, asking to be hit, and Victoria duly dispatched it, off the middle of the bat to the mid-wicket boundary. The crowd was stunned, but reacted with surprise and delight. Mr Keenan looked a little bemused, but said nothing as he ambled back to his mark. His second ball, another gently delivery, was again short, but this time on the line of the leg stump. Victoria rocked onto her right foot, swivelled and struck the ball sweetly along the ground to the square leg boundary. This time there was a roar of approval from the crowd. The third ball, noticeably faster than the first two, was a full toss. This was met with a firm straight bat, and two more runs were added to the total. Victoria had scored ten runs off just three deliveries.

The spectators, scarcely believing what they were seeing, were on their toes, cheering and crying out for more. Mr Keenan though, was not amused. He started to bowl with the speed and determination he had shown against his male opponents. It made little difference. Straight balls were met with a solid defensive stroke, and anything loose was dispatched to the boundary. It was a fascinating David and Goliath contest, Victoria cool and compact at the wicket, concentrating on every ball with admirable resolve; Mr Keeley, a giant in comparison, becoming increasingly frustrated, ever redder in the face, attempting to bowl each ball faster than the last, but only succeeding in getting wilder. One full toss whistled straight back over his head. It landed short of the rope, but still reached the boundary for another four. The crowd loved every minute of it. The more bad balls he bowled, the more rapidly the score mounted. Victoria was not physically big, nor powerfully built, but her timing was immaculate. She simply used good technique and the speed of the ball to score at will. Although wickets continued to fall occasionally at the other end, Victoria's inning was chanceless, and she had hit an undefeated 46 by the time the last over was bowled. She left the field to a standing ovation. The junior doctor's final score was 130 for the loss of eight wickets. Richard declared himself satisfied. He felt reasonably certain the total was beyond the reach of the consultants.

During the interval between the two innings, there was a further demonstration of the community spirit that bound the staff together, and was such an attractive feature of hospital life at this time. The catering staff had organised refreshments. Standing behind trestle tables that the porters had carried to the edge of the field, they smiled and chatted, as they served players and spectators with tea, cakes and biscuits.

When the match resumed, Professor Butterworth walked to the

crease to open the batting for the consultants' team. Accompanying him was the GP 'ringer', who had taken three wickets in a couple of overs when the junior doctors had been batting. It quickly became apparent that not only was he a demon bowler, he was also an accomplished batsman. Not so the Professor, who scarcely knew which end of the bat to hold. To the delight of the crowd, he swished enthusiastically at every ball he received, completely missing most of them, all the while laughing heartily at his own incompetence. He was the beneficiary of two very dubious umpiring decisions, both given by Fred. The first was an appeal for 'leg before wicket', which looked plumb, but there was no way that the fawning clerk to the consultants committee was going to give a decision against the university professor. The appeal was turned down almost before it was uttered. On the second occasion, the visiting GP, clearly accustomed to batting with players as nimble as himself, called for a quick single. Prof Butterworth, gasping for breath, and lumbering like a carthorse, looked to be at least two yards short of the crease, when the wicket was broken. The appeal was emphatically rejected.

'Come on, play the game,' muttered one of the housemen.

'Definitely not out,' repeated Fred. The Professor clearly regained his ground.'

The Professor's charmed life continued. Once again, the general practitioner, not having learned the lesson from the previous episode, turned a ball to square leg where Victoria was fielding. He called for a quick single. Victoria picked up the ball, and threw it accurately to the stumps where Richard caught it in both hands. Prof Butterworth was still halfway down the pitch. Unaccountably, the ball slipped through Richard's hands, and then he fumbled in his attempt to retrieve it. This allowed the Professor, now too short of breath to run, plenty of time to walk sedately to safety. Obviously, Richard, who had previously worked in the Professor's University Department, and was dependent on him for his next reference, did not regard it in his best interests to dismiss his boss! *'Why kill the goose that might lay you a golden egg'* he admitted afterwards! However, the batsman's reprieve proved to be short lived. A couple of balls later, his innings finally came to an end. Having missed most of the deliveries that he had received, he actually managed to put bat to ball, only to see the ball lob gently to be caught in the gully. The junior doctors wondered whether Fred would dare to call a much-delayed 'no ball', but he didn't. Instead, he apologised.

'I am most terribly sorry Sir, but I'm afraid you must be out this time.'

The Professor though, wasn't in the least perturbed, and grinning from ear to ear, having enjoyed himself immensely, walked off the field to a generous round of applause.

Although Professor Butterworth had added little to the total, the GP at the other end was scoring freely. After a chanceless fifty, perhaps aware that there was a danger that he might win the match for the consultants single-handed, he started to hit the ball in the air, to give catches to the fielders. The first couple were dropped, but eventually Richard accepted a chance, and the 'ringer' left.

After only seven overs, the score had already reached 70 for the loss of only two wickets. The junior doctor's total of 130 was beginning to appear inadequate, and Richard became concerned. With little idea of the competence of the members of his scratch team, he looked around the field, and then tossed the ball to Mohammed Khan, probably more in hope, than in expectation.

With the ball in his hand, Mo looked completely at ease. Standing at the bowler's end, he quickly reorganised the field, all the while spinning the ball casually from hand to hand. Then, walking gently to the wicket off a two-yard approach, he bowled a slow delivery that looped deceptively through the air, landed exactly on a length, and then fizzed viciously off the pitch toward the wicket. Paul thought at first, that the ball must have hit a bump to behave in such a fashion, but Mo repeated the trick time and time again, and it quickly became apparent that this quiet unassuming man was in fact, an extraordinarily skilled cricketer.

'You've played this game once or twice before,' Paul commented as they passed at the end of the first over.

Mo smiled modestly. 'Yes,' he said, 'I used to play a little at school and at college. In fact, I played a couple of times for the Indian under 19's team, but that was a long time ago. I thought I'd lost the knack.'

'Why didn't you have a bat?' Paul asked.

'This is the house officer's day,' he replied, 'a day for them to enjoy. I'm just a visitor today.'

His second over was just as effective as the first, and as wickets fell, the consultant's score slipped to 82 for five. Things were looking brighter for the junior doctors. This appeared to be a good time for Richard to put himself on to bowl, to capitalise on Mo's success. However, he continued to hold himself back.

When the sixth wicket fell, Mr Potts strode confidently to the wicket accompanied by some clapping and ribaldry from the spectators on the boundary.

'Show them what you are made of, Mr Potts, Sir.'

'Let's see if you're as good as you say you are,' cried a less charitable voice, safely hidden in the midst of the crowd.

Whether Mr Potts heard these remarks or not is difficult to say, but he did raise his bat and then his cap, in recognition of the applause.

When Richard saw Mr Potts coming to the crease, he brought himself onto bowl. Evidently, he had saved himself for this moment. He brought the fielders in close, clustering them around the bat then marched back for a 15 yard run, a venomous look on his face.

Richard's first ball to his ex-boss was fast and straight, a 'yorker'. It was aimed directly at the consultant's feet. It carried with it, all the anger that had built within Richard when he was working for Mr Potts. Mr Potts' instinct was for his personal safety, particularly to get his ankles and toes out of the firing line. He managed to keep his bat on the ground to protect his wicket, but with both feet in the air, and a startled look on his face, he gave a fair impression of a pole vaulter at the point of take-off. The ball, travelling at great speed, nicked the edge of the bat, whistled passed the stumps, and raced to the boundary. Richard appeared not to mind that four runs had been added to the consultant's total. There was a look of satisfaction on his face. The next ball was equally fast but slightly off line. It whistled passed the batsman and the wicket, narrowly missing both, before being caught in the wicket-keeper's gloves. The third ball of the over was even faster than the previous two. Short in length, it rose off the pitch, passing within two inches of Mr Potts' left ear as he ducked out of the way at the last minute. Up to this moment, the game had been played in a good spirit, everyone enjoying themselves in the sunshine. There had been light-hearted banter between the opposing teams, and whilst both sides were keen to win the match, everyone understood that the result was not of prime importance. Whilst Paul could understand Richard's anger, this display of aggression was misplaced. It would not impress Sir William or the numerous consultants who were watching. Doctors were expected to demonstrate self-control at all times. Even if Richard did not intend to continue with a career in hospital medicine, perhaps preferring to work in public health or to practice in the community, he still needed a reference. Richard was in the process of committing professional suicide, and besides, there was a danger that Mr Potts might get injured.

Paul exchanged an anxious glance with Mo who had seen enough. Mo called for the wicket-keeper to throw the ball to him, and then walked to the bowler's end, to hand it to Richard. Quite a long discussion between the two ensued. To a casual observer, it might have appeared as if a captain and his bowler were discussing how a field should be set for a new batsman, but clearly this was not the case. Paul was not party to the conversation, but understood exactly what was being said.

Then there was another development. It became clear that Mo was not the only one concerned for Mr Potts' safety. His wife, evidently overlooking, at least for the moment, the manner in which her husband had been greeted by his glamorous, young ex-house officer, came running onto the pitch.

'Leslie, Leslie, Leslie. You must put this on,' she shouted, waving a cricketer's box high in the air. The spectators, who had watched Richard's aggressive bowling in silence, dissolved into gales of laughter, and inevitably there were more catcalls.

'Got to protect the crown jewels.'

'You might need that equipment later tonight, Sir. Better safe than sorry!'

'That will give Richard something to aim at!'

Mrs Potts ran to the middle of the pitch, and then handed this vital piece of protective equipment to her husband. The crowd loved it. Seeing a senior consultant loosen his belt, then slip the box down his trousers to protect his genitals in the middle of the cricket field, in plain view of so many young nurses, was a spectacle that became a talking point within the hospital for many weeks to come. After this short delay, Richard, accepting the wisdom of the advice he had been given, bowled the rest of his over in a more conventional style.

At this stage, the consultant's score had slipped to 98 for seven; it was going to be a close match, And so it proved; with four overs remaining, twenty runs were needed, and then eleven from the last two overs. When the ninth wicket fell, four runs were required from the last four balls. It was at this point that Leslie Potts Junior came to the crease, his father at his side. Unfortunately for Paul, he was the bowler. As Junior went to the crease, and took his guard in a very confident manner, Mr Potts approached Paul.

'Andrew has really been looking forward to this game,' he said. 'It would do his confidence the world of good if he were able to score a run or two.' He put his hand in his pocket, and for one dreadful moment, Paul thought he was going to produce a five-pound note. He didn't. Instead, he handed Paul a tennis ball.

'You will treat him gently won't you, Lambert.' Mr Potts' words were clearly an instruction, not a request. Then he patted Paul on the shoulder, and walked away, shouting '*Good Luck*' to his lad as he left.

Paul wondered what on earth he was supposed to do. He was twenty-seven years old, reasonably fit and athletic, with only a nine-year-old boy standing between him and a win for his team. Yet he was also a surgical trainee, ambitious and eager for promotion, and the obstacle between him and victory was the son of his boss. And his boss clearly wanted Paul to allow his son to '*score a run or two.*' Paul decided that the only appropriate course of action was to bowl very slowly, but reasonably straight, and let fate take its course. If Junior missed the ball, and it chanced to hit the wicket, then that was just too bad. Paul also thought it best to bowl underarm, then even if Andrew was bowled, at least it would appear that he had tried to oblige his boss. Paul though, was unaccustomed to the lighter weight of the tennis ball, and his first delivery was far too gentle. It bounced three times before coming to rest at Junior's feet. He took a swipe at it, but only managed to return it to Paul along the ground. Now there were only three balls left, and the consultants still needed four runs for victory. Then Paul had a brainwave, a moment of inspiration. A good strategy would be to allow Junior to score a single, and then bowl the last couple of balls overarm with a proper cricket ball to the consultant at the other end. With this in mind, he pushed the fielders back, almost to the boundary, and then threw the ball higher in the air, hoping that Andrew would hit it into one of the large unprotected areas where a single was perfectly possible. Unfortunately, however, he bowled far too high, and a little too fast. The ball landed two thirds of the way down the pitch, and then bounced clean over Junior's head. He waved his bat at it gallantly, but it was quite out of his reach.

'Hey, you,' Junior shouted at Paul, in much the same tone that his father used to address his staff, 'that's not fair.' Then he turned towards his father, who was watching eagle-eyed on the boundary.

'Dad, tell this man to bowl properly.'

All eyes turned to Mr Potts to see what his response would be, but he was wise enough to stay silent. Meanwhile Sir William had signalled a wide for the last delivery. The consultants now needed three more runs to win, and there were still three balls left. Once again,

Paul tried to bowl a ball from which Junior could score a single. This time, the tennis ball reached him at just the right height for a gentle push, into any one of the empty spaces Paul had left for him to score. Paul was delighted. His plan was working. But Junior had other ideas. He opted for a wild slog. The contact of bat on ball was perfect. The ball sailed away off the middle of the bat, high into the air, clearly visible in the bright light against the cloudless blue sky. It flew straight into the hands of Mohammed Khan, the international cricketer, who was fielding on the square leg boundary. It was the simplest of catches, but mysteriously it slipped through his fingers, and then bounced twice, before crossing the ropes for a boundary. Four runs and a victory to the consultants, with just two balls to spare. Junior did a war dance of delight, and then whooping happily and waving his bat high in the air, he ran back to his father.

'I did it, Dad. I did it, and we've won.'

Ruefully Paul turned to Sir William, who handed him his cap.

'Well-played, Lambert. Well-played.'

Then he looked Paul in the eye and smiled. 'Surgery can throw up some difficult dilemmas, can't it?'

'It most certainly can, Sir.'

Thoughts for the day

Cricket is basically baseball on valium

Robin Williams 1952 – 2014

Personally, I've always looked upon cricket as organised loafing.

William Temple 1881 - 1944

Chapter 31   The Lady with the Lump

26th July 1971

'If you're training to be a doctor, you've got to look like a doctor, not like some scruffy labourer from the local building site. Jeans and an open neck shirt are not suitable apparel. Leave at once, and don't come back until you're properly dressed.'

Leslie Potts was in the outpatient clinic with the medical students, and one of the young men was learning the hard way that the consultant expected certain standards to be maintained. On this occasion the consultant's reprimand was justified; having been advised previously of the accepted code of dress, he should have known better. The student left red-faced and angry.

'Now let's get back to work,' Mr Potts said to the remaining students. 'I've got a letter here from one of our local GPs. I'll read it to you, and then we'll go and see the patient.'

Dear Mr Potts,
Re. Anne Nichols
This pleasant lady is the wife of a local farmer, and has noticed a lump in her left breast. The lump is not painful and does not vary with her periods. Two years ago, she had a lump in the opposite breast, which proved to be benign.
I should be grateful if you would kindly see and advise on her further management.
With thanks
David Evans

'No attempt to offer a diagnosis, you'll notice,' commented Mr Potts drily, as he beckoned Sister to show the patient in. 'What else is missing from this letter?'

He addressed the question to James Cassidy, a quiet, diligent student who, although highly intelligent and well-read, lacked self-confidence. Had James been in an examination hall with time to consider his response, he would have had no difficulty in suggesting the GP could have given the patient's age, stated how long the lump had been present, whether it was increasing in size, and half a dozen other pieces of information. But in the presence of the patient, a couple of nurses and surrounded by his fellow students, and with Mr Potts glaring at him, he became flustered.

'I, er, um, well, I'm not sure, Sir,' James stuttered. 'Perhaps whether she's married, or has a family.'

'I told you she's married to a farmer. That was one of the few things the GP did say in his letter. My God, when I saw you standing there in your white coat, I thought you were training to be a doctor, but if you're part of the maintenance staff come to do a bit of decorating, you should have waited until the clinic was over.'

He turned to one of the girls. 'Miss Johnstone, you look as though you're a bright young thing, for heaven's sake, help him out.'

Mr Potts believed that such criticism stimulated the students to work harder, but it had the opposite effect. It crushed the confidence of the unfortunate victim, filled his fellow students with apprehension, and embarrassed the patient.

Mrs Nichols proved to be a pleasant woman, 36-years-of-age, who had kept her figure, despite having two young children. Wearing a plain, thick, woollen skirt and a chunky roll-necked sweater, and with her rosy cheeks and broad, calloused hands, her appearance spoke of a healthy life of hard work spent in the open air.

In response to Mr Potts' interrogation, she described how she had noticed the lump a few weeks earlier. It had gradually increased in size, but hadn't been painful. She acknowledged she did a lot of physical work, but had no recollection of having bumped or knocked her breast. Apart from the contraceptive pill, she was not taking any medication.

'Nothing there to suggest what the problem might be,' Mr Potts remarked to the students before asking Sister to take Mrs Nichols into one of the examination cubicles.

In the privacy of the cubicle, Mrs Nichols enquired whether she would be seen by Mr Potts alone, or whether all the other young men with him would also be present.

'If you like, I can ask him to see you on his own,' Sister replied, though the inflection in her voice indicated she was not optimistic that she would be successful. In fact, her request fell on deaf ears.

'I have brought a number of young doctors with me today,' Mr Potts began when he entered the cubicle. 'They do have to learn, you know, so that they will be able to look after patients with breast problems in the future. Now, if you would care to remove that dressing gown.'

Hesitatingly, Mrs Nichols did as she was told.

For a moment, Mr Potts stood back and regarded his patient. 'Now sit up straight and show me where this lump is.'

'Frugis ruris vero largae sunt,' Mr Potts remarked, a smile on his face, and with a sideways glance at his students. Some of the medical students who had studied Latin at school were amused, some were annoyed, but all were surprised at the remark. Non-Latin scholars looked puzzled. Mrs Nichols, realising that a personal comment about her appearance had been made, looked hurt, her eyes turning to Sister appealingly. Sister also conscious that an inappropriate remark had been made, though not understanding what had been said, looked daggers at Mr Potts but said nothing.

'Right, let's see what this lump is all about.'

He examined Mrs Nichols quickly, though thoroughly. He was about to instruct one of the students to examine Mrs Nichols as well, but Sister beat him to it. In a flash, she had the dressing gown back in place.

Mr Potts stood back, a grave look on his face. 'I'm afraid that you have a bit of a problem there,' he said. 'Dress up and I'll come and have a chat with you in a minute.'

Without waiting for a response, he led the students out of the cubicle.

'What did that Latin phrase mean?' one of the students whispered to his colleague.

'The fruits of the countryside are truly bountiful,' he was told.

Whilst Mrs Nichols dressed in the cubicle, Mr Potts spoke to the students. 'I'm afraid that's rather a large tumour,' he said.

He then went on, in a question-and-answer session, to explain that it was unusual to find such a large cancer in a young patient, and unfortunately, the prognosis was poor.

'Sister obviously didn't want you all to examine her today, but when she comes in for her surgery, I want each of you to take the opportunity to examine her. Then you will get to know what a breast cancer looks and feels like. Now,' he said, looking at his watch, 'we're running behind schedule. You go and read up about the conditions that you've seen this morning, whilst I have a word with Mrs Nichols, and then finish the clinic.'

****

Sister Rutherford on the female ward was worried. Anne Nichols, the lady with the ominous lump in her breast, had been admitted to have a mastectomy. Although Malcolm had 'clerked her in', Mrs Nichols had a number of questions he had felt unable to answer.

Sister rang Paul. 'Do you have time to pop to the ward to talk with Mrs Nichols?' she asked. 'She's extremely anxious because she believes that many patients die of breast cancer despite having surgery.'

The operation was planned for the next day, and Sister hoped Paul would be able to offer some words of encouragement and reassurance.

Paul found Anne Nichols to be a likeable and uncomplicated lady who asked little more of life than to be able to care for her husband, and her two young children. She had previously had a lump in her breast which had proved to be a cyst.

'That only required a tiny operation,' she explained, 'I was home within 24 hours, and back at work within a couple of days.' She had been horrified to learn that on this occasion, she had not been so lucky having been told by Mr Potts in the clinic that removal of her breast was required.

Paul was painfully aware that the prognosis for patients who developed breast cancer at such a young age was particularly bad; regrettably, the majority of patients would succumb to their cancer despite surgery and x-ray therapy.

'Obviously, I don't want to lose my breast,' Mrs Nichols said, 'but no doubt I shall get used to that.'

'I'm sure that you will,' Paul replied. 'It's an operation we have to perform quite commonly. Unfortunately, we're seeing more and more patients with this problem these days. If it will help, we can introduce you to one of our patients who has already had a mastectomy. You could have a chat with her, and she could show you how to disguise the operation. When you're dressed with a pad in your bra, no-one will be any the wiser.'

'I'm sorry, Doctor, I'm not making myself clear. It's not me that I'm worried about.'

'You're married, aren't you,' Paul replied, still not understanding Anne's principal concerns. 'Well, obviously, you won't be able to disguise it from your husband, but if he truly cares for you, he will understand.'

'Of course, my husband would prefer that I didn't have to lose my breast, but that's not what's worrying me. It's the children. They're so young; still at primary school. John is nine and Becky's only six. At that age, they need a mother, and will do for many years to come. Left on his own, my husband won't be able to give them the support that they need.'

Mrs Nichols went on to say that her mother had died of breast cancer when she was a teenager. She still harboured painful memories of watching her lose weight, and seeing her in distress and pain. She remembered hearing her moaning as she tossed and turned in the night. Sometimes, she would go and try to comfort her mother, but was always sent back to her room. She used to cover her head with her pillow because she couldn't bear to hear her mother suffer.

Towards the end, when she was confined to bed, her mother developed bed sores. The smell of those terrible skin ulcers still haunted Mrs Nichols and she didn't want her children to have a similar experience. She desperately wanted to see them grow up; she needed to stay healthy until they were old enough to look after themselves; old enough to be independent.'

Belatedly Paul realised that any concerns she had about her body image were overshadowed by her fears of dying of cancer, and leaving her children without a mother.

Sitting at the bedside with the screens drawn, despite knowing the odds were stacked against this young patient, Paul explained that many patients with breast cancer did survive, indeed they lived into old age; but Mrs Nichols, in her own mind, equated a diagnosis of breast cancer with death from breast cancer. She begged Paul to promise that when she was dying, he would arrange for her to be admitted to the hospital, so that her children would not witness the terminal stages of her illness.

Again, Paul tried to reassure. 'The majority of patients with breast cancer are cured by the operation,' he said.

Although this statement was true, taken literally, Paul felt guilty. Given her age, it was misleading in this particular case.

'Admittedly, the operation is somewhat radical,' he continued, 'but that's the price to be paid for being rid of the problem.'

'But what happens when the cancer returns?'

'You mustn't assume it will return.'

'But it usually does come back, doesn't it, Doctor?'

'In most cases, it doesn't,' Paul replied, again conscious that he was guilty of verbal deceit, 'but even if it did, we should still be here to help you.'

But Mrs Nichols was not to be reassured. Regrettably, the consultation ended with the patient in tears. Paul prescribed a large dose of a sedative, and arranged for sleeping tablets to be available should they be needed that night, before he left her with one of the nurses attempting to comfort her with kind words and the inevitable cup of tea.

Victoria, Paul, together with Sister Rutherford, a staff nurse, and two junior nurses accompanied Mr Potts as he left the office to review his patients. This was to be Paul's last ward round with Mr Potts before he left to take up his new post and continue his surgical training at the neighbouring Middleton Hospital. They were followed by the eight medical students who shuffled along in an untidy group.

The students were apprehensive. They had each been allocated two patients, and were expected to be well informed on all aspects of their disease and its management. They knew that if their knowledge was found to lacking, they would face criticism.

Many of the patients were also anxious as they waited in their beds for the round to begin. Many questions were running through their minds. 'What did my investigations show? Am I to have an operation, and when is it to be?' 'What did you find at my operation? Was it anything serious?' And the question that was all-important to them; 'Can my problem be cured?' Different questions in the minds of individual patients, each question important to their health and happiness, perhaps even pivotal to the life of the person concerned, all to be answered in the next few moments.

Except that not all the questions had definite answers. 'We're still waiting for the results of your tests.' 'Many patients with your problem never have any more trouble, but unfortunately, a few do.' Then the phrase that is meant to reassure, but often doesn't, 'Don't worry. We shall continue to keep a close eye on you in the clinic so we can deal with any problems that may arise.'

On this occasion, Mr Potts was in a hurry. Occasionally, he explained some aspect of a patient's condition to the students, but to their great relief, never once did he ask them to present their allocated patients to him.

When he arrived at Anne Nichols' bed, the screens were drawn, and Mr Potts instructed that Mrs Nichols' nightdress be removed. Despite the attempts by Paul and Sister Rutherford to offer reassurance, anxiety was etched into her face. As she sat vulnerably and exposed, it seemed Mr Potts was unaware this might be embarrassing for her, and as the consultation continued, it became apparent he was equally unaware, or possibly unconcerned, about any feelings she might have. No wonder that Anne should burst into tears.

'No need to cry, my dear,' Mr Potts remarked impatiently. 'No-one is going to hurt you. We just want to sort out this little problem for you.'

The abnormality of her breast was very obvious. The lump within it was so large that it caused the nipple to be distorted, and pushed to one side. It appeared to have increased in size since her clinic appointment ten days earlier. The overlying skin was stretched and pale.

Mr Potts examined Mrs Nichols and then invited Victoria to examine as well. Then, retreating to the foot of the bed, he turned away from the patient, and addressed the medical students.

'A fairly large mass, typical carcinoma, about two inches across. Pretty big, really. It's a good job she's big busted. It's always easier to do a complete operation if the patient has large breasts. The best plan will be to whip off the breast and remove the glands in the armpit.' His voice was loud enough, not only to be heard by Mrs Nichols, but also by those in neighbouring beds, the screens insulating from sight, but not from sound.

Paul and Victoria glanced at each other, the same thought passing through each of their minds. Other consultants such as Sir William would never behave like this. They would put the patient at ease, restrict the number of people around the bed, and then discuss the position quietly and sensitively, rather than bellowing like a foghorn for half the ward to hear. How could Mr Potts be so insensitive? Surely, if his own wife had been subject to such lack of feeling, he would have been furious, and the first to complain.

Paul wondered how someone who behaved in such a manner could have risen to become a consultant. Had he perhaps hidden his true feelings towards patients when he was being supervised as a trainee? Or had he become insensitive by virtue of having seen so many cancer victims, that he had forgotten that they were human beings with human feelings? Perhaps he had come to regard them merely as academic problems? He wondered if there was any higher authority to whom he could express his concerns, but of course, there wasn't. The consultants were the highest authority; that was what enabled some of them to act as Gods!

When Victoria had completed her examination, she stood back and Sister Rutherford immediately helped Mrs Nichols to replace her nightdress, just as Sister had done in the clinic. She then sat on the bed, offering words of comfort, her arm around her patient's shoulders.

Victoria looked worried. She turned to Mr Potts, and then spoke quietly and hesitantly. 'Do you think, Sir, it would be wise to take a sample of the lump as a first step? That would enable us to confirm the diagnosis before the whole breast was removed.'

Mr Potts however, was adamant. 'There's no need to do that, Miss Kent. There's really no doubt about it.'

Then he turned back to Mrs Nichols, 'Don't you worry about a thing, my dear. We'll remove your breast tomorrow. You'll be fast asleep. You won't know a thing about it. The appliance lady will sort you out afterwards. The 'falsies' are pretty good these days. We'll have you home in a week or so, and nobody will know you're a bit lopsided.'

A voice inside Paul wanted to scream, 'her husband will know, and in any case, that's not what she's worried about. She's worried she's going to die a painful death from her cancer, and leave her children alone in the world without a mother.' But, fearful of a public verbal lashing, he didn't.

As Mr Potts moved on to the next patient, Mrs Nichols again began to cry. Sister indicated that the screens should be left around the bed, and that one of the nurses should remain with Mrs Nichols to comfort her. For a brief moment, before following the consultant down the ward, Victoria took hold of Mrs Nichols' hand and whispered, 'I'll be back as soon as I can, to explain it all to you.'

However, Victoria was not the only one aware of the distress that had been caused. Sister asked one of her staff nurses to ring for her husband, and a patient from the opposite side of the ward was already moving across to offer support.

Thirty minutes later, back in the office, the ward round over, Victoria again expressed her concern about Mrs Nichols' proposed operation.

'Do you think, Sir, that there's a possibility the breast lump might be benign?' she asked tentatively, by which she actually meant, wouldn't it be wise to take a biopsy of the lump first, before being committed to a full mastectomy?'

Paul wondered if the consultant would explode at having his decision questioned a second time. He didn't, but as before he was unyielding, his view unchanged.

'That would simply mean two operations and two anaesthetics; one to take the biopsy, then a second to remove the breast. It would also give the patient false hopes that would inevitably be dashed. It will come to the same thing in the end, so we might as well get on with it.'

Paul was not sufficiently qualified or experienced to question the consultant's diagnosis, but he could see that Victoria remained unconvinced. Furthermore, bravely she was prepared to stand her ground.

'She's had a breast cyst in the past, Sir, although I admit that was on the other side. Don't you think we should stick a needle in it first and see?'

Paul recalled the history he had taken from the patient, and knew that a minor operation had cured Mrs Nichols' previous breast cyst.

'Look, Miss Kent, do that if you must, if it will put your mind at rest, but I don't want you spreading any cancer cells around. With big tumours like this, the prognosis is bad enough as it is.'

Mr Potts was concerned that if a needle was inserted into the tumour, cancer cells might be displaced from the lump, and seeded into the surrounding tissues. Paul though, was sufficiently experienced to realise that this argument was false. If the patient subsequently had a mastectomy, all the surrounding tissue would be removed anyway.

Mr Potts looked at his watch, and turned to leave. 'Now, I must be off. I'm committed to removing a gall bladder in the private wing in a couple of minutes. Perhaps you would care to assist me, Miss Kent.'

As Victoria departed with the consultant, she whispered urgently to Paul, 'Put a needle into that lump, Paul. If it's solid, then I accept that it's probably a tumour, but I still think there's a chance it's just another cyst.'

As soon as they left, Sister Rutherford shooed the medical students out of the office, despatched her nurses to their routine tasks, and then turned to Paul. 'I'll swing for that man one day! How can he be so insensitive?'

Together, Sister Rutherford and Paul walked back down the ward. The screen remained drawn around the bed, and within Mrs Nichols was still being comforted by one of the nurses, yet another cup of tea on the bedside locker, this one being ignored and going cold.

She was distraught; her face streaked with tears.

'It's not the operation that worries me,' she wailed. 'I don't care about that. My husband's a good man. He'll get used to it. You can take both of them off for all I care. It's the children; they're both so young. They need me. My husband has to work long days on the farm. I've lost my Mum and Dad, and there's no-one else to help. I need to be there for them.'

Paul attempted reassurance. 'You're still assuming that all patients with cancer die. They don't. The whole purpose of the operation is to remove the tumour, to get rid of it so that you can be healthy afterwards.'

'But many patients do die, don't they?'

Paul couldn't deny this. But he didn't want to get involved in a discussion on the success rate of surgery until he had done the needle test.

'Yes, that's true,' he admitted, 'not everyone is cured of cancer, but many people are. But first, Mr Potts has agreed that we do a little needle test on this lump for you. Let's get that over first. We can talk about other things afterwards.'

Once again, Sister helped Mrs Nichols to remove her nightdress, and then asked her to rest back on the bed, and lie with one arm above her head. In this position, the lump was so prominent, distorting the overlying skin, that it amazed Paul she had only noticed it recently. Mrs Nichols must have read his thoughts.

'I always examine myself at my period time. Five weeks ago, the lump was tiny. At first, I wasn't even sure there was a lump there. Now it's enormous.'

'This will only take a couple of minutes,' Paul said as he attached a needle to a large, empty syringe. 'You'll feel a sharp pin-prick in the skin, like the one when we take blood from your arm. I suggest you look away while we do it.'

Fixing the lump firmly with his left hand, so that it would not run away from the needle, Paul swabbed the skin with an antiseptic solution, and then plunged the needle into the heart of the mass. Immediately, the barrel of the syringe started to fill with pale yellow fluid. As he aspirated more and more fluid, he could feel the lump getting smaller, collapsing beneath his fingers. He felt exhilarated. A feeling of pure joy swept through him. Victoria had been right. This wasn't a cancer at all. It was an enormous cyst. It would have been an absolute disaster to perform a mastectomy. He glanced at Sister Rutherford, and saw all the anger and frustration melt from her face.

Soon the syringe was full, and Paul had to replace it with a fresh one as the cyst continued to empty. When all the fluid had been removed, the breast looked and felt entirely normal. Two minutes earlier, there had been a large, hard mass in the heart of the breast. Now the lump simply didn't exist, and there were 70 millilitres of clear, pale, yellow fluid in the dish on the bedside locker. Nursing sisters are trained not to show emotion, but Paul was sure that he saw moisture in Sister Rutherford's eyes. There was certainly a tear of happiness in his own eye. Ever so gently, Sister took Mrs Nichols free hand, and carefully placed it over her breast, and asked her to feel for the lump. It was a delight to watch her face as her fingers probed in vain for the lump that was no longer there.

At first, her expression was one of bewilderment, then incredulity, and finally one of enormous relief. The last time Paul had seen such joy on a patient's face had been during his student days at the maternity hospital when he had placed a new born baby into a mother's arms.

'It's gone!' she exclaimed.

'Yes, it was a cyst, just like the last one. It wasn't a cancer at all,' Paul said, and showed her the fluid on the bedside locker. Without warning, and still naked from the waist up, Mrs Nichols threw both her arms around Paul's neck, and dragging him to her, gave him a most tremendous bear hug.

'Hey,' he said, 'be careful; your husband's due at any minute.' But it was too late. At that very moment, Mr Nichols appeared through a gap in the screens escorted by one of the nurses.

'What the bloody hell is going on here?' he exclaimed, his face showing surprise and anger.

With difficulty, Paul tried to extricate himself from her embrace, but Mrs Nichols was not for letting go. She kissed him on both cheeks before releasing him.

Paul stood back, red-faced and flustered. 'I think you'd better explain to your husband what's happened,' he said.

He had been hoping to make a quick getaway, but Mrs Nichols clung on to his hands. She looked at him through tear-streaked eyes, 'Thank you, Doctor, thank you so much, and you too, Sister.'

A junior hospital doctor's job was hard work. There were long hours on duty, disturbed nights, and there were times when you were so exhausted you could scarcely think straight, but events such as this made it all worthwhile.

'It's Miss Kent you need to thank,' he said quietly, 'not me. She's the one who insisted that this needle test should be done.'

With a spring in his stride, he walked to the office, picked up the phone and spoke to the staff in the operating theatre.

'Tomorrow's mastectomy operation is cancelled,' he said, 'the lump in the breast has disappeared.'

****

At the end of the day, Paul called on Sir William to thank him for the training and support he had been given, he said goodbye to Sister Ashbrook, Sister Rutherford, Victoria and many other members of staff, then gathered together his various belongings, and left the hospital for the last time. He would be sad to leave; as a medical student, then as a house officer, and more recently as a surgical registrar, he had been around the place for the best part of ten years. He knew though, that if he was to advance his career he had to move on. At the Middleton he would gain more experience, and learn to carry greater responsibility which hopefully in a further five years or so, would see him appointed as a consultant.

He didn't go straight home, instead he drifted into the municipal park adjacent to the hospital, sat on one of the benches, and gazed at the City General Hospital in the early evening sunshine. The buildings looked timeless. Built in solid Victorian brick, they had been there for a hundred years, and no doubt would still be there for the next hundred. From the outside, the three-story blocks with their linking corridors looked cold, inanimate and forbidding. Inside however, it was warm; the hospital had its own life, its own social spirit, fellowship and camaraderie. For Paul, it had been both home and workplace for many years, a place where he ate, drank, slept, but most of all a place where he'd worked hour after hour, day after day, week upon week. And he was not the only one; he was just a small cog in a team of nurses, doctors and paramedical staff; the physiotherapists, radiographers, dieticians, laboratory technicians and all the other key members of staff without whom the hospital could not function; the cooks, porters, cleaners, administrative staff, all essential to the vital function of caring for the sick.

Paul looked again at the hospital; perhaps it would not change much on the outside as the years slipped by, but would it be the same on the inside? No doubt therapies would improve as new medicines becoming available, new operations were devised and as cures found for conditions that at present were untreatable. If medical practice developed in the next fifty years as quickly as it had in the last fifty, hospital routines would be very different in the future, but there was much that would not change. The hopes and fears of the staff would remain, as would the anxiety of newly qualified young doctors. Nurses would always be essential, maybe in time extending their skills to undertake some of the tasks currently performed by doctors, but hopefully still showing the care and compassion that epitomised their role. And of course, there would still be the patients; many like Anne Nichols to be relieved of their anxieties and cured, but others tragically, like little Rosie, that lovely ray of sunshine, to die. Those solid, brick Victorian walls would continue to bear witness to the hundreds of little incidents and dramas that make up hospital life.

Thought for the day

All's well that ends well.

Late 14 C Proverb

Peter continues to publish new stories on his blog at www.medicaltales.org where you can Sign On/Subscribe and receive future tales, free of charge, direct to your email inbox.

Printed in Great Britain
by Amazon